WITHDRAWN

The Presidency of
WILLIAM HOWARD
TAFT

AMERICAN PRESIDENCY SERIES

Donald R. McCoy, Clifford S. Griffin, Homer E. Socolofsky
General Editors

George Washington, Forrest McDonald
John Adams, Ralph Adams Brown
Thomas Jefferson, Forrest McDonald
John Quincy Adams, Mary W. M. Hargreaves
Martin Van Buren, Major L. Wilson
James K. Polk, Paul H. Bergeron
James Buchanan, Elbert B. Smith
Andrew Johnson, Albert Castel
James A. Garfield & Chester A. Arthur, Justus D. Doenecke
Benjamin Harrison, Homer E. Socolofsky & Allan B. Spetter
William McKinley, Lewis L. Gould
William Howard Taft, Paolo E. Coletta
Warren G. Harding, Eugene P. Trani & David L. Wilson
Herbert C. Hoover, Martin L. Fausold
Harry S. Truman, Donald R. McCoy
Dwight D. Eisenhower, Elmo Richardson
Lyndon B. Johnson, Vaughn Davis Bornet

The Presidency of
WILLIAM HOWARD
TAFT

by
Paolo E. Coletta

THE UNIVERSITY PRESS OF KANSAS
Lawrence / Manhattan / Wichita

To
my Mother and Michael,
and to
Maria and the children,
Bernarr and Paula Maria

Editors' Preface

The aim of the American Presidency Series is to present historians and the general reading public with interesting, scholarly assessments of the various presidential administrations. These interpretive surveys are intended to cover the broad ground between biographies, specialized monographs, and journalistic accounts. As such, each will be a comprehensive, synthetic work which will draw upon the best in pertinent secondary literature, yet leave room for the author's own analysis and interpretation.

Each volume in the series will deal with a separate presidential administration and will present the data essential to understanding the administration under consideration. Particularly, each book will treat the then current problems facing the United States and its people and how the president and his associates felt about, thought about, and worked to cope with these problems. Attention will be given to how the office developed and operated during the president's tenure. Equally important will be consideration of the vital relationships between the president, his staff, the executive officers, Congress, foreign representatives, the judiciary, state officials, the public, political parties, the press, and influential private citizens. The series will also be concerned with how this unique American institution—the presidency—was viewed by the presidents, and with what results.

All this will be set, insofar as possible, in the context not only of contemporary politics but also of economics, international relations, law, morals, public administration, religion, and thought. Such a broad approach is necessary to understanding, for a presidential administration is more than the elected and appointed officers composing it, since its work so often reflects the major problems, anxieties, and glories of the nation. In short, the authors in the series will strive to recount and evaluate the record of each administration and to identify its distinctiveness and relationships to the past, its own time, and the future.

Donald R. McCoy
Clifford S. Griffin
Homer E. Socolofsky

Acknowledgments

My thanks are due to many for aid with this study. Roy S. Basler, chief, Manuscripts Division, Library of Congress, and Paul T. Heffron, specialist, Twentieth Century Political History, steered me into the letter collections of the important political and military men of William Howard Taft's time. Dr. Dean Allard, head, Operational Archives, Naval History Division, Washington, D.C., and Mrs. Kathy Lloyd provided the records of the General Board of the Navy and various letter collections. Professor Richard A. Evans, librarian, U.S. Naval Academy Library, Theodore E. De Disse, Periodicals Division librarian, and Mrs. Eileen E. Baltimore, of the Inter-library Loan Desk, proved indefatigable in making available or acquiring needed references. Professor Gerald E. Wheeler, chairman, Department of History, San Jose State College, San Jose, California, offered constructive suggestions on Chapters 10 and 11. A sabbatical leave generously granted by the superin-tendent, U.S. Naval Academy, made it possible for me to concentrate upon research and writing for an academic term. Last but not least I must thank my wife, Maria, and the children for their patience when at times it seemed as if I lived more for Taft than for them.

Paolo E. Coletta

U.S. Naval Academy
Annapolis, Md.

Contents

1

★★★★★

THE APOSTOLIC SUCCESSION

I

William Howard Taft won a place as a possible presidential candidate via the appointive rather than elective route. Born in an outlying section of Cincinnati, Ohio, in 1857, into a family of moderate wealth and some legal and political distinction, he became impregnated with the conservative attitudes so often associated with an upper-middle-class society. He graduated as salutatorian from Yale University in 1878, after being exposed to the laissez-faire teachings of William Graham Sumner; he gained admission to the Ohio bar after completing his studies at the Cincinnati Law School. Except for the year 1880, when he was a newspaper reporter, and the years 1883–1885, when he practiced law, all of the positions he held until elected as president were appointive offices—assistant prosecuting attorney at Cincinnati, 1881–1882; collector of internal revenue in the same Queen City, 1882–1883; assistant county solicitor, 1885–1887; judge of the State Superior Court, at Cincinnati, 1887–1890; solicitor general of the United States, 1890–1892; United States Circuit Court judge, 1892–1900; president of the Second Philippine Commission, 1900–1901, and first civil governor of the Philippines, 1901–1904. He was then secretary of war, 1904–1908.[1]

It has been asserted that a fall from a buggy when he was nine years of age dented Taft's skull into his pituitary gland, thereby contributing to his growth to great size. "Big Lub," as he was called when a boy, was more than six feet tall and weighed 332 pounds at his inauguration as president at the age of fifty-two years

1

in 1909. As a college boy, "Big Bill" was not too active in athletics. Later in life he gave up riding horseback as exercise, which he took only in order to keep his weight down. (Theodore Roosevelt said it was dangerous for him and cruelty to the horse!) He then became almost addicted to golf, in which he became quite adept but which provoked public vilification as fit only for the effete rich with time on their hands. Although corpulent, he was extremely light on his feet, and an excellent dancer. As his military aide while Taft was president, Archibald Willingham (Archie) Butt, put it, "I have found out three things he does well. He dances well, he curses well, and he laughs well."[2] On the other hand, his corpulency made him sensitive to heat and increased his natural lethargy. Often after a meal his head would fall on his chest and he would go sound asleep for ten or fifteen minutes, awaken, and then continue the conversation where he had left off. Almost invariably he fell asleep in church. He would leave to others or postpone the making of decisions which he himself should make, forget promises he had made, and procrastinate the tackling of a task until the last possible moment, when he would reveal a tremendous amount of energy in completing it. He confessed after his term as president that he did not accomplish more than he did in part because of "too much love of personal ease."[3]

Lacking a brilliant mind, Taft mastered learning by persistent application; by citing innumerable precedents in his legal pleading or judicial decisions he appeared to be erudite. He was a good and avid conversationalist, but he read narrowly rather than broadly and developed a ponderous and verbose writing style. He liked music and enjoyed playing cards but had no interest in art. In great part because of parental teaching he never smoked and only occasionally drank beer or wine. Even less often did he lose his temper and reveal his capacity to let fly with a round oath or two. Rather, he loved to laugh and to share his laughter with those about him. Rarely critical of others, he had a sense of humor that enabled him to enjoy jokes of which he himself was the butt. And he was tender-hearted enough actually to cry over some sentimental scene in a play.

In 1886, Taft had married an intelligent, charming, often critical, sometimes possessive if not dictatorial young lady named Helen but called "Nellie" Herron, of a moderately wealthy Cincinnati family. If money meant little to him—he was human enough to overdraw his checking account occasionally and confessed that upon their moving into the White House they had saved only about

$5,000—it meant much to her, for she paid the bills, bills which increased as the three children came. If he pined for high judicial office, she kept her eye on even higher political office. As it turned out, both were eventually made happy.

Like so many other lawyers, Taft acknowledged that he learned more about the law in practicing before the bar than in law school. He also learned much about what went on in the local courts as the local reporter on Murat Halstead's *Cincinnati Commercial.* Unfortunately, he did not maintain the journalistic associations of his youth, reveal qualities of showmanship, or harbor political ambitions. Nevertheless, his father's prominence and his own tilling in the city and state Republican vineyard won him the appointment of post after post. It helped, too, that the governorship of Ohio and the presidency of the United States, except for Grover Cleveland, lay in Republican hands for almost three decades after he graduated from Yale, and that during his two years in Washington as solicitor general he met most of the leading Republican politicians as well as members of the Supreme Court. Although the exact date of their first encounter has been lost, it was during these years that he met Roosevelt, one of the Civil Service commissioners.

In the judgment of his best biographer, the mature Taft was "an ardent Republican and therefore conservative in his political and social views."[4] The liberal views that infected Grangers, Greenbackers, Populists, and the Bryan wing of the Democracy, and eventually inoculated the insurgent (or progressive) wing of the Republican party left him quite untouched. While his decisions on both the state and federal bench reveal that he was not a pro-corporation judge, they do point to an illiberal view of organized labor. He thought, for example, that it would be "necessary for the military to control some of the mob before trouble [in the Pullman strike] can be stayed," and he sent to jail for six months a lieutenant of Eugene V. Debs for contempt of a court injunction he had issued. Largely overlooked were instances in which he championed workers against employers in accidents caused by the failure to provide safety devices and in which he countered the "assumed risk" and "contributory negligence" doctrines of employment.[5] In part because he was known as an "injunction judge," he discounted suggestions that he aim for high political office. More important, he aspired not for the presidency but for a post on the Supreme Court—an ambition not achieved until Warren G. Harding became president. He always admired the jurist more than the statesman.

At a time when Melville Fuller's Supreme Court was rigorously applying the doctrine of laissez faire, as in the *E. C. Knight* decision of 1895, Taft took a liberal rather than conservative attitude toward enforcement of the Sherman Antitrust Act of 1890. He found that the six cast-iron pipe manufacturing companies, even though they manufactured only 30 percent of the annual production of pipe, effectively controlled prices and thus were a combination in violation of the terms of the Sherman Act. Moreover, the companies were undoubtedly engaged in interstate trade, hence subject to regulation by Congress. Taft thus edged toward the control of trusts he would exercise as president.

On the income tax that appeared as part of the Wilson-Gorman tariff, Taft agreed with the Supreme Court that it was unconstitutional—a stand unchanged throughout his career. With respect to the currency issue, which so enlivened and also embittered the campaign of 1896, he favored gold over silver but admitted that he knew little about the money question. If Ohio's William McKinley was not the best candidate the Republicans could have chosen, William Jennings Bryan was a Socialist and anarchist as well as free silverite. Those Democrats who voted for him were "crazy."

McKinley's victory blasted Taft's hope for appointment to the Supreme Court, for McKinley appointed Joseph McKenna. He spoke with the president about a post for his friend Roosevelt. "The truth is, Will," McKinley replied, "Roosevelt is always in such a state of mind."[6] He nevertheless granted Roosevelt the position of assistant secretary of the navy, a step he may have rued in 1898. Paradoxically, the fruits of the Spanish-American War, in which Taft revealed no interest, bent his career away from the supreme bench for twenty years.

II

As president of the Second Philippine Commission, then as the first civil governor of the Philippines, 1901–1904, Taft gained executive experience, broadened his knowledge in such matters as finance, sanitation, taxation, currency, educational systems, civil service, and tariffs, and learned what real heat was. The only time he stopped perspiring, he wrote to Mrs. Taft, who remained at Yokohama during his first summer, was when he perceived the frigidity of General Arthur MacArthur, who would remain as military governor of the islands until Taft became civil governor. MacArthur's actions deepened his distrust of the military point of view.

While he did much to improve the standard of life in the Philippines, Taft was convinced that the Filipinos would not be ready for independence for decades. He gave them great freedom in conducting their domestic affairs, and he handled the Friar Lands question very well. He nevertheless provided another excellent example of his lack of political astuteness in sanctioning political parties that advocated either that the Philippines become a state in the Union or that they be granted independence.

The assassination of McKinley brought to the presidency Roosevelt, with whom Taft was on a first-name basis. He thought that Roosevelt would make an excellent president and defended him against charges of "impulsiveness and lack of deliberation." But he again revealed his political naïveté by asserting that Roosevelt lacked "the capacity for winning people to his support that McKinley had."[7] Although he was pleased when Roosevelt several times mentioned him as fit to be president of the United States, his ambition lay not in political campaigning but in sitting on the supreme bench. Therefore he asserted in one instance that the Republican party could "hardly take a weaker candidate than I should be, with my record as a federal judge in labor troubles."[8] Yet his sense of duty in the Philippines determined him again and again to decline Roosevelt's offer of an appointment to the Supreme Court and also to resist suggestions from his wife and from the various members of the large Taft family that he seek the presidency. Brother Henry Taft was more sanguine than the many other Tafts that his brother would become president. He noted the value of William's being in Washington and in addition the fact that Roosevelt, deeply involved with the Northern Securities case, needed an adviser on "industrial" and labor questions. Indeed, Taft was mentioned as a possible contender with Roosevelt for the nomination in 1904 by those hostile to Roosevelt because of his antitrust and presumably pro-Negro activities. Taft was "disgusted" by such a proposal and firmly declined even to run for governor of Ohio in 1903 as a stepping stone to the presidential nomination in 1908.

Taft's determination to finish his job in the Philippines was finally broken when Roosevelt asked him to replace Secretary of War Elihu Root, who would resign in 1904. He accepted the appointment because as secretary of war he still would be in charge of Filipino affairs, and because amoebic dysentery threatened to undermine his health. Brother Charles offered to add $6,000

5

or more a year to his cabinet salary of $8,000 if he needed it. And Mrs. Taft was now very pleased.

III

Roosevelt wanted Taft in his cabinet less because he needed a good lawyer to head the War Department, for he himself ran the army, than because he needed sound legal advice and could use a spellbinder during the campaign of 1904. "He is, of course, the greatest imaginable comfort to me here, and I think the only man in the country who could have taken Root's place," he admitted.[9] To the British historian Sir George Otto Trevelyan he wrote in part:

> I wish you knew Taft, whom I have had acting as Secretary of State as well as Secretary of War in Hay's absence. He was Governor General of the Philippines. He is the man through whom I have been doing my work about the Panama canal. He has no more fear in dealing with the interests of great corporate wealth than he has in dealing with the leaders of the most powerful labor unions; and if either go wrong he has not the slightest hesitation in antagonizing them. To strength and courage, clear insight, and practical common sense, he adds a very noble and disinterested character. I know you would like him. He helps me in every way more than I can say. . . .[10]

It helped, too, that Taft had already twice visited Japan, whose competition for supremacy in the Far East with Russia might affect United States interests therein, particularly if the freely predicted war between Japan and Russia occurred. With respect to Taft's work in the Philippines, Roosevelt stated that "a more high-minded and disinterested man does not live; and he represents as high-minded and disinterested, aye, and as successful, an effort to keep a people as any recorded in history."[11]

As befitted his placid character, one that craved tranquillity, Taft found cabinet meetings uninteresting because they were largely devoted to politics. Except for John Hay, who upon his death was succeeded by Root, and possibly P. C. Knox, none of the other cabinet men was particularly notable in any way. Hence Roosevelt depended heavily upon Taft, and in his frequent moods of blue desperation he would turn to him. Taft was his major trouble-shooter, in his absence "sat on the lid" at Washington, was acting secretary of state when Hay was ill, and in utterly partisan fashion expounded the Roosevelt cause when on the stump, even to the extent of upholding him on his "rape" of Panama from Colombia. Although Roosevelt said that he took his election in 1904 as a second term, Taft spurned suggestions that he himself run in 1908 and looked instead toward the chief justiceship of the Supreme Court. "I hesitated a little between Root and Taft, for Taft as you know is very close to me," Roosevelt wrote to Henry Cabot Lodge about a successor for the deceased Hay, adding that he was happy that Root would be the new secretary of state and that he would now have both Root and Taft in his cabinet. Illuminating, too, is Roosevelt's comment at this early date with respect to his thinking about Taft for the presidency:

> Taft is a great big fellow. He urged me to bring Root into the Cabinet. Of course the papers with their usual hysteria have for the moment completely dropped Taft, whom they were all booming violently up to three weeks ago, and are now occupied with their new toy, Root. They are sure that he has come into the Cabinet for the purpose of making himself president, and the more picturesque among them take the view that he stipulated this before he accepted and that I in effect pledged him the Presidency—omitting the trifling detail that even if I had been idiot enough to feel that way, he would not have been idiot enough to think that I had any power in the matter. As a matter of fact I am inclined to think that Taft's being from the west, together with his attitude on corporations, would for the moment make him the more available man. Of course no one can tell what will be the outcome three years hence.[12]

In 1904, Taft stated that "a national campaign for the presidency is to me a nightmare." By 1905, however, he spurned an associate justiceship offered to him by Roosevelt. He was now giving more time to politics than to the department he was supposed to run, and in his utterances on current issues he became almost another Roosevelt. At first opposed to the Monroe Doctrine, in 1905 he upheld Roosevelt's corollary to it by which Roosevelt by executive agreement established a customs receivership over Santo Domingo. Through his department Taft saw to it that the customs were collected. In Roosevelt's absence he carried on the negotiations with respect to the Algeciras Conference, came to see the hatred that existed between England and Germany, and absorbed some of the fear that Roosevelt had that Germany somehow threatened the security of the United States. As secretary of war he supervised the building of the Panama Canal. He helped to pacify Cuba, which was torn by political upheaval, by temporarily becoming its provisional governor and by maintaining American troops there from 1906 to 1909. He persistently sought to improve conditions in the Philippines. At Roosevelt's bidding he dismissed without honor the three companies of Negro troops allegedly involved in the shooting fray at Brownsville, Texas, on August 13, 1906. As secretary, too, he helped the victims of the tragic earthquake and fire at San Francisco in 1906. All in all he had proved his executive capacity. He now enjoyed Washington society, and was of course happy when Congress raised cabinet salaries from $8,000 to $12,000 in 1907. He was even happier when a prolonged diet supervised by a physician reduced his weight from 326 to 250 pounds, with consequent improvement in his health but a huge bill for clothing alterations. As for the national issues which he propounded on Roosevelt's behalf in the congressional elections of 1906, he upheld his warfare against the trusts and praised the advance in railroad control provided in the Hepburn Act as well as both the Pure Food and Drugs and the Meat Inspection acts of 1906. When he wished to go beyond Roosevelt, who knew little about the tariff, in suggesting that improvement in the business conditions of the country since 1897 dictated a reduction of the schedules of the Dingley tariff, he acquiesced to the president's blue-penciling of a speech he had prepared for delivery.

In the meantime, while on his way to visit the Philippines in the summer of 1905, Taft had followed Roosevelt's instructions to stop at Tokyo, where he made the Taft-Katsura "agreed memorandum" which approved of Japan's suzerainty over Korea in exchange for a nonaggression pledge toward the Philippines. In seeking to balance Russia against Japan, Roosevelt had closed the Open Door a bit. Roosevelt rather than Taft bore the responsibility for the settlement achieved in the Portsmouth Conference, the honor for smoothing over the anti-Japanese agitation in California of 1906 in the Gentlemen's Agreement of 1907–1908, and the exhibition of strength in his sending of the fleet around the world in 1907–1909. Yet on the eve of his sending Taft again to Japan, in July 1907, he wrote to Taft that perhaps the Philippines should be freed, because the United States could not defend them. Indeed, "The Philippines form our heel of Achilles. They are all that makes the present situation with Japan dangerous. . . ."[13] Much more bellicose than Taft, and surer that a war with Japan was inevitable, Roosevelt was far more concerned with the buildup of the American army and navy than Taft was. In Tokyo, however, Taft smoothed ruffled Japanese-American relations and paved the way for the later Root-Takahira Agreement.

Several factors had great repercussions and invited bitter recriminations later on. The first was that Roosevelt selected Taft to be his successor and gave him vital support during the campaign of 1908 on the understanding that he was the best man to continue the "Roosevelt policies." As he told Archie Butt on July 24, 1908, "I do not think Taft would be as aggressive as I have been, but there will be no backward step under Taft."[14] Second, Taft, although rotund, jolly, and famous for his infectious chuckle, lacked Roosevelt's political skills, especially his capacity for achieving political compromise. Third, despite almost thirty years of judicial and administrative experience, he lacked qualities of executive leadership.

How did Taft and Roosevelt think about each other as Taft took over the presidency? Late in 1907, Taft stated that he had supported Roosevelt because they both had the same ideas, ideals, and objectives, saying:

> Is it possible that a man shows lack of originality, shows slaving imitation, because he happens to concur in the views of another who has the power to enforce those views: *Mr. Roosevelt's views were mine long before I knew Mr. Roosevelt at all.* You will find them expressed in my opinions in so far as it was proper to express them in judicial opinions, and I am not to be driven from adherence to those views.[15]

After Taft's election, Roosevelt wrote to Trevelyan that

> Taft will carry on the work substantially as I have carried it on. His policies, principles, purposes and ideals are the same as mine and he is a strong, forceful, efficient man, absolutely upright, absolutely disinterested and fearless. In leaving I have the profound satisfaction of knowing that he will do all in his power to further every one of the great causes for which I have fought and that he will persevere in every one of the great governmental policies in which I most firmly believe.[16]

But Roosevelt had changed over the years and would change still more in the future. From 1901 to 1904 he had sought only moderate reforms in limited areas in order not to set the Old Guard against him and so to insure his own nomination and election in

9

1904. Once elected in his own right, he went forward steadily in what has been called "his middle-of-the-road, middle-class program of mild reform."[17] Despite all his frenetic activity and bluster, the only legislative reforms he could get from his uncooperative congresses were the Elkins Act (1903); Hepburn, Pure Food and Drugs, Meat Inspection, and Employers' Liability acts (1906); the 1907 act prohibiting corporation contributions to campaign funds; and the 1908 law limiting trainmen's hours. He had achieved that much in part by appealing over the head of Congress to the people, in part by performing, between the advocates of revolution and of reaction, a marvelous balancing act designed to obtain what he felt was politically possible, a square deal for everyone. Capitalism must be curbed lest it endanger labor and stimulate socialism; on the other hand, labor must be curbed lest it become so powerful as to challenge capitalism. As a realist, he had worked with the Old Guard in both House and Senate. When in 1908 he suggested liberal reforms anathema to the Old Guard—such as laws for workmen's compensation, an inheritance tax, and the physical valuation of railroad property—he was laughed away by those who saw them as the expected outcry of an outgoing president. Moreover, many congressmen were unhappy because the people tended to give him rather than them the credit for legislation and, frustrated by their subordination, vowed that Taft would not beat them in similar fashion. Finally, he had no great respect for the Supreme Court, which did not always agree with what he thought was right.

IV

The major domestic issues Roosevelt had faced were with few exceptions the same ones that Taft would confront, and it is well to note specifically what Taft had to say with respect to them before he became president.

Labor. Labor has a legal right to organize, to strike, to enforce its demands by any peaceful method. In some respects, the courts had abused their injunction powers to oppress labor. . . . The boycott in labor disputes is illegal.

Capital. It must be forced to obey the law. . . . The capitalist system is the best thus far devised, however, and should be preserved.

Panic of 1907. The disturbance was caused, at least in part, by irregularities, breach of trust, stockjobbing, overissues of stock, violations of law "and lack of rigid state or national supervision in the management of some of the largest insurance companies, railroad companies, traction companies and financial corporations. . . ."

Currency Reform. The existing currency system was defective in that it was "not so arranged as to permit its volume to be increased temporarily to counteract the sudden drain of money by hoarding in a panic."

Trusts. The fight of the Roosevelt administration had been on the combinations which violated the law providing free competition. . . . The time had come for a new, more specific statute [than the Sherman Antitrust Act].

Railroad Regulation. The control gained by the Roosevelt administration had been justified by such abuses as rebating and other illegalities whereby the common carriers had combined with the large trusts to undermine free competition. The Interstate Commerce Commission should have power to fix maximum rates, but these should not be effective until after review by the courts.

Government Ownership. The railroads should remain under private ownership. Government ownership meant "state socialism, an increase in the power of the central government. . . ."

Socialism. The answer to the "very humane and kindly theories" which bore this name was that it was not possible "to carry on a business as economically and with the same production of profit by a government as it is under the motive of private gain."

Tariff. In general, the rates should not be greater than the difference in the cost of production abroad and in the United States.

Income Tax. The Supreme Court had ruled against the right of the federal government to pass such a tax. However, the Constitution should be amended. An income tax might be wise. . . .[18]

Where Taft disagreed most notably with Roosevelt, as will be shown, was not in objective but in method and in interpretation. Of vital import was the difference in their conception of the office of president. According to Roosevelt, writing in his *Autobiography:*

The most important factor in getting the right spirit in my administration . . . was my insistence upon the theory that the executive power was limited only by specific restrictions and prohibitions appearing in the Constitution or imposed by Congress under its constitutional powers. My view was that every executive officer, and

11

> above all every executive officer in high position, was a
> steward of the people bound actively and affirmatively to
> do all he could for the people. . . . I declined to adopt
> the view that what was imperatively necessary for the
> Nation could not be done by the President unless he could
> find some specific authorization to do it. . . . Under this
> interpretation of executive power I did and caused to be
> done many things not previously done by the President
> and the heads of the departments. I did not usurp power,
> but I did greatly broaden the use of executive power.[19]

He had, for example, appointed a number of extralegal, unsalaried
commissions and denied the right of Congress to limit him in
seeking advice from them. He used executive agreements with
abandon and denied the right of the Senate to advise him on his
executive duties, although it of course must approve nominations
and treaties. When he sent the fleet around the world, he knew
that it could reach Japan but no farther, thereby forcing Congress
to appropriate extra money for its return. "While President I have
been President emphatically," he said after leaving the office. "I
have used every ounce of power there was in the office and I have
not cared a rap for the criticism of those who spoke of my 'usurpation of power'; for I know that the talk was all nonsense and there
was no usurpation of power."[20]

In contrast to Roosevelt, who would expand state power, Taft
would limit government in order to grant full and free rein to
personal and property rights. He also had a juridical rather than
political conception of the presidency. As he expressed it after
his term,

> The true view of the executive function is, as I con-
> ceive it, that the President can exercise no power which
> cannot be reasonably and fairly traced to some specific
> grant of power or justly implied or included within such
> express grant as necessary and proper to its exercise. Such
> specific grant must be either in the Constitution or in an
> act of Congress passed in pursuance thereof. There is no
> undefined residuum of power which he can exercise be-
> cause it seems to him to be in the public interest.[21]

Especially with respect to conservation measures, Taft thought,
Roosevelt had used dubious legal procedures. As the *Wall Street
Journal* of July 29, 1908, editorialized about Taft's acceptance
speech: "Most of the criticism of Roosevelt has been directed not
so much at what he has done or attempted to do, but at the methods

of speech and action he employed in doing them. . . ." Second, Roosevelt's reform legislation had upset the business community in particular. The time had come to consolidate the progress he had made and to quiet the popular clamor he had excited. In his acceptance speech, which Roosevelt himself had approved, Taft had stated that

> the chief function of the next administration, in my judgment, is distinct from, and a progressive development of that which has been performed by President Roosevelt. The chief function of the next administration is to complete and perfect the machinery . . . by which the lawbreakers may be promptly restrained and punished, but which shall operate with sufficient accuracy and dispatch to interfere with legitimate business as little as possible. Such machinery is not now adequate. . . .[22]

Taft was fortunate in having Bryan as his opponent, for Bryan even more than Roosevelt sought to incite the popular clamor for additional reform and by so doing made Taft appear to be more conservative.

Upon his return from a world tour in late August 1906, Bryan at Madison Square Garden had devoted only about two minutes of a two-hour speech to reading six paragraphs devoted to the railroad question. What he said was that the Democracy should study the proposal to provide for the government ownership of railroads if effective railroad regulation could not be obtained. "I have already reached the conclusion," he said, "that the railroads partake so much of the nature of a monopoly that they must ultimately become public property and be managed by public officials . . . in accordance with the well-defined theory that public ownership is necessary where competition is impossible." The opposition press reacted as though he had spoken about government ownership alone and substituted "immediate" for "ultimate" ownership. In the face of the Hepburn Act, which answered his demand for better railroad regulation, and because of objections of the states-rights South, Bryan dropped the issue, but his opponents did not. Yet Taft had to answer Bryan's assertion that he rather than Taft was Roosevelt's logical heir because Roosevelt had stolen his reform planks from Bryan and because Bryan had supported the president in achieving these reforms.[23] Taft thereupon distinguished between Roosevelt, and presumably himself, and Bryan. As he wrote to Roosevelt:

What I am most anxious to do is to meet Mr. Bryan's proposition that you have stolen his clothes and are only carrying out his policies. . . . The main differences between you and Bryan are, first, that when he proposes a thing it is merely to catch votes, and not with any sense of responsibility as to the possibility of carrying it out, or the effect of carrying it out; consequently, that he is always opposed to wealth, property, and its accumulation under the protection of a strong government. He is in favor of the punishment of the rich, but opposed to a strong government which shall punish both the poor and the rich. In other words, his tendency is toward the rule of the mob.

I, with deference, have never met a man more strongly in favor of a strong government than you are and more insistent that courts shall not only have power to enforce the law, but should enforce the law. Bryan's attitude is that of one who would weaken the sanction of all government, would reduce the army and navy, would take away all power in the courts to increase their own orders; and would reduce the government to a mere town meeting by whom the laws should be enforced against the rich, but should be weakened as against the poor. . . .[24]

Bryan probably erred, too, in campaigning under the shibboleth of "Shall the People Rule?" and dealing with a plethora of issues rather than with a "paramount" issue. He possibly could have done better to concentrate upon a tariff-for-revenue-only, thereby putting Taft on the defensive and hastening the Republican split over the tariff reform issue that occurred early in Taft's administration.

In 1912, Roosevelt would complain that Taft had rigged their party's convention in favor of himself by the use of the patronage. It is therefore necessary to note what Taft had to say about the methods used in his own behalf in 1908, particularly about the use of the "rotten boroughs" in the South:

The South has been the section of rotten boroughs in the Republican national politics, and it would delight me if no southern state were permitted to have a vote in the National Convention except in proportion to its Republican vote. . . . But when a man is running for the presidency . . . he cannot afford to ignore the tremendous influence, however undue, that the southern vote has, and he must take the best way he can honorably to secure it. In the past it has been secured too frequently by pure purchase. Of course I would never stoop to that method.[25]

14

It is enough to add that of the 491 delegates needed for a majority in the convention, 125 were federal officeholders and 97 of these were pledged to Taft.

Notice should also be taken of several issues arising out of the convention itself. First, Taft said nothing when a minority platform offered by La Follette's Wisconsin delegation was refused because it demanded tariff reform, a tariff commission, and the valuation of railroad property for purposes of taxation, hence was "socialistic and Democratic." On the other hand, because the platform adopted called for tariff revision and contained an antitrust plank, and since Taft promised progressive legislation, the midwestern Republicans said nothing. Second, Taft was originally adamantly opposed to a compromise anti-injunction labor plank, against "reckless use of the ex-parte injunction." He told the national chairman that he would "rather cut my hand off" than take the power to protect property from the courts; on the other hand, some judges had abused the use of injunctions in labor cases. However, he had finally agreed to the compromise plan, thereby earning the enmity of organized labor. Samuel Gompers, president of the American Federation of Labor, who dubbed Taft the "Father of Injunctions," had thereupon gone to Denver and succeeded in having the Democrats adopt his anti-injunction plank. Third, a forty-nine-minute acclamation following the mention of Roosevelt's name by Permanent Chairman Henry Cabot Lodge caused Mrs. Taft, at least, to suspect that Roosevelt wanted himself rather than Taft to be named. Fourth, Taft would have preferred as his running mate a man like Senator Jonathan P. Dolliver, of Iowa, whom he looked upon as a conservative with progressive leanings. But he did not fight for a progressive and agreed to take the political hack Senator James "Sunny Jim" Sherman, of New York. Then, although complaining that there was not enough time to think, he vacationed for two months before taking to the stump and, as usual, prepared his speeches too late to be able to give them the careful editing they required. Being conciliatory rather than aggressive by nature, he could not make himself over, as Roosevelt perhaps wanted him to do, into a pugnacious fighter. Moreover, he interpreted parts of the platform to suit himself. The platform was silent on contributions by corporation officers and directors to political parties, but Bryan was making much of his demand that such contributions be barred, and Taft sought to avoid the receipt of contributions from corporations that might later be involved in litigation with the government. While he disagreed with Bryan that contributions should be publicized prior to election day, he wanted them to be made public after the election. He stood with La Follette and other midwestern progressives in demanding the physical valuation of railroads as the basis for the setting of rates, yet he opposed Bryan's proposal, already in effect in Kansas, for the guarantee of bank deposits and favored instead a postal savings bank system that would serve the needs of the poor. Although he confessed that the great weight he would have to carry in the campaign was "Cannonism" and that he would be pleased if another Republican would replace Joe Cannon as Speaker of the House of Representatives, he said nothing publicly against him. In contrast, as soon as William Randolph Hearst had smeared Joseph B. Foraker with Standard Oil money, he refused to appear on the stump with him. Finally, he interpreted the Republican platform plank on tariff revision to mean revision *downward*, thereby attaching to himself the progressive faction of his party.

V

Born into a large family of moderate wealth and some political influence, Taft came into national prominence as a judge, administrator, and presidential counselor rather than by engaging in politics. Republican leaders like Foraker, McKinley, and especially Roosevelt befriended him. Big, bluff, hearty, and thoroughly honest, he was clean in both his private and public life. To twist an old saw, he was too lazy to hunt and Roosevelt too restless to fish. Roosevelt was quick, aggressive, emphatic, decisive; Taft was slow, deliberate, judicial by temperament. Roosevelt would make the presidency the most important of the three branches of government; Taft would seek to keep the branches in equilibrium. Yet two more different men could hardly have enjoyed a closer friendship—at least until 1909. Denying that he was merely a shadow of Roosevelt, Taft was convinced of the righteousness of Roosevelt's reforms, although he was not as friendly toward labor as was the president and disagreed with some of his methods. By the rule of elimination, he, rather than Philander C. Knox, Charles Evans Hughes, and certain lesser lights, appeared to be the best choice for presidential candidate in 1908—Root refused to run—and it may be said with some justice that Roosevelt both chose and elected him, as Jackson had Van Buren, without really violating any proprieties except in the mind of the Democratic opposition.

In turn, Taft had denied aspirations for the presidency in favor of appointment to the Supreme Court and then revealed a keen sense of obligation and duty by denying such appointment in order to serve Roosevelt in other ways. Trained in the law rather than in the jungle of politics, he often erred in his political judgments. Because he was trained in the law, which he admired as providing ordered liberty, and believed should be modified slowly, he desired to consolidate and to put upon a sound legal foundation the changes Roosevelt had made.

Despite Taft's conception of himself as the impartial judge acting without bias under the law, he tended to invest only the Republican party with virtue and to attribute all vices to the Democrats. If he scorned masters of capital who tried to twist the law to their own benefit, he also looked with contempt upon reformers who demanded "nostrums" and "panaceas" beyond the capacity of the governed to understand and use, especially if they were paternalistic. Thus he looked upon the law as an absolute rather than as a social device, saying in one instance that "undoubtedly the government can wisely do much more than [the laissez-faire school] would have favored to relieve the oppressed, to create great equality of opportunity, to make reasonable terms for labor in employment, and to furnish vocational education for the children of the poor. But . . . there is a line beyond which government cannot go with any good practical results in seeking to make men and society better." Therefore, "enthusiasts" who wished to eradicate poverty and the ugliness of city life erred, for they "have lost their sense of due proportion, and spend their energies in forward legislative plans for the uplift of the suffering and the poor and for the mulcting of the fortunate, the thrifty, and the well-to-do that are impractical and will only result in defeat, and increased burden of taxation."[26]

This is not to say that Taft opposed all additional reforms, for he sponsored many and was perhaps too consistent in pushing for the consummation of his major demands. But he often said privately what he refused to say publicly, or said publicly what might have been better said in private. In sum, despite his long and fruitful experiences at home and abroad, his avid desire to be a progressive reformer along lines laid out by Roosevelt, his having at hand a powerful club in the presidential office, particularly in the patronage, and his many legislative achievements, his administration was often marred by political ineptitude in both domestic and foreign affairs.

Taft was conservative by instinct, regular by training. If his legal learning caused him to avoid complete entrapment by the devotees of Social Darwinism, he was intuitively and ideologically conservative in his support of business rather than of labor, in seeing as inseparable the rights of the individual and the rights of property, and in his love of peace, quiet, stability, and order. As he put it in his Cooper Union address during the campaign of 1908:

> The capitalist, however wealthy, who is willing to devote his nights and days to the investment of his capital in profitable lawful business or manufacture and who studies methods of reducing the costs of production and economizing expenses should be regarded with favor by the workingman, because, while his motive is merely one of accumulation, he is working not only for himself but for labor and for society at large. . . . Their sole motive has been one of gain, and with the destruction of private property that motive would disappear, and so would the progress of society.[27]

That four years as president did not change his attitude is revealed in his writing in 1913 that

> the right of property guaranteed by the Constitution . . . united with that of personal liberty, has contributed more to the growth of civilization than any other institution established by the human race. . . . [I]f it is to be eliminated from our country . . . we shall see a halt in thrift, providence, industry, and mental and physical energy because they will no longer command the rewards that have heretofore stimulated them. . . .[28]

Yet Taft was optimistic about man's possibilities for improvement. While he held man to be "perfectible," he believed that generations if not centuries of the necessary educational and political processes would be needed to achieve this goal. Like Nicholas Murray Butler, Lodge, Roosevelt, and Root, he feared the tyranny of the majority, the passion of the mob, and the power over the people of a demagogue. As he put it in a lecture, "The principles of right and justice, and honesty and morality, are not merely conventional." They came from a "higher source more accurately than any which can be devised by man." And the best instrument to support and preserve that law was the judicial system, not as Roosevelt and the progressives believed, by state action or direct primaries or the initiative or other methods through which change was demanded by the people.[29] To expand the democratic base was particularly reprehensible because newly enfranchised voters or those using indirect methods might deprive holders of their properties. In vetoing the Arizona Constitution because it permitted the recall of judicial officials, he would say that "the people at the polls no more than kings upon the throne are fit to pass upon questions involving the judicial interpretation of the law" and that "the rule of the people would degenerate into anarchy and revert to despotism as the only way of escape."[30]

That such a philosophical devotee of laissez faire as Taft, who has been compared favorably with Grover Cleveland, should have promised to support Roosevelt's policies has been explained by his personal friendship with Roosevelt, his party loyalty, his unfortunate habit of permitting those closest to him to make his decisions for him, and his lack of contact with, indeed dislike of, reformers and progressives even before he became president. Despite his support for an income tax, corporation excise tax, conservation, direct election of senators, a postal savings bank system, and an antitrust crusade, he became stereotyped as the defender of the status quo, protector of property rights, and opponent of social democracy. In contrast, as a jurist he single-mindedly, dynamically, and imaginatively strove to make the courts more efficient instruments of justice. As has been said, he sought improved judicial administration as a bulwark against the rising tide of social democracy: "One way to undermine the social reformer's crusade was to meet his legitimate demands for evenhanded justice. Leveling gross inequalities between rich and poor at the bar of justice would remove a major source of social unrest. Improved judicial machinery would make courts potentially more effective safeguards of private property and, perhaps, help disarm its most dangerous enemies— socialists, communists, and progressives."[31] In the meantime, the nobless oblige of the rich and leisured class would lessen the burdens and sufferings of the poor and improve their opportunities for self-betterment. Harboring middle-class ideals, he devoted himself to the preservation of middle-class political, economical, and social institutions.

Irwin Hood "Ike" Hoover, who had begun serving as an usher at the White House in 1891, had seen a jolly and good-humored Taft come often to seek Roosevelt's advice during the campaign of 1908, then noticed that he rarely called between his election and inauguration. His duties at the reviewing stand completed on March 4, 1909, Taft returned to the White House. He had lost his good nature and seemed cross. He threw himself into a comfortable chair and prefaced his first order with the remark, "I am President now, and tired of being kicked around."[32] Unfortunately for him, he persisted in moving right while Roosevelt and much of the country moved left.

2

★★★★★

THE COUNTRY AND THE CHALLENGE

I

What was the material and spiritual condition of the United States that William Howard Taft inherited from Theodore Roosevelt?

Fortunately for Taft, by December 1907 the nation had weathered the panic that began in August. It then enjoyed an unbroken period of prosperity throughout his administration even though there was a slight recession in 1911. Bank deposits and capital, imports and exports, mineral production, manufactures, agricultural production, and insurance, among the many other indices of well-being, all showed increases over 1900. But the wealth of the nation was inequitably distributed. It was estimated in 1900 that 1 percent of the population owned more of the nation's wealth than did the other 99 percent. The situation had not improved much by Taft's time, when it was determined that seventy Americans each owned properties of $35 millions or more, or one-sixteenth of the total wealth of the nation. Because of this tremendous variation in personal or family income, those at the bottom of the economic scale, including color minorities and immigrants, lived very poorly.

The consolidation movement in industry which had blossomed under William McKinley continued despite Roosevelt, thanks in part to the weakening of the Sherman Antitrust Act by the courts. The United States Steel Corporation, 1901, was America's first billion-dollar enterprise. Had Roosevelt permitted the Northern

Securities Company, also 1901, to live, it would have dominated the railroad industry from Chicago to the Pacific Northwest. For legal reasons, the larger consolidations preferred the holding company to the trust form. Despite competition on a scale and of a type previously unknown, in 1910 1 percent of the industrial companies were producing 44 percent of the total manufactures, and railroad transportation lay in the hands of a small number of oligopolists. Favorable franchises similarly permitted monopoly in the urban and interurban trolley-car lines. With the Ford Motor Company (1903) and the General Motors Corporation (1908), the automobile manufacturing industry also became big business. Although they dealt with perishable products, beef, dairy, and other "trusts" made part of agriculture big business also.

Unlike the major European countries, which tolerated a degree of cooperation, combination, and monopoly, nineteenth-century America was dedicated to individualism and competition. So rampant was the unrestrained growth of industrial enterprise that state courts and legislatures had intervened to restrain monopolistic practices. The social legislation passed by Massachusetts soon after the Civil War and the Granger laws of the states of the Middle West are illustrative. Congress entered the picture with the Interstate Commerce Act, 1887, and the Sherman Antitrust Act, 1890. However, by declining to judge the latter strictly, and especially by deciding in the E. C. Knight case (1895) that maufacturing was not commerce, the Supreme Court excluded a large sector of the economy from judicial purview. Simultaneously, proposals for a civil service, the single tax, cooperatives, and currency inflation were among a number made to reform America and restore her individualistic moral society.

Following where the Populists and the liberal Democratic adherents of William Jennings Bryan had dared to tread, many of the progressives of Taft's day challenged the laissez-faire doctrine and what they believed to be the businessman's domination of both politics and government. Although masters of capital frequently fought one another—importers against exporters, for example—farmers and small-town businessmen of every section could readily point to metropolitan magnates nearby who controlled their financial destinies. "Wall Street," however, perceived as a living entity, was characterized as the chief villain. Progressives demanded a government strong enough to regulate business practices and also to assume long-range responsibilities in many other areas in order to assure that the promise of American democracy would be realized. Among their major demands were a regulation of the economy that would more equitably distribute the national wealth, a modification of government so as to make it more responsive to the wishes of the voters, and aid to the dispossessed without crushing their individual initiative. Priority was given to regulation of the economy.[1]

Preferring collective to individual action, big business naturally had its own outlook toward labor, the antitrust laws, and its relations with the state and federal governments. It tended to favor cooperation with the federal government—for state regulations were uneven—and even regulation from Washington, because its interests were national in scope and it avidly desired long-range stability. Smaller businessmen, however, responded more easily to the appeal of the trade association, which also had stability as its prime objective and voiced their particular outlook toward labor, the antitrust laws, and relations with the state and federal governments.[2] If the nation's businessmen did not speak with one voice, neither did they react in the same way to Taft's attempt to improve upon the Sherman Antitrust Act.[3] That labor opposed the stability sought by both large and small businessmen is understandable, for stability—achieved by price-fixing agreements, curtailing production, and lobbying at state capitals as well as at Washington— would benefit the associated employers rather than workers. It is also understandable that employers looked upon labor unions as being in violation of the antitrust laws and desired to destroy them.

In Taft's time, there was evidence of a shift from industrial to finance capitalism. J. P. Morgan and Company and Kuhn, Loeb, and Company, for example, for fat fees shuffled often watered stocks to put together manufacturing and/or communications giants, either controlling them directly or through a system of interlocking directorates.[4] Edward H. Harriman, who in the twentieth century maintained the public-be-damned attitude of the nineteenth-century tycoon, acquired such extensive holdings in the railroads of the East, South, and Pacific Northwest that his rails were enough to girdle the earth three times. If death had not intervened in 1909, he might have extended his American rail lines by joining trans-Pacific steamers with those of the Trans-Siberian in the Far East and thus proceeded westward in a globe-circling system. The extent of the growth of finance capitalism and its impact upon government as well as upon business was revealed by the Arsène Pujo subcommittee investigation, which began its work during Taft's last year and of which more will be said later.

As for the recessions of 1907 and of 1911, they were looked upon as unavoidable parts of the business cycle, hence not amenable to legislative action even if the temper of the times had permitted political tinkering with "immutable economic law." On how to deal with business "bigness" men disagreed. Some looked upon bigness as inevitable and called for government control; others proposed not only the federal control of trusts but a vigorous anti-trust program. The latter favored a return to the old competitive system of small units, arguing that in this way a regulatory bu-reaucracy would be avoided and individualism would be encour-aged. The battle between the individualistic and paternalistic schools and the search for a compromise position between them, such as that offered by the Socialists, would continue throughout Taft's term, as it indeed would under Woodrow Wilson and many later presidents.

Paralleling the consolidation movement in both industry and finance were the numerous new trade associations already men-tioned. These mushroomed in consequence of the continued flour-ishing of unionized labor and of the advantages already gained in a half-century of experience summarized by A. J. Eddy's *The New Competition* (1912). Similar objectives animated the National As-sociation of Manufacturers (1895–) and the Anti-Boycott Association (1902–). Not only did these organizations oppose the closed shop and restriction of output or of the number of apprentices; they also helped to defeat Taft's attempts to limit the issuance of labor in-junctions, and they worked mightily to defeat prolabor state and national representatives.[5] Yet many of them also sponsored various reforms, particularly of the "boomer" variety.

If industrial and financial concentration, management consoli-dation, and trade associations did not serve the needs of the average American, neither did much of the organized labor movement, which in 1910 included less than 10 percent of the workers. The perennial president of the American Federation of Labor, Samuel Gompers, rejected socialism, stoutly defended the capitalistic sys-tem and "pure and simple unionism," persistently followed an op-portunistic philosophy, catered only to the skilled portion of labor, and until 1908 eschewed direct political action.

In addition to the approximately two million men in the AFL, perhaps fifty thousand others were members of such unaffiliated unions as the United Mine Workers (1890–) and International Workers of the World (1905–), with other thousands in the four Railroad Brotherhoods. By the time of Taft's inauguration, when the IWW enrolled about sixty thousand men, its leadership resided in the one-eyed former cowboy and miner William "Big Bill" Haywood. While it had most success in the West, it invaded the East and conducted such bitter and violent strikes in Lawrence, Massachusetts, and Paterson, New Jersey, that Taft appointed an Industrial Commission to study the causes of such violence. But never during his four years did he use his powers or influence to prevent or settle a strike. The greatest labor gains in the East, in part because of victories of strikes in 1909 and 1910, came to the International Ladies' Garment Workers' Union, one of the first to win agreement with employers to use arbitration as a method of settling labor disputes.

Organized labor faced many conservative judges. Especially those on the federal bench looked upon unions as combinations in restraint of trade and readily issued injunctions against them when they sought to strike, or upheld yellow-dog contracts. Though he was not listened to at the moment, Associate Justice Oliver Wendell Holmes dissented in favor of labor. In other cases, judges used the Fifth and Fourteenth Amendments to protect property rather than persons or, by holding corporations to be "persons" at law, prevented their control by either federal or state law. The verdict in 1910 in the *Danbury Hatters* case, which had been before the Connecticut courts for six years, hit labor hard by causing the Union Hatters of North America, which had conducted a boycott, to pay the company almost a quarter of a million dollars. Taft appointed many new judges, sought to improve the administration of justice, and tried also to limit the use of injunctions in labor cases. While his personnel choices were happy and some betterment occurred in judicial administration, it cannot be said that he improved in any way the legal lot of labor.

II

The average annual wage of the American worker, $600, and the national per capita income of $227 at the time of Taft's inauguration sound low by comparison with figures of later years. However, the latter was still $46 better than the average for Great Britain and $66 greater than that of France. Moreover, Frenchmen paid an average tax of 12 percent, Britons of 9 percent, and Americans of only 3 percent. Yet in terms of real wages, of what goods and services the worker could buy, he was no better off than he had been in 1900. Indeed, the average annual cost of food for a worker's family rose from $309.19 in 1900 to $374.75 in 1910, with higher consumer prices beginning in 1910 often blamed upon the Payne-Aldrich tariff Taft dared to approve. The high cost of living —20 percent higher in 1910 than in 1901—was an international as well as a national phenomenon. It provoked enough articles on its causes to stock a small library and even investigations by state commissions and by the United States Senate. Middlemen, trusts, the tariff, the exhaustion of natural resources, and the increased money supply were among the many factors to which it was ascribed. Most pertinent was the fact that while profit plowback into future production remained steady during the decade, per worker productivity increased by 50 percent, yet wages remained firm. Thus more was produced than the worker could afford to purchase.

In contrast to the worker, the farmer was better off in every year of Taft's administration than in 1900. For him, the year 1908 was the most prosperous in history. In that year he produced crops valued at almost $8 billion—four times the value of all the minerals including oil extracted from below ground—and in 1910 almost $9 billion. In 1910, the value of his land and of his total holdings was double that of 1900, and his prices were 50 percent higher. Mechanization and specialization were progressing rapidly, with the result that corn, cotton, dairy, livestock, and wheat "belts" were clearly discernible and often spoke with variant political voices, as Taft learned to his regret when he tried to change the tariff rates.

By the time Taft took office, although there were many county and state agricultural societies and the remnant of the once powerful Patrons of Husbandry, little was left of such older farmers' organizations as the Alliances or even of the Populist party. There would be no real organization of political spokesmen for farmers outside of special-interest lobbyists until the Farm Bloc was established in 1921. Although many farmers left the states of the upper Mississippi Valley for cities in industrialized states, those who remained found the asperity and loneliness of farm life, so well described by Hamlin Garland, Ole Rolvaag, and Maria Sandoz, among others, largely dissipated by burgeoning postal, telegraph, telephone, and railroad lines and the beginnings at least of a road network.

Many issues of the progressive movement, which began at the turn of the twentieth century, continued the demands of the agrarian-oriented Populists; others reflected problems arising out of the growing industrialization and urbanization of the nation.

By Taft's time, the shrill denunciations of the inequities in American life by such Western Populists as Ignatius Donnelly, Mrs. Mary E. Lease, William A. Peffer, "Sockless" Jerry Simpson, Tom Watson, and James Baird Weaver, and of the liberal Democrat Bryan were muted by "better times," a less rigorous farm existence, and the accomplishment of some of the reforms they had demanded. To city dwellers, country people now appeared to be "hicks" or "rubes" rather than "radicals" or "anarchists." Similarly, the Socialist-oriented demands of Henry Demarest Lloyd and his minority-following in Populism had given way to an urban-based, more middle-class reformism dedicated to the improvement of the position of labor and of city life in general. Moreover, many businessmen demanded reform either because they sincerely wished it or because they feared labor violence or government control as alternatives. Finally, some energetic and ambitious federal administrators, including Dr. Harvey Washington Wiley, of the Department of Agriculture, Gifford Pinchot, of the Forestry Service, and Frederick Newell, of the Bureau of Reclamation, sponsored very practical reforms. In any event, whether agrarian- or urban-based, and while not overlooking the possibility of reform on the local and state level, progressives of all parties demanded a greater intervention by the federal government than did the Populists. They sought federal intervention in the solution of moral, economic, and political problems, especially of national problems unamenable to state action, such as antitrust legislation and railroad control, and they sought presidential rather than congressional action.[6] With few exceptions, Taft proved unwilling to support federal intervention.

With respect to population, the Census of 1910 showed that the continental United States contained 91,972,266 persons, an increase of 21 percent since 1900. The trend of population continued to be westward, especially to the Pacific Coast states, but the most populous states were New York, Pennsylvania, Illinois, Ohio, and Texas, in that order. Moreover, since only 45 percent of the people in 1910 lived on farms or in towns of fewer than twenty-five hundred persons, Taft would govern an increasingly urban rather than agrarian country and be charged with solving the myriad problems of a land of sprawling and formless industrial cities.

Some of the problems facing America's cities in Taft's day were caused by the as yet quite "open" immigration policy. Of the immigrants who still continued to flock in at a rate of approximately a million a year, most shunned the South, where wages were lower and the Negro provided economic competition. They thereby failed to leaven this heavily agrarian section with their usuable industrial labor, native intelligence, and perhaps new ideas. The vast majority of immigrants went instead to the slums of eastern cities, thereby exacerbating labor, union, housing, school, and sanitation problems, to mention only the most obvious ones. By far the greatest number of them were of the "new" immigration, from Italy, Austria, and Russia; these were generally abjectly poor and mostly illiterate. In 1910, one out of every seven Americans, or about fourteen million, was foreign born. In the same year, the vast preponderance of the seventy-two thousand Japanese lived in the West Coast states, many of which discriminated against them at the risk of involving the federal government in trouble with Japan. Organized labor, to a growing extent employers, and those who doubted the efficacy of the "melting pot" demanded the restriction of immigration. Congress passed a literacy-test requirement in 1912, but Taft vetoed it. Meanwhile settlement houses in the largest cities undertook to Americanize the immigrant without destroying those parts of his heritage which fit into and enriched American society.

Negroes in 1910 composed almost 11 percent of the total population. Four-fifths of them were in the states of the Old South, where they lived as though the Fourteenth and Fifteenth Amendments had never been adopted. They therefore questioned whether they were living in a democracy. They faced almost insuperable obstacles to exercising the right to vote and were segregated under Jim Crow practices in churches, labor organizations, and in the use of public facilities, in keeping with the "separate but equal" doctrine of Plessy v. Ferguson (1896). They did not enjoy the equal protection of the laws and were often subjects for lynchings. Their illiteracy rate was still very high. For example, in 1910 in Virginia, 10.9 percent of the native whites and 44.6 percent of the Negroes were illiterate. In 1900, when the national average expenditure per school child was $21.14, Massachusetts spent $39.10 per child and Alabama $3.10, North Carolina $4.56, and South Carolina $4.62. Moreover, southern states spent $4.92 for white and only $2.21 for Negro children. By 1910, a veritable educational revolution had occurred in the South: school revenues doubled, the school term was lengthened, more white and Negro children attended school, and the illiteracy rate dropped still further. Despite these accomplishments, southern mass education still lagged behind that of the North. Lower property values and the larger number of children compared to adults helped to account for the lag, but even more important was the fact that the South persisted in segregating white and Negro children in separate school systems and continued to spend more on white than on Negro children.

One type of Negro leadership was that provided by Booker T. Washington (d. 1915), who offered the hand of Christian conciliation and counseled that economic and eventual political progress could be made by vocational education, hard work, thrift, and acquiescence in social segregation. Another type was offered by the Massachusetts intellectual, William E. B. DuBois, who advised professional training and an uncompromising push for equal civil and social rights including that of the ballot. With others both Negro and white, DuBois helped in 1909 to establish the National Association for the Advancement of Colored People and through his editorship of the *Crisis* continued to counter the tactics pursued by Washington.

Negroes were making demonstrable economic gains, some via the tenant system, others through the outright ownership of land, still others by migrating to the North and obtaining industrial employment.[7] That they were still being exploited by whites was the thesis of Ray S. Baker, although George K. Turner held that both Negroes and whites were being exploited.[8] While Negro illiteracy dropped from 44 to 30 percent between 1900 and 1910, those Negroes who migrated to the North quickly learned that they were no more welcome to northern than to southern whites, for Jim Crow was born and reared in the North before it moved to the South.[9] Moreover, the popular northern conception of the Negro was that concocted by Baptist clergyman Thomas Dixon, of North Carolina and New York. In *The Clansman* (1905), Dixon pictured the Negro as a degraded creature lusting after white women and the Ku Klux Klan as the defender of white women and of Anglo-Saxon civilization. These characterizations were retained in the film version of the book, *Birth of a Nation* (1915), which coincided with the reorganization of the Klan that same year. By Taft's time, then, those southern liberals who would treat the Negro as an equal in all ways and those conservatives who would guarantee him at least his political and civil rights were in danger of being overwhelmed by racists. Jim Crow laws adopted by the southern states between 1898 and 1907 are a case in point, as are various studies of the time concluding that the Negro race was inferior to the white and that legislation could not change the mores governing their interrelations.[10] In consequence, a few blacks pessimistic about their future in the United States acquired "emigration fever" and returned to Africa.

Taking umbrage at the fact that the states controlled the educational system and the federal government had only limited power of intervention, Taft leaned more toward the Washington than the DuBois school, saying that Negroes should be trained in industrial work with only a few of their leaders going on to a university education. In the South, more attention should be paid to sanitation, hygiene, and education. In the end, he said, "The greatest hope that the Negro has, because he lives chiefly in the South, is the friendship and the sympathy of the white man with whom he lives in that neighborhood." Finally, "It seems to me that the future is in the hands of the race itself." He appointed a number of Negroes to public office, particularly in Washington, but "without the sacrifice of any interest of my own party," adding that "what I have not done is to force them upon unwilling communities in the South itself."[11] By agreeing that the solution of the Negro problem in the South lay with the dominant southern whites, Taft let the Negro be "kept in his place," that is, subordinated, exploited, and ostracized—except when white politicians needed their ballots wherever they were permitted to vote. He thus failed to see or follow the humanitarian mission historically associated with the Republican party, with the result that Negroes both North and South began to drift toward the Democratic party.

III

Many keen investigations of the American way of life, and various suggestions for improving it, were made in Taft's day. There was the pragmatism of John Dewey as applied to education and that of Holmes as applied to the law. A challenge to the sanctified Constitution was made in *The Spirit of American Government* (1907) by J. Allen Smith, while Lee Thorndike imparted novel ideas to pedagogy in his monumental work, *Educational Psychology* (1913). The study of sociology received a boost in William Graham Sumner's *Folkways* (1906), and the ideas concerning history of Frederick Jackson Turner, James Harvey Robinson, and various others ushered in a new kind of history. Charles A. Beard introduced an element of economic determinism in his early historical writings, while Thorstein Veblen revealed great irreverence toward orthodox economics. The revival of a neo-Hamiltonian philosophy may be credited largely to Herbert Croly and to the Theodore

Roosevelt of post-presidential years, and the name of Walter Rauschenbusch loomed large with respect to the Social Gospel movement.

In *The City: The Hope of Democracy* (1905), Frederick C. Howe detailed his vision of a planned urban democracy; in *The Bitter Cry of the Children* (1906), John Spargo called for reforms designed to improve the chances for a healthful and fruitful life for future generations. Dewey's "progressive" ideas for educating for social efficiency rather than learning by rote were beginning to take hold in many private schools and were even filtering into public ones. In most schools and colleges, furthermore, curricula were becoming increasingly secularized, and the number of elective courses continued to grow. Pragmatism extended also to the law, which many jurists saw not as fixed and immutable but as adjusting itself to social changes. Holmes, for example, said that "the life of the law has not been logic; it has been experience." The "sociological jurisprudence" of Louis D. Brandeis soon found a proponent in the teaching of law by Roscoe Pound. Finally, Frederick W. Taylor's program of industrial management found a happy home in the center of an efficiency craze that included a scrutiny of personal qualities and relationships between materials and between investment and revenue. Most importantly, it sought a "social harmony" that would provide "social efficiency." Among many others in various ways, Brandeis, Herbert Croly, and Walter Lippmann included in their writings about it their social outlook as well. Each concluded that greater governmental intervention and control was needed in the social order and that this control could come only from professional experts—men whose technical knowledge, training, and discipline established a leadership of the competent.[12]

Most of the ideas proposed by the men mentioned above were beyond the understanding of the common American. However, the average American easily believed criticisms of an economic system which permitted an imbalanced distribution of the national wealth. If Veblen perhaps too severely castigated all captains of industry as men who lived ostentatiously, they understood what he meant by "predatory wealth" and the vulgarity displayed by those who flaunted their riches before the eyes of the poor. They understood Edward A. Ross, who called attention to such "sins" as stock watering, which was not covered by law. They understood Bryan, who held that men with money corrupted everything they touched from legislatures to colleges. Less irreverent than the criticisms by economists like Veblen were the easily comprehended

31

strictures of Richard D. Ely, a lay leader in the social gospel movement.

The ideas of the men mentioned above as well as of others were widely spread by the mass-circulation media. Many daily newspapers in the largest cities had a circulation of well over one million. Some of them, like the *New York World*, often crusaded for reforms in political and governmental affairs as well as engaging in yellow journalism. However, the *World* was easily outdone by William Randolph Hearst, who by the end of Taft's term had newspapers in Atlanta, Boston, Chicago, Los Angeles, New York, and San Francisco. If sedate journals of opinion like the *Nation* were read by only the most literate and socially concerned Americans, more popular periodicals like the *American Review of Reviews, Collier's Weekly*, the *Forum, Harper's Weekly*, the *Literary Digest*, the *North American Review*, and the *Saturday Evening Post* had large circulations. It was perhaps less important that Thomas E. Watson, Robert M. La Follette, and Bryan could sell up to 150,000 copies of their weekly or monthly newspapers, though this revealed that personal journalism was still possible, than that their issues during Taft's term were largely devoted to an excoriation of his policies and his politics.

By Taft's day, the country press and Chautauqua were quite stereotyped, yet the latter had a color and appeal that beckoned to millions. The radio and cinema, invented at about the turn of the century, served relatively few as yet, and particularly those persons living in the hinterlands obtained their culture under canvas tents or in the "ol' opry house." For fifty cents, or less if he had a season ticket, one could enjoy the gamut from trained animal acts and Swiss yodelers all the way up to the serious political deliveries of La Follette or the morally inspiring and extensive disquisitions of Bryan. As yet, too, numberless thousands turned out to hear spellbinders orate on Memorial Day, the Fourth of July, and Labor Day, attended summertime political picnics, and formed vast audiences for those campaigning for election to office. As a cabinet officer, presidential contender, and then as president, Taft had an excellent forum for reaching the public. As will be shown, as president he got a bad press, and he failed to evaluate properly the propaganda value of the journalistic estate.

Of special interest are the muckrakers who appeared about the turn of the twentieth century, and by Taft's time may have passed their peak, yet still exerted a great deal of influence.[13] The writings of Ray S. Baker, Thomas Lawson, David Graham Phillips, Charles

Edward Russell, Lincoln Steffens, Mark Sullivan, and Ida Tarbell, to mention only the best-known writers, were published by the *American, Arena, Cosmopolitan, Everybody's, McClure's, Munsey's,* and a number of other magazines sold at popular prices, and Taft often felt their sting. Only occasionally, the novel voiced discontent with things as they were, as in the depictions of the ruthlessness of the American businessman found in Theodore Dreiser's *The Financier* (1912) and especially in *The Titan* (1914). According to a survey of 1911, the topics discussed by the magazines included better tenements, improved safety conditions in mines, fresh air campaigns, education about tuberculosis and other diseases, war on flies and other insect pests, pure food, abolition of white slavery, workmen's compensation, city government, rescue of poor children, juvenile courts, agricultural improvements, and police problems[14]— problems with which Taft did not concern himself except for eventually using his influence against rather than for "Boss" George B. Cox of his own home city of Cincinnati.

IV

If organized and unorganized workers, critics of conservative courts, heads of families hard put to obtain food for their children, Negroes, scholars, and journalists found much wrong with Taft's America, so did those who adhered to the Social Gospel. At least among the 186 Protestant denominations (of churchgoers in 1910, there were 12,000,000 Roman Catholics, 18,500,000 Protestants, and 150,000 Jews), religion centered upon the literally inspired Bible and concentrated upon winning souls for Christ. This was especially true in rural areas of the South and West, where "fundamentalism" still barred acceptance of Darwinian evolution and other scientific findings, where the manners and morals of the city were deemed to be wicked, and where the Reverend William A. "Billy" Sunday and other revivalists called many sinners to repentance during evangelistic crusades and, as Sunday put it, to "hit the sawdust trail." Except for eradicating the saloon, Sunday and his kind largely overlooked the economic and social abuses of their day. Such institutions as the Salvation Army, the Young Men's Christian Association, the Young Women's Christian Association, and the Young People's Society of Christian Endeavor (which had 2,700,000 members in 1911.), had strong social as well as religious programs, and various urban churches also became "institutionalized," that is,

33

tried to serve the daily needs of their people by providing shelter for athletic, social, and educational as well as religious activities.

The social gospel church, however, was devoted to the reform of society itself. The Reverend Washington Gladden, for example, eschewed the old-time individual pietism for Christian capitalism. He would make the church an active agency in advocating economic and social reform in the factory, in business, and in trade to the end that Christian ethics would dominate production. More radical were George D. Herron and Walter Rauschenbusch, who would destroy "amoral" capitalism by abolishing private property, create a cooperative socialistic "Christian democracy," and form a kingdom of righteousness on earth. If they failed to do so, they at least stimulated the growth of the institutional Protestant church. A similar group in the Roman Catholic Church led by Father John A. Ryan tried to make that church also a social service agency. In 1908, a general conference of the Methodist Episcopal Church asserted that labor unions were "of great benefit to society at large." The Federal Council of Churches of Christ in America, established that year, in its "social creed" adopted from the Methodists, urged the abolition of child labor, shortening of the work day, provision of old-age insurance, and "the most equitable division of the products of industry that can ultimately be devised." Similar economic and social reforms were also demanded by the Baptist World Alliance.[15]

It was only natural that Protestant rural America rather than heavily Catholic and Jewish urban America would support the fundamentalist faith and that Modernism flourished in the cities. Modernism might flower in the "country club" church, whose divines did not believe in the Bible as written and denied the necessity of belief in its miracles, but the devotees of the "old-time religion" would have none of it. Between 1909 and 1912 *The Fundamentals*, a series of 135 pamphlets, were published. These stressed the inerrancy of the Bible, the Virgin birth, substitutionary atonement, the physical resurrection, and the imminent second coming of Christ. Some three million copies of these pamphlets were distributed, and the World's Christian Fundamentals Association and similar organizations were formed to defend and spread their tenets. Among many others, Bryan subscribed to them. On the other hand, the mantle of "the great agnostic" Robert Ingersoll was being sought by Clarence Darrow among others, so that it may not be too far fetched to say that the Scopes trial of 1925 was made possible if not inevitable by events transpiring in Taft's day.

Closely allied with the Protestant churches was the prohibition movement. The Methodist Church in the North and all Protestant denominations in the South, where a particular objective was to keep liquor from Negroes, were joined after 1893 by the Anti-saloon League, which soon had a powerful lobby in Washington as well as in most state capitals. The league simply held that a man who drank was unfit to hold public office. Under the leadership of William H. Anderson and Wayne B. Wheeler, by 1909 it had won its first victories, in four southern states, and by the end of Taft's term could assert that half of the American population lived in dry territory and that national prohibition was not far off.

Many of the women in the Woman's Christian Temperance Union (1874–) also fought for woman suffrage, labor reforms, world peace, and other "moral causes," such as the protection of women's rights in marriage (or the right of divorce) and in the professions, "equal pay for equal work," a single standard of morality, and even birth control. Most of their earlier successes were on the state level. It was not until 1908, for example, that the United States Supreme Court, convinced by Brandeis's "sociological jurisprudence" method, upheld an Oregon law restricting the working hours of women in industry (but not of men) to ten a day. It thereby negated the freedom of contract guaranteed by the Fourteenth Amendment in favor of the police power of the states. In any event, by 1910 woman suffrage was permitted in six states, and in seven in 1911, and in fourteen in 1912, and the leaders in this movement correctly predicted that an amendment to the Constitution was within grasping distance even if Taft was rather hostile to the idea. Although he dignified the movement by addressing the annual convention of the National American Woman Suffrage Association, at Washington, he was hissed when he said that most women were not interested in obtaining suffrage, and if they did, the ballot would be controlled by women of the "less desirable class."[16]

As head of the Denver Juvenile Court, Judge Ben B. Lindsey had begun his experiment of listening to youthful offenders without lawyers and juries present and was sparking needed police and prison reforms. By 1909, a juvenile "psychopathetic institute" (forerunner of the child-guidance clinic) had been established in connection with Chicago's juvenile court and, despite the violent opposition of special interests in both political parties, a law was passed prohibiting the employment of children in dangerous occupations. By 1913, seventeen states had joined pioneer Missouri in granting pensions to mothers and widows who might not otherwise be able to rear their children in their own homes, and Taft's administration had added a Children's Bureau to the Department of Commerce and Labor to do research into and to gather data on problems affecting children.

V

That the political process was in many instances adapting itself to the economic and social changes of the "good years" was in evidence on the local and state levels before it affected national politics. Even though Lincoln Steffens graphically illustrated inefficiency, corruption, and waste in *The Shame of the Cities* (1904), thousands of "corrupted and contented" local governments paid no heed to reform. Whether the machine was Democratic or Republican made no difference in cities either large or small. As Jane Addams had concluded before him, Steffens believed that the voters rather than the "system" needed reformation. On the other hand, such mayors as Brand Whitlock in Toledo (1904–1914), Tom Johnson (1901–1909) and Newton D. Baker (1911–1915) in Cleveland, and several Socialist mayors fought successful battles against graft, privilege, and corruption, particularly against traction and utility rings. Like the leaders in the business-dominated municipal research bureaus, they favored a more businesslike and efficient government, one which often owned its own utilities or exerted tight control over private companies and over tax assessments. Galveston, Texas, was the first city to adopt the commission form of government, one in which a number of well-trained and expert commissioners for fire, police, education, and the like administered the government and the mayor was relegated to a figurehead post. Staunton, Virginia, was probably the first to adopt the city-manager plan, with other cities soon falling in line because of the appeal of taking their government out of politics and putting it on a "businesslike" basis. In 1908, more than sixty cities with a total population of three million had adopted some form of commission government. By 1912, the number of cities with this form of government had grown to 207.[17]

Steffens also wrote about the corruption in the states, and reforms proceeded on a grander scale and at a faster pace on the state than on the city level. The chief targets for reformers were the usually corporate business interests and their ally, "the boss" of the political machine. In this "invisible government," the

36

boss obtained whatever legislation business wanted or, more likely, killed attempts to set maximum hours or minimum wages for labor or to obtain other forms of social legislation. The cure for the ills of democracy, many believed, was more democracy, more popular control of the instrumentalities of government, more home rule. For example, direct primaries, first adopted in the Middle- and Far West, spread soon to the East and by 1913 were used by fifteen states.

Others, however, would reconcile expertism and democracy by heightening nonpartisanship, using stronger executives, and separating politics from administration. Belief that the partisanship which caused people to split into two parties on the national level should not be transferred to municipal affairs led to the adoption of the nonpartisan local ballot and the commission form of city government. A strong executive was looked upon as a protector of the people against organized interests and seekers for special privilege. Professor Frank J. Goodnow led the movement to separate the ends of government—politics and legislation—from the means—impartial, nonpartisan, and scientific management. After Wisconsin established an efficiency commission in 1911, fifteen other states adopted the plan by 1917.[18]

Many reform governors who were Taft's contemporaries demanded that all citizens participate in government and that the state governments use their police powers to achieve social betterment. Among them were Albert B. Cummins, Iowa (1900–1906); Joseph W. Folk, Missouri (1905–1909); Charles Evans Hughes, New York (1906–1910); Hiram Johnson, California (1910–1912); Robert La Follette, Wisconsin (1900–1906); George Sheldon (1906–1908) and D. H. Aldrich, Nebraska (1910–1912); and Woodrow Wilson, New Jersey (1910–1912). The acme of good administration was portrayed in *Philip Dru, Administrator* (1912). Although it was rumored that Theodore Roosevelt wrote the book, Edward Mandell House later claimed its authorship.

The progressive movement also flowered early and blossomed widely in the states of the South, where its devotees were paradoxically racists who equated white supremacy with progressivism.[19] In any event, the panic of 1907 and the short depression that followed it acted as a catalyst and caused reformers who had concentrated upon local government to adopt a national orientation. In 1908, for example, the AFL moved into national politics, the Vreeland Act foreshadowed the Federal Reserve banking system, Roosevelt nationalized his demands for the conservation of natural resources, and the founding occurred of the National Association for the Advancement of Colored People, the National Urban League, and the Federal Council of Churches of Christ in America.[20]

Progressives used states as social laboratories. Because of the prominence of La Follette, the program included in the "Wisconsin idea" is worthy of note. Direct primary elections were used to take political power away from the bosses. Business corporations were brought under strict control, railroad taxes were raised to represent a fairer share of the state's burden, and the use of railroad passes by public officials was made illegal. A progressive tax was laid upon inheritances, provision was made for employer liability and workmen's compensation in case of industrial accidents, and conservation laws were applied to forests and to water power. The expert in government was welcomed rather than feared, and good use was made of administrative commissions staffed by experts in the fields of taxation, industry, banking, conservation, and insurance, among others.[21] Meanwhile many other states adopted the initiative and referendum and the recall of state officials, extended the suffrage to women, and adopted preferential primaries for senators until the Seventeenth Amendment was added to the Constitution in 1913. Except in the South, the most egregious evils of child labor were mitigated. In contrast, the state supreme court of Arizona found unconstitutional the first law establishing an old-age pension system.

Throughout the progressive era, much was heard about making government "businesslike," about giving government the same singleness of purpose, leadership, discipline, and efficiency as a corporation. Frederick W. Taylor, in his *Principles of Scientific Management* (1911), suggested that an efficiency expert be added to a president's cabinet in order to promote efficiency in all government departments. Although the suggestion was not adopted, Taylor's ideas were followed in two "model cities," New York and Philadelphia.[22] As will be seen, Taft did more than any president before him to make the federal government "efficient." It was no coincidence that he chose Frederick A. Cleveland, the technical director of the New York Bureau of Municipal Research, to head the Commission on Economy and Efficiency he appointed in 1912. But such was his innate conservatism that he opposed the extension of more democratic political methods.

Vachel Linday charged that Roosevelt "cursed Bryan and then aped his ways." To a degree, Roosevelt had put into practice Bryan's demand for an interventionist government, one that would at least discipline the unrestrained economic order. He had provided the executive direction needed to accomplish some progressive reforms, as in trust busting (though this fizzled out quickly), new railroad legislation, and the conservation of natural resources. He also obtained the prohibition of corporation contributions to campaign funds, social legislation affecting labor and the consumer, as in the Pure Food and Drugs Act, and the creation of a Bureau of Corporations that would investigate corporate practices. Finally he threatened the criminal prosecution of businessmen lawbreakers. He spoke about revising the tariff and the currency and about the federal control of all interstate corporations but did nothing about them. Nor did his administration indict criminally a single corporation executive. Thus much remained to be done. Indeed, Bryan, often looked upon as a "yardstick of reform," charged that Roosevelt had won his greatest popularity by filching his platform planks. Bryan also declared that the small town middle classes and the farmer of the West and South were "on fire" for a progressive revolution, that "the more freely you allow the people to rule, the more quickly will every abuse be remedied," and that the prime economic problem to be solved was "the more equitable distribution of wealth."[23] Bryan added that La Follette should have been nominated by the Republicans in 1908 because he was a proved reformer, and Taft was not. Did Roosevelt have any assurance that Taft as president would oppose predatory wealth and monopoly? As Bryan saw Taft, he was a judge who had aroused the hostility of labor and an administrator who had not made himself popular with the Filipinos, the American soldier, or the American people.[24] Others predicted that his administration would be a shadowy repetition of Roosevelt's, a Hamlet without the Prince of Denmark.

The Republican party's unbroken victories from 1896 to 1908 made at least the business community stick steadfastly to it as the party of safety and prosperity. However, the panic of 1907 reduced businessmen's reverence for Roosevelt and caused them to welcome Taft as president because he was thought to be conservative and, while continuing the best of the Roosevelt policies, would not be so violent and disruptive. But Republican dominance in government was more apparent than real. Although it may be held that the returns for 1908 as well as for most other presidential years reveal sentiment, resentment, or conviction in the voters' minds rather than sectionalism, geography does play a significant part and votes do show that sectionalism is important.[25] For many years, economic factors such as a protective tariff enabled the Republican party to dominate the states of the East, none of which voted Democratic from 1896 to 1908. While the more agricultural South and the Middle West suffered from a consciousness of being in a "colonial" status, the South gave about 40 percent of its presidential vote to the Republican party. The Border States, which enjoyed a diversity of economic enterprise, slowly shifted from the Democratic to the Republican party. However, by Taft's time the growth of industrialism in the states of the Old Northwest tied that section to the Republican party too—it won every election therein between 1896 and 1908. Similarly, most of the fifteen states of the Far West were Republican rather than Democratic; in the six elections held between 1888 and 1908, the Republicans lost only one of them. By definition, then, the Republican party was a sectional party with its greatest strength in the East and Middle- and Far West. Even though Democratic businessmen in the South could be considered to be "assistant Republicans," the Republican organization rarely if ever won public office in the South and did little if anything to bring that section into the fold beyond dispensing some patronage. On the other hand, that contender for the presidential nomination who controlled the "rotten borough" southern states enjoyed great support in the national convention.

Very important for Taft's presidential career were the death of O. H. Platt in 1905, the refusal of John C. Spooner to stand for reelection, and the increasing disaffection of William B. Allison. These occurrences left Nelson W. Aldrich pretty much alone to lead the Senate's Republican majority against the small insurgent minority that nonetheless could show its power when allied with the minority Democrats. Only the need for unity in the elections of 1908 had prevented the outbreak of internecine party warfare— warfare which became public and intensified with the inauguration of Taft. As will be indicated, the warfare was based largely upon variant sectional attitudes toward the major reforms Taft would support or initiate—the tariff, conservation, post office, postal savings banks, railroads, income tax, efficiency in government, tariff reciprocity with Canada, and currency and banking.

When Taft assumed office, it appeared more important to him to assimilate the reforms undertaken by Roosevelt than to enlarge the degree of federal intervention in the economic and social life

40

of the nation. Since he believed American civilization to be basically sound, he need improve it only a bit here and there. But would the progressives be satisfied with piecemeal reform of problems besetting both agrarian and urban America? Would he not seem to abdicate leadership in the progressive movement if he stood pat?[26]

VI

Taft's experiences in the Philippines and in the cabinet should have given him an excellent background for dealing with foreign relations. To understand how his conduct differed from that of Roosevelt, a brief account is necessary of the major Roosevelt policies.

Though he had capable secretaries of state in John Hay and Elihu Root, Roosevelt largely determined the foreign policies of the United States and in addition conducted them as much by executive action and as little with congressional consent as possible. A realist, he had concentrated upon possible challenges to the security and interests of the United States from the large powers of the world, namely Great Britain, France, Russia, and Japan. Primary objectives to him were the defense of the American empire in the Caribbean and in the Pacific and the building of an isthmian canal so that the United States could be a Pacific as well as an Atlantic power. A necessary corollary, in keeping with the Monroe Doctrine, was the protection of that canal, which included the defense of Central and South America from external aggression. The nation he feared least was Great Britain, for he well knew that Canada served as a hostage for Anglo-American friendship. The nation he feared most was Germany, which "menaced" various nations in the Caribbean, was reputedly seeking to acquire the Danish West Indies, was rapidly building up its navy, and, as revealed in the Venezuela episode of 1902–1903, was eager to extend its influence in South America.

Even if McKinley provided a threshold to American internationalism,[27] Roosevelt was the first president to shun the traditional policy of noninvolvement in the affairs of Europe and to assume for the United States a positive role in world affairs. His efforts at Portsmouth and Algeciras are cases in point. Despite his frequent moral blusterings, his threats to "stand the Kaiser on his head," and his decision to increase the size and power of the navy, he would use military power not only to protect the interests of the United States but to preserve world peace. The most egregious exception to this strategy was his "taking" of Panama, in 1903. A second exception was his intervention in Santo Domingo. Thus, rather than denying European powers the right to interfere in the Americas, as Monroe intended, he unilaterally exercised an international police power in the Western Hemisphere. As has been said, it was a negative, homeopathic imperialism against European imperialism.[28] Roosevelt forced Santo Domingo to agree to American control of her finances, thus obviating the need for European intervention. When the Senate rejected the arrangement in treaty form, he implemented it by executive order for two years before excellent work by Root got the Senate to approve a treaty modified so as to lessen the grounds on which the United States could intervene. On the other hand, although he sent American troops twice to Cuba, as he could under the Platt Amendment to maintain order, he twice removed them. Moreover, he generously admitted that he had followed much of the advice of Root, who as secretary of war had established the colonial policies of the United States and as secretary of state from 1905 to 1909 had administered the colonies in humanitarian rather than paternalistic or despotic manner and in addition sought to foster the Pan-American movement. Better than Hay, Root had cooperated with Congress in matters dealing with foreign affairs. Finally, he had made one of his most important contributions in reforming the Consular Service by extending the merit system to it. With respect to the Department of State, which remained separated from the Consular Service until 1924, at Taft's urging he had authorized the creation of a Division of Far Eastern Affairs, precursor of numerous other "geographical desks" Taft and Knox would establish.

How would Taft react to the numerous challenges that faced him upon his assumption of the presidency?

It was often assumed that Taft, an "edited" version of Roosevelt, would merely continue Roosevelt's domestic policies. Every president, however, develops his singular "style," and Taft was already on record as desiring to place upon a sounder constitutional or legislative basis some actions Roosevelt had taken by executive order. Note has already been made that organized labor and the Negro could expect little help from him. Would he or could he provide a more equitable distribution of the national wealth, control big business in the national interest, and keep peace between capital and labor? Could he level out the ups and downs of the

42

business cycle? If it fell to him to nominate new judges, especially to the Supreme Court, would he reverse tradition and choose men who preferred to protect the rights of persons rather than of property? Would that court stop its arbitrary use of labor injunctions? What would he do about the high cost of living, which bore particularly hard upon breadwinners? If he was not interested in solving the myriad problems that beset both city and country life, what would his attitude be toward the most critical problems facing the nation—an income tax that would raise revenue but also serve as a redistributor of the national wealth, the control of big business so as to provide free competition, and reform of the tariff, currency and banking, and conservation of natural resources along "scientific" lines? Each of these issues reverberated with divisive sectional as well as political overtones. Did he have the skill to force political compromises on them? Even if he did, would the result that was acceptable politically necessarily be the *best* solution for the nation? Finally, would he favor the improvement of democratic government by the admission of more democratic methods and/or more efficient administration? Would he try to nationalize the Republican party by winning converts and thus victories in the South as well as in the North and also reform the rules of the national convention so that all Republicans would be represented equally therein? Would he succeed in quelling the incipient insurgency movement against standpat Republicanism in Congress or become a victim of it? Most of this study is an attempt to answer these questions.

Would Taft be his own secretary of state, as Roosevelt had been, or would he delegate the making of policy and the conduct of diplomacy to subordinates? Would his policies be as realistic as Roosevelt's or more idealistic? Would he keep the military forces of the United States, particularly the navy, at the degree of strength and efficiency to which Roosevelt had brought them, augment them, or weaken them? What ramifications in both military and diplomatic contexts would have faced him if the Panama Canal were completed during his term? Would he continue to use the Big Stick or design policies suited to restore or enhance world peace? Would the Anglo-American friendship and the German-American confrontation continue? What would be his attitude toward the apparent contest for hegemony in the Orient between Japan and Russia? We shall deal with these questions in chapters 10 and 11.

3

★★★★★

"THE BEST TARIFF BILL"

I

A natural showman, Theodore Roosevelt was fascinated by being president. "When you see me quoted in the press as welcoming the rest I will have," he wrote to William Howard Taft on January 1, 1909, "take no stock in it. I . . . like my job. The burdens . . . will be laid aside with a good deal of regret."[1] Determined to leave Taft alone to run his administration, the still young Roosevelt—he was only fifty years of age—made his final preparations to go hunting in Africa for a year. Worried lest his experiences had not sufficiently fitted him to be the chief executive, Taft confessed to Roosevelt that he looked "forward to the future with much hesitation and doubt . . . but if we put our shoulder to the wheel and follow the course marked out by you . . . I am very hopeful that, while we may not accomplish all we have promised, we shall give evidence of an earnest and sincere attempt to do so."[2]

Taft clearly stated his objective on February 23:

> Mr. Roosevelt's function has been to preach a crusade against certain evils. He has aroused the people to demand reform. It becomes my business to put that reform into legal execution by the suggestion of certain amendments of the statute in the governmental machinery. . . . The people who are best fitted to do this, without injury to the business interests of the country, are those lawyers who understand corporate wealth, the present combination, its evils, and the method by which they can be properly re-

45

strained. I am hopeful, moreover, that the suggestions that we shall make to the first regular session of Congress will be received with respect and a desire to support them by those men—leaders in Congress—who would certainly oppose recommendations made by a Cabinet consisting of the more radical members of the party. What I am anxious to do is to do something, and not to make a pronunciamento, and then at the end of my administration have nothing to point to. . . .[3]

Two items in this letter should be stressed: Taft's proposal to use in his cabinet corporation lawyers who would respect the rights of the business interests of the country, and his reference to opposition expected from the "more radical members of the party," those called "insurgents."

The word "insurgency" is used here to denote the actions taken by a group of dissentient Republican congressmen who revolted against taking dictation from their leaders either on questions of procedure or on specific legislative measures. In particular, they opposed Taft on the Payne-Aldrich tariff, the Ballinger-Pinchot conservation controversy, and the Mann-Elkins railway rate bill of 1910. Although used as early as 1901, the term "insurgent" was popularized during the months between Taft's election and inauguration by the four journalists Ray Stannard Baker, Mark Sullivan, Judson C. Welliver, and William Allen White. During Taft's term, insurgents included mostly progressives who preferred Roosevelt's policies to Taft's. They will be referred to herein as either insurgents or progressives, depending upon the context, and often synonymously.

Several forebodings of the eventual Taft-Roosevelt split occurred at inauguration time. On the afternoon of March 3, while Taft played golf, Mark Sullivan called to bid Roosevelt goodbye. As they walked toward the door, Sullivan asked Roosevelt, "How do you really think Taft will make out?" Roosevelt replied, "He's all right, he means well, and he'll do his best. But he's weak. They'll get around him." Pressing against Sullivan's shoulder with his own and pushing him gently back, he added, "They'll, they'll lean against him."[4] The evening of March 3, after the Tafts had accepted an invitation to stay overnight at the White House, was one of the most miserable ever spent by the Tafts and Roosevelts. Although Roosevelt had approved of Taft's inaugural address and said nothing about his cabinet choices, both men found it difficult to talk in the lighthearted way they usually did. Elihu Root, generally known as an unemotional man, was said to have dropped tears into his soup at dinner because Roosevelt was leaving the White House. Mrs. Roosevelt, upset because Mrs. Taft with unbecoming lack of grace asserted that she intended to make certain personnel and other changes at the White House, happily joined her husband in retiring early. Their sleep was later broken by the howling winds of a snowstorm. Taft meanwhile attended a Yale alumni gathering at which he said "I will do my best; I feel it in my bones that I will make good."[5]

Some jocularity was restored the following morning. Roosevelt said that the storm would soon be over, that "as soon as I am out where I can do no further harm to the Constitution it will cease." Taft retorted: "You're wrong. It is my storm. I always knew it would be a cold day when I became President of the United States."[6] They then proceeded to the inauguration ceremonies, which were held in the Senate rather than outdoors because of the storm. He recognized his "heavy weight of responsibility," said Taft, adding that he had helped

> to advise Roosevelt, to hold up his hands in the reforms he has initiated. I should be untrue to myself, to my promises, and to the declarations of the party platform on which I was elected to office if I did not make the maintenance and enforcement of those reforms a most important feature of my administration. . . . They were directed to the suppression of the lawlessness and abuses of power of the great concentrations of capital invested in railroads and in industrial enterprises carrying on interstate commerce. . . . To render the reforms lasting, however, and to secure at the same time freedom from alarm on the part of those pursuing proper and progressive business methods, further legislative and executive actions are needed.

He would see to the enforcement of the antitrust laws, to the conservation of the nation's natural resources, to the protection of workmen against the abuses of industrial life, and to the building of the army and navy to the point where they could be useful in supporting peace. He would try to bring some flexibility into the currency system, to advance the status of the southern Negro, to stop abuse of the labor injunction, and to revise the Dingley tariff downward.[7]

Protocol called for the incoming and outgoing presidents to return to the White House, but Roosevelt vetoed protocol and went directly to Union Station while Mrs. Taft violated precedent by riding back to the White House with her husband.

While under the spell of the dynamic Roosevelt, Taft had appeared to be a progressive cut from the full Roosevelt cloth. With Roosevelt gone he would return to his basic conservative self and thereby earn the odium of the progressives as one who had deserted their cause. Meanwhile, helped by Captain (later Major) Archibald Willingham Butt, who was continued as the president's military aide, Mrs. Taft instituted her changes. She placed liveried Negro footmen rather than frock-coated white men at the door to announce visitors and direct sightseers, replaced the male steward with a female housekeeper, and in general refurbished and resupplied the establishment and even pastured a cow on the White House lawn. She had her problems, of course, for she never knew how many guests her husband would bring to lunch, or whether he would arrive a half hour early or an hour late. With meticulous care she arranged for the numerous state and informal dinners and receptions, for receiving her callers on three afternoons a week, and for an amazing number of teas, luncheons, musicales, dinner parties, garden parties, and dances. In addition, the Tafts went out as often as they could. They knew the city and occasionally escaped their guards and called upon their own close friends. The result for her was a breakdown in health which began in May 1909 and lasted for about a year, until she recovered from a stroke that had affected her speech and the use of her right arm and right leg. After her recovery, however, she resumed her social obligations by giving musicales, attending dancing classes, and introducing daughter Helen, a student at Bryn Mawr, to society. She also arranged to have musical concerts given on the Mall, supervised the planting of Japanese cherry trees along Potomac Park and started the Cherry Blossom festival, and ordered the installation of an extra large bathtub in the White House after Taft got stuck in the regular one. So busy was she that she decided to stop giving her husband political advice—a grave error because her judgment was often superior to that of the conservative counselors Taft gathered about him.

From the social point of view, Washington rarely had four happier years. If the Tafts did not drink, they served good food and wine; being the first to enjoy a $75,000 rather than $50,000 salary, they were able to entertain effectively and, in summer, to rent a cottage, really a mansion, at Beverly, Massachusetts, where he would get in at least one golf game a day. Now granted a traveling allowance, Taft also became one of the most peripatetic of presidents, with some of his tours lasting for several months and covering many thousands of miles. Indeed, his travels and his participation in so many social functions and persistent banqueting raised the question in many minds whether he was truly serving the nation's needs or seeking personal pleasure. At the annual Gridiron Club dinners, for example, he was severely taken to task for his junketing and eating. And the *Outlook* was only one of many periodicals that asserted that while he should go out and meet the people it might be better if he stayed at Washington to give direction to national policy and also to settle controversies before they reached the crisis stage.

One of the reasons often alleged for the eventual Taft-Roosevelt "break" was Taft's choices for his cabinet. If he were to carry out Roosevelt's policies, should he not retain his personnel? In the flush of excitement following his nomination, he had implied rather than pledged that he would keep the members of Roosevelt's cabinet and also retain the services of the diplomatist Henry White. He then probably forgot what he had said. However, since Secretary of State Root and Secretary of the Navy Truman Newberry wished to retire to private life, and Secretary of the Treasury George B. Cortelyou was not considered capable of working with him, he asked only four or five members—James Garfield, George von L. Meyer, Oscar Straus, and James Wilson, and possibly Luke Wright—to stay on. "I must get the best men," he told a friend. "I mean by that I must get the best men with the best qualifications for the place."[8] He later asserted that he had made up his own cabinet and had not conferred with anybody except as to the secretary of the treasury and the secretary of state, thereby assuming full responsibility for his actions. But he had talked with more men than he was willing to admit. When Root declined to stay on, he asked him to suggest a successor. Root named P. C. Knox and at Taft's request approached him and won his consent.[9] Taft had also taken counsel with Nelson W. Aldrich, Knox, William Nelson Cromwell, and John Hays Hammond but had not sought the advice of Roosevelt or that of a number of powerful party leaders. Hammond, who had been two years ahead of him at Yale and was now a rich retired mining engineer, had helped with his election by revitalizing the National League of Republican Clubs. After his election, Taft offered Hammond the secretaryship of the navy, which he declined, and talked with him about the various cabinet posts. Hammond recalled that Taft, in his expansive way, had intimated that Roosevelt's cabinet should also help him "in the new job the President has picked for me" but that he had made no specific promises to appoint any one of them to a particular position. He would give Meyer a post so that he could not contest the congressional seat Henry Cabot Lodge wanted for his son-in-law, Augustus P. Gardner. He also needed to reward national chairman Frank Hitchcock. It was Hammond who personally made Taft's offer of secretary of the interior to Richard Achilles Ballinger, who declined it, whereupon Taft had his own brother Henry win Ballinger over. If by selecting Ballinger he meant to recognize the claims of the Far West, he soon learned that sectionalism of this kind could have disastrous results. In the end, Taft switched Meyer from Post Office to Navy; replaced Wright, War, with Jacob McGavock Dickinson; Cortelyou, Treasury, with Franklin MacVeagh; Attorney General Charles J. Bonaparte with George W. Wickersham, a partner in Henry Taft's law firm; and Garfield, Interior, with Ballinger. Charles Nagel, of Missouri, legal counsel to Adolphus Busch, succeeded Oscar Straus as secretary of commerce and labor, most likely as a reward to a Taft patron and to likeminded businessmen. With the perennial James Wilson in Agriculture, the cabinet was complete.

In January 1909, Lodge visited Taft at Augusta, Georgia, where he had gone to vacation almost immediately after his election. He reported to Roosevelt that "it was evidently the intention to get rid of every person who might keep President Taft in touch with the Roosevelt influence."[10] While all of Taft's men were quickly confirmed by the Senate, the public was immediately struck with the fact that seven of the nine had studied law, that five were lawyers well seasoned with corporation atmosphere, and that only three—Hitchcock, Meyer, and Wilson—had served Roosevelt. Taft's selections disappointed the insurgents, and Roosevelt realized that conservative if not reactionary lawyers would not advise Taft to support his policies, yet he said he did not care. "Taft is going about this thing just as I would do," he told Butt, "and while I retained McKinley's cabinet the conditions were quite different. I cannot find any fault in Taft's attitude to me."[11] "Ha, ha! *you* are making up your Cabinet. *I* in a lighthearted way have spent the morning testing the rifles for my African trip. Life has compensation!" he had written Taft on December 31, 1908, and on January 4, 1909, he had written that Taft should tell those whom he would not reappoint that they should begin to seek employment elsewhere.[12]

Typical of the letters Taft wrote to those in Roosevelt's cabinet he did not keep is that he wrote to Garfield:

> The most painful duty I have to perform is the selection of a Cabinet for my own administration. The circumstances under which I enter upon the duties of a new administration are quite different from those of a retiring administration, and they require that the complexion of the new Cabinet should be somewhat different from the old because of a difference in function that the new administration is to perform in carrying out the policies of the old, as I explained in my letter of acceptance. It means that I cannot retain in my Cabinet a good many who served Mr. Roosevelt in that capacity, although I have for them a warmth of affection and a great respect. . . . The truth is that in the selection of my Cabinet I have tried to act as judicially as possible and to free myself altogether from the personal aspect, which has embarrassed me not only with respect to you, but with respect to the members of the body of which we both formed a part.[13]

To the opposition press Taft was guilty of a breach of faith with respect to Garfield, Straus, and Wright, and their headlines screamed that "Taft Has Surrounded Himself with Corporation Attorneys" and that "Taft Has Made Studied Effort to Repudiate Things Predecessor Stood For." Moreover, Republican partisans were greatly disturbed with his having brought two Democrats, Dickinson and MacVeagh, into the cabinet, where they assumed that political affairs as well as public policy would be considered. However, if Taft had appointed Dickinson, "the finest type of Southern Democrat," to "honor the South," he considered MacVeagh, who had supported Lincoln, McKinley, Roosevelt, and himself and voted for Cleveland only because of the tariff, to be a "Progressive Regular" Republican—whatever that meant.[14] None of his cabinet, however, was either a reformer or a progressive. It was popularly held that corporation lawyers could not be in sympathy with the aspirations of the people; Taft's premise was that the best kind of lawyer was often employed by the great corporations and that he needed lawyers who knew the corporations if they were to enforce the laws against them. In some instances, however, and particularly in the case of Ballinger, strict construction of the law did not always fit in with the spirit of what Roosevelt had tried to do. Furthermore, once trouble brewed between Taft and Roosevelt, Dickinson felt out of place because as a Democrat and a southerner he could bring his chief no political support. When he resigned, Taft named Henry L. Stimson, intimate friend of Roosevelt, as his successor.

Difference of opinion also surrounds Roosevelt's reception of a letter and farewell gift Taft sent to the S. S. *Hamburg* via Archie Butt on March 23, 1909. Taft had addressed the letter to "My dear Theodore" and begun by saying, "If I followed my impulse, I should still say 'My dear Mr. President.' I cannot overcome the habit. When I am addressed as 'Mr. President,' I turn to see whether you are not at my elbow." He bade Roosevelt farewell and a safe journey. Then:

> I have no doubt that when you return you will find me very much under suspicion by our friends in the West. . . . I knew . . . I should make a capital error in the beginning of my administration in alienating the good will of those without whom I can do nothing to carry through the legislation to which the party and I are pledged. [Joseph G.] Cannon and Aldrich have promised to stand by the party platform and to follow my lead. They did so, I believe, for you in the first Congress of your administration and this is the first Congress of mine.

He would do nothing as president, he continued, without having a "mental talk" with Roosevelt, but he confessed that he lacked Roosevelt's facility for

> educating the public as you had through talks with correspondents, and so I fear that a large part of the public will feel as if I had fallen away from your ideals; *but you know me better and will understand that I am still working away on the same old plan* and hope to realize in some measure the results that we both hold valuable and worth striving for. I can never forget that the power that I now exercise was a voluntary transfer from you to me, and that I am under obligation to you to see to it that your judgment in selecting me as your successor and in bringing about the succession shall be vindicated according to the standards which you and I in conversation have always formulated. . . .[15]

Besieged as he was by well-wishers, Roosevelt could not read the letter at the moment, but as his ship steamed down the Hudson River he telegraphed Taft: "Am deeply touched by your gift and even more by your letter. Greatly appreciate it. Everything will turn out all right, old man. Give my love to Mrs. Taft."[16] However, according to James Watson, the Senate whip, who got the story from Colonel William Ward, for forty years a leader of the Republican party in New York State, Roosevelt sent everyone but Ward out of his stateroom and exploded about Taft: "He mentions his brother Charles in connection with me? . . . I'll show him. I'll get back in time for the next presidential election. I'll teach him to mention his brother Charles along with me. . . ."[17] Apparently, Roosevelt confused Taft's letter with one Taft had sent him some time earlier which mentioned Charles and Roosevelt together as responsible for Taft's election.

Taft normally began his day with physical exercise at seven o'clock. At breakfast he would read his favorite newspapers, the *New York Sun, Times,* and *Tribune,* and *Washington Post.* Upon arriving at his office at about 9:30, he would read the *Charleston News and Courier* because he liked its style, then hold a brief public reception in which he could say a few words and shake hands with from 150 to 200 people in ten minutes. Formal appointments followed and were supposed to end at 1:30 P.M., but frequently ran late because he would tarry to talk with interesting or favored callers. Much of his free afternoon time he spent signing commissions and dispatching other business. On Tuesday and Friday afternoons he held cabinet meetings and received members of the diplomatic corps. Generally free by 5:00 P.M., he would sometimes go for a drive or a walk before going home, although he often called for a stenographer after dinner and worked far into the night. Much of the correspondence load was lifted from him by secretaries who let him see only the name of a correspondent and his subject and replied on standardized forms. The chief mail clerk helped by preparing a "yellow journal" of daily newspaper clippings, keeping a record of outgoing letters, and handling all packages and periodicals.

By spending altogether too much time deciding which one of say four or five candidates should have a job, Taft postponed the filling of offices and earned some criticism from the press. More importantly, he did not gather a broad sample of opinions, as Roosevelt had from the variety of men who frequented the White House during his seven years. Mrs. Taft, his brothers Charles and Henry, and Aldrich and Cannon apparently gave Taft most of the advice he heeded, with his brothers exercising a conservative influence upon him and with Mrs. Taft feeding him his brothers' suspicions with respect to Roosevelt. Taft's later lament that

"Roosevelt has no one to advise him of the conservative type, like Root, or Moody or Knox or myself, as he did when in office" was as revealing of himself as of Roosevelt.[18] Early in his term, Taft used his cabinet as a group of general counselors. In many instances vigorous discussions were held on major policy decisions, but those were usually made on the conservative side. Stimson recalled, for example, that he and Walter Fisher, who succeeded Ballinger, "represented a sort of liberal wing in the cabinet and, although the President always listened with good will and was himself not basically averse to the ideas, he generally avoided decisive support of their position."[19] Taft admired the wit of Wickersham, listened officially to MacVeagh, grew nervous under the placid demeanor of Meyer, but loved Dickinson, who regaled him for hours on end with funny stories.

If Taft asked his cabinet for counsel, he sometimes failed to inform them about his actions. For example, he and Knox negotiated the tariff reciprocity agreement with Canada so quietly that Nagel, whose Department of Commerce and Labor would feel the brunt of the measure most acutely, learned about it from the newspapers. When war threatened with Mexico, he consulted only with Dickinson and Meyer. And he accepted Ballinger's resignation and released the news to the press without either asking or informing the cabinet. It is no wonder, then, that the cabinet did not long remain a unified body and that Taft did not use it as a true advisory group or staff agency.

Unfortunately for Taft, he found no one who could even approximate the technical or political skills of Roosevelt's private secretary William Loeb, Jr. In his four years he used four different men, none of whom served in a particularly distinctive way except the last for a few months. Fred W. Carpenter, a painstaking little man who had already served Taft for many years in the Philippines and the War Department, had no political sense and no more discrimination than Taft himself in handling callers at the White House. After he resigned in 1910 to become the American minister to Morocco, he was succeeded by Charles Dyer Norton, a former Chicago journalist and insurance man who for a short time was assistant secretary of the treasury under MacVeagh. He was young, enthusiastic, and eager—especially to build an empire for himself. Taft spoke more freely to him than he did to some of his cabinet members, but Norton was as out of place as a raw oyster in a cup of tea. He did not understand his job or the people he dealt with and knew less about politics and politicians than Taft did. Calling himself assistant to the president, he wanted to build his office into a permanent group of career officials, and even tried to change Taft's personal work habits and to reorganize the Republican party. Taft first cautioned him to stop acting like an "under-president" and finally let him go. His office staff sang the Doxology as he went out the door! Taft's most circumspect secretary was Charles Dewey Hilles, who did not fear to tell him about things as they were and handled congressional relations well. Hilles served for about a year and went on to become chairman of the Republican National Committee, 1912–1916. He was succeeded by Carmi Thompson, who had both legislative and administrative experience and raised the level of his office almost to the level achieved by Loeb.

Nor did Taft know how to make effective use of the press so as to mold public opinion favorably toward himself and his administration. According to William Allen White, he was "as insensible of public opinion and of the currents of public thought as an Oriental satrap,"[20] a conclusion concurred in by such journalists as Oscar King Davis, Henry L. Stoddard, Charles W. Thompson, and Arthur Wallace Dunn. Dunn said that secretary Carpenter faithfully and without discrimination kept reporters away from Taft, which was the way Taft wanted it. Once Dunn approached Carpenter for an interview on which to base a series of articles on Taft's first six months in the White House. When he appeared, he was told merely that Taft saw newsmen on Wednesdays. Dunn waited patiently with other reporters and overheard Taft snarl to Carpenter: "Must I see those men again! Didn't I see them just the other day?" Carpenter motioned the reporters forward. They met a Taft with "the smile that wouldn't come off," and Dunn never published his articles.[21]

While Roosevelt was in office, newsmen wrote about his many doings. If not at work he played tennis or went horseback riding or rowed a boat or chopped down a tree or took a hike. With Taft the news was almost always the same—he played golf with this business tycoon or that, or he made the round of the links, or his score was such and such—with the result that his golf games became anathema to the press and to the people as well.

For his first two years, Taft explained his actions to the people on junkets about the country, with poor results. Often, however, he refused to speak out when he needed public support, and erred in his choice of words. He was therefore frequently referred to as "Mr. Malaprop" and "Mr. Blunderer" and quickly used up the small store of good feelings he had brought to the White House. His skin was simply too thin to take criticism. When the *New York Times* criticized him, for example, he stopped reading it and read only the *New York Sun* and *Tribune,* which consistently flattered him. Woodrow Wilson took his measure well when he said on November 5, 1910, "If I were to sum up all the criticisms that have been made of the gentleman who is now President of the United States, I could express them all in this: The American people are disappointed because he has not led them. . . . They clearly long for someone to put the pressure of the opinion of all the people of the United States upon Congress."[22]

II

At the risk of beginning a battle that would jeopardize his entire legislative program and further split his party, but in keeping with his promise to revise downward the rates of the Dingley tariff, Taft called the Sixty-first Congress into special session for March 15, 1909. As is often the case with platform pledges, the tariff statement was so ambiguous that one could read it to mean nothing or, as Senator William E. Borah put it, that "revision was understood in the public mind to be revision downward, but always within lines of sufficient protection to American industry and American labor."[23]

Since the Civil War, the Republican party had been singularly attached to the principle of protection, its members arguing that American industry would be stimulated by prohibiting competing imports and that labor in consequence would enjoy higher wages. Disbelieving this principle, Cleveland during both of his presidential terms had tried to lower the rates to a tariff-for-revenue-only basis in order to augment international trade, lower the cost of living for ordinary workers, and destroy a system of special privilege granted only to the favored industrial class. Presented in 1894 with the distastefully high Wilson-Gorman tariff, the child of Democratic as well as Republican protectionists, he had registered his protest by letting it become law without his signature, for the alternative was a return to the even higher McKinley tariff of 1890. Although McKinley was the author of the 1890 law and was pleased originally with the higher Dingley tariff of 1897, as president he began to see that the benefits of protection went to the manufacturer rather than to the worker and consumer and that the tariff hindered American overseas trade. Moreover, since domestic production exceeded the demands of the national market, profits could accrue only by the winning of overseas markets. While industrialists generally stood by protection, or would go along with only a slight lowering of the tariff rates, some businessmen believed that protection caused domestic prices to rise, favored the formation of trusts, and nourished monopolies. Not only exporters of agricultural products but producers of finished goods as well recommended tariff reduction, with importers wishing to lower duties on raw materials and ocean shippers and railroads eager to obtain the greater traffic promised by freer trade. Producers of raw materials, especially in the South and Middle- and Far West, naturally opposed. In 1901, McKinley had suggested a reduction of rates by means of reciprocal agreements with other nations. Few agreements were actually made, however, and for seven years Roosevelt had done nothing about the tariff except to shun it as a politically explosive subject. Taft was thus the first Republican president since 1861 to seek a downward revision of the tariff schedules. His intention in calling a special session of Congress was to secure "a genuine and honest revision," to demand a "substantial revision downward," for like McKinley he believed that any excess in the difference between the costs of production of articles at home and abroad "offers a temptation to those who would monopolize the production and the sale of articles in this country, to profit by the excessive rate."[24] To the great dismay of partisan protectionists, in his inaugural address he had approached the Democratic position of a tariff-for-revenue-only, saying that "in the making of a tariff bill the prime motive is taxation and the securing thereby of a revenue."[25] He hoped, too, that the new tariff bill would include "a provision for a permanent Tariff Commission, which would make its investigations and report each year the facts respecting products whose schedules should be increased or decreased."[26] Finally, he let it be known that he would veto an objectionable bill and fight those who continued to demand protection designed to exclude foreign competition. But had he conjured the opposition he would receive from those who looked upon protection as a wise and patriotic policy necessary to the prosperity of the country? First newspaper reports on the bill offered by the House Ways and Means Committee indicated pleasure from both Democratic and Republican sources, with some warning, however, that the House bill would be rewritten by the Senate in line with the special interests which for many years therein had been quite effectively represented.

The House of the Sixty-first Congress contained 219 Republicans and 172 Democrats, and the Senate, 61 Republicans and 32 Democrats. Although it was a foregone conclusion that Cannon would be reelected as Speaker and that Aldrich would continue as the Senate leader, opposition to these men was rapidly building up. In the House, which had a majority of only forty-seven men, approximately thirty insurgent Republicans threatened control, and it has been said that the Payne-Aldrich tariff bill was to progressive senators what Cannon and the Rules were to the House insurgents.[27]

Cannon had been elected by the Fourteenth Illinois District to Congress in 1872, when he was thirty-six years of age, and had missed serving only one term since then. In one breath he would quote the Bible, in the next tell a dirty story, and he was long known as "Foul-mouth Joe" before he became "Uncle Joe." Coarse and uncultured, yet humorous, witty, and a master of ridicule, with a disdain for popular opinion, he was variously called a "despot," a "Tory," a "tyrant," the "Iron Duke," and "the strangler." He had had twenty-eight years of service before he was elected as Speaker in 1903 at the age of sixty-seven years. He used the "Reed Rules" in an altogether arbitrary and dictatorial manner. If from 1903 to 1909 he had been "innovative," after that time he was "regressive."

Cannon controlled the assignment of members and chairmen to committees, transferred members from committee to committee, and abused his great power of recognition. As one of the three majority members of the five-man Committee on Rules he insured that only bills that pleased him reached the floor and brushed off attempts to liberalize the rules. The House, rather than being a popular legislative body, produced only the laws Cannon wanted. His defense was that only by these methods could the majority rule, and that it would only take a majority vote to unseat him. A firm believer in self-reliance and in weak government, his answer to demands for governmental intervention in economic and social affairs was curt: "I am god-damned tired of listening to all this babble for reform."[28] Of all the laws he would preserve inviolate, for he equated it with prosperity, he chose the Dingley tariff.

While he was president, Roosevelt had respected Cannon's great power and cooperated with him rather than fighting him. Should Taft now fight Cannon, or cooperate with "an old man of the sea," as he had called him during the campaign of 1908, when Cannon's antics had reduced the Republican vote in the West?

After his nomination, Taft had gone to Hot Springs, Virginia, for a working vacation in which he made plans for entering the presidency. What to do about Cannon? Both Vice-President-elect James Sherman and Roosevelt advised him not to support those Republicans who opposed Cannon's reelection as Speaker. Roosevelt said, "I do not believe it would be well to have him in the position of the sullen and hostile floor leader bound to bring your administration to grief, even tho you were able to put someone else in as Speaker. . . ."[29] Upon receiving these words of caution from Roosevelt and similar ones from Root, too, Taft told Root, with reference to the impending tariff battle:

> I have not said anything for publication, but I am willing to have it understood that my attitude is one of hostility toward Cannon and the whole crowd unless they are coming in to do the square thing. . . . Cannon's [high tariff] speech at Cleveland was of a character that ought to disgust everybody who believes in honesty in politics and dealing with the people squarely, and just because he has a nest of standpatters in his House and is so ensconced there that we may not be able to move him is no reason why I should pursue the policy of harmony. I don't care how he feels or how they feel in the House. I am not going to be made the mouthpiece of a lie to the people without disclaiming my responsibility.[30]

Just before Taft's inauguration, Roosevelt told Nicholas Longworth, in Taft's presence, that "he had not believed formerly in the contention of the insurgents in the House, but that he had come to the conclusion that either Congress itself should elect its committees or else elect its committee on rules. Mr. Taft said he had had the same change of heart, and while he did not think the Speaker should be deprived of all power of appointment, yet he should agree with the President that the House should elect the steering committee."[31] But on March 11, when Representative W. Bourke Cockran asked Taft whether he would support Cannon against the insurgents, Taft replied that, much as he disliked doing so, he must support Cannon against the insurgents in order to win his strength in the battle for tariff reform.

After polling enough congressmen to learn that Cannon could not be defeated, at Roosevelt's suggestion Taft had an interview with Cannon from which he concluded that Cannon would loyally assist him to carry out the pledges of the Chicago platform. Rather than keeping this conclusion to himself, however, he publicized it, thereby alerting the insurgents, who had hoped to unhorse Cannon at the special session, that they would get no help from him. In this way the course of Taft's administration was set, for Cannon, angered with the insurgents' assaults upon him, would kill any moves that looked toward reform. On the morning of March 9, Cannon, Aldrich, and Payne had personally warned Taft that they must defeat the House rebels lest the tariff bill be endangered. Taft could have stayed out of the fight but decided to back Cannon, and the insurgents wondered how he meant to achieve progressive reforms by supporting the conservatives.

In the Senate since 1878, Aldrich had rapidly gained power and eminence because of his keen mind, knowledge of the tariff, and honest adherence to conservative political and economic beliefs that greatly pleased the masters of capital. One of the twenty-one millionaires in the Senate, and chairman of the Committee on Finance, he controlled legislation, had a large voice in the distribution of patronage, and carried weight in the direction of Republican party affairs. Rather than representing people, he spoke for economic constituencies, for employers, manufacturers, banks, railroads. An aristocrat with luxurious tastes he could indulge from his growing fortune—his daughter married a Rockefeller—Aldrich was repelled by reform and reformers. He had opposed the creation of the Interstate Commerce Commission and tariff reform during the Cleveland administrations, written the Republican substitute for the Mills bill that provided the basis for the McKinley tariff, and with Arthur P. Gorman and Calvin S. Brice raised the rates of the Wilson-Gorman tariff. American industry must be protected from foreign competition. An income tax, he believed, was designed to saddle the costs of government upon the rich, and international bimetallism and the gold standard were better than free silver. He thus appeared to stand for the creditor against the debtor classes, for the rights of property over those of the people, and "Aldrichism" was much used as an epithet, especially by mid-westerners. Those who criticized Aldrich for representing his financial and industrial constituencies were of course equally busy representing their own farm constituencies—cotton, wool, lumber, and the like—so that both they and men like Aldrich were culpable of adhering to protectionism and of reflecting certain interests rather than the people as consumers. As Senator Elihu Root told Whitelaw Reid, the "great obstacle to securing reductions arises from the fact that most of the men who are earnestly advocating them are as earnestly insisting upon retaining or increasing the Dingley duties on the products in which their own states are interested."[32] It should be added that Root, who earlier had advocated tariff revision, now voted for what Aldrich wanted.

Roosevelt had created working arrangements with the leaders of both House and Senate that left him in command of everything except economics and finance. Taft, who had already reached accord with Cannon, found it much easier to agree with a refined if politically ruthless gentleman like Aldrich, particularly since Aldrich had consistently championed his own views with respect to the Philippines and was on his way to becoming an expert on currency and banking matters. In *The Republican Command,* the Merrills speak of the years 1907–1908 as those of the "Roosevelt-Aldrich-Cannon Triumvirate" and of the year 1909 as that of the "Taft-Aldrich-Cannon Triumvirate."[33]

Just two days after the elections of November 8, 1908, the Ways and Means Committee began formal hearings on tariff revision destined to last until December 24. In an interview with Cannon and the Republican members of the committee on December 9, Taft was advised by Cannon not to interfere with the bill until it had gone to conference. This advice was concurred in by Payne, chairman of the committee, and by Aldrich. In the interim the president could confer as needed with these legislative leaders. Taft did consult with Cannon and Aldrich quite often, but erred gravely in not trying to give them directions or to threaten them with his powerful patronage club. Taft felt that the branches of government were coordinated and that he should not intrude upon the work of the lawmaking department. When his vice-president suggested that he shut off all patronage, not merely that of recalcitrants, he resisted doing so unless he had to. When he did intervene, it was too late. As has been said: "No single issue looms so large in the story of Insurgency as the revision of the tariff during the special session of 1909. The conservation question rallied more sympathetic adherents throughout the country, and the struggle for an equitable railroad rate bill struck deeper toward economic fundamentals, but the Payne-Aldrich tariff debate cut the first gaping groove into Republican solidarity. Other issues followed naturally along the lines of this schism."[34]

Instead of sending Congress a trenchantly worded state paper or electrifying the country by a personal appearance on the Hill, as Wilson would do in 1913, Taft on March 16 sent Congress a 324-word message asking merely that the tariff law be disposed of quickly lest business be disturbed and Congress fail to take up many other matters during the special session. Insurgents gasped at the brevity of the message and wondered if Taft had abandoned his crusade. Instead, Taft had consciously shunned a dramatic presentation in order to preserve party unity, avoid feuding with Congress, and escape censure for appearing to pressure Congress. On the next day, after Cannon had been elected as Speaker, a position in which he could reward those who had helped him quell the insurgent revolt against him, Payne introduced his bill, which was immediately referred back to his committee and on the eighteenth was reported to the House.

Payne was a stanch but not fanatical protectionist. He and his colleagues on the Ways and Means had held hearings for two months. Despite the offering of much misinformation by protectionist-minded witnesses, they had become convinced of the need of lowering some duties for the benefit of the consumer. The Dingley rates on lumber, print paper, zinc ore, pig iron, coal, shoe-leather hides, petroleum and petroleum products, and sugar, for example, were removed, and progressives generally applauded their work. But in keeping with Cannon's order, they boldly responded to sectional and local protectionist interests and reported a bill that would pinch the consumer even more tightly than the Dingley measure. It even included a duty on gloves that Taft believed Cannon had insisted upon in order to pay off a political debt to a New York industrialist, Lucius Littauer. Because of the demands of congressmen from the South and the Pacific Northwest, lumber would be taxed at $1 a thousand feet and petroleum at 24 percent. The rates were raised not only on sugar, other foodstuffs, and fibers but on such finished products as the aforementioned gloves and hosiery, razors, and silks. The invincible alliance between wool growers and wool manufacturers had also produced a wool schedule Taft thought was much too high. The result, as George Norris put it, was that "the Middle West, my home, was exploited and bled white."[35] Exceptions were free wood pulp, an extended raw materials free list, and a cut of two-thirds of the duty on newsprint. A novelty was a small federal inheritance tax of 1 percent on $10,000 or more.

Out of a total of four thousand imported articles considered, the Payne bill raised the duties on seventy-five and reduced them on four hundred, thus promising a very slight reduction downward. When Champ Clark sought to recommit the bill to committee and make it square with the Democratic tariff-for-revenue-only pledge of 1908, protectionist Democrats joined the insurgents in voting against him. They wanted only a downward revision that still preserved the protectionist rates, albeit some insurgents like Joseph L. Bristow desired to vote against the Payne bill unless its rates on such items as gloves and hosiery were reduced and steel, lumber, and leather were placed on the free list. Taft thought that the bill, which on April 9 was sent to the Senate by a vote of 217 to 161 over the strenuous objections of the insurgents, came "as near complying with our purposes as we can hope."[36] He thereby over-looked the fact that by special rules Cannon had restricted the offering of amendments to 90 percent of the bill and limited the entire debate to about three weeks. Nor was his conclusion shared by either the House or Senate insurgents. On the day before the final vote on the bill in the House, Norris moved to lower the petroleum rate from 25 to 1 percent. When Cannon ruled him out of order, Norris appealed over his head and the House overruled Cannon by a vote of 322 to 47. Then La Follette called to tell Taft that the Payne bill did not comply with the platform pledge. Were it not made to do so, Taft replied, he would veto it. But when La Follette urged him to send Congress a message stating that the bill neither fulfilled the platform pledge nor served the public interest, he said, "Well, I don't much believe in a President's inter-fering with the legislative department while it is doing its work. They have their responsibility and I have mine. And if they send that bill to me, and it isn't a better bill than it is now, I will veto it." The cocky and indomitable La Follette retorted that it would do little good to veto a completed bill and that he should speak up. Thumping his desk to emphasize his attitude, Taft replied: "You and your associates in the Senate go ahead, criticize the bill, amend it, cut down the duties—go after it hard. I will keep track of your amendments. I will read every word of the speeches you make, and when they lay that bill down before me, unless it complies with the platform, I will veto it." La Follette predicted that the Senate would offer him a worse measure than the Payne bill. "Well," said Taft, "I will show you."[37] With the objective of clubbing the protectionists toward center, he then urged Senators Jonathan Dolliver and Albert Beveridge, both of whom had given him strenuous support during the campaign of 1908, to fight for a downward revision of the tariff.

The Senate Finance Committee worked on the Payne bill as it was first reported to the House literally from sunup to sundown for many days, with Lodge writing to Roosevelt that

we shall bring out the Dingley bill in the main as it stands, with some improvements in details and classifications . . .

63

and a good many reductions from the Dingley rates, but they are not of a character to come home to the mass of the American people. The really important and valuable parts of the bill will be outside of the rates and schedules; the adoption of the maximum and minimum—which we shall put in proper form in the Senate; the establishment of a customs court and a bureau of tariff experts made up of Treasury officials to get us the facts, and not have lay commissioners to agitate for tariff revisions every six months.

He added that "I have never come so close to tariff making before, and the amount of ruthless selfishness that is exhibited on both sides surpasses anything that I have ever seen."[38] Whereas Taft wanted the maximum-minimum provision to mean that the maximum rates would be lowered for countries that removed discriminations against the United States, the Senate put the matter "in proper form" by establishing minimum rates with power to apply the maximum to countries which discriminated.

Aldrich kept the Payne bill in his Finance Committee for only two days while representatives of protected industries crowded inside its closed doors for secret sessions. Then, without an oral or written report or explanation, he submitted a bill containing 847 changes including 600 increases and demanded immediate consideration of the three-hundred-page document so that delay would not disturb business. In a speech of April 19, moreover, he made it clear that he desired no controversy between those who opposed or desired the bill. But La Follette immediately objected, saying that the senators needed time to study the bill before acting upon it, thus starting a summer of debate which for the oratory it provoked and the consequences that followed ranks with the League of Nations of 1919 and Franklin D. Roosevelt's attempt to "pack" the Supreme Court in 1937. Determined to prevent study of the bill and thus to railroad it through, Aldrich obtained a ruling that the Senate would remain in session without recess or adjournment from 10:00 A.M. to 11:00 P.M., and for long weeks during the late spring and far into the hot summer the progressives worked until the small hours of the morning at the risk of endangering their health. They divided the schedules, mastered their intricacies, and battled against Aldrich until he left the floor whenever one of them spoke. If they could not move Aldrich and other standpatters, they publicized the iniquities of the Payne-Aldrich tariff throughout the country in the most critical attack ever made upon a high tariff by Republican representatives.

The progressives publicly renounced the leadership of Aldrich and pointedly noted the difference between themselves and the "regular" Republicans, tools of Eastern corporations and trusts. On July 8, ten of them voted against a bill which to them represented, as La Follette put it, "the consummation of privilege more reprehensible than had ever found a place in the statutes of the country."[39] When Aldrich read them out of the party, they had to depend upon their constituents for continued public life, and they fully intended to tell these constituents their side of the story.

When the bill was passed by a juncture of stalwart Republican and protectionist Democratic votes and went to conference—the vote was 45 to 34—Taft took his distress over it to the golf links rather than try to influence the conferees. Under the necessity of making his own decisions, he had lost his vaunted good nature and become irritable. When Medill McCormick, of Chicago, warned him that the West would bolt and defeat him for reelection, he pounded a table and swore angrily, as defiant as a man can be who knows he is wrong but cannot help it. When La Follette called upon him on July 12, however, he said, "Come and sit down. I want to talk with you about the tariff. What am I to do with this bill?" He saw that it was "not in compliance with the platform" and considered vetoing it.

"Mr. President," La Follette replied, "you ought to veto it. You remember you said you would unless it was a better bill than when it passed the House. Instead of being a better bill, it is much worse. Hundreds of increases have been made in the Senate."

"Well, suppose I find that I can't do that. What changes ought I to insist upon in conference?" Picking up pad and pencil, he added, "Tell me what things ought to be reduced in duty." He wrote as La Follette talked and then asked him to send him a letter recapitulating "the things that you think ought to be done." This La Follette did.[40] Taft thanked him and after a meeting with various members of the House publicly but belatedly declared that he "was committed to the principle of downward revision."[41] But he was like a child in the hands of cunning politicians. As Dolliver put it, "Taft is a very large body entirely surrounded by men who know just what they want,"[42] and Taft himself wrote to Mrs. Taft that "I am dealing with very acute and expert politicians and I am trusting a great many of them and I may have been deceived."[43] To Secretary Meyer he added: "I fear Aldrich is ready to sacrifice the party, and I will not permit it. I am not very anxious for a second term, as it is, and I certainly will not make any compromises to secure one."[44]

Aldrich was the first to betray Taft, saying that he was unaware that the party was pledged to revision downward. Though knowing about this "most unfortunate" repudiation, Taft did nothing to challenge the Rhode Islander. Instead he became angry with the insurgents, the very men who were fighting his fight, because he believed that their criticism of Aldrich was also leveled at himself. It may be, too, that while he noted that midwesterners like Beveridge, Bristow, Moses E. Clapp, Albert B. Cummins, Dolliver, La Follette, and Knute Nelson quite consistently voted against the Aldrich schedules, such insurgents as Borah, Jonathan Bourne, and George S. Nixon voted to protect the range and mining empires of the states of the Northwest. Beveridge, though honest and able, was now a "selfish pig. He never talks. He only preaches." La Follette, Cummins, and Dolliver were "equally objectionable . . . blatant demagogues" and "yellow dogs."[45] On July 25 he wrote to Mrs. Taft: "I don't know what the insurgents are going to do; whether Beveridge and his crowd are going to vote for the bill or vote against it. It would be better for us if they were to vote for the bill, but I don't know how much better."[46] While saying that "he would like to tell some of the members that they could go to Hell,"[47] he battled Aldrich and Cannon privately to the point where he believed he had "defeated" them. As Butt put it, instead of being "duped" by Aldrich and his following, the president had "chloroformed" them.[48]

First, Democratic Senator Joseph Bailey, of Texas, supported by Republican insurgents Borah and Cummins, on April 15 introduced an amendment to the tariff bill calling for a flat 3 percent tax on individual and corporate incomes above $5,000 a year as a substitute for the inheritance tax in the Payne bill which Aldrich had deftly deleted (lest the raising of too much revenue justify the lowering of the tariff rates). Taft approved of this income tax as a way to make up the deficit expected from the lower tariff rates but opposed it on the ground that the Supreme Court would find it unconstitutional, as it had a similar law in 1895. He therefore preferred to obtain a constitutional amendment on the subject. He knew that Aldrich opposed both inheritance and income taxes and that he would not agree to the taking of a vote on an income tax before the tariff bill had passed. Why not, he then suggested, place a tax on corporations? Cummins had moved to amend the tariff bill with a progressive tax of 2 to 6 percent on both corporate and personal incomes ranging from $5,000 to $100,000 a year. When he and Bailey compromised on a bill placing a 2 percent tax on all incomes of over $5,000, there was a fair chance that the Democrats and insurgent Republicans could pass it. When nineteen insurgent Republicans said they would help Bailey and the Democrats pass an income tax bill, Aldrich won postponement of consideration of the income tax amendment to the tariff bill and turned to Taft for help, a position Taft enjoyed immensely. Aldrich would agree to the submission of an income tax amendment to the Constitution and even go along with a corporation tax limited to two years, after which he thought the new tariff would provide sufficient revenues, for he was interested in government revenues, not in measures designed to provide a more equitable form of federal taxation by taxing the rich more than the poor. Taft objected, Aldrich backed water, and on June 16 Taft shocked the insurgents, who had been kept in ignorance by Taft of his dealing with Aldrich, by asking Congress to enact as part of the tariff bill a 2 percent tax on all corporations except those engaged in banking, and also for the submission of an income tax amendment to the Constitution. The alternative, he told the members of the Finance Committee, was the Democratic-Insurgent income tax bill and possible defeat of the tariff bill. On June 25, Aldrich presented the corporation tax amendment to the tariff bill. Feeling that Taft had let them down on the income tax, the insurgents offered a resolution calling for an income tax amendment to the Constitution and had it adopted by the Senate on the twenty-eighth. On July 2, the Senate accepted the corporation tax by a vote of 60 to 11, and on the fifth it adopted the income tax amendment by unanimous vote. In the House, the latter was adopted on the twelfth by a vote of 317 to 14.

Taft favored a corporation tax over an income tax because he wished to spare the Supreme Court from criticism. Nevertheless, having defeated Aldrich in this instance, he should have gone on to demand improvement in the tariff bill, but he did not, and the insurgents arraigned him for having made a deal with Aldrich and having abandoned a Roosevelt policy. Moreover, having made one concession, Aldrich could not be budged from his high tariff position. Taft was then stung when Cannon and Aldrich on July 9 betrayed him again in their appointments to the conference committee, which was destined to sit for ten days. Cannon did not "play square," he complained, by naming protectionists as six of the nine House members. Five of the eight Senate conferees were also high protectionists, and insurgent members found in this action another reason for seeking to overthrow "Cannonism" and "Aldrichism," particularly when the Republican members of the conference committee left the Democrats out of their meetings and reached conclusions that pleased only themselves. The interested "ultimate consumer" looked to Taft as a judge with a jury, as able to settle the differences between the House and Senate. Although he knew of the rising ire of the insurgents in both houses, he still refused to put pressure on the committee, saying that his vetoing of an unsatisfactory bill would lose him the support of the congressional leadership he would need in obtaining other reforms in the following session of Congress. Insurgents also noted that patronage was going to "standpatters" rather than to them and that many post office appointments were being delayed. When La Follette complained about this fact in person, Taft replied, "Well, I can't take this matter up until after the tariff bill is passed." Feeling that his constituents were behind him, La Follette refused to be intimidated.

Taft abhorred the idea of vetoing a bill that reduced the tariff and contained a corporation tax and hoped against hope that the insurgents would defeat the conference report. When he was urged to appeal to the people over the head of Congress and to threaten a veto unless Congress gave him the kind of bill he wanted, he demurred on the ground that while he might gain personal popularity he would split his party. However, he served notice on several senators and threatened those who would not withdraw some of their demands that he would force an inspection of the wool schedules—a threat worse than any other the senators could anticipate. "I have told them all," Taft told Butt,

> that free hides is the keynote for this bill. I will have nothing less than free hides. I also want free iron ore, free coal with reciprocity, free oil, and less duty on lumber. I am also opposed to the duty which they have put on gloves and stockings. This is not the time to talk of building up new industries by protection, and it is foolhardiness to run counter to shibboleth and that is what the opposition to this duty on stockings and gloves amounts to.[49]

Payne explained the changes made to his original bill in his report from the conference committee to the House on July 30. On the thirty-first, the House approved of the report by a vote of 195 to 183, with 20 Republicans voting against, only 2 Democrats voting for it, and Champ Clark saying that "not all the perfumes of Araby the Blest can sweeten the Payne-Aldrich Tariff Bill to please the nostrils of the American people."[50] The Senate, acting on August 5, adopted the conference report by a vote of 47 to 31, with ten insurgents—Beveridge, Bristow, Clapp, Crawford, Cummins, Dolliver, La Follette, Brown and Burkett of Nebraska, and Nelson of Minnesota—voting against it. The tariff bill now passed, Cannon finally announced the membership of the House committees.

Taft was fairly happy with a number of the rate changes made in the various tariff schedules. Many compromises were of course made by the conferees, and he himself had forced some compromises on some rates. The Dingley rate on lumber, for example, was $2 per thousand feet. The House reduced this to $1; the Senate raised it back to $2. Taft told Aldrich that $1.25 was all the duty that he, their party, or the country would accept. Cannon threatened to adjourn the House without taking any action on the bill, and Aldrich suggested to Taft that he should accept $1.50— but the president stood firm and finally threatened to call Congress immediately into special session if it did not produce an acceptable bill. Since Congress would be blamed by the public if he did so, Aldrich and Cannon preferred to shift the responsibility for an unsatisfactory bill to him and adopted the committee report.

In addition to modifying the old Dingley rates, the new tariff contained a number of novelties. With Taft openly favorable, Beveridge had sponsored a tariff commission bill. This was referred to Aldrich's Finance Committee and eventually was added to the Payne-Aldrich tariff. The new tariff also contained a "maximum-minimum" provision whereby 25 percent of the value of an imported article could be added by the president to the minimum rate if a foreign country "unduly discriminated" against the United States in some way. Taft found no such discrimination, hence only the minimum rates were ever applied. Moreover, although the Tariff Commission was authorized to work only on data concerning the maximum-minimum rates, Taft meant to use it as an advisory body on competitive costs and on tariff legislation in general and soon won congressional appropriations for the body. In theory, at least, tariff rates would now be made "scientifically" and "efficiently" by detailed studies of costs of production at home and abroad.

On July 30, when Butt had gone to the White House in answer to Taft's invitation to play golf, he felt that the tariff battle had resulted in "a complete victory for the President." He found a deathly silence that indicated that something unusual was happening, and Taft told him what he had done. The conferees, who would report on the morrow, had again appealed to him to recede from his position on gloves and lumber. He had replied that he would not sign a bill that carried more than $1.25 on lumber and more than the amount on gloves specified in the Senate bill. "They have my last word," he said, "and now I want to show my scorn for further negotiations by spending the afternoon on the golf links. . . . " Early in the evening he was informed that the conferees had accepted the limits he set. "Well," he said, ". . . this makes me very happy." Said Butt, "Mr. President, I have watched the struggle, and I congratulate you."

"Did you expect me to weaken, Archie?" asked Taft.

"Hardly that, sir, but I was afraid they might convince you," replied the military aide.[51]

During a weekend at Beverly, Taft said to his friend Hammond:

> I can veto this tariff bill as Cleveland did the one presented to him [sic]. Perhaps such an action would make me popular with the country, as it did Cleveland, but it would mean a hostile Congress for the rest of my term. Furthermore, if I should send a veto message, the confidence of the country, which is just recovering from the panic of two years ago, would probably get a setback. More important still, perhaps, is the deficit of $100,000,000 which can best be made up by the revenue features in the new bill. The Tariff Board and the minimum and maximum features will allow us to make adjustments.[52]

What Taft did not know was that Hammond and others of his kind had surreptitiously arranged for clubs, chambers of commerce, and newspapers in the West to demand that he sign the tariff bill.

Lodge beautifully summarized for Roosevelt the conservative Republican view of the part Taft had played as follows:

> The President refrained from saying anything or doing anything while the bill was passing through the Houses, which I thought was wise and I told him so and I am still of that opinion, but when the conferees met they went to him and said they would like to know what his views were and he gave them his views very freely. He stood very firmly for what he demanded and forced a number of reductions which ought to have been made. I think his influence has been salutary in a high degree and his action has strengthened the Party with the Country, strengthened him and, I think, has made a bill which is really a very

good one and contains some very valuable provisions and is much better liked than it would otherwise have been.[53]

At about 5:00 P.M., on August 6, Taft went to the president's room in the Senate and signed the bill. Newspaper reports commented that a terrific thunderstorm that suddenly broke was a forecast of the storm of protests he would receive from the country. Harmony could hardly be expected from the regular and insurgent wings of the party spawned by the tariff fight. New life had been infused into the Democratic party. European merchants naturally were grieved by the retention of many of the old Dingley rates, and Republicans would be blamed if a rise in consumer prices followed. Instead of the "honeymoon" expected during his first hundred days, Taft had lost the initiative, and the wounds inflicted in the acrid tariff debate never healed.

III

It was not really immodest for La Follette to write in his autobiography (1913) that in 1905 he was "alone in the Senate," that is, the only progressive insurgent, for he was at the time the only recognized Republican political figure committed to every progressive principle. However, he was soon joined by Beveridge, who had been in the Senate since 1899, Clapp (1901), Dolliver (1901), Bourne and Nixon (1907), Borah and Cummins (1908), and Bristow (March 1909). The fight over the tariff brought these men together, won them deserved credits from their constituents, and made their names known throughout the country. Taft's signing of the Payne-Aldrich tariff was in itself enough to determine them that he should not be renominated for president in 1912.

Taft had appeared to heed most the man he liked least, Cannon, to have lost mastery over himself and his party to the Speaker, and to place party regularity before his platform promises. Never realizing that he had been captured by the protectionists rather than having captured them, he was so inordinately happy over the few concessions he had forced upon them that he had abandoned his veto threat. While he had done more about the tariff in a few months than Roosevelt in seven years, one editor could state that "the simple fact is that the Payne tariff is the most thoroughgoing high-protectionist measure that has ever been enacted in this country or in any other land."[54] On the other hand, the government would now collect a corporation tax, the Philippines would have free trade with the United States, a Tariff Com-

71

mission had been provided for, an income tax amendment was before the states, and high protectionist proponents were definitely on the defensive. "The close . . . was very peaceful and sweet," Taft wrote to his wife. "I gave a dinner to both committees, and I think everybody left with a good taste in his mouth, except possibly Cannon."[55] He had not, however, invited any of the insurgents. Perhaps he was right about the "good taste," for he had received little public criticism except from the newspapers, criticism which he discounted because it came, he said, from the denial of free newsprint in the tariff. If he was right, then the progressives and scholars who have written about the Payne-Aldrich tariff are wrong. If he was right, moreover, then how does one account for his decision to explain the tariff, along with speaking about other subjects, on an extensive personal tour about the country?

With his penchant for doing good things in a bad way, Taft undertook in the months between the close of the special session in August and the opening of the regular session in December to "jolly the people," to explain the Payne-Aldrich tariff to them, to put out the flames of insurgency that engulfed the West, and particularly to save the political life of standpatter James A. Tawney. Most Americans in the summer of 1909 knew nothing and cared less about the details of tariff making. On the other hand, many were worried because the new tariff would not reduce the high cost of living, which on August 1 hit the second highest figure in history, because they heard of the compromises which had been made and of the "jokers" which had been slipped into it, and because they feared that it would do nothing to reduce the incidence of monopoly. Midwesterners were particularly incensed because tariff cuts were made largely on their raw materials and therefore helped the eastern manufacturers and trusts.

Before starting on his tour, Taft rested for about a month at Beverly, playing golf or otherwise recreating himself rather than preparing with great care the speeches he would deliver, although he did spend some time on the serious squabble over conservation that will be discussed in the next chapter.

"If it were not for the speeches," Taft told Butt, "I should look forward with the greatest pleasure to this trip." Butt well knew that few if any speeches would be ready before he entrained, but when he nudged the president, Taft replied: "I would give anything in the world if I had the ability to clear away work as Roosevelt did. . . . I am putting off these speeches from day to day."[56] As Butt had commented as early as March 10: "If the President continues to transact business as he is transacting it now, he will be about three years behind when the fourth of March, 1913, rolls around. . . . He moves very slowly, and I defy anyone in the world to hurry him."[57] Meantime Taft ate his unhurried beefsteak breakfasts, played golf, and won no laurels with the insurgents by socializing with Henry Clay Frick. Moreover, he neither employed speechwriters nor submitted his writings to anyone for editing.

Taft started at Boston on September 14 and immediately provoked the insurgents by praising Aldrich as the real leader of the Senate and as one of the ablest statesmen in financial matters in either house. In Chicago, he spoke about labor and the writ of injunction and about the need of reforms in the judicial system. In Milwaukee, Wisconsin, where it would have helped him had he acknowledged at least the honesty and courage of La Follette and his fellow midwestern insurgents, he spoke instead of the need of a postal savings bank system. He had proved his ineptitude as a conciliator. "Tomorrow Milwaukee and Winona [Minnesota]. Hope to be able to deliver a tariff speech at Winona but it will be a close shave," he telegraphed Mrs. Taft, and on the next day, "Speech hastily prepared, but I hope it may do some good."[58] If he had in mind the support he would give to Congressman Tawney, who had voted for the tariff and was now opposed by his constituents, he erred badly.

To the audience that crowded into the Winona Opera House on September 17, Taft explained that he had dictated his speech on the train and that he read it because the tariff was a subject "that calls for some care in expression." His legislative history of the bill was good, and he was honest in his contention that he had not expected every rate to be lowered, certainly not to the point where prices would be reduced "by the introduction of foreign competition. That is what the free traders desire. That is what the revenue tariff reformers desire; but it is not what the Republican party wished to bring about." He agreed that some of the rates, such as those on wool, were too high, and correctly asserted that the cost of living had gone up in free trade as well as in tariff-protected countries. If the Payne-Aldrich tariff did not do everything he had wanted, he had been willing to agree to a few high rates in order to maintain party solidarity. Then he added in a fatal and supreme blunder the words that soon blazoned forth in various ways in newspaper headlines: "When I do say without hesitation that this is the best tariff bill that the Republican party has ever passed, and therefore the best tariff bill that has been

73

passed at all, I do not feel that I could have reconciled any other course to my conscience than that of signing the bill."[59] Ever afterwards he defended the correctness of his statement and blamed the press for taking it out of context, misrepresenting it, and perverting it. But the damage had been done. "Shades of Theodore Roosevelt! May ghosts of the animals he has killed in Africa ever haunt him for having foisted on the country this man Taft," cried the *Des Moines News*. Representative Asher C. Hinds, of Maine, said that "Massachusetts never went away from Congress carrying more in her craw than she got in that tariff bill." The *St. Paul Pioneer-Press* defiantly asserted that "those western representatives have made up their minds that they are not going to be ruled by New England and for New England."[60] Several days later, Butt said to Hammond, "It is too bad you weren't with him. He bubbled all over and has done himself great harm." Said the *Nation*: "President Taft's Winona speech in apology for the revision of the tariff was the wettest blanket he has cast over the party," and Dolliver wrote to La Follette:

> Poor Taft made a sad mess of it at Winona. I knew he was good natured but I never dreamed he was so dull. . . . It is like taking candy from children for Aldrich to confer with Taft. Is he ignorant of the fact that Aldrich himself organized the proceedings around the textile schedules, every paragraph drawn by the parties in interest, and made up the bill by attracting a majority, to vote for the *citadel* in exchange for the privilege of naming the other rates? This is not legislation. It is rank interchange of reciprocal larcenies. . . .[61]

Taft had revealed his lack of preparation in drafting his speech and ignorance of certain aspects of tariff making, for Payne had fought against accepting various compromises and Aldrich was honest about a tariff's being a patchwork of trades made between conflicting interests. He himself had intervened only at the conference stage and had received very little criticism for signing the bill. Now he seemed to be set against any tariff revision in the near future, to be reading from his party the insurgents who had opposed higher tariff rates, and to be providing his foes with excellent ammunition for the campaign of 1910.[62] He then further angered the insurgents, while in Utah, by praising Senator Reed Smoot, who had voted for the tariff; by permitting himself to be photographed with Cannon, who made part of the trip with him, and by referring to him in complimentary terms; by suggesting that Congress in the coming session could devote itself to no more important subject than providing a ship subsidy; by asserting that he would put a lid on pork-barrel legislation; and by consorting almost exclusively with the conservatives of his party. He further provoked the question whether his trip was worth the time, money, and neglect of public business that it cost.

Taft had received an unprecedented reception in the South only because he had avoided Negroes whenever he could and made it plain that he would do nothing to placate them and that he would eliminate them from politics if he could. Yet he was convinced by the largeness of the crowds that came to see and hear him and the comments of sycophants that the people were not only friendly but satisfied with him and that the outcries of the insurgents were of no account. He was wrong, for the insurgents were finding that while the people had generally upheld and praised him before his Winona address, they were now turning away from him to such a degree that they predicted the overthrow of the Republican party in the elections of 1910 if not in 1912. By aligning himself with the conservatives of his party, Taft had also opened the door to demands that Roosevelt be reelected in 1912, and as the demands for Roosevelt increased, he veered ever closer to the conservatives as men who better appreciated him.

4

★★★★★

CRISIS OVER CONSERVATION

I

The battle over the tariff had not yet ended when William Howard Taft was caught in the center of another. This battle, over conservation policy, engendered a mountain of controversy and had fantastic political repercussions.

For over a century, land policy had been geared to building up a great country with a great population. Land had been given to individuals, to corporations, and to states; the last had in turn given them to individuals and corporations. In 1891, when most virgin timberlands were already in private hands, Congress authorized the president to create forest preserves by proclamation. Despite demands for the scientific use of these preserves, they were originally closed to commercial operations. Then in 1897 Congress empowered the secretary of the interior to regulate their occupancy for mining, grazing, lumbering, and water power purposes. It is often held that because they feared the exhaustion of natural resources and hoped to deny control over what was left of the national domain to "trusts," many public-spirited citizens demanded a conservation, or "preservationist," program by the turn of the twentieth century. To a degree this was true, for many conservation crusaders equated conservation with "thrift," patriotically sought to reduce the power of the "interests," which customarily assumed a corporate form, and saw public ownership as the only solution to the problem.[1] But other factors were antecedent and more important before Taft's time.

The conservation movement began in the West, particularly

with water development plans offered by John Wesley Powell's *Lands of the Arid Regions* (1878). After various congressmen blocked Powell's plans, a mining engineer turned hydraulic engineer, Frederick H. Newell, of the United States Geological Survey, was a prime mover of a federal water power development program including irrigation, power, navigation, and flood control. In 1907, Newell became director of the Reclamation Service, in the Department of the Interior. A California lawyer who was an expert on water law, George H. Maxwell, popularized the need of federal support for irrigation so well that in 1900 both major political party platforms called for the federal construction of irrigation works. Meanwhile Newell and Gifford Pinchot, chief of the Bureau of Forestry, found it easy to win Theodore Roosevelt to the cause of a national conservation program. Roosevelt was the first president since John Quincy Adams to have a personal interest in science. He had lived in the West and knew of its water problems; as governor of New York State he had shown great interest in its natural resources. As president, he characterized conservation as "my policy," the most important contribution he had made to domestic administration.

Of the plans suggested by various western congressmen, those of Representative (later Senator) Francis G. Newlands, of Nevada, were adopted in particular because Roosevelt urged their adoption. Among other terms, the Newlands Reclamation Act, approved on June 17, 1902, provided that the federal government would finance irrigation through a Reclamation Fund, the money for which would come from the sale of western lands, and that the secretary of the interior would administer the program. However, he could withdraw from private entry in proposed irrigation project areas only those lands not taken up under the homestead laws.[2] To head the Reclamation Service, a new branch of the Geological Survey, Roosevelt appointed Newell, who was immediately opposed on the one hand by people in the western states who wished to use their own water and complained of federal interference, and on the other by land speculators.

Because watershed vegetation affected water supply, timber cutting and grazing were prohibited in national forests and a need developed for scientific forest management which would provide a sustained tree yield. Thus irrigation and forest programs were intertwined. Newell, for example, demanded the protection of forests, and Pinchot promoted federal irrigation. Roosevelt appointed both men to the Inland Waterways Commission he established in 1908 with the hope that it would become a central planning agency which would coordinate the work of the numerous bureaus concerned with conservation and also provide new plans. Both Newell and Pinchot, among others, supported Roosevelt's demand for a thoroughgoing revision of the public land laws. These had been designed to dispose of natural resources to individuals. An improved law would not only stop illegal entry and speculation; it would permit the application of comprehensive land management concepts which would in turn result in orderly resource development. Public ownership was merely a means to the end of orderly, efficient, and maximum development. Finally, all public questions should be put under the supervision of a single federal department and be administered by experts rather than by politically appointed officials.

Rather than by the masses, therefore, the conservation movement was sponsored originally by hydrologists, forestry experts, agronomists, geologists, and the like, men of science who demanded rational plans with which to develop resources efficiently. They also demanded that these plans be drawn and executed by them, as experts, rather than by politicians. The goal was not limitation or retrenchment but planned and efficient progress in the name of the public interest.[3] However, by 1908 Roosevelt found further advance in his conservation program blocked by Congress—it refused to authorize his Inland Waterways Commission, for example —and by such men in the executive departments as his secretary of war, Taft. With President Taft, Congress, and the executive departments and the Army Corps of Engineers still opposed in 1909, support of the Roosevelt brand of conservation depended more and more upon the general public, which tended to equate it with the antitrust movement.[4]

With great energy and persistence, and with the help of Senator Newlands, after March 4, 1907, of Secretary of the Interior James Garfield, and of Pinchot, Roosevelt had withdrawn from public settlement sixteen million acres of timber and mineral lands and water power sites in the Northwest, caused an inventory to be made of the nation's natural resources, classified public domain resources, and on January 29, 1909, sent to Congress the report of the National Conservation Commission he had appointed. Although congressmen had headed the commission's committees, the real work was done by government scientist administrators. The magnitude of the withdrawals and of their local importance may be measured by the fact that the forest, coal, phosphate, and water reserves in Idaho alone covered one-half of that state and totaled an area equal to the size of New York State. More important to the Taft-Roosevelt controversy was the spirit of Roosevelt's conservation crusade, which was to encourage the commercial use of natural resources yet to conserve them by scientific methods. Furthermore, he wanted national and state agencies to cooperate in conservation in order to assure the permanent welfare of the people. In keeping with this spirit, he had proceeded to do whatever was necessary, and not specifically prohibited by law, to protect the public domain, despite opposition from Western grazing, lumbering, and mining "interests." In so doing, he, Garfield, and Pinchot had stretched what authority Congress had granted them over conservation far beyond the intent of that body.[5]

Taft agreed wholeheartedly with Roosevelt on the need of conservation, saying in one instance that "as a people, we have the problem of making our forests outlast this generation, our iron outlast this century, and our coal the next; not merely as a matter of convenience or comfort, but as a matter of stern national necessity."[6] He disagreed with him, however, on his use of the executive order to accomplish his purposes and promised during his campaign to regularize Roosevelt's actions by appropriate legislation. Roosevelt was pleased when he understood that Taft would keep Garfield as secretary of the interior, for Garfield had enthusiastically supported the Roosevelt conservation policies, indeed had been chosen for his post because he did so. The first of a series of actions that led Roosevelt to suspect that Taft would not follow "my policy" occurred when Taft, who needed a western man in his cabinet, replaced Garfield with Richard Achilles Ballinger. The second was Taft's refusal to continue the work of the National Conservation Commission.

The problem of conserving the nation's resources was taken very seriously in Taft's day, for alarming pictures were drawn, most probably overdrawn, of a starving and shivering population, of gross waste in exploitation, and of oligopolistic if not monopolistic holdings. Nearly one-half of the timber resources, for example, were owned by 195 holders, with three—the Southern Pacific Company, the Weyerhauser Timber Company, and the Northern Pacific Railroad Company—together holding 11 percent. Few critics knew, or cared, that the last two companies had obtained advice from the Bureau of Forestry and followed scientific forest management programs. By this time, however, the conservation movement had lost the character of a scientific and rational program of resource use and become a moral crusade devoted to combating exploitative materialism. Rather than being led by technical men it was directed by urban middle-class reformers such as William Kent and Walter L. Fisher. Reform-minded citizens, including many businessmen, now attacked wasteful commercial exploitation of natural resources, rejected laissez faire, and demanded the adoption of scientific methods in the public interest. Only efficiency, scientific management, and social planning could insure the perpetuity of civilization and preserve the welfare of the present and future generations. As Roosevelt himself had told the Conference of Governors, convened in Washington on May 13–15, 1908, to discuss all phases of conservation, ". . . let us remember that the conservation of natural resources . . . is yet but part of another and greater problem . . . the problem of national efficiency, the patriotic duty of insuring the safety and continuance of the nation."[7]

Three avenues of action on conservation could be followed: (1) unregulated exploitation by private capital; (2) state ownership and regulation; (3) federal ownership and regulation. Roosevelt strongly urged federal control, Taft, state control, saying in this connection that "in these days there is a disposition to look too much to the Federal Government for everything."[8] More specifically, Roosevelt would have the federal government act whenever the states were unable or unwilling to do so, retain possession of water, coal, and timber lands, permit exploitation of natural resources only in keeping with federal regulations, and have the government reclaim arid and swamp lands. He thus spoke for the progressive brand of conservationist who placed physical values above market values yet invested those physical values with social and moral interests. Unwilling to address himself to the issue of conservation in the emotional tones of a preacher of righteousness, Taft approached it as a jurist. He would lease timber, coal, oil, gas, and phosphate lands for exploitation by private capital, let Congress determine whether water power and water itself should be under federal or state control, and undertake reclamation projects only on lands within the national domain. He thus spoke for private exploitation, preferred congressional to presidential leadership in the conservation movement, and would restrict congressional action to only those lands the federal government controlled. Moreover, he construed congressional conservation statutes more narrowly than did the courts, took a limited view of the power of the presidency itself, and was determined to regularize what he considered to be Roosevelt's extralegal methods regardless of the results for conservation.

Ballinger, a fiercely upright, self-made man, classmate of Garfield at Williams College, and reform mayor of Seattle (1904–1906), had organized the state of Washington for Taft in 1908. A member of the Republican National Committee, chairman of the Washington delegation to Chicago, and a member of the Committee on Resolutions and a campaign strategist, he deserved reward. His appointment was a serious disappointment at least to Roosevelt, Garfield, and Pinchot. Taft's "promotion" or transfer of subordinates who had shaped their conservation policies to posts outside of the departments of Agriculture and the Interior also sat badly with them. So did Taft's taking of advice from his brother Henry, a member of the law firm that included Attorney General George Wickersham, who opposed Roosevelt's water conservation policy, and Taft's dependence for advice on resource affairs upon the Corps of Engineers.

An expert on mining and land law, Ballinger in January 1907 had accepted an invitation from Garfield and practically a command from Roosevelt and, at considerable financial sacrifice, served a year as commissioner of the General Land Office. After reforming its bureaus and making the office efficient, he retired to private law practice. While he supported Roosevelt's conservation policies, during his year he had clashed with Newell, of the Reclamation Service, and with Pinchot, of the Forestry Service, by questioning the legality of some of their actions. He was also unhappy with Roosevelt's directing the secretary of the interior to let the secretary of agriculture decide questions of fact with respect to claims in forest reserves. By a law of 1905, control of forests went from the Land Office to the Department of Agriculture, but the Department of Interior was still responsible for granting titles to the land, including mineral claims in the national forests. Pinchot therefore practically controlled the work being done in another department. By a law of 1906, the Department of Agriculture determined what land in national forests could be given as homesteads by the Interior Department, with the Land Office again getting short shrift. Resentment that flared between Ballinger and Pinchot was increased when Ballinger, spokesman for the struggling small entrepreneur of the West, opposed Pinchot's program on several grounds outside of jurisdictional matters. Ballinger would sell rather than lease coal lands and water power sites and guard against eastern monopolists those small investors who risked their capital in the West. A progressive in many, many areas, he objected to the Roosevelt conservation policies, according to Pinchot, largely because of his dislike of Roosevelt's willingness to let big business live so long as it behaved itself. As Ballinger put it in his first annual report, "The best thought of the day is not that development shall be by national agencies, but that wise utilization shall be secured through private enterprise under national supervision and control."[9]

Ballinger had accepted the post of secretary of the interior only after Taft had pressured him to do so. The kind of strict constructionist lawyer and devotee of responsible and efficient administration Taft wanted in this post, he was immediately made the target for criticism by those who believed he would reverse Roosevelt's conservation policies. One of his first acts was to stop granting water power permits in the public domain.

Without specific congressional authority, Roosevelt and Garfield had withdrawn from settlement lands along rivers and streams in the Northwest and by intent or inadvertence failed to inform Ballinger. Upon complaint from people farming in these lands, within ten days of his taking office Ballinger began to restore the right of private use and directed the Geological Survey to specify water power sites for future preservation. "Conservation without development has no substantial reason for existence," he said.[10] Despite Pinchot's personal protests to Taft on April 19 and 20, 1909, Taft supported Ballinger, adding that Congress, not the executive, could withdraw lands for conservation purposes and that he would not violate the law even to achieve reform. Upon the careful studies provided by the Geological Survey, Congress at Taft's request between 1910 and 1912 set aside all valuable water power sites. Taft thus regularized and legitimatized the work begun under Roosevelt, but he had repudiated Roosevelt's method if not countered the spirit of his earlier actions. According to Robert La Follette, Taft had given water power magnates the lucrative opportunity to get in after blocking the development of water power in the public domain in the West for two years.

In the name of efficiency, to get rid of "sloppy administration," and to create a staff that would be personally loyal to him, Ballinger sought to institute other substantial changes in policy, as in irrigation and in the relations between the Department of the Interior and the Forestry Service. In irrigation, for example, he would curtail federal and expand private reclamation work. Newell quickly fell into disgrace. Pinchot was no longer welcome when he called at the Interior Department and learned that Ballinger would talk only with the secretary of agriculture, James Wilson. Ballinger also ended various informal cooperative arrangements between the Department of Interior and the Forestry Service. Pinchot was therefore no longer able to act as a coordinator of the broad conservation program. In addition, both Ballinger and Taft wished to change the Roosevelt policy concerning water power on public lands and navigable streams.[11] In these cases Ballinger clearly revealed his differences with Roosevelt on objectives, saying that the federal government could not dictate to a state how its nonnavigable waters must be used. Moreover, by demeaning their ability, he tried to discredit Roosevelt appointees. The battle that resulted between Pinchot and Ballinger is told below in terms of personalities because the people were interested in the persons involved, especially Taft, not in bureaus, departments, institutions, or even perhaps policy. Beneath it all, of course, were important disagreements over resources policy exacerbated by an administrative organization that divided responsibility for conservation and made cooperation on policy extremely difficult. "The crux of the issue," it has been said, "lay in the fact that former officials resisted changes which newer officials desired to institute."[12] It has also been said that "Ballinger's changes threatened a working program, and precisely because the program was in full operation he was bound to run into opposition from the bureau chiefs who had most at stake in the perpetuation of established policies."[13] It is understandable that Taft did not relish the idea of having Pinchot act as an unofficial department head for conservation and perpetuate the Roosevelt methods. One can also sympathize with him because, by seeking to play the part of the conciliator between Ballinger and Pinchot and their adherents, he earned the reward usually given to conciliators—criticism from both sides.

II

It was the coal lands problem that created a severe political crisis for Taft. Roosevelt, knowing that speculators under dummy entries had obtained 160-acre homestead claims and merged them in order to exploit the coal that lay beneath, had in 1905 appointed a committee to suggest revisions in mining laws. The committee had suggested the leasing, not the sale, of public lands for coal mining. In 1906 and 1907 he had withdrawn from entry approximately 66,000,000 presumably coal-bearing acres, of which 7,680,-

000 were in Alaska. One Clarence Cunningham had obtained various claims along the Bering River, twenty-five miles inland from Controller Bay, Alaska, and then sought financial support to begin mining operations, for his 5,280 acres were exempted on the ground that they had been acquired earlier in "good faith." These simple facts were soon blown up into fantastic stories about the impending rape of Alaska's mineral resources by unscrupulous Wall Street interests.

In 1906, Cunningham's request for approval of his claims and for permission to form an operating corporation had been granted routinely. However, Horace T. Jones, a special agent for Ballinger who was then commissioner of the General Land Office, suspected that other Alaska claims might fall into the hands of the J. P. Morgan and Guggenheim interests, interests which, among others, Roosevelt had hoped would help to develop Alaska. Jones voiced his suspicions to another special agent, Louis Russell Glavis, who was working the Pacific Coast. Although he was but twenty-four years of age in 1907, Glavis was placed in charge of investigating. He was told by Ballinger, however, that Cunningham's claims were legal. When Glavis protested this conclusion, Ballinger consulted Garfield and then immediately rescinded the approval order. Thus matters stood while Ballinger retired to his law practice and then was selected by Taft to be his secretary of the interior.

Once in his new office, Ballinger asked Glavis to forward his report on the Alaska coal claims. During a call on Ballinger in May 1909, Glavis voiced his suspicion of corruption in a Cunningham-Guggenheim deal. Ballinger directed that an investigation be made and accepted the report of his assistant secretary that no evidence of fraud existed. Now convinced that the Cunningham claims impinged upon a forest preserve, Glavis improperly asked for help from the Forestry Service headed by Pinchot, which was in the Department of Agriculture. Glavis stated that he had "damaging and conclusive" evidence of the "official misconduct" of Ballinger and of his land commissioner, Fred Dennett. "The department of the interior has charge of all public lands and does not intend that the forestry bureau, a part of another department, should run the department of the interior," Ballinger sputtered,[14] while Pinchot, upon learning that Ballinger had been an attorney for Cunningham, saw a chance to force him out of office. At a conservation congress in Spokane and elsewhere in the West, he mentioned no names but derided those who insisted upon a strict interpretation of law and thereby favored "the great interests as against the people," adding that "the people, not the law, should have the benefit of the doubt."[15] Then, worried lest his words be taken as being critical of Taft, he wired the *New York Times* that he intended no reflection upon the president. Privately, however, he confessed that ". . . I think I have probably forced Taft to take his stand openly for or against the Roosevelt policies in act as well as in words."[16] No wonder that Butt described Taft's mood as "black and pathetic," for while he felt keenly the fact that his party was dividing, "he feels more than anything else in a political way . . . the efforts which the Pinchot people are making to drag him into the investigation."[17] Indeed, Taft said to Butt:

> For a long time I did not believe the reports that the whole trouble is the outcome of a well-organized conspiracy on the part of Garfield and Pinchot to discredit my administration, but I am beginning to believe it to be true. I have tried to have this investigation impartial and conducted on legal lines, but I am to be forced to enter the fight, and if I do, I shall make public such facts as will utterly annihilate Garfield and those who are behind this matter.[18]

In characteristic fashion, however, he kept quiet while his opponents got the headlines, did what he thought was his duty without fighting for what he believed was right.

By 1909, Pinchot had deservedly won recognition as the leader in the national movement for forest conservation and was probably more widely known than any other government administrative officer in the country except for the president. After studying at home and abroad, he had put his ideas on practical forest management to work at the famous Vanderbilt estate, Biltmore, near Asheville, North Carolina. In 1898, he headed a small branch office called the Division of Forestry in the Department of Agriculture which included only two foresters among its eleven employees. Soon he had four hundred men working in six field offices, and in 1905 he was given control over work transferred to him from the Department of the Interior. In 1898, there were 19 national forests covering 20,000,000 acres; in 1909, there were 149 national forests covering 193,000,000 acres.

Under Roosevelt, Pinchot had been much more than the chief forester. He had been a prominent member of the Public Lands Commission, which provided a general public lands policy for the nation. He had also mapped the forestry policy for the Philippines and had suggested that conservation policy be broadened to include water, minerals, and land as well as forests. He had favored the leasing of coal lands to private developers, whereas Ballinger, as commissioner of the General Land Office, had favored outright sale. Ballinger had also unsuccessfully objected to Pinchot's desire to establish the Chugach National Forest in Alaska, in which Cunningham's claims lay. More importantly, he had for seven years been a member of Roosevelt's "tennis cabinet" and had grown accustomed to having Roosevelt accept his advice. An excellent public relations man, he had also successfully lobbied his ideas through Congress and had been the chairman of the committee that arranged for the conference of governors on the subject of conservation held at the White House on May 13–15, 1908.[19]

All this does not mean that "Sir Galahad of the woodlands," as Harold Ickes later called him, had no opposition. Farmers, grazers, and water-power people of the West, where most of the forests were, finally succeeded in February 1907 in transferring from the president to Congress the authority to establish national forests in the states of Colorado, Idaho, Montana, Oregon, Washington, and Wyoming. With ingenuity, great speed, some inaccuracy with respect to boundary lines, and against the better judgment of Secretary of Agriculture James "Tama Jim" Wilson, Roosevelt and Pinchot prepared a presidential proclamation for "midnight forests" covering sixteen million acres just before the bill went into effect. In Idaho alone, three million acres of agricultural land were included, but the Roosevelt administration was slow to remove them from the reserves. At any rate, that Roosevelt was highly pleased with Pinchot is illustrated by his writing to him just two days before he retired from the presidency: "I cannot think of a man in the country whose loss would be a more real misfortune to the Nation than yours would be. . . ."[20] Conversely, with Roosevelt gone and a westerner, Ballinger, as secretary of the interior, "Pinchotism" became the hated target especially of western anticonservationists.

Taft had known Pinchot since his days at the War Department, when Taft had championed the work of the Army Corps of Engineers rather than of the Forestry Service and thought Pinchot somewhat of "a radical and a crank." Taft had, however, given him very high praise for the work he had done in the Philippines and appreciated his stumping for him in the campaign of 1908. A "fanatic" conservationist who utterly worshiped Roosevelt, the

high-strung Pinchot, like Roosevelt, immediately followed an idea
with action. Personally modest although independently wealthy,
"the millionaire with a mission" was a dogged fighter, yet he had
the unfortunate habit of ascribing unworthy motives to whoever
disagreed with him. With Taft's approach to the White House,
he was afflicted with a "sickening doubt" whether Taft would
promote conservation as strongly as Roosevelt had. When Roosevelt
called him and Taft into conference soon after the election of 1908,
Taft said he would support conservation vigorously. Pinchot's
suspicions were aroused, however, when at a conservation conference held at Washington in December 1908, Taft had declined to
use a speech Pinchot had prepared for him and perhaps in jest
stated that "the imagination of those who are pressing [conserva-
tion] may outrun the practical facts." Pinchot thereupon concluded
that Taft would carry out Roosevelt's policies "on a shutter."[21]
"After T.R. came Taft," he later wrote. "It was as though a
sharp sword had been succeeded by a roll of paper, legal size."[22]
Although he would remain as the chief forester and Wilson as
secretary of agriculture, he believed that Garfield's replacement by
Ballinger boded ill for conservation and he asserted that he and
Ballinger might "clash." It may be that Pinchot was peeved with
Ballinger because he refused his request that land be withdrawn
for the establishment of "administrative sites" for ranger stations,
a technique he confessed was used to withdraw water power sites.
Ballinger also blocked his attempt to bring Indian forest reserva-
tions under the Forestry Service, and seemed to prefer to have the
national domain exploited by monopolists rather than by the common man. Because Ballinger differed with him on procedures, he
was a "yellow dog," a traitor to conservation.[23]

Although a law of 1902 authorized the withdrawal of water
power sites for use in connection with federal reclamation projects,
Roosevelt had acted in keeping with his belief that a president
could take any step necessary for the public good unless specifically
prohibited by the Constitution. Under color of this belief, he and
Pinchot had created the "midnight forests" and Garfield had withdrawn more than four million acres of water power sites to insure
that they would not be acquired illegally. Roosevelt left to Congress only to pass protective laws. Taft's outlook on a president's
powers differed from Roosevelt's considerably, as revealed in his
writing to Representative William Kent that

> we have a government of limited power under the Consti-
> tution, and we have got to work out our problems on the

basis of law. Now, if that is reactionary, then I am a reactionary. . . . Pinchot is not a lawyer and I am afraid he is quite willing to camp outside the law to accomplish his beneficent purposes. I have told him so to his face. . . . I do not undervalue the great benefit that he has worked out, but I do find it necessary to look into the legality of his plans.[24]

Upon learning of Glavis's charge that Ballinger had incorrectly approved of the Cunningham claim, which impinged upon an Alaska forest preserve, and after talking with Glavis, Pinchot suggested that the whole matter be taken up with Taft rather than being made public. Bearing an introduction from Pinchot, on August 18 Glavis called upon Taft at Beverly and submitted a fifty-page report. Ballinger, to whom Taft sent the report for reply, called, too, and left a thousand-page report. Butt overheard Taft tell still another caller that "Pinchot is a fanatic and has no knowledge of discipline or interdepartmental etiquette," and that he would "not stand for such insubordination as he has been guilty of,"[25] while Ballinger, in a bellicose mood, told newspaper reporters upon his return to Washington: "Incidentally, I propose to kill some snakes."[26]

Taft read the documents, turned them over to Attorney General George Wickersham, discussed the whole problem with him and two other cabinet members, and concluded that jealousy between the Forestry Service and the Department of the Interior had caused the quarrel. He then asked those officials Glavis had implicated for a full statement about them, studied them, and decided that Glavis's charges were not well founded and concurred with Ballinger that Glavis be fired "for disloyalty to his superior officers in making a false charge against them. . . ."[27] He sent a copy to Pinchot, who called it "the whitewash letter." On the same day, Taft wrote to Pinchot that Ballinger was a true friend of conservation and that the best friend of conservation was one "who insists that every step taken in that direction should be within the law and buttressed by legal authority." He had the utmost confidence in Pinchot's desire to serve the public and to carry on the conservation crusade, he added. However, he insisted

that the action for which I become responsible, or for which my administration becomes responsible, shall be within the law. I write this letter in order to prevent hasty action on your part in taking up Glavis' cause, or in objecting to my sustaining Ballinger and his subordinates within the Interior Department as a reason for your withdrawing from the public service.

I should consider it one of the greatest losses that my administration could sustain if you were to leave it, and I sincerely hope that you will not think that my action in writing the inclosed letter to Secretary Ballinger is reason for your taking a step of this character.[28]

During his speaking tour, Taft tried to be conciliatory by praising Ballinger on the one hand and giving full credit to Roosevelt for initiating and nationalizing conservation policies. He put himself squarely behind those policies, yet he would not enforce more policies until he was sure he had the law on his side. Publicly, he praised Ballinger for his "efficiency and integrity"; privately, he believed that the accusations against him were generated by insurgents and muckrakers.[29] In the meantime, subordinate officials in the Forestry Service leaked some of Glavis's charges to the press and helped Glavis to write an article about them; and on September 20 Glavis wrote directly to Taft that "duty" required that he publish the facts he had collected. He would not accept pay for the article but agreed to have it published in *Collier's Weekly*, a moderately muckraking magazine with a circulation of about five hundred thousand. In the issue for November 6, editor Norman Hapgood severely criticized Ballinger for having approved of the Cunningham claims, thereby misrepresenting the interests of the people, and concluded that in "whitewashing Ballinger" Taft had been "outrageously misled." In the following issue, under lurid captions supplied by Hapgood's office, Glavis presented his side of the case, including a tortured narration of the Morgan-Guggenheim interest in the Cunningham claims. He also made a number of charges, among them that Ballinger had acted improperly both as land commissioner and as secretary of the interior. Particularly inciting to the public mind was the allegation that Ballinger had acted as a paid attorney for Cunningham and other coal speculators during the year after he had resigned as land commissioner and before he became secretary. The damaging superficial fact was that Ballinger had worked to legalize Cunningham's claim and thereby violated the regulation which prohibited a former officeholder to appear for a fee before his own agency with reference to claims made while he had been in office. The truth was that he had spent more money than he had received on what he had considered to be perfectly honest work. While the anti-Ballinger and anti-Taft chant was taken up by such muckraking magazines as *Hampton's* and *McClure's*, Taft, always willing to give a man the benefit of the doubt, held him to have been scrupulously honest in the matter and also correct in having dropped his connection with Cunningham once he became secretary. To Senator Jonathan Bourne he remarked:

> Well, I find on my return [from his tour of the country] everybody full of despair and predicting all sorts of evil. One member of the Cabinet tells me that there is a cabal of the Roosevelts' friends to force an issue between us and another that Pinchot has got to be dismissed. Still another tells me that the reformers don't believe I intend to push any of the reform measures instituted by Roosevelt and that hell is to pay everywhere. The trouble is that they don't believe me when I say a thing once. . . . I have told the Cabinet that if I had done anything to be ashamed of or had said anything which might have brought on them all this gloom, then I would feel some regrets possibly. But I have done nothing that I would not do over again, and therefore I must feel that their troubles are either imaginary or else someone else is to blame.[30]

Rather than springing publicly to Ballinger's defense, however, and rather than dismissing Pinchot for abetting Glavis, Taft praised Ballinger in private. He also asked Ballinger to direct his subordinates to leave Pinchot's name out of any statement they might make if the evidence in the case was called for by Congress and told Pinchot he had done so. Above all, he wanted to stop the controversy. "I must bring public discussion between departments and bureaus to an end. It is most demoralizing and subversive of governmental discipline and efficiency. I want you to help me in this. I can enforce teamwork if I can keep public opinion out of newspaper discussion," he told Pinchot.[31]

Pinchot admitted that Taft's letter to him was "one of the finest . . . one friend could write to another" and agreed to meet with the president at Salt Lake City. During the evening of September 24 and again on the morning of the twenty-fifth, Pinchot wrote down the major points of an interview which never would have been held except for "the old friendship between us." When Pinchot said he would not resign, Taft was greatly relieved. When Pinchot added that he "might find it necessary to attack Ballinger," in whom he lacked confidence, and promised to provide Taft with a bill of particulars against him, Taft retorted that his "zeal was so great he tended to think that any man who differed as to method was corrupt" and that the press bureau of the Forestry Bureau was responsible "for fuss about this fight." Pinchot did not think Ballinger corrupt, but he told Taft that he "looked at the whole question from legal standpoint" and that while he himself sought to avoid trouble, he might have to cause some and Taft "might be forced to fire him." Each man then approved of the other's carefully guarded statement to the press about their meeting. Taft confirmed his support of conservation and expressed his wish that Pinchot remain in office; Pinchot praised Taft's promise of support for conservation and said he would remain in office.[32] The squabble appeared to be over, but Pinchot saw a way to keep up his fight for conservation.

What Taft overlooked was Pinchot's penchant for martyrdom, his willingness to risk being discharged in order to dramatize the difference in attitude toward conservation between Taft and Roosevelt. Ballinger, he stated in a letter he had promised Taft at Salt Lake City, was "actively hostile to the conservation policies." Unless Ballinger was "vigorously friendly" to these policies, private interests would gain and the public would suffer. His indifference and hostility would differ little in the final result. With some flamboyant exaggeration, he concluded that "the effect of Secretary Ballinger's action . . . was actively harmful to the public interest in the most critical and far-reaching problem this Nation has faced since the Civil War. . . . I am forced to regard him as the most effective opponent the conservation policies have yet had."[33]

Taft gave Pinchot's letter and another written by Garfield to Ballinger for comment. On November 15, Ballinger presented his side of the case, which commended itself to Taft, who then sent the letter on to Pinchot and on November 24 wrote him a personal letter in which he indicated that his confidence in Ballinger remained unshaken and that the continuation of the controversy was not "in the interest of the public service." Since Ballinger was carrying out the conservation policies, why could not he and Pinchot live together in the same government?[34] Pinchot thought the letter "friendly" but saw in it the "growth of tension," for the president had addressed him as "My dear Mr. Pinchot" rather than "Dear Gifford." Moreover, he did not believe that there was room in the government for both him and Ballinger. Perhaps the Angel Gabriel could cooperate with Ballinger, he suggested, for he could not. Since he had promised not to resign, he must arrange for Taft to dismiss him. The first step in this process had come with the publication of Glavis's article in *Collier's*. When Pinchot then attacked Taft openly in a speech at the University Club of New York and in a letter to Jonathan Dolliver, chairman of the Senate Committee on Agriculture and Forestry, he courted dismissal but insured that the crisis over conservation would not die. Rather, it would be investigated by Congress and thus become a national issue.

In his letter of early January 1910, written he said in answer to Dolliver's request for information and with the approval of Tama Jim Wilson, Pinchot stated that he had reprimanded those subordinate officials who had helped Glavis publicize the Cunningham claims but that "they broke no law and at worst were guilty only of the violation of official propriety." Moreover, "A public officer is bound first to obey the law and keep within it. But he is also bound, at any personal risk, to do everything that law will let him do for the public good."[35]

Ballinger's annual report for 1909 had suggested government rather than private control of natural resources, as also did an article by Pinchot entitled, "The A B C of Conservation."[36] These men thus agreed in objective but not in method. In any event, as Taft prepared a special message asking that a law be passed to legalize the withdrawal of lands from entry which Roosevelt had accomplished by executive order, to prevent monopoly of water power sites, improve waterways, and carry on the work of the Reclamation Service, Charles Taft told him that he was "getting tired of this Forestry Bureau business, and I don't know but it would be a good thing to let Pinchot out!" Taft replied:

> If the whole contention is the result of some sort of con-
> spiracy, Pinchot's dismissal would only bring about what
> they are trying to do, an open rupture between Roosevelt
> and myself, and I am determined if such a rupture is ever
> to be brought about that it shall not be through any action
> of mine. Theodore may not approve of all I have done
> and I don't expect him to do so, but I shall try not to do
> anything which he might regard as a challenge to him.
> No, Charlie, I am going to give Pinchot as much rope as
> he wants, and I think you will find that he will hang
> himself.[37]

To Butt, Taft looked "haggard and careworn . . . like a man almost ill," for by dismissing Pinchot he might create a rupture with Roosevelt and stimulate a "Back from Elba" movement which would be supported by the insurgents. He had asked Elihu Root to go over the record of the case, and Root had suggested to him that "there is only one thing for you to do now, and that you must do at once."[38] In his best judicial tone, Taft noted in a letter to Pinchot the imputation that he had approved of fraudulent claims, adding:

> Your letter was in effect an improper appeal to Congress and the public to excuse in advance the guilt of your subordinates before I could act, and against my decision in the Glavis case before the whole evidence on which that was based could be considered. I should be glad to regard what has happened only as a personal reflection, so that I could pass it over and take no official cognizance of it. But other and higher considerations must govern me. When the people . . . elected me president, they placed me in an office of the highest dignity and charged me with the duty of maintaining that dignity and proper respect for the office on the part of my subordinates. Moreover, if I were to pass over this matter in silence, it would be most demoralizing to the discipline of the executive branch of the government.
>
> By your own conduct you have destroyed your usefulness as a helpful subordinate of the government, and it therefore now becomes my duty to direct the secretary of agriculture to remove you from your office as the forester.[39]

When the letter was delivered to his home, Pinchot knew what it contained. He waved it toward his doting mother and said, "I'm fired." With eyes flashing, her head flung back, and waving an arm over her head, she cried, "Hurrah!"[40]

Three days after firing Pinchot, Taft plaintively complained that "I would not have removed Pinchot if I could have helped it."[41] Pinchot, however, remained unabashed. From the "narrowly official angle," he said, his letter to chairman Dolliver had been "insubordinate," for "it condemned the action of another Department, and even criticized publicly an official decision of the President of the United States. On that basis Taft was perfectly justified in firing me. I had asked for it, I could not complain when I got it, and as a matter of fact I never did. Officially we were quits." Extremely enlightening are the words that followed:

> But from every other angle I was right and Taft was wrong. As an executive he should never have let the issue reach any such point. Since he was supporting Ballinger, he should have told me long before to shut up or get out. As President he should never have approved my aggressive and defiant statement at Salt Lake. And as a man

he was in honor and in duty bound to stick to his word, given to T. R. in my presence, and call off Ballinger's attack on T. R.'s conservation policy.[42]

III

Taft had hoped that Congress would investigate the charges against Ballinger, as Ballinger himself demanded. Such an investigation would show just how lenient he had been toward Pinchot, yet he would not push the issue, saying, "Roosevelt would have come back at those preferring the charges and would by now have them on the run, but I cannot do things that way. I will let them go on, and by and by the people will see who is right. . . ."[43]

When Senator Wesley L. Jones, of Ballinger's own state, moved to provide for the investigation a joint committee of twelve members, six to be appointed by the vice-president and six by the Speaker, Norris objected and demanded that the House elect its own members, for he feared that Taft men would manipulate the investigation and whitewash Ballinger. With the aid of other insurgents and of Democrats eager to embarrass the administration, he was able by three votes to give Cannon a stinging defeat and provide for an investigation which would have the confidence of the American people.

To Taft it appeared that the insurgents were backing Pinchot, whereas the insurgents saw Taft as allying himself with the Old Guard and trying to repudiate the Roosevelt policies, for Cannon thoroughly opposed conservation measures and sided with Ballinger. In any event, with Senator Knute Nelson, of Minnesota, as chairman—he was bitterly anti-Pinchot—and Root included "to do the serious thinking and give respectibility," as Norman Hapgood put it,[44] the joint committee on Ballinger held hearings from January 26 to May 20, 1910, in what was popularly called the "American Dreyfus case." Everyone knew that the hearings were being held less for the edification of the committee or even of Congress than of the entire country and that the findings were to be more in accord with partisan considerations than with the evidence. The committee exonerated both Ballinger and Taft of evil-doing, yet revealed that Ballinger had little real enthusiasm for conservation. It appeared that Ballinger's strict constructionism usually resulted in favors for private enterprise and for the exploitation of the resources desired by the West, and that in justifying his actions he had at least by implication criticized the Roosevelt conservation program. These points were well driven home by a minority report made by the four Democrats on the committee and another prepared by the Republican insurgent E. H. Madison. The whole matter could be seen as "a tilt between Taft and Ted," as one newspaper put it. But a curious set of circumstances then changed what should have been an affirmation of Taft's integrity into a widespread denunciation of him for having sought to white-wash Ballinger in part by the use of a predated document.

Fearing a million-dollar libel suit if Ballinger was exonerated, the editors of *Collier's* had hired Louis D. Brandeis to defend Glavis. Ballinger was at first unrepresented by counsel. Taking Taft's advice to get a lawyer but not a western one, he retained Taft's friend John J. Vertrees, of Tennessee. Vertrees, a genuine anticonservationist, did more to harm than to help Ballinger. Ballinger damaged his case further in his own testimony, which was directed toward defending his reputation and upon occasion cast ridicule upon Roosevelt's conservation policies. His touted respect for the law withered when Brandeis elicited the information that appointments to the Department of the Interior not made by Taft were made only after consultation with Taft's patronage broker, Postmaster General Frank H. Hitchcock.

In studying the evidence while the hearings were in progress, Brandeis suspected that Taft had used a predated report prepared by Wickersham on which to dismiss Glavis and that he had not given the case the attention it deserved. He was then able to learn that Taft had not depended upon Wickersham's report but upon a preliminary report prepared by Assistant Attorney General Oscar W. Lawler, who was assigned to the Department of the Interior and was a loyal supporter of Ballinger. Ballinger, in his testimony, denied that he knew anything about the Lawler memorandum even though he had read it and approved of it. Then when Ballinger and Wickersham finally acknowledged the preparation of the memorandum, Taft, ignorant of this disclosure, denied the fact and said that he himself had dictated the statement in question. With his innate penchant for procrastination, Taft waited too long to reply to the charge of mendacity leveled against him, even if it pointed to the making of a mistake rather than wrongdoing. What had happened was that Lawler had come with Ballinger to visit at Beverly on September 6, 1909. Because he would soon leave for his transcontinental trip, Taft directed him to prepare an opinion on the Glavis case "as if he were president." Wicker-sham brought Lawler's work with him to Beverly on the twelfth, but Taft was unhappy with it and preferred an opinion that Wickersham himself completed on the twelfth. Unable because of his impending departure to write his own opinion based upon Wickersham's work, on the thirteenth Taft drafted his own letter and directed Wickersham to "embody in a written statement such analysis and conclusions as he had given me, file it with the record, and date it prior to the date of my opinion, so as to show that my decision was fortified by his summary of the evidence and his conclusions therefrom."[45] In consequence, Wickersham had dated the opinion September 11 and filed it with the other documents, but did not include the Lawler report with the papers which he submitted at the request of the investigating committee. When Brandeis ferreted out that Wickersham could not possibly have produced his report in the five or six days available to him—Ballinger's report alone included a half-million words—Taft was laid wide open to charges of being a liar and forger in the public press, which thereupon "convicted" him and "vindicated" Pinchot and Glavis.

Even more important than the relevation of Taft's "mistake" was the fact that Pinchot, eager to state his version of the affair to Roosevelt, first wrote to him, on December 31, 1909, and then hastened to Europe to talk with him, as did Hapgood. Pinchot told Roosevelt that Taft had turned "directly away from the Roosevelt policies." He had chosen a cabinet of lawyers who could not possibly follow those policies; did not oppose attacks made upon Roosevelt in Congress; sought the advice of only those congressional leaders who opposed Roosevelt's policies; in the appointment of Ballinger had named a man opposed to conservation; and had handled the Payne-Aldrich tariff in a disgraceful manner.[46] Instead of defending himself in strong terms, Taft wrote to Roosevelt, who would leave England in June 1910: "The Garfield-Pinchot-Ballinger controversy has given me a great deal of personal pain and suffering, but I am not going to say a word to you on that subject. You will have to look into that wholly for yourself without influence by the parties, if you would find the truth."[47]

The truth was that Taft had lost politically by dismissing Pinchot and retaining Ballinger. Even if innocent of corruption, Ballinger was not a dedicated conservationist and was a liability to him, yet Taft was unwilling to sacrifice him to a conspiracy he believed was aimed at himself. Although he said that he would never desert him, late in July he asked Senator Murray Crane, of Massachusetts, to propose to the Republicans of the state of Washington that they elect Ballinger as senator and also to convince

Ballinger to run. On August 4, Taft's personal secretary, Norton, who thrived on intrigue, spoke on the telephone with Crane and reported jubilantly to Taft, "I think we have got Ballinger."[48] Although Norton had argued that the retention of Ballinger would result in the defeat of thirty-five candidates for the House of Representatives and loss of the House to the Democrats in the elections of 1910, he overlooked the fact that the insurgents were after Taft rather than Ballinger and that the mere ousting of Ballinger would not satisfy them.[49] Furthermore, Ballinger refused to cooperate, saying that he would not leave the cabinet unless Taft asked him to resign, that he would "not allow his enemies to force him out" and thus provoke public condemnation of him. Taft thereupon told Norton, "Then we will wait till we see old Pussyfoot [Crane]. Norton, I don't care much whether Ballinger gets out or not. . . . He has suffered enough, it seems to me, without having the dagger driven into his heart by me."[50]

Once Congress granted him authority to withdraw lands temporarily from entry, Taft's record of withdrawals almost equaled that of Roosevelt. By July 1910, 71,518,558 acres of coal lands had been withdrawn in the United States and about 770,000 acres in Alaska. On July 3, Taft signed a bill withdrawing 8,495,731 acres of water power, phosphate, and petroleum lands, an area equal to that of the states of New York, Pennsylvania, and South Carolina. He had proved his faith as a conservationist. Moreover, these withdrawals were the first to be legally authorized. Congress also authorized the expenditure of $20,000,000 to complete reclamation projects already under way. Furthermore, he weathered charges that he was permitting the Guggenheim Alaska Syndicate to obtain a monopoly on coal transportation in Alaska and that he took 12,800 acres from the Chugach National Forest and opened them to development. But after his dismissal of Pinchot no one paid much attention to what he said or did about conservation.

As president, Taft insisted upon his right to administer the conservation program in his own legal manner rather than taking directions from those who preferred the extralegal Roosevelt way, and in the end he kept his promises to regularize Roosevelt's conservation measures by appropriate legislation. However, by wrecking the interdepartmental arrangements between Interior and Agriculture that had existed under Roosevelt and Pinchot, strengthening the power of Interior over conservation, and depending more and more upon the Corps of Engineers, he had fragmented the comprehensive Roosevelt conservation program. He had replaced Garfield, in whom both Roosevelt and Pinchot placed great faith, with Ballinger, whose devotion to the cause of conservation they doubted. He had allowed the split in his party made evident by the tariff to widen further by his stubborn support of Ballinger against overwhelming demands that he be dismissed. He had let Pinchot remain in office long after he could have dismissed him on the ground of insubordination, and then let him become a martyred hero to progressives. He had permitted an interdepartmental squabble which he could have solved quietly and effectively to balloon into astronomical proportions, let his inefficiency as an administrator be used as a key to the charge that he opposed conservation. Rather than determining for himself whether Ballinger was an adequate executive officer, he had permitted Congress to decide. Although favoring efficiency in other areas, as in demanding machinery for deciding upon "scientific" tariff rates, reforming the administration of justice, and appointing a committee to suggest methods for improving the administration of the executive branch, with respect to conservation he seemed to place strict construction of the statutes and neat organization charts before scientific management. Ballinger did not help by saying after he resigned that he had conformed with Taft's ideas on conservation even though he disagreed with them, for he opposed rubber-stamping the Roosevelt policy of federal landlordism which Taft followed.[51]

The insurgents had added Pinchot, Garfield, and their supporters to the anti-Taft ranks and hoped soon to bring Roosevelt to their side also. Taft was not helped when he bowed to the demands of his cabinet and the advice of his brother, Charles, and accepted "with great reluctance" Ballinger's proffered resignation, in March 1911, in which he spoke only of ill health and the decline of his law practice. Taft then acted inconsistently by appointing as his successor Walter L. Fisher, a friend of Garfield and of Pinchot whom he had lately characterized as one of the "foul conspirators" in the Ballinger affair. Furthermore, he knew Fisher was determined to open to development the water power sites Ballinger had withdrawn from use two years earlier. While he gave Fisher freedom to determine policy, nothing Taft or Fisher could do would win back western progressives.[52]

The crisis over conservation, after all, affected ideology and politics more than it did conservation itself. To Roosevelt, "conservation" meant government management by experts in the interest of efficient resources development, whereas Taft preferred a freely competitive market and a minimum of governmental interference—one a Hamiltonian idea, the other Jeffersonian. Roosevelt would take whatever steps not prohibited to him to push conservation; Taft stuck to the letter of the law. Pinchot had tried to discredit Taft, Ballinger to discredit Pinchot. Rarely had the thesis that politics and administration were interdependent been offered such excellent proof. Roosevelt had supervised and administered conservation by a bureaucracy that, as Pinchot's actions revealed, was not disinterested but power-hungry. This policy was anathema particularly in the West, which preferred state to federal conservation programs. Ballinger questioned "the elitist assumptions of bureaucracy and expertise which were the underpinnings of the new regulatory state" and was therefore a threat to "every effort to forge the executive into an effective instrument for the central control of resource use."[53] But in the end it was Taft who suffered the most. His bungling first on the tariff and then on conservation insured that the House would lose its Republican majority in the elections of 1910 and also provided issues for the presidential campaign of 1912. His dismissal of Pinchot drove a deep wedge between himself and Roosevelt, who now saw him a failure as a leader. Whether the insurgents would look to Roosevelt instead for leadership was a question which could, of course, be answered only after Roosevelt returned from Europe. At the moment, he hoped that Taft would regain a position of leadership and renounced any thought of again entering the lists. But, he said, "our own party leaders did not realize that I was able to hold the Republican party in power only because I insisted on a steady advance, and dragged them along with me. Now the advance has been stopped. . . ."[54]

5

★★★★★

THE DENOUEMENT OF 1910

I

On February 3, 1910, William Allen White wrote Taft that

> if you will just let the insurgents alone they will come
> home like little Bo-peep's sheep. They are not against your
> administration. For the most part they favor your legis-
> lative program. They are not mixed up in any return from
> Elba conspiracy. . . . The insurgents so far as I know
> them would rather see you successful for two terms than
> not.
>   But they will not work with Senator Aldrich and Mr.
> Cannon. . . . It is not your fault, not fundamentally.
> You have to take things as they are. The leadership of
> the party remains under the present status with Senator
> Aldrich and Mr. Cannon. You are more or less bound to
> take their advice, and of course their advice is for disci-
> pline. But it will be hard on majorities next November.[1]

Some time later White called at the White House and had
lunch with the president, Mrs. Taft, and his half-brother, Charles.
White wanted to "show him that if he would give us fair treatment,
we should be glad to work with him." Mrs. Taft, he said, "regarded
me as a curious kind of horned toad," brother Charley knew exactly
what he wanted, and Taft steered him away from any serious talk.
White tried to find a way to wean Taft from the reactionary crowd
with which he was surrounding himself. Taft was courteous, con-
siderate, cordial, yet whenever White mentioned Aldrich or Cannon, "I could see his eye behind his smile veiling with almost the

hint of a serpentine glitter" and White left the White House knowing that "I and my kind, the whole progressive lot, were anathema—
outlawed from his counsel. He would have none of us. . . . He
was convinced that we were mad. He was a consistent, honest,
courageous, most intelligent conservative. He believed in the
existing order. . . . He deeply resented the hands that would touch
the Ark of his Covenant." Time and again White tried by letter
and messenger "to make him understand how serious was the uprising against his creed and crowd. Possibly he knew, for he was
sensitive. But if he knew, he was unmoved. He walked to his
doom 'a gentleman unafraid'!"[2]

In Europe, meanwhile, Gifford Pinchot and Norman Hapgood
poured into Theodore Roosevelt's ears their version of William
Howard Taft's apostasy. What would Roosevelt do upon his return?
He had never avoided taking a position on national questions and
was known to prefer war to peace; a poll taken in February 1910
of the Republican editors west of the Mississippi showed that he
was preferred to Taft for president; and progressive speakers were
demanding that he run in 1912 on a third-party ticket. The *New
York Herald*, an independent paper, asserted that he would run
and thus offer the people "the choice between Caesarism and constitutionalism," and most Democratic journals shuddered at the
thought of having again as president the "Man on Horseback."
Republican papers divided, some saying that the personal friendship of Taft and Roosevelt was so strong that nothing could sunder
it, others that Roosevelt would either support Taft or give up
politics altogether.[3] As though in anticipation of Roosevelt's running, Taft in a Lincoln-day speech in New York frankly admitted
that his party was divided, but pleaded for solidarity on the ground
that Republicans had "either substantially complied with" or were
"about to perform within the present session of Congress" the promises contained in the party platform. He alleged that the Payne-
Aldrich tariff was a substantial downward revision, the best revenue
producer of all tariffs, and one that could not be blamed for increases in consumer prices, and repeated his assertion of Winona
that it was the best tariff ever passed. The railroad regulation and
antitrust crusades he had recently begun, moreover, were in the
Roosevelt tradition.[4]

Taft sought to solidify his party for the forthcoming congressional elections, but he could neither reconcile his party to the
Payne-Aldrich tariff nor get Roosevelt out of his mind. Roosevelt
was going to have a "hard time" when he returned, he alleged,

for "every man with an ambition, every new movement, will try to drag to him and to it the ex-President, and whether he will be able to keep out of all I don't know." But he was certain that Roosevelt would never be president again because of the anti-third-term sentiment. The strongest man the party could offer, he continued, was Charles Evans Hughes, and if the party demanded Hughes he himself would gladly stand aside.[5]

In March 1910, Taft had completed a full year in office. What had he done that warranted continued support and renomination by his party? Although no president escaped unscathed from a tariff revision, the country was prosperous. He remained the unquestioned leader of his party, and the implementation of the reforms he had suggested to Congress early in the year, including such "Bryanite" proposals as an income tax and a corporation tax— which endeared him to liberal Democrats—should win him laurels as a reform president. He must not be judged before he had completed his labors and without taking into consideration the Congress with which he had to work, said his apologists, who quickly added that no man who had followed seven years of Roosevelt could avoid injurious comparison, especially since Taft's leadership was considered to be judicial, philosophical, or intellectual and Roosevelt's moral. To insurgents, however, his support of the Payne-Aldrich tariff and of Richard A. Ballinger in particular, his failure to uphold the Roosevelt policies in general, his siding with reactionaries on railroad regulation and other legislation, and his denying of patronage to them were the major reasons he had lost the confidence of the people and divided his party. That he should have sided with the vast majority, the regulars, was understandable; so was the decision of the progressives, who until the primaries of 1910 had kept private their criticisms of the administration, to declare open war.

Roosevelt's refusal to speak publicly stimulated diverse and irreconcilable conjectures as to his plans, with some editors asking "What shall we do with Roosevelt?" and others "What will Roosevelt do to us?" He happily submitted to the great reception given to him upon his return to New York on June 18 and cheerfully greeted Pinchot but declined Taft's invitation to visit the White House. Despite importunities from many newspaper reporters to say where he stood with respect to Taft and the progressives, he kept quiet. While he had no intention of reentering public life, he began to change his mind about Taft. After hearing many criticisms of Taft from Pinchot and others, he became convinced that the Republicans could neither win Congress in 1910 nor reelect Taft as president in 1912. While he would "probably" help in the campaign to rename Taft, in April 1910 he said that he could not support Taft's administration or his bid for reelection. On the other hand, he meant neither to take sides in the battle between regulars and progressives nor to run himself. He sought to put the public good before the welfare either of himself or of Taft, telling Henry Cabot Lodge,

> Very possibly if Taft had tried to work in my spirit, and along my lines, he would have failed; that he has conscientiously tried to work for the objects I had in view, so far as he could approve them, I have no doubt. I wish . . . to give Taft the benefit of every doubt. . . .
> But it puzzles me to see how I can help him or Congress to victory. . . . I very earnestly hope that Taft will retrieve himself yet and . . . I most emphatically desire that I shall not be put in the position of having to run for the Presidency. . . .[6]

When Elihu Root spoke with Roosevelt in May, he asked him not to take sides between Taft and the progressives and came away with what he believed was Roosevelt's promise to stay out of politics for two months after his return. "If he had done as he had promised me—keep out of things political—we should have been saved much of our past trouble," Root later said.[7] Roosevelt also promised Lodge that he would keep quiet about the political situation for sixty days after his return, albeit he noted that ". . . Taft, Cannon, Aldrich, and the others have totally misestimated the character of the movement which we now have to face in American life. I am not at the moment striving to apportion praise or blame . . . [but] I finally have to admit that [Taft] has gone wrong on certain points. . . ."[8]

On Easter Sunday, Archibald Butt saw Taft as looking "very badly. . . . He is white-looking and his pallor does not seem healthy. . . . It is hard on any man to see the eyes of everyone . . . turning to Roosevelt."[9] But why should Taft be uneasy? Given Pinchot's actions, could he have done anything but dismiss him? Had not Roosevelt told him to cooperate with Nelson W. Aldrich and Joseph Cannon, as he himself had done? Once he had discussed "most frankly every act of the administration" with Roosevelt, he added, Roosevelt would see that he had acted correctly.[10] Were he angry with Roosevelt he would not have sent secretaries George Meyer and James Wilson, both of whom had served Roosevelt, to greet him officially upon his arrival at New York. Nor would he have written a letter to be delivered by Butt in which he pleaded for Roosevelt's sympathy and understanding.

During his thirteen months in office, Taft confessed in his letter, he had had "a hard time." He did not know whether he had had "harder luck than other presidents but I do know that thus far I have succeeded far less than have others. I have been conscientiously trying to carry out your policies, but my method of doing so has not worked smoothly." The illness of Mrs. Taft, he added, had placed a terribly great strain upon him for almost a year. As for the Payne-Aldrich tariff, while "not as radical" as he had wanted it, it was "a real downward revision" and the revenues from it had been "remarkable." But he admitted that the high cost of living continued because of the price of items on which rates had not been lowered, and both the Republican and Democratic press opposed him because the duty on printing paper had not been lowered more. On other measures, such as railroad regulation, postal savings banks, and protection for railroad employees, restoration of the president's power to withdraw lands from the public domain, and the admission of Arizona and New Mexico as states, he predicted success. He blamed especially the progressive senators for having made it difficult for him to comply with the promises of the party platform and for making the election of a Democratic House in 1910 probable and the election of a Democrat as president in 1912 possible. Finally, he asked Roosevelt to visit him in Washington.[11]

Roosevelt had replied to Taft just before leaving Europe—in the first letter he had written to him since March 1909—that he did not know the situation at home, was much concerned about some of the things he was told, and intended "to keep my mind as open as I kept my mouth shut!" Then followed an expression of pleasure at Mrs. Taft's recovery.[12]

II

Two days after landing at New York, Roosevelt wrote to Taft to thank him for the letter delivered at New York by Butt, for words of welcome he had written for the *Outlook*, and for having sent Meyer and Wilson to greet him. Although he declined his invitation to visit him at the White House, he praised him for the progress he was making, for by this time the House had reformed its rules and Taft had obtained new railroad legislation, a postal savings bank bill, and new laws which gave practical effect to Roosevelt's conservation policies. Perhaps with these accomplishments in mind, he had categorically told Meyer at the New York reception that "of course I am for Will's nomination and his reelection; there can be no question about it."[13] But he kept his promise to keep his mouth shut for sixty days for exactly four, for on June 22 he talked with newspaper reporters at Sagamore Hill. When he then held conferences with Pinchot, Albert J. Beveridge, James Garfield, Robert M. La Follette, and other progressives, Taft, who assumed that Roosevelt had formally invited them to his home, accepted Butt's suggestion and cautioned his cabinet to speak warily, telling them that "it is just as well to wait until the situation shall *open* itself; at least, we do not desire to create any situation. We may very well content ourselves with standing upon our record until circumstances arise calling for further action."[14] When he went to sign some bills at the Capitol when the Congress adjourned, on June 25, he noticed that none of the progressive senators bade him goodbye. He did not expect a break with Roosevelt to come, however, and intended to learn about Roosevelt's attitude when he met with him at Beverly on June 30.

At Beverly, perhaps because neither man wished to be alone with the other, Taft had Mrs. Taft and his daughter Helen at his side while he spoke with Roosevelt and Butt talked with Lodge and Taft's secretary. Roosevelt's telling of his experiences while in Europe drew booming laughter from Taft, but nothing political beyond the situation in New York was discussed during the two-hour meeting, and the reporters waiting outside were told merely that the meeting was a purely social one. Mrs. Taft did not share her husband's faith in Roosevelt's friendliness, but Taft revealed complete trust in his old friend by telling Butt, "Well, Archie, that is another corner turned. I think he felt just as I did, that it was best . . . not [to] give any opportunity for confidences which might be embarrassing."[15]

What Taft did not know was that Roosevelt believed that Taft's bungling leadership had split their party and made Democratic victories possible in November. To weld the two wings of the party together without supporting either side against the other now became Roosevelt's objective, and he cautioned Pinchot particularly not to make a "factional attack" on Taft lest he make it difficult for him to win renomination and reelection. "He has not been a good leader," he wrote, but would be better than any Democrat who could be named against him. "As you know," he added, "Taft has passed his nadir. He is evidently a man who takes color from his surroundings. He was an excellent man under me, and close to me. For eighteen months after his election he was a rather pitiful failure because he had no real strong man on whom to lean, and yielded to the advice of his wife, his Brother Charley, the different corporation lawyers who had his ear, and various similar men." However, Taft had learned some bitter lessons and in the future would try "to look at things more from the standpoint of the interests of the people, and less from the standpoint of a technical lawyer. . . ." Thus, he concluded, Taft with new advisers would redeem the past and, if he did not do everything that the progressives wanted, would turn out to be a "very respectable President" who should be renominated and reelected.[16]

Roosevelt's experiences in New York State revealed the difficulty of trying to draw the two wings of his party together. Charles Evans Hughes had been elected as governor of New York in 1906 with help from both Roosevelt and Taft and had made direct primary nominations and other electoral reforms his major objectives. After an overnight visit with Hughes at Albany in March 1910, Taft decided that in order to win New York in November, Hughes must run for a third term and that he, Hughes, and Root must defeat Republican State Chairman Timothy Woodruff, William Barnes, Colonel William Ward, and other Old Guard followers who opposed Hughes in particular and good government in general. When Hughes met Roosevelt at a Harvard class reunion, on June 29, he convinced him to enter the fight for a direct primary law which would end control by party bosses. Roosevelt joined both Taft men and progressives against the Old Guard, only to be defeated. At the suggestion of Hughes and also of Lloyd C. Griscom, a Taftite who had recently become the chairman of the New York County Republican Committee, he then promised to take his fight to the state convention, of which he hoped to be the temporary chairman in order to obtain a "clear-cut progressive program." After talking with both Roosevelt and Taft, Griscom stated publicly that the two men were in complete agreement on state issues.

Now Taft took a step that made it appear that he was deserting Roosevelt, for in offering Hughes a seat on the Supreme Court he made it impossible for him to help Roosevelt in New York. Moreover, he began to question the sincerity of Roosevelt's offer to help the Republican party. Rather than replying to his letter of welcome at New York with kind words for his administration, Roosevelt had said that he would keep quiet for two months. "I don't care if he keeps silent forever. Certainly the longer he remains silent, the better it will please me," Taft snapped.[17] He believed that he was following Roosevelt's policies and deserved commendation, never realizing that Roosevelt could not in good conscience endorse him. Roosevelt's associating with numerous progressives at Oyster Bay made him believe that he had abandoned him and that he would seek the presidential nomination in his own right. He told Butt on July 6 that

> I do not see how I am going to get out of having a fight with President Roosevelt. . . . I hardly think the prophet of the square deal is playing it exactly square with me. . . . But I shall do nothing. I shall let matters shape themselves in his mind and give him every chance to whip around if he sees he is making a mistake. I shall take no notice of it until it absolutely forces itself on me or the Administration.[18]

When he read to Mrs. Taft a dispatch in which Roosevelt was reported as favoring in Washington State the election as senator of Miles Poindexter, a leading insurgent, her innate distrust of Roosevelt was deepened, and she said, "Well, I suppose you will have to fight Mr. Roosevelt for the nomination, and if you get it he will defeat you. But it can't be helped. . . ."[19] And on August 15, Taft told Butt: "Archie, it is coming as sure as we are sitting here. And when it does come, we must depend on some of the South to help us out to hold the country from absolute socialism."[20]

Taft could do several things: help Roosevelt, oppose him, or bargain with him. Had he supported Roosevelt, he would have placed him under personal obligation and perhaps drawn him closer to him, but with characteristic political ineptitude he chose the last course and offered him a deal: in return for his endorsement of his administration he would drop Aldrich and Cannon as advisers and let him suggest a replacement for Ballinger. Were Roosevelt not to comply, he would fight him. However, if Taft was throwing overboard the old crowd from whom he had accepted advice thus far, he had not yet included some progressives among the new ones, thereby angering both the regulars and the progressives.

On August 16, the New York Republican executive committee named to be the keynoter of the state convention not Roosevelt but Vice-President James Sherman, close friend of Woodruff. While it is doubtful that Taft engineered the surprise, he probably acquiesced in it because the New York Old Guard promised to deliver the state delegation to him in 1912.

"Did you see what they did to Mr. Roosevelt today?" Taft's secretary, Charles Norton, asked Butt. Butt, who was so loyal to Roosevelt that he was considering leaving Taft's service, replied, "I did, and I am very sorry for it."

"Why?" asked Norton. "It is a great victory for the Administration."

"I don't regard it as such," Butt replied. "Moreover, it simply puts Mr. Roosevelt on his mettle, and he will clean out the entire lot sooner or later, and I don't see how they can help involving the President."

Later in the day, while motoring with Butt and Norton, Taft said casually, "Have you seen the newspapers this afternoon? They have defeated Theodore."

Norton began to chuckle and the President to laugh, and Norton said: "We have got him—we've got him—we've got him, as sure as peas we've got him."

Butt felt like saying "Like hell you've got him," but managed to keep his mouth shut.[21]

After stating that he would continue the battle on the floor of the state convention, which would meet late in September, Roosevelt took to the stump in a sixteen-state western tour to announce the policies of the New Nationalism and thereby to help the western progressives. Taft meanwhile appealed for support for his administration lest the Democrats win the November elections and "reject the Republican doctrine of protection,"[22] but at Beverly he played golf with Henry C. Frick and held conferences with J. P. Morgan, Aldrich, and Murray Crane, among others known to be anathema to the progressives.

If Roosevelt intended by his speaking to bring his party together, he accomplished exactly the opposite. Out of office and unfettered by responsibilities, he was now as free as William Jennings Bryan ever was to voice his opinions. Partly because of Bryan's ideas, and of La Follette's, and perhaps also those of Herbert Croly as expressed in his book *The Promise of American Life* (1909), he had moved considerably to the left under the shibboleth probably taken from Croly of "the New Nationalism," but he could not be all things to all men. In any event, before the Colorado legislature he demanded advanced social legislation and branded the Supreme Court as a barrier to the achievement of social justice, as in its *Knight* and *Lochner* decisions. The Court erred, he said, in permitting to exist a twilight zone between state and federal powers in which rich evildoers enjoyed immunity. At Osawatomie, Kansas, in a speech Pinchot had written, he asserted without mentioning Taft, that a statesman who broke his word should be hunted out of public life. He also demanded the strengthening of the federal government to the point where it could obtain social justice, particularly through an executive who would be the "steward of the public welfare" and to whom the courts would be subordinate. In seeking a "square deal" for everyone, he placed the rights of persons before those of property and the rights of labor before those of capital and concluded that "the man who wrongly holds that every human right is secondary to his profit must now give way to the advocate of human welfare, who rightly maintains that every man holds his property subject to the general right of the community to regulate its use to whatever degree the public welfare may require it." Because labor was "the chief element of wealth," the government should regulate the conditions of its use "in the interests of the common good." He then endorsed the graduated income tax, the inheritance tax, workingmen's compensation laws, the regulation of child and woman labor, a thoroughgoing revision of the tariff, and increased powers over corporations for both the Bureau of Corporations and the Interstate Commerce Commission.[23]

Eastern conservatives reacted to Roosevelt's radical proposals as they had to Bryan's platform of 1896. He had in attacking property and the courts assailed the bulwarks of civilization and become an anarchist and communist, and his wish to augment the powers of the president revealed him to be another Napoleon. In contrast to him, Taft appeared to be the conservator of all worth saving. At any rate, having won the progressives to his side, Roosevelt now sought to attach the conservatives to him as well, as by praising Taft's work in conservation, and so to unite the party. Upon his return East, for example, he supported both Lodge and Beveridge for reelection and said that Taft's tariff commission and the postal savings bank measure were examples of the kind of legislation called for by the New Nationalism. He also agreed to meet with Taft to show the public that they were in agreement on the New York State situation.

Taft mused that Roosevelt was using strange ways indeed to help him. "If I only knew what the President [sic] wanted . . . ," he told Archie Butt on August 19, "I would do it, but you know he has held himself so aloof that I am absolutely in the dark. I am deeply wounded." Furthermore, he asserted that the trouble between him and Roosevelt had begun with a letter Butt had carried from him to Roosevelt when he had sailed for Europe. Without mentioning the source of his information, which was Colonel Ward, he told Butt that Roosevelt was angry because he had included his brother Charles in the same class with Roosevelt as being responsible for his nomination and election.[24] He also wrote to a friend that "I don't know whither we are drifting, but I do know where every real thinking patriot will stand in the end, and that is by the Constitution."[25] Shocked and bewildered in seeing Roosevelt as one who would destroy the Constitution, he withdrew even more closely into his conservative shell. In a letter to his brother Charles, who was abroad, he commented that Roosevelt

> has proposed a program which it is absolutely impossible to carry out except by a revision of the federal Constitution.
> He has attacked the Supreme Court, which came like a bolt out of a clear sky, and which has aroused great indignation throughout the country on the part of the conservatives. His tour through the West has been one continual ovation. . . . In most of these speeches he has utterly ignored me. . . . His attitude toward me is one that I find difficult to understand and explain.

If, he concluded, Roosevelt disliked him because he had coupled him with Charles for having made his nomination and election possible, "I venture to say that a swell-headedness could go no further than this."[26]

A week later Taft told another brother, Horace, that part of Roosevelt's trouble was that he "has no one to advise him of the conservative type, like Root or Moody or Knox or myself, as he did when he was in office . . ." and that "the thing of all others that I am not going to do is to step out of the way of Mr. Roosevelt when he is advocating such wild ideas as those in . . . the Osawatomie speech."[27]

During the days from August 23 to September 11 that Roosevelt was on the stump, Taft grew increasingly sullen, and his golf game deteriorated. One day he swore a terrific oath and threw his club twenty-five yards from him in such anger that even the caddies were astonished. When Butt reminded him of his having said publicly that he liked golf because it helped one to control his feelings, he snapped, "All of which goes to show that it is easier to preach than to practice."[28]

Both Taft and Roosevelt addressed the National Conservation Congress held at St. Paul in the first week in September, but Taft vetoed the suggestion of meeting with Roosevelt and spoke on the day before he did. However, in a second personal meeting, which took place at the Henry White home in New Haven, Connecticut, on September 19 at the suggestion of Griscom, he promised to help him against the New York Old Guard. Any advantage he may have gained from the meeting was then lost when Norton publicly asserted that Roosevelt had asked for the meeting because he was in trouble in New York and that Taft had been magnanimous to him. This, of course, greatly embarrassed Roosevelt, who publicly denied Norton's statement. When Taft was also told tales true and false about Roosevelt's having said that he had not followed his policies, Taft told Butt that he and Roosevelt had evidently come to the parting of the ways. Roosevelt conceded that Taft might redeem himself, but he was certain that the Republican party could not be saved.

"We're going to beat them to a frazzle," Roosevelt told the crowd that met his train at Saratoga, site of the New York State Republican Convention, and rapidly overwhelmed the stalwart opposition to him as the temporary chairman. In his keynote address he praised Taft's achievements, even with respect to the tariff, thus giving the lie to those who asserted that he wanted to be the keynoter in order to control the committee on resolutions and bar any endorsement of Taft. In turn, Taft said that he could not support Woodruff, Barnes, and the rest of the "dead lot," dumped the Old Guard, and sided with Roosevelt against Sherman. He sent Root to Saratoga to act as his hatchet man. "I hope," he wrote to Mrs. Taft, "you saw the proceedings of the Saratoga convention and the very satisfactory resolution endorsing your husband. Roosevelt made a speech praising me also, which must have gone a little hard with him, but which indicated that he found it necessary."[29] But in part because of Roosevelt, the convention did not endorse his renomination for president, and Roosevelt called Henry L. Stimson, who was named for governor, "a man of my type." Butt cheered that Roosevelt had "beat them all to a frazzle," and believed that fully half the cabinet secretly rejoiced at his victory.

Under the circumstances, it is difficult to ascertain who was defecting from whom, although Roosevelt told many friends, anent Taft's "duplicity," that any support for his renomination would be given "simply as the best thing that conditions present."[30] At any rate, Roosevelt's attempt to ride two horses at once was bound to fail, for the West complained about his support for Taft and the Payne-Aldrich tariff and the East criticized him for the doctrines he had enunciated at Osawatomie. Perhaps in desperation, Roosevelt continued to try to unite his party by speaking for conservatives as well as for progressives in various states of the East and of the Middle West, albeit he refused Taft's request to speak in his name in Ohio. But Taft, too, changed direction in an attempt to cement party unity. More progressive advisers would replace Aldrich, Cannon, and Ballinger; Cannon would not be supported again for Speaker; the Payne-Aldrich tariff, he confessed, was not a "complete compliance with the promises made"; the patronage would no longer be used as a club against the progressives.[31] When Norton offered him a list of appointments which would help to elect Republicans, including many names for the South furnished by Postmaster General Frank Hitchcock, he said with a show of temper aggravated by a case of the gout that he would not swerve an iota from his policy toward the South. "I shall not appoint Negroes to office in the South and I shall not appoint Republicans unless they be good men . . . and if I cannot find good Republicans for the offices, then I will fill them with Democrats."[32] In strict privacy he contributed $5,000 to the Ohio campaign, got Andrew Carnegie to send an extra $5,000 there, and sent his cabinet to stump his home state during the last days of the campaign under the shibboleth of "A vote for Harding is a vote for Taft." For two days in New York City, too, he himself sought to bolster the election of Stimson, for he feared disaster if he failed to carry Ohio and also lost New York to Roosevelt.

III

In the late spring of 1910, because of their opposition to his legislative program, Taft decided to launch a campaign against the congressional insurgents, particularly middle westerners like Beveridge, Albert B. Cummins, Jonathan P. Dolliver, and La Follette, and Hiram Johnson in California. In addressing the National League of Republican Clubs at Washington, D.C., he said that, while no man had the right to read another out of the Republican party, "he reads himself out if he is disloyal and if he cannot by his own works show his colors." He then asked Republicans of all brands to support his administration. On the same day, speaking in Chicago, Attorney General George Wickersham asserted that treason should not be rewarded and that those who called themselves Republicans but supported Democratic policies and sought to subvert the president should join the Democratic party. But were the insurgents the traitors they were said to be? In suggesting that they were, Taft made one of the worst mistakes of his political career, for in confusing "insurgents," narrowly defined as congressmen who opposed Cannonism, with "progressives," he drove away men of long standing in their party and split his party by supporting only its conservative wing.

Could not both sides see that they were seeking the same objective, the fulfilling of the pledges of their platform? According to insurgent Victor Murdock, of Kansas, "The House insurgents have insisted that the President's legislation should be passed. . . . If the Administration really wishes to accomplish results, the better way would be to quit lambasting the insurgents and turn attention to the men who are holding up the bills in committee." Dolliver, to whom the Payne-Aldrich tariff was what a red flag is to a bull, delivered in the Senate only weeks before his death in mid-October a speech still considered to be the best defense of insurgency ever uttered. If indeed both wings sought the same objective, why should Taft repay those who supported him with threatened exile?[33]

An important fact Taft overlooked was that the impending retirement of Aldrich and Eugene Hale would free him from the influence of two powerful conservative advisers. The leadership of the Senate would now most likely be collective rather than individual and party control would shift from New England to the Middle West. Under the circumstances, should he not consider cooperating with rather than opposing progressive Republicans, particularly when they and their Democratic allies were demolishing such of his proposals as the railroad rate bill and rewriting them to suit themselves? As of mid-May, not a single one of the nine bills he had suggested had yet passed Congress. Finally, he must make up for expected losses from the East and depend for victory in the November elections upon the insurgents who, if opposed, were still partisanly loyal. Fortunately for him, his stock increased when by the end of June the amended railroad bill, the most important of his conservation measures, the postal savings banks bill, statehood for Arizona and New Mexico, and an appropriation for the Tariff Board made it possible to speak of the "Triumph of the Taft Program," which was the Roosevelt program, and of having obtained more reform legislation in two years than Roosevelt had in seven.

An elated Taft asserted that he and his party had "kept its contract . . . and the Republican party has a good record to take to the people in the coming elections."[34] He also made a hit with thinking people at least by saying that he would sign no more "local spoils" river and harbor bills written on the old pork-barrel plan in which small appropriations were made for large numbers of projects with the expectation that future congresses would provide the rest of the funds.

Insurgents and progressives had countered Taft's campaign against them by denouncing the president not only privately but publicly. Progressive orators, a progressive press and new "Progressive Republican" clubs vied in calling attention to Taft's "betrayal" of Roosevelt. Particularly effective were *La Follette's Magazine*, which was founded in 1909 as an unofficial insurgent organ, and speeches delivered by numerous insurgents at the Chautauquas of 1910 in which they demanded control of the party by western progressives rather than by eastern conservatives. With perhaps a more intellectual approach, they restated the old demands of the Grangers, Greenbackers, and Populists and the demands Bryan Democrats had been making since at least 1896.

The internecine battles in the Republican primaries were so bitter that the Democrats were practically forgotten, and in the end Taft lost. Great interest had centered upon Indiana, the first northern state to hold primaries, where the tariff was a major issue. Despite the organizational work of former Senate Whip James E. Watson, Beveridge was chosen as the keynote speaker of the state convention. After he specifically arraigned the Payne-Aldrich tariff, the convention adopted a platform which promised to support Taft only when he tried to secure progressive legislation. When Beveridge later called at the White House, Taft became very angry. Although Beveridge was endorsed for another term by Republicans of all kinds and Roosevelt spoke for him, Indiana went Democratic and Taft had his revenge.

In Michigan, stalwart Senator Julius Burrows, who was slated to succeed Aldrich as chairman of the Finance Committee, was defeated for renomination by a progressive, and the progressive Chase S. Osborn was named for governor. Taft endorsed an unusual Wisconsin preprimary stalwart Republican conference designed to purge La Follette's influence from the state, and Vice-President Sherman went to Milwaukee to tell the conferees that progressives should be expelled from the party. But Taft was hoping for too much, for La Follette had Democratic help offered by Bryan as well as Republican support, and in the primaries he won by a majority of fifty thousand over the standpatters in one of the most sweeping victories of his career. The split in the national Republican party in 1912 was thus foreshadowed in Wisconsin in 1910.

Anti-Cummins and anti-Dolliver work by Taft men in Iowa resulted in the creation of a statewide network of Taft clubs. With Cummins stating that a Republican party "permanently half Progressive and half Standpat" could not endure, the progressives also organized clubs. Thereupon Taft denied the progressive Iowa representatives patronage and sent Cannon and Secretary of Agriculture Wilson, among others, to stump the state against them. However, he received another rebuff. All the progressives were renamed in the primaries, whereas two of the four standpatters were defeated. Even the governorship went to a progressive. In Nebraska, in contrast, stalwart Senator Elmer J. Burkett repelled the charge of an insurgent for his seat and George Norris was the only insurgent from all the Congressional districts to win a nomination.

In Kansas the fight was plainly one between standpatism and insurgency and drew national attention. Walter Roscoe Stubbs, a Lawrence contractor without political experience, had opposed machine politics since his entry into the state legislature in 1903. Rallying about him as a "boss buster" and supporter of Roosevelt's "trust busting," Kansas progressives had battled the conservative forces led by various officeholders and leading railroad men and elected him as governor. Of great value to him was the support of Arthur Capper, who popularized the progressive side in his *Topeka Daily Capital* and in a number of farm journals. Now Stubbs, Bristow, William Allen White, Henry Allen, Murdock, and Edmond H. Madison countered the Taft organization. The primaries, held on August 1 and centering on the tariff issue, dumped six of the state's eight representatives who were regular in favor of insurgents and renamed Stubbs for governor.[35]

Progressives in western Pennsylvania wanted P. C. Knox to run for governor. Knox was willing, but Boies Penrose, who bossed the regular state organization, was not. Penrose spoke to Taft, who talked with Knox, and Knox remained in the cabinet. The Pennsylvania state platform subsequently praised Taft to the skies, but stalwart victories were by such close margins that the primaries were characterized as marking the passing of the old order.

Although Warren G. Harding revealed no political ideals or policies, Ohio Republican conservatives championed him to defeat Roosevelt's friend Garfield for the gubernatorial nomination and the contest for election with Democratic Governor Judson Harmon, exponent of moderate reforms who had far outpolled Taft in 1908. Whether Senator Charles W. F. Dick would be challenged for his seat by Charles P. Taft was still moot. In any event, the regulars were able in state convention to endorse Taft's administration unequivocally, including high praise for the Payne-Aldrich tariff, to read out of the party those who dared to criticize the measure, to name the "regular" Harding for governor, and with indiscriminate superlatives to endorse Taft for renomination in 1912. Taft also gained when Minnesota endorsed him and his administration and voted down a resolution condemning the Payne-Aldrich tariff, and when the Republicans of Missouri and of Oklahoma preferred regulars to insurgents.

Soon after suffering defeat in the most important midwestern states, Taft's forces lost California to Hiram Johnson and his Lincoln-Roosevelt Republican League. In Washington, Poindexter, one of the most aggressive House insurgents and a favorite of Pinchot who had vigorously criticized Ballinger, carried every county and was named for senator in what Taft called a "body blow." Taft thereupon asked Ballinger to help "save the country from the disaster of Poindexter."[36] Meanwhile perhaps a fourth of the Republicans of Vermont revealed their apathy by staying away from the primaries or their disgust by voting for Democratic hopefuls, and the Democrats swept Maine in a "political earthquake" which dumped two of the four Republican congressmen and promised to send a Democrat to the Senate for the first time since 1853.

Of the forty-one incumbent Republican congressmen defeated, only one was an insurgent; all progressive senators were renominated and would soon be joined by three more, Judge John D. Works, California, Asle J. Gronna, North Dakota, and Poindexter. The insurgent uprising early in the year against Cannon had swelled into a party revolution in which announced progressives had defeated standpat Republicans in almost every instance. Democrats had been named for governor in two traditionally Republican states; and Uncle Joe Cannon was no longer considered to be a serious candidate for reelection as Speaker. Moreover, a liberal slant had been given to such legislation as that pertaining to railroads and to postal savings banks, and a promise was made by the insurgents to continue their efforts to wrest the control of politics from the special interests both in Congress and in the Republican party and to give it back to the people. On election eve, Taft had said that the Republican party was no longer conservative but "progressive," as proved by its legislative record, and predicted that it would win the states of the Middle West—where insurgency was strongest—but have trouble in the East, "where discontent exists, but without organized leadership in the Republican ranks" and that the House would remain Republican even if by a reduced majority.[37] The elections refuted him.

When Knox referred to the returns as a "landslide," Taft replied, "Well, from what you tell me I should say it was not only a landslide but a tidal wave and holocaust all rolled into one general cataclysm."[38]

In the Republican Waterloo of November 8, Vermont went Republican by reduced majorities and the progressive Robert Perkins Bass won the governorship in New Hampshire. In Maine, a Democrat replaced Hale and the Democrats won the governorship, control of the state legislature for the first time in thirty years, and two of the four congressional districts. In governors like Simeon E. Baldwin, Connecticut, Eugene N. Foss, Massachusetts, and particularly Woodrow Wilson, New Jersey, the Democracy had found new leaders of presidential stature. In Ohio, the greatest Democratic triumph on both the state and congressional tickets in two decades was a thorough rebuke to Taft Republicans. Taft thought very highly of Ohio's Harding. With his defeat, Judson Harmon also appeared as an outside presidential possibility, with Taft saying that ". . . if Harmon is reelected and I am renominated, I would rather have him as an opponent than any man the Democrats could put up."[39] Since Indiana and the border states of Maryland, Kentucky, and Missouri were added to the Democratic column, Republicanism had survived only in Pennsylvania (by a very narrow margin) in the East and in the western states, where progressives won the victories. Taft was especially hurt by the defeat of James A. Tawney, of Minnesota, in whose district he had delivered the Winona speech, and the predictable return of La Follette to the Senate by a progressive Republican Wisconsin state legislature, and was particularly distressed by the victory of Poindexter over his opposition, results he attributed directly to Roosevelt's influence. He had predicted the loss of the House by from twenty to twenty-five men. The results brought a Democratic majority of fifty-nine. The House of the Sixty-second Congress would contain 165 Republicans, 225 Democrats, and the Socialist Victor L. Berger from the Milwaukee district. Champ Clark, of Missouri, was slated to be the new Speaker; six Democrats would replace six Republicans as committee chairmen, and Cannon, who survived the Republican disaster, would be sent to be the junior Republican on the Appropriations Committee he had chaired before becoming Speaker. Since the Republican majority in the Senate was reduced from 25 to 12, Taft would face a Congress in which either house could block his demands for legislation. Moreover, with the House Democratic, for the first time since 1893, and Republican progressives holding the balance of power in the Senate, progressives believed they could take the nomination away from Taft in 1912.

When pressed to make a statement about the elections, Roosevelt said:

> So far as I am concerned, I have nothing whatever to add or to take away from the declaration of principles which I have made in the Osawatomie speech and elsewhere, East and West, during the past three months. The fight for progressive popular government has merely begun, and will certainly go on to a triumphant conclusion in spite of initial checks and irrespective of the personal success or failure of individual leaders.[40]

The only solace Taft may have had was that Roosevelt had been solidly defeated in New York and that only two of the men he had supported had been elected, with Stimson losing to a Democrat by more than fifty thousand votes. However, when the coterie about him began to belabor Roosevelt as being responsible for the Republican debacle, Taft explained, "Well, that may be all so, and I fear Roosevelt did not help the ticket very much, but I am inclined to think that even had he remained in Africa the result would have been just the same."[41] At the same time Roosevelt told Lodge:

> From my personal standpoint, the bright spot in the business is that I think it will put a stop to the talk about my being nominated in 1912, which was beginning to make me very uneasy. I am not really responsible for the present situation, and I don't want to have to take the responsibility.[42]

119

When asked to account for his lowered plurality, Sereno E. Payne replied that at this time silence was golden. Both Democrats and Republicans believed the tariff and the high cost of living popularly ascribed to it were the chief factors in the Republican defeat. Others mentioned the expected swing at midterm against the party in power, the fact that the new progressive movement was as obvious in the Democratic as in the Republican party, and that the revolt against Cannon in the House and against boss rule in many states as well as the Ballinger affair worked against Taft. Some blamed the defeat in part upon Roosevelt's intervention in the campaign, asserting with glee that "the everlasting noisemaker" and the "New Nationalism" had been pitched into the grave and that Taft's "Judas Iscariot" was no longer to be considered as a presidential possibility in 1912. Others agreed with Taft that Roosevelt's intervention made no difference but that Taft's surrender to "tariff extortionists" was a prime reason for his party's discomfiture and that if Roosevelt could be blamed for the results in New York, he had not intervened in Taft's home state, which Taft lost by a hundred thousand votes.[43] Disagreement also existed over whether the election indicated a preference by the people for "radicalism" or "conservatism," with Pinchot saying that it "was an overwhelming rebuke to the reactionaries" and the regular Republican *Kansas City Journal* commenting that the tree of insurgency had borne only bitter fruit. Charles Taft's *Cincinnati Times Star* alleged that the Republican party could not stand if divided and that progressive rather than radical or reactionary ideas must be infused into it. The *New York Journal of Commerce* came closest to the nub, perhaps, in saying that the election would serve to make the Democratic party more conservative and the Republican party more progressive.[44] But how would Taft get along with a more progressive party?

6

★★★★★

THE PERILOUS PROGRESS OF PROGRESSIVE REFORMS

I

With the end of the second session of the Sixty-first Congress on June 25, 1910, President William Howard Taft had brooded about his lack of success and gloomily admitted that the Republicans would lose the elections of 1910 if not those of 1912. He had failed to convince the nation that the Payne-Aldrich tariff was the "best bill that the Republican party ever passed" but persisted as late as February 1910 in saying that it was.[1] In the Ballinger-Pinchot controversy he had brought down upon himself the wrath of Theodore Roosevelt and his supporters. He was also charged with looking both ways with respect to the insurgent revolt against Uncle Joe Cannon. The result was that his administration had few enthusiastic friends. Public opinion was critical. The conservatism of his policy was clear, and he exercised little leadership over Congress. Democrats opposed to him tried to foment dissension; regular Republicans tainted as reactionaries for supporting him tried to maintain party unity; and insurgent Republicans seemingly opposed him by trying to infuse his administration with a spirit of progressive reforms.

Taft desired the defeat of Cannon for Speaker but, as he told Attorney General George W. Wickersham, would "do nothing to *force* his resignation."[2] House insurgents thereupon took matters into their own hands. On March 16, 1910, Cannon ruled that a resolution dealing with the taking of the census was privileged

121

because the Constitution made a census mandatory. On the seventeenth, George Norris used the same tactic in moving that the House rather than the Speaker name the Committee on Rules. If Cannon ruled the motion in order, he would immediately be stripped of his power; on the other hand, he would be overruled if he denied that the motion was privileged. He finally ruled against Norris, who appealed and was upheld by the House. Norris and several other insurgents wished Cannon to remain as the Speaker but to have the House elect the Committee on Rules. With the galleries jammed and various senators in attendance, on March 19 he demanded that popular government be restored to the House. By a vote of 191 to 155, with 23 Democrats joining 41 Republican insurgents, his resolution passed. Although Cannon would remain as Speaker, the House would elect an enlarged Committee on Rules of which he could not be a member. The insurgents were motivated by principle but also by a desire for revenge upon Cannon, who had denied them the committee assignments they wished, whereas Taft looked upon their victory as providing the freedom they sought to oppose his legislative program. However, when he was urged to return to Washington from a speaking tour in order to defend Cannon, he declined to do so, for he believed that the insurgents had timed their coup during his absence in order not to involve him. To his military aide, Archibald W. Butt, he said, "Well, Archie, I think they have got the old fox this time." Yet he revealed his admiration for Cannon by adding, "But it is fine to see how he is fighting. That is the quality I admire most in Uncle Joe: he does put up a good fight."[3] Taft had taken good measure, for Cannon for the rest of his tenure refused to compromise his principles, stoutly opposed reform legislation, and attacked the insurgents for being disloyal to their party. In turn, the insurgents heightened their attack against him, with Taft in the middle because he sought reform legislation but placated the worst enemy of reform, Cannon.

II

Despite the opposition of the insurgents to Cannon, Taft was on his way to achieving more legislative reforms in his four years than Roosevelt had achieved in seven. Some of these came while Cannon remained as the Speaker and the new Committee on Rules was still composed of regulars rather than of insurgents. During the Sixty-first Congress, after all, the few insurgents had power only when joined by the Democratic minority. Moreover, as partisans they would still vote for Republican rather than for Democratic measures. Paradoxically, additional reforms came from the Democrats who controlled the House of the Sixty-second Congress and had the cooperation of a Democratic-insurgent bloc in the Senate. Taft's tragedy was that his sincere efforts to achieve reforms rebounded against him and split his party.

In his annual message of December 7, 1909, Taft described the state of the Union but failed to recommend legislation. In special messages, however, he outlined the measures he wished passed. By the end of the Sixty-first Congress on March 3, 1911, approximately fifty new laws had been added to the statute book, and he was elated with the fulfillment of a large number of the pledges made in his platform of 1908.

In special messages to the first regular session of the Sixty-first Congress, which opened on January 4, 1910, Taft noted that there would be a revenue surplus of $34,000,000 for the fiscal year ending June 30 and that the departments had so pruned their expenditures as to save an additional $40,000,000. Disbelieving that the maximum-minimum tariff rates would lead to tariff wars with foreign countries, he pleaded for time in which to demonstrate the effectiveness of the work of the Tariff Board, asked that its power be extended, and requested $250,000 for it for the next year. He thereby admitted that the Payne-Aldrich tariff was a logrolling measure that needed to be improved by scientific study of costs of production at home and abroad. Yet he was supporting not only such businessmen as those in the National Association of Manufacturers, which after the panic of 1907 demanded a permanent tariff fact-finding commission, but those progressives who wanted government "efficiency" and expected a tariff commission to follow "scientific" rate-fixing procedures. If such a commission worked well, Congress must base its tariff policy upon its recommendations rather than upon the often biased information offered it at hearings. Taft in essence was asking Congress to give up logrolling in favor of science. He failed to see that he was also seeking to divorce political policy from administrative practice. The result was that Congress appropriated money for the Tariff Board but denied it authority to make the studies he wanted.

Among other things, Taft then asked for authority to appoint a commission to study ways of simplifying and speeding up court procedures; that a limit be placed upon the issue of labor injunctions; that Arizona and New Mexico be admitted as states; that ship subsidies be granted; that postal savings banks, parcel post, and federal budget systems be established; that a commerce court be created to hear cases arising from decisions reached by the Interstate Commerce Commission; and that federal incorporation be permitted for corporations engaged in interstate commerce.

Taft placed heavy emphasis upon the need of reforms for the Post Office Department. He blamed the deficit of $17,000,000 in 1909 primarily upon losses incurred in delivering magazines and newspapers and in serving those who lived on free rural delivery routes. The government charged a penny a pound for second-class delivery for newspapers and magazines which it had to pay railroads nine cents a pound to carry. The obvious solution was to increase the postage on magazines to nine cents a pound or charge more for the advertising they carried than for material which fit the description of "diffusion of general intelligence." He thereby overlooked the fact that express companies made good profits by carrying second-, third-, and fourth-class mail for less than a penny a pound on short hauls, and that perhaps Postmaster General Frank H. Hitchcock could learn something about business management from them—a point heavily underscored by the Publishers' Association of America.

The department, said the opponents of higher rates, was organized in a cumbrous and antiquated way and lacked a parcel post system. Moreover, the administration should stop attacking "education." Taft retorted that the government was granting an enormous subsidy to newspapers and magazines and to those enjoying free rural delivery. He then made matters worse, at a time when the muckraking magazines were attacking Richard A. Ballinger, by saying publicly in essence what he told a friend, that "if we wish to contribute a subsidy of $50,000,000 to the education of the country, I can find a great deal better method of doing it than by the circulation of Collier's Weekly and Everybody's Magazine."[4]

Roosevelt had declined to embroil himself in the vexatious question of postal reform. Taft courageously faced it, as he had tariff reform, on the unpopular side and raised another controversial issue for the duration of his term. He aroused the insurgents, who refused to sanction higher rates, and also the hostility of those who he alleged "control the news they give and the editorial opinions they express."[5] That Hitchcock meanwhile had improved the efficiency of his department was proved by the fact that the deficit for 1910 was only $6,000,000, or a drop of 60 percent over 1909, and that it was in the black by $219,000 in 1911—the first time in twenty-eight years the department had a surplus. Moreover, his demand for a parcel post system, which reflected the popular demand to get rid of the four large express companies that monopolized the field, was answered in 1912. On January 1, 1913, the postmaster in Washington, D.C., inaugurated the service by sending a silver loving cup to his counterpart in New York. Designed to kill the express companies, the system succeeded beautifully in doing so. Yet by causing the railroads to carry parcels, even those including eggs, milk, cream, and butter, as part of the regular mail, it also placed an intolerable burden on the railroads.[6]

Taft also endorsed a postal savings bank system in which money could be deposited with the government but earn a very low interest rate. The idea drew the fire of Nelson W. Aldrich, of Cannon, and of the nation's bankers as being unnecessary, vicious, and paternalistic. Cannon told Taft that "I am getting so damned tired, Mr. President, of this everlasting yielding to popular outcry against wealth that unless we put a check on it somewhere there is no telling where it will lead."[7] Taft disagreed, saying that he was not a paternalist or socialist but that "we have passed beyond the time of . . . the laissez-faire school which believes that the government ought to do nothing but run a police force."[8]

Much of the argument over postal savings centered about use of the deposits. The Aldrich Monetary Commission proposed a new central bank to replace the old national banks, which held more than $73,000,000 worth of 2 percent bonds, bonds upon which most of the national bank notes were issued. By purchasing these bonds with postal deposits, the way would be cleared for the central bank plan. Insurgents countered that Aldrich's plan would concentrate local funds in the financial centers of the great eastern cities. Taft in turn objected to their demands for various guarantees and local rather than federal control, charging them with "loading down the bill with impossible conditions" and making it almost as "socialistic as Bryan's guarantee deposit plan." With the Aldrich proposal deleted, the House insurgents helped to pass the bill by a vote of 195 to 102, with the insurgents crediting Taft with making victory possible and every Republican and even one Democrat voting for it in the Senate. The law which Taft signed on June 25, 1910, was a compromise in which the deposits would be placed in local banks under the supervision of a government Board of Trustees, thus pleasing the insurgents. However, in an emergency the deposits could be used to purchase government bonds, a stipulation which pleased conservatives like Aldrich. In this instance Taft had performed a unique feat in driving the opposing sides toward center. Moreover, the amount of deposits proved to be so negligible that those who had opposed the plan approved of it soon after it went into operation on January 3, 1911, with a bank in each state.

III

On February 13, 1909, Franklin K. Lane, a West Coast progressive member of the Interstate Commerce Commission, wrote to his brother, "The Harriman crowd seems to think that they will all be on good terms with Taft, but unless I'm mistaken in the man, they will be greatly fooled."[9] Lane prognosticated correctly, for on January 7, 1910, Taft asked Congress for improvements in the Hepburn Act of 1906, for advanced regulation of interstate industrial corporations in general, and for the establishment of a United States Court of Commerce. In the last, five men who would rank as federal circuit judges would hear cases arising under the Interstate Commerce Act. They would relieve the lower courts of highly technical cases, introduce uniformity into decisions, build up a body of law relating to railroad regulation, and speed up the judicial process. Appeals from their decisions would go directly to the Supreme Court whenever a constitutional question was involved. Taft believed the regulation of railroads a judicial matter. His idea for a commerce court, however, was immediately opposed by those who knew what the courts had done to the original powers of the ICC and looked upon railroad regulation as an economic and political subject.

The panic of 1907 had severely shaken the heavily watered financial structure of the railroads at the same time that they needed a massive injection of capital not only to improve their service but to expand it for a burgeoning passenger and freight traffic. Roosevelt had demanded new railroad control laws on March 25, 1908, but stated that a rate increase was politically impossible. Moreover, a newly founded National Industrial Traffic League spoke for shippers in demanding that the ICC be empowered to suspend proposed rate increases and also to fix rates prior to judicial review. Convinced that shippers rather than consumers would have to absorb any rate increases, a nationwide Shippers' Association hired Louis D. Brandeis to argue against the railroads before the ICC, whose membership was notoriously antirailroads.

In the *Eastern Rate* case, Brandeis, fresh from the conservation controversy, asserted that the railroads did not need a rate increase. Rather they should adopt scientific management methods, and he promised to show them how they could save a million dollars a day if they did so.[10]

Taft might have helped heal the split in his party had he managed to induce the insurgents to cooperate with him on railroad reform legislation and to reveal his independence not only from the railroads but also from Aldrich and Cannon.

In a bill written by Wickersham in his name, Taft would lift the antitrust laws and permit railroads to cooperate in drafting freight rates and passenger fares, which had risen little since the depression of the 1890s, provided these were filed with the ICC. But the ICC was empowered to suspend proposed rate increases for as long as sixty days while investigating their reasonableness. Railroads would in addition be prohibited from acquiring stock in other lines, and the commission must approve of the amount of stocks and bonds the lines could issue. Finally, railroad workmen must be protected by the provision of safety appliances.

On this bill, introduced at request by Representative James Mann, Taft courted criticism from railroad men as well as from leading congressmen. Various senators knew the facts and figures of the railroad industry. Perhaps because many of them, especially Jonathan Dolliver and Albert B. Cummins, were known to "hate" railroads and were suspected of opposing Taft for political reasons, none of them was called to the hearings held on it. Therefore to them the bill was immediately suspect; it must be strengthened where weak or defeated if bad.

Knowing that Aldrich favored the Taft-Wickersham measure, insurgent and Democratic members of the House Committee on Interstate Commerce quickly amended the bill to bar railroad mergers and to prohibit a greater charge for a short than a long haul, to include telephone and telegraph companies as common carriers, and failed only by a tie vote to delete the commerce court. In the Senate, meanwhile, Moses Clapp and Cummins sided with Democrats on the Committee on Interstate Commerce in a minority report in the belief that they were helping Taft obtain more effective regulation. Instead Taft took their aid as opposition. With Cannon and Aldrich, whom he called to the White House on March 1, he decided to make the original bill a test of party loyalty. Certain insurgents, particularly Cummins and Robert M. La Follette, responded so strongly, however, that the regular leaders could not obtain a majority in the party caucus they called and sent a cry for help to Taft, who happened to be away. Upon his return, Taft tried to convince the recalcitrants, and Aldrich sought in vain to win over the insurgents until he found an opportunity for compromise with the Democrats. Taft had recommended statehood for Arizona and New Mexico. Both regular and insurgent Republicans had opposed the move because the new states most probably would be Democratic. But Aldrich would agree to statehood if the Democrats would approve of a railroad bill lacking control over railroad security issues, and he won Taft over to the compromise. The insurgents had succeeded so well in changing Taft's original bill that they joined the regular Republicans in passing it in the House.

When the Senate Committee on Interstate Commerce reported the Elkins bill practically unchanged, insurgents led by Cummins offered more than two hundred amendments to what they considered "a long step backward." In this instance, their cooperative effort contrasted mightily with their division over the tariff. Despite Wickersham's attempted intervention, the Senate on May 2 knocked out those sections of the bill authorizing traffic agreements and railroad mergers. On May 13 Aldrich's lieutenant Reed Smoot defected by coming to terms with the Democrats and prohibited a greater charge for a short than for a long haul. And on the twenty-seventh the bill was made to cover telephone, telegraph, and cable companies and in addition railroad terminals, bridges, and ferries. The greatly changed Mann-Elkins Act passed the House by a vote of 200 to 16 on May 10, the Senate on June 3, by 50 to 12, and the conference report received the solid Republican vote of both houses on June 18. Although La Follette's physical valuation plan failed—at which Taft exclaimed "Bully! Bully!"[11]—it was added in 1913; although government control of the issue of railroad securities was not provided for, it too would come later. After a fight that lasted for three months, the insurgents had won the best bill they thought they could obtain.

But Taft had played a part, too. Four days before Mann introduced his railroad bill, Taft had denied demands made by J. P. Morgan and the presidents of a number of eastern railroads. When twenty-five western railroads joined together to raise their rates, on May 31, he had had Wickersham obtain an injunction against them, thereby provoking a storm of howling from eastern as well as western Republicans. After the presidents of several western lines conferred with Taft and Wickersham, on June 6 and 7, they had rescinded their rate increases and promised to follow the new regulatory procedures, and Wickersham had stopped legal action against them. In great part because of Brandeis, early in 1911 the ICC denied rate increases. Although the bill that Taft signed on June 20 was a vast improvement over both the Hepburn Act of Roosevelt's day and the Taft-Wickersham proposal, he looked upon the attempts of the insurgents to improve the original bill as an antiadministration move, enough to cause him to seek their defeat in the elections of 1912.

IV

Although businessmen were generally pleased with Taft because he wished to give them time to adjust to new regulatory laws and to judicial decisions affecting them, they were even happier with him when he decided to devote his energies to such areas other than trust busting as efficiency in government, currency and banking reform, and taking the patronage out of politics.

In his inaugural address Taft had stated, "We want economy and efficiency; we want saving, and for a purpose." In his annual message of 1910, he asserted,

> I believe it to be in the interest of all the people of the country that for the time being the activities of government, in addition to enforcing the existing [antitrust] law, be directed toward the economy of administration and the enlargement of opportunities for foreign trade, the conservation and improvement of our agricultural lands, the building up of home industries and the strengthening of confidence of capital in domestic investment.

According to the *New York Evening Mail* (Independent Republican), these paragraphs contained "the most steadying words that have come out of the White House in eight years," and businessmen followed Taft's suggestion "to reflect the view of American business" by creating the Chamber of Commerce of the United States. As will be noted later, however, they were distressed when Taft's antitrust crusade proceeded full blast for another two years and no new legislation on the relations of government and business was forthcoming. To progressives, of course, Taft's strictures could have been written by Aldrich, for while economy in administration, enlargement of trade opportunities, and strengthening the confidence of capital might win him the support of the business community, he had no words of cheer for the political, economic, and social reforms the progressives sought. Taft nevertheless was in

129

agreement with those progressives who demanded efficiency in government and with businessmen in general, for the latter made efficiency and economy their watchwords.

Taft pushed forward with his program, some of it excellent, some of it questionable. Various reforms resulted from the Democratic-insurgent coalition in the Sixty-second Congress; others were proposed too late to be effected during his term; a few so angered the progressives that they felt driven to revolt.

When he took office, Taft found that the federal government spent about a billion dollars a year, yet no one really knew how it was organized or functioned. There was a considerable overlapping of duties between bureaus, record keeping was such a bewildering maze that cost of products or services could not be gauged, and some methods adopted with the founding of the Republic were long outdated and extremely inefficient. Each of the nineteen bureaus of the Department of the Treasury, for example, used different accounting systems.

By the end of 1910, certain reforms enabled Taft to abolish four hundred positions in the Treasury Department and another hundred in the Philadelphia mint. More efficient methods of collecting customs would soon be put into effect. He made large cuts in the military services; the estimates for 1911 expenditures were $53,000,000 less than in 1910. He also sought to introduce some planning, coordination, and centralization into the executive department. Above all he needed exact and prompt information upon which to reach decisions of an administrative nature. To put his ideas into effect, he demanded an executive budget, a central purchasing system which would establish standards and specifications, and a staff to serve as a planning agency to coordinate the administration of the executive office, Congress, and the budget office.[12]

Nothing had come from the first comprehensive presidential inquiry into governmental administration, Roosevelt's Keep Commission of 1905–1909, and Taft had had so much trouble as secretary of war in obtaining the accurate information he needed that he confessed that he did not know what went on in his own department.[13] He was thus the first president to have the federal administration studied in detail as one mechanism. His efforts won him the title of "efficiency engineer" and established a policy followed by succeeding Republican presidents, particularly by Herbert Hoover.

At Taft's request, Congress in September 1910 appropriated

$100,000 for a preliminary inquiry into what ground should be covered and what staff and organization would be required. These matters decided and additional funds made available, in June 1911 a Commission on Economy and Efficiency went to work. Taft sent its *Report* to Congress on January 8, 1913, with a message stating that its adoption would save the government money and also save the time and energy of public officials. Congress also granted his request for a moderate amount of money to continue the commission at work.

The *Report,* nine hundred pages long, included eighty-five reports to date and showed Taft how much each department and bureau spent on personnel, services, and supplies. By the end of January there were 110 reports, many of them carrying recommendations for constructive legislation which Taft passed on to Congress. It was amply clear that he wanted to reduce appropriations and the number of federal employees to the lowest possible points; diminish the public works program and rectify rivers and harbors appropriation bills; copy the best cost accounting and other management control devices used by the business world; and reorganize where necessary departments and agencies but sternly object to their proliferation. He would also adopt a budget system for the federal government which would provide a financial plan for its activities and a bureau of central administration that would help draft the budget and evaluate the efficiency of the personnel in the departments and the results achieved by the departments themselves. Finally, he would devote a minimum of expenditures to social welfare projects. The last was a sore point with progressives, but in the end Congress spurned Taft's recommendations largely because they weakened its power over the purse and reduced the areas of control its committees had over federal finances and administrative policies. When Taft, on July 10, 1912, asked the heads of federal agencies to prepare two budgets, one along customary lines and one following the recommendations of the Commission on Economy and Efficiency, Congress tried to prevent preparation of the latter. Relying upon his constitutional power to seek information from administrative officers, Taft asserted that Congress could neither prevent nor forbid the preparation of a federal budget. He demanded that the information he desired be forwarded, and on February 26, 1913, he sent Congress a budget for the fiscal year 1914. Rather than asking merely for appropriations, however, his budget included suggestions for changing laws, management procedures, organization, business methods, and even personnel of the executive branch. Congress took no action and the United States remained the only important nation in the world as yet without a federal budget.[14]

Taft's conception of administration was nevertheless mechanistic; he visualized little more than a formalistic structure as an end in itself and was not prepared to give the leadership and spirit management requires. More importantly, he looked upon his term as president as a period in which to perfect extant governmental machinery to consolidate the Roosevelt reforms, not to sponsor his own machinery, and rarely associated administration and policy. In fact, in keeping with the recommendations of early pioneers in the study of administration, such as Frank J. Goodnow, he would disassociate administration and policy if he could. In any event, he wished to regularize the labyrinthine mass of overlapping and duplicating departments, bureaus, and agencies that made interdepartmental strife possible, as in the Ballinger-Pinchot affair. For example, since each had the same duties, he wanted the Life Saving Station Service and Bureau of Lighthouses consolidated. He would also put all health services under a Bureau of Public Health. By similar grouping of related functions he could thus control the administrative agencies of the government. Since the power to create and reorganize administrative agencies lay with Congress, however, his attempts were foredoomed.

Although the Department of State was reorganized in 1909, that reorganization really consisted of superimposing five new divisions upon its already sprawling structure. In other departments, as in War and Navy, reorganizations occurred by the administrative rather than legislative route. The United States Postal Savings Bank System, approved June 25, 1910, originally an independent agency, was later shifted to the Post Office Department. Taft himself reorganized the Customs Service by executive order until his badgering of Congress resulted in authority being granted him to accomplish his purpose. Although he signed during his last days as president the act creating the Department of Labor, he lamented the proliferation of departments and again asserted the need of a thorough reorganization of the executive structure.

Taft asked the special session of the Sixty-second Congress, which met on April 1, 1911, to reconstitute the Tariff Board as a permanent, independent, and nonpartisan tariff commission. The House gave him exactly what he wanted in early February, but opposition from the Democrats to the measure as amended by the Senate and the inexorable working of the clock on March 4 killed it. He would have to try again.

Many other Taft demands were answered by the special session even though he had called it to deal primarily with Canadian reciprocity. In four and a half months, it provided for Canadian reciprocity, the admission of Arizona and New Mexico as states, the reapportionment of the House membership from 391 to 433, free trade with the Philippines, postal savings banks, and campaign publicity. It also created an Industrial Bureau, strengthened the Pure Food and Drugs Act, and increased the power of the Interstate Commerce Commission to regulate railroad rates, provided for an eight-hour day on federal projects and for compensation for workers injured on interstate railroads, and created a Bureau of Mines that would specialize in safety. Taft, however, was lukewarm toward the direct election of senators, vetoed the admission of Arizona because its constitution provided for the recall of judges, and in vetoing the tariff revision bills hurt himself and his party in the campaign of 1912.

Progressive Democrats like William Jennings Bryan and Populists had demanded the direct election of senators. Some progressive Republicans soon took up the chant and Taft in 1908 supported it as a nonpartisan issue rather than from the heart. By 1911, many states had preferential voting for senators, so that their legislatures really reflected the popular will. Woodrow Wilson's fight against James Smith, Jr., in New Jersey, control over the election of New York's senators by Tammany's Charles F. Murphy, and the William Lorimer case, discussed below, heightened public interest in the issue and pointed directly to the Senate as the nemesis of this reform. In any event, a House resolution required that the power to supervise the election of senators be transferred from Congress to the states. With this section deleted by a Senate amendment, the House passed a direct election bill by a vote of 296 to 16 and William E. Borah announced on January 11, 1911, the Senate Judiciary Committee's favorable report on it by a vote of 10 to 2. The senators then cast 64 votes for it to 24 against it. Taft had not come out strongly for it, and only the affirmative vote by Vice-president James Sherman gave it the required two-thirds vote.

Taft made another false start in the Lorimer affair. Lorimer, the "blond boss" of Chicago who was backed by big business and could be expected to vote "right" on the tariff, was elected as senator in Illinois in May 1909 by a combination of fifty-three

Democrats and fifty-five Republicans even though some Democrats confessed to taking bribes on his behalf. The question whether a Senate seat could be bought transcended state lines and aroused the interest of the entire nation. Lorimer denied that he had obtained his office by dishonorable means and insisted upon keeping it. When Roosevelt refused to attend a banquet where he would be present, Taft criticized him as prejudging his case. A majority report of the Senate Committee on Privileges and Elections in December 1910 found evidence of bribery but gave Lorimer a clean bill of health for the curious reasons that they could not prove that he was personally involved and that not enough men had been bribed to make his election otherwise impossible. Since four Democrats by this time had confessed to accepting bribes to vote for him, Taft quickly changed his tune; he now regarded the majority report with disdain, stated that the Republican party must not condone such nefarious undertakings, and urged Elihu Root and various other senators to speak against accepting the report. However, after an exhaustive debate, the Senate voted 46 to 40 in Lorimer's favor. Unsatisfied with the majority report, La Follette demanded a new and sweeping investigation. In May 1912, a report was issued in favor of Lorimer. However, a minority report asserting that corrupt methods invalidated his election and adopted by the Senate by a vote of fifty-five to twenty-eight practically called for his explusion. Finally on July 13, 1913, with Taft already out of office, the Senate by a vote of fifty-five to twenty-eight declared Lorimer's election invalid.[15]

As in the Lorimer affair, Taft had to wiggle out of a predicament he might have avoided in the Wiley case. The chief of the Bureau of Chemistry in the Department of Agriculture was Dr. Harvey W. Wiley, who had done much of the research on which Roosevelt had based his demand for pure food and drug legislation. To retain the services of the reputedly best pharmacognosist in the country, Dr. H. H. Rusby, Wiley agreed to a salary arrangement which was not harmful either to the Treasury or to the drug service but which technically violated the law. The Committee on Personnel in the Department of Agriculture recommended to Taft that Wiley be dismissed, and Attorney General Wickersham agreed that Wiley deserved "condign punishment." Taft was trapped. He must execute the law even though Wiley had only technically violated it. But his disciplining of a man who had a strong hold on public opinion would have untoward political reverberations. Moreover, most influential newspapers demanded not the ouster of Wiley but of the solicitor of the Department of Agriculture and of Secretary James Wilson himself, who was charged with impeding Wiley's enforcement of the food and drug law. Finally, investigation revealed that the arrangement whereby the departments of Agriculture, Commerce and Labor, and Treasury cooperated in the enforcement of the pure food and drug law was as poor as the one in which Agriculture and Interior shared responsibility for conservation. However, the retirement of the solicitor and certain personnel changes soon strengthened Wiley's hand in enforcement matters and Taft not only completely exonerated him of any wrongdoing but upon his retirement in March 1912 after twenty-nine years of service praised him highly and asked him to suggest a capable successor. Nevertheless, Democrats and Progressive Republicans charged that Wilson rather than Wiley should have resigned and called for a reorganization of the Department of Agriculture. Had Taft fired Wilson, some said, then Wiley could not, as Gifford Pinchot did, arm the progressive enemies of Taft with ammunition to use in the campaign of 1912. Taft bungled again by stating that the department needed drastic reorganization and that he would look into the matter *after* the election of 1912.

Taft continually bickered with the leaders of the special session of Congress on the tariff issue. Although he praised the Democrats and their progressive Republican allies for their "statesmanlike course" with respect to Canadian reciprocity, he charged them with seeking "not tariff for revenue only, but tariff for politics only." The only correct way to reform the tariff was on the basis of the "scientific" data to be furnished by the Tariff Board, he concluded, and he promised to submit new tariff reduction bills "made with a full knowledge of the facts as found by an impartial investigation."[16] Champ Clark retorted that Canadian reciprocity would not have passed Congress except with Democratic-insurgent votes and that he and Oscar W. Underwood had warned Taft that if he called an extra session the Democrats would pass whatever bills they thought desirable. Moreover, Democrats favored a tariff board which would serve as an adjunct to the Ways and Means Committee, not "a tariff board or commission under the control of the President alone and responsible to him only."[17] Thus the battle over tariff revision would continue when the second session of Congress met in December and would spill over into the campaign of 1912.

Additional controversy occurred over how to reform the banking and currency system. In consequence of the panic of 1907, a National Monetary Commission had been appointed, Aldrich chairman. After two years of study it made its tentative report public on January 8, 1911, and on the seventeenth it unveiled a comprehensive reform program. Briefly, Aldrich would create a great central bank with Reserve Association branches in numerous districts, all under the direction of private bankers, and issue an untaxed assets currency. The plan was immediately attacked by those who feared the concentration of loanable funds in the largest cities in the districts, especially at New York. Others decried banker rather than public control; demanded credit facilities for farmers; and insisted currency should be issued by the government rather than by banks. Nevertheless, on January 29, Taft asked Aldrich to put his plan into legislative form. Even if the Democrats rejected it, he added, the next Republican Congress might accept it. Aldrich believed that the Republicans would support his recommendations and that the opposition of the Democrats and insurgent Republicans would be of no consequence. He erred, but he provided the bill, and Taft endorsed it heartily, telling a meeting of the New York Bankers Association that "there is no legislation— I care not what it is—tariff, railroad, corporation, or of a general political character, that at all equals in importance the putting of our banking and currency system on the sound basis proposed in the National Monetary Commission plan."[18]

The fate of the bill depended mainly upon agreement on the character of the national board of directors, a uniform discount rate for the entire country, the relation of the banking system to the government, and prevention of monopoly through purchase of bank stock. Aldrich wanted a central national bank like the Bank of England and a board of directors in which the secretary of the treasury, secretary of commerce and labor, and the comptroller of the currency represented the government. In truth, he would give the government knowledge about banking affairs but not control over them, yet his plan included various provisions which would make a "money trust" unlikely if not impossible. These provisions were added in part at the request of Taft and of Secretary of the Treasury Franklin MacVeagh.

National rather than sectional or local control over banking sat very badly with both liberal Democrats and insurgent Republicans, who quickly ended the life of the monetary commission. Bryan and his friends in Congress said they would flatly reject any plan which did not give control over banking and currency to the government rather than to the bankers, and it was clear that the Aldrich Plan would be rejected by Congress. Taft had not pushed currency and banking reform vigorously, and the retirement of Aldrich from the Senate in 1911 meant that other and later hands must struggle with it.

So important was currency and banking reform that by early 1912 four standing committees of the House began investigating the "money power." Particularly revealing was the testimony of Samuel Untermyer before the Committee on Rules, which contended that while there was no "money trust" as such there did exist a vicious but legal "money oligarchy." The real fireworks occurred in the so-called money-trust inquiry conducted by a subcommittee of the House Committee on Currency and Banking chaired by Arsène Pujo (Democrat, Louisiana). However, the Pujo Committee did not submit its report until January 1913, too late for Congress to act upon it before the expiration of Taft's term and of its own life on March 4. At any rate, the Federal Reserve Act adopted by the Wilson administration was not based upon it but rather upon conclusions reached by a second subcommittee of the House Banking and Currency Committee, one headed by Carter H. Glass (Democrat, Virginia).

Taft was familiar with the civil service because as governor general of the Philippines he had drawn up the Philippine Civil Service Act of September 19, 1900, and also handled personnel management problems while secretary of war. Yet his attitude as president toward personnel management was ambivalent. He would not use the patronage power in order to get regulars to support him on the Payne-Aldrich tariff, then used it against the insurgents. Although his cabinet of lawyers did not particularly sponsor the merit system, he pleaded for an extension of it to all but the most important administrative officers of government. While he would oust the unfit, he would add a pension plan to the civil service system. His call for these changes, made in the name of increased economy and efficiency, won no action from Congress. In 1910, however, by executive order he placed under civil service assistant postmasters and clerks in first- and second-class post offices and extended the merit system to consular officers and to subordinate diplomatic officials. He wanted to cover not only first-, second-, and third-class postmasters but all local officers whose nomination was subject to Senate confirmation. He admitted that the suggestion was "not intended to win votes and make platforms to carry elections" but was rather a sincere attempt to benefit the whole country. Were his wish granted, the costs of administering the government would be reduced greatly, the "pie counter" would disappear, the administration machine which supposedly controlled Republican conventions would be smashed, and 59,518 officials, mostly postmasters, would be freed of dependence upon political patronage. Had he won his point, he would have accomplished more for the cause of civil service reform than all presidents from Cleveland to Roosevelt. He would also have made his renomination impossible. Congressmen reacted to his suggestion as though the Statue of Liberty was rocking on its pedestal until they realized that he had made it as a threat and would withdraw it once appropriations were made to continue the work of the Economy and Efficiency Commission.[19]

In 1912, Taft placed under the merit system twenty thousand skilled workers in the navy yards, but the cabinet would not agree to Wickersham's proposal to place all assistant attorneys under the merit system and the Civil Service Commission did not recommend the action to the president. In the end, Taft's greatest extension of the classified service came in his covering in 1912 of thirty-five thousand fourth-class postmasters. While he also showed great strength in preserving the system by vetoing a bill that would limit the terms of all classified employees to seven years, it is doubtful that the government service was as efficient or as free of political influence as it had been under Roosevelt.

V

Because of his unwillingness to talk with reporters, Taft's "authorized interview" with Francis E. Leupp in late November 1911 is especially important. Taft had just returned from a forty-nine-day trip during which he delivered 306 speeches and was resting at Hot Springs, Virginia. With respect to the Sixty-first Congress, he had fought for three main objectives: a railroad bill, the postal savings bill, and conservation measures. While the insurgents had changed the first two, he had won on the last. He was very pleased with the Tariff Board, he went on, with the work of his efficiency commission, with the scaling down of governmental expenditures, and with the corporation tax and the submission of the Sixteenth Amendment. Under unfinished business he listed reductions in the wool and cotton and possibly metal schedules and the development of Alaska without infringing upon conservation. In his annual message he would deal with the money question and "other live future policies." While he confessed that he was disappointed with the failure of Canadian reciprocity, he still favored it, indeed, "I see no objection myself to free trade between the two countries . . . ," but he knew that the issue was dead.[20]

If Taft was fairly pleased with his accomplishments, it was amply clear that both Republican progressives and regulars were unhappy with him. In a written statement, Cummins listed a bill of particulars: Taft had aligned himself with reactionaries rather than with progressives; pronounced the Payne-Aldrich tariff the best bill ever passed; tried to foist a poor interstate commerce bill upon Congress; supported the large cities rather than small towns in the postal savings bank system; substituted a corporation tax for the income tax; opposed true conservation; had urged Canadian reciprocity; had failed to obtain a real advance in international arbitration; and had vetoed the woolen and free list bills and also the admission of Arizona and New Mexico.[21] Speaking for the regulars, editor George Harvey spoke of Taft's "volte-face" in which he had veered from the "cardinal" Republican policy of tariff protection and "blundered . . . into a quagmire of apostacy" from which he could extract himself only with the greatest difficulty.[22] Finally, the editors of the *Outlook*, Roosevelt spokesmen, found three reasons why popular discontent with Taft was widespread. First, Taft had allowed himself to become identified in the public mind with the standpatter wing of his party that opposed progress in the field of human rights and merely believed that "the prime function of party government is to promote material prosperity or mere money-making." Second, he was more interested in the machinery of government than in promoting human welfare. He deserved praise for crystallizing public opinion with respect to such matters as the tariff, commerce court, and judicial procedures but had not furnished leadership on the "vital questions" facing the people, on such problems as the draining of the country population into the city, reclaiming desert lands for homesteading, decent hours and wages for labor, lynchings, pure food, and the protection of children. Third, he was primarily an interpreter of laws rather than an administrator of laws. One with the ability to make quick executive decisions would never have let crises such as those involving Ballinger and Wiley reach the ear of Congress. Taft should learn that human rights must be made to fit the Constitution rather than trying to fit the Constitution to human rights.[23]

The reforms achieved during Taft's first three years are too numerous to repeat here, but mention should be made of his putting the Post Office Department on a paying basis, of his attempts to lower the tariff rates, to obtain efficiency in government, to regularize and extend Roosevelt's conservation measures, and to reform the banking and currency system. Mention must also be made of the postal savings bank system and of the Mann-Elkins Act and of the submission to the states of the Sixteenth Amendment to the Constitution. Yet it was a rare instance when he pleased both regular and progressive Republicans or, as in the battle over the postal savings bank law, succeeded in leading them toward center.

Rather than aiding the insurgents to unhorse Cannon, Taft had chastised those most likely to support his reforms. In seeking postal reforms, he won the enmity of newspaper and magazine publishers. In the Canadian reciprocity matter he violated his stated belief in the separation of powers, tried to drive congressmen to his support, and also deviated from his principle that tariff changes should be made only upon the recommendations of the Tariff Board. His laudable effort to obtain efficiency in government sat badly with those who lost their jobs and with congressmen who would have fewer spoils to bestow. If it pleased businessmen, it angered those who believed that he reflected the desires of the business community more than any other segment of American life. Cold and calculating, his effort lacked heart and sentiment, they felt, contributed little to the welfare of the people, and could be achieved only by weakening the military defenses of the nation. While his desire to bring order out of the ramshackle government structure was admirable, he failed to see the dynamic aspects of administration and did not or could not inspire administrative officials to support executive policies. Unlike Roosevelt, he would of course keep inviolate the chain of authority delineated in formal organization charts.

He came out badly in the Ballinger, Lorimer, and Wiley affairs, sided with Aldrich rather than progressives on the vitally important banking and currency question, and really did little to improve the civil service. With the aid of the Democratic-insurgent coalition, he had nevertheless accomplished a large number of reforms. It was not the reforms that he demanded but the persistent fumbling in his attempts to achieve them that alienated Republican progressives and stimulated La Follette and his small band to form a third party.

We shall return to the continuing intraparty contest after assessing Taft's work in foreign affairs and as commander in chief.

7

★★★★★

TARIFF RECIPROCITY WITH CANADA

I

In his annual message of December 5, 1910, President William Howard Taft reported on the state of the Union rather than offering a legislative program to the Congress that would expire the following March. He knew that Canada looked upon the maximum-minimum provision of the Payne-Aldrich tariff as "a new and large club" and that the Liberal party premier, Sir Wilfrid Laurier, was threatening to impose an export duty on Canadian pulp—a move that would immediately result in the closing of some twenty paper mills in New Hampshire alone. Among other things, therefore, he stated that the adjustment of the maximum-minimum rates with Canada under the Payne-Aldrich Act had proved to be beneficial and that efforts were justified to seek "readjustment of the commercial relations of the two countries, so that their commerce may follow the channels natural to contiguous countries and be commensurate with the steady expansion of trade and industry on both sides of the boundary line."[1] On January 10, 1911, he advised Theodore Roosevelt that he intended to seek a reciprocity treaty with Canada which would reduce domestic complaints about the high cost of living, open Dominion markets to American products, and prevent a threatening tariff war. He predicted that his proposal would antagonize Republican agrarians, but he planned later to placate them by recommending reductions in the schedules for manufactured goods in accordance with findings of the Tariff

141

Board. Roosevelt replied that his proposal was "admirable" and that the Republican party would surely benefit by it in the end.[2]

In consequence of Taft's demand, on January 28, 1911, Representative Samuel Walker McCall (Republican, Massachusetts) introduced a Canadian reciprocity bill which one reporter called "the first Taft policy," a policy Taft designed in the hope that effective leadership in its consummation would salvage some advantage from the Payne-Aldrich tariff, quiet the snapping of newspapers at his heels, and restore his personal and party prestige. Soon thereafter, Senator Albert B. Cummins began a battle over tariff revision by resolving that the rules be changed to permit the Payne-Aldrich tariff itself to be amended schedule by schedule. He found support for this method in Nelson W. Aldrich and Henry Cabot Lodge in the Senate, from Sereno E. Payne in the House, and also from a few Democrats, although a vast majority of Democrats preferred to write an entirely new reform bill once they were in control of Congress after March 4, 1911. Unfortunately for Taft, he paralleled his demand for Canadian reciprocity with another in which he suggested raising the postal rates on newspapers and magazines, which had done so much to publicize the inadequacies of the Payne-Aldrich tariff.

Canadian proposals for reviving the Elgin-Marcy Reciprocity Treaty of 1854 had been made many times since the United States had abrogated it in 1866. Tired of being rebuffed by the United States, Canada had determined on "making no more pilgrimages to Washington," raised her tariffs, granted bounties to certain industries, and explored the alternative policy of obtaining recognition as a partner rather than a subordinate in the British Empire.

The Payne-Aldrich tariff was the most generous American tariff to apply to Canada since the reciprocity treaty abrogated by the United States in 1866. Taft, however, wished to spare Canada the embarrassment of applying the maximum tariff rates against her at a time when she had a special trade agreement with France. At Albany, New York, on March 18, 1910, he and Secretary of State P. C. Knox talked with Canada's finance minister, Hon. W. S. Fielding, about ways of reducing for Canada some of the rates of the Payne-Aldrich tariff. Talks then held at Washington resulted in a decision to let only the minimum rates apply to Canada and the expression of hope by both sides that a comprehensive arrangement encompassing more liberal terms could be reached. In consequence of arrangements made by Taft and Knox, American and Canadian diplomatic and financial experts met in Ottawa. After a short, secret meeting, Earl Grey, the Canadian governor-general, on November 17, 1910, said he hoped that a satisfactory agreement with the United States could be reached, a conclusion echoed by Laurier and by Taft. The British ambassador to the United States, James Bryce, who handled Canada's diplomacy, was also favorable.

Much depended upon how each country expected to benefit from such an arrangement. The United States could look for increased sales of manufactures, greater access to Canadian raw materials, and cheaper foodstuffs for the American consumer. Businessmen from Boston to Duluth eagerly expected unlimited profits from reciprocity. Opposition was expected from the American farmer, who competed with the Canadian wheat grower; from American producers of raw materials; from American workers, who feared lower wages if not less employment; and from the New England fishermen, who showed their objection to the free entry of Canadian fish by flying their flags at half-mast. Canada in turn could hope for greater sales of agricultural products to the United States, a reduction of the cost of imported American manufactures, with a consequent drop in taxes and in the cost of living, and generally increased mutual trade. Opposition was expected from those unhappy with various fishery and canal arrangements, the loss of East-West Canadian trade to North-South Canadian-American trade, the slowdown in growth predicted for native manufactures, the increase of American capital invested in Canada, the destruction of the benefits of imperial preference with Great Britain, and prospective increases in the price of food and of agricultural implements. Many Canadians in addition believed that reciprocity should come only when the American tariff, almost twice as high, should be made equal to Canada's; that American trusts would enlarge their operations in the Dominion; that the United States was so dependent on Canada's raw materials that reciprocity was unnecessary; and that doing away with the tariff and bounty systems would seriously hurt Canadian industry, the banks associated with it, the major railroads, which ran east and west, and the mining community. With 1866 in mind, they asked what would prevent the United States from again abrogating a treaty and leaving Canada then to find new markets for its surplus products? Finally, old "loyalists" who preferred closer relations with Britain displayed an inherited antagonism to the United States, while Roman Catholic French Canadians feared the loss of state financial support for certain work undertaken by their church if Canada were annexed by the United States.

If these arguments in opposition were not enough, the fact remained that a treaty must run the gauntlet in the parliaments of two nations. Could Taft, defeated in large part because of the Payne-Aldrich tariff in the elections of 1910 and with a Democratic Senate after March 4, 1911, find enough votes for a treaty that would redound to the benefit of the Republican party?

From January 7 to 21, 1911, Knox talked at Washington with Canadian emissaries and reached a "legislative agreement" rather than a treaty. On the twenty-sixth, Taft sent a special message to the Senate asking for its approval but indicating no urgency in the matter. However, in referring to Canada, he said that "it has an active, aggressive, and intelligent people. *They are coming to the parting of the ways.* They soon must decide whether they are to regard themselves as isolated permanently from our markets by a perpetual wall or whether we are to be commercial friends." Although he obviously referred to trade only, his words were soon distorted by Canadian opponents of reciprocity into a threat to the political solidarity of the British Empire.[3]

Although the agreement had been initiated by diplomatic circles, like any other revenue measure it must originate in the House of Representatives. In this case, however, the bill began in the Senate and was then sent to the House early in February with a demand that it be passed without amendment. It was also unusual that Republicans could assert that Republican presidents from Lincoln through Roosevelt had favored reciprocity while Democrats could applaud reciprocity as a step toward tariff reform.

Dropping the complacent approach revealed toward the writing of the Payne-Aldrich tariff until it went into conference, Taft tried to jam Canadian reciprocity through without giving Congress time for thorough discussion and by depending for success upon Democratic rather than Republican votes. He directed various cabinet members to speak and to write letters applauding it, put pressure upon various congressmen, and then appealed to the people over the head of Congress in a western speaking tour. He told Republican Senator William O. Bradley, of Kentucky, for one, that "I regard this as the most important measure of my administration. . . . I can say to you that I shall be very bitterly disappointed if I can't count on your support when I need it. . . ."[4] He told one large farm delegation opposed to reciprocity that they were "seeing ghosts," warned the public that "insistence on too much protection will arouse an opposition in the country that will know no moderation," and defied both regular and progressive Republicans, neither of whom wanted to be pressured on reciprocity.

Such sincere advocates of reciprocity as Cummins failed to see the need for emergency action and resented Taft's virtual coercion of Congress, while many public men blamed the pressure for passage upon the demands of the newspapers for free access to Canadian newsprint paper and pulp. Cummins wrote to Albert J. Beveridge, for example, that newspaper clamor favoring Taft would not produce votes for him and that

> every member of the Senate, no matter how he feels about reciprocity, is dispirited and somewhat sullen. We are in no temper to legislate properly, and yet we must crawl through the hot days of July and probably August in order to reach an end that will satisfy nobody. I congratulate you on being out of it all.[5]

Moses Clapp too believed that "Mr. Taft has weakened himself terribly throughout the country with the Canadian bill."[6] Others asked why, even if the preservation of American forests was considered, the better quality paper used by magazines as well as newsprint should not enter free. And why should Canadian cattle and wheat but not beef and flour enter free? If, as Jonathan Dolliver once said, an insurgent was one who insisted that a bill at least be read before it was passed, Taft must give Congress time to consider the measure. Taft, however, took prospective Speaker Champ Clark to be his partner in the matter and discounted his warning of great opposition he must expect particularly from Old Guard members on the Committee on Rules. By dint of great personal pressure, he won the necessary rule from the committee, then asserted that "this is the lowest politics I have ever seen played in Congress and, damn them, it is my own party which is playing it."[7] In the end, the bill passed the House on February 14 by a vote of 221 to 92 without debate, with the sullen support of the minority Republicans but with the hearty support of the Democrats, who saw reciprocity as hastening the downfall of the Republican high-protection system and a partial abrogation of the Payne-Aldrich tariff. Only 5 Democrats voted against the bill while 143 supported it; the division of Republicans was illustrated when 78 of them voted for it and 87 against it.

The Senate was preoccupied with passing the appropriation bills, a permanent tariff commission bill, and a direct election of senators bill, and with debating the Lorimer case. Moreover, the

Finance Committee, despite Aldrich's support for Taft, would go only as far as to report a reciprocity bill without recommendation. When the appropriation bills were passed but no vote was taken on reciprocity prior to the end of the Sixty-first Congress, Taft, though every man in both houses objected, promptly called the Sixty-second into special session for April 1 to deal almost exclusively with Canadian reciprocity, thereby indicating that he had virtually abandoned the tariff commission bill. However, progressive senators led by Beveridge and certain Democrats passed this bill shortly before adjournment. When various Republicans warned Taft that the Democratic-controlled Congress might pass legislation on the tariff and other matters that might embarrass him, he disbelieved them. Champ Clark, who would be elected as Speaker of the House, told him that the Democrats would pass the reciprocity bill "and any other bill that we thought proper, including tariff [reduction] bills." Taft disbelieved Clark also.[8] By calling Congress into extra session he dug deeper his political grave.

II

On April 1, the House Democrats revived the power of the caucus, wherein policy decisions could be adopted only by a two-thirds vote. As expected, Clark was chosen as Speaker. He would not, however, as had been the case for the past fifty years, be a member of the Committee on Rules, which was expanded from ten to eleven members, seven Democrats and four Republicans, and his power of recognition was circumscribed. The right to name members to the standing committees was shorn from him and given to the Democratic members of the Ways and Means Committee who, acting as a Committee on Committees, must obtain caucus approval for their nominations. As chairman of Ways and Means, chairman of the Committee on Committees, and also the majority floor leader, Underwood would be a more powerful figure even than Clark. Furthermore, the Democrats permitted the bypassing of committee chairmen by means of a discharge petition, largely overlooked the seniority rule in the appointment of committee chairmen, and transferred fifty-eight members among seventeen major committees in order, as Cordell Hull put it, "to strip each committee of every possible vestige of special privilege."[9] While southerners chaired thirty-nine of the fifty-five committees, length of service, experience and ability, and geographic equity were also taken into account. On the other side, the Republicans dumped

Joseph G. Cannon as minority leader and chose instead James R. Mann, of Illinois, who made no distinction between regulars and insurgents in making the committee assignments.

The Sixty-second Congress convened on April 4. It was the first time that a Democratic House of Representatives had assembled in sixteen years and also the first time that a Democratic House had been called into extra session by a Republican president to act upon an administration measure which a Republican Senate had refused to consider.

Without even mentioning reciprocity, Clark outlined the Democratic legislative program. This would include changes in the House rules to make them more democratic, economy in public expenditures, statehood for Arizona and New Mexico, the direct elections of senators, publicity for campaign contributions prior to elections, and an intelligent downward revision of the tariff so that the rates "will not destroy fair and honest competition in the home market," thereby rendering ineffective any reciprocity agreement with Canada based upon the Payne-Aldrich rates.[10]

On April 5, Taft's message urging early approval of the "purely commercial and economic" Canadian reciprocity agreement was read to both houses. A few days later, Underwood favorably reported a reciprocity bill from the Ways and Means Committee but also introduced a measure placing on the free list more than a hundred manufactured articles used by farmers in order to compensate them for expected losses under reciprocity. Democrats like Claude Kitchen, of North Carolina, supported reciprocity while Speaker Clark promised undying opposition. Whether out of chauvinism, a hope to defeat Taft's purpose, or pure bungling, Clark stated that "I am for this Bill, because I hope to see the day when the American flag will float over every square foot of the British North American possessions clear to the North Pole." Republican insurgents orated in defense while regulars like Cannon, Joseph W. Fordney, John Dalzell, and Payne opposed. On April 21, the House passed the bill by a vote of 265 to 89, but the vote well illustrated the split in the Republican party. Of the 160 Republicans present, 66 voted for and 78 against the bill, with 16 not voting. Representatives from manufacturing states voted for it while those from states bordering Canada voted against it. However, Taft said that 57 of the 92 senators favored it, thereby insuring its passage, yet he also told his personal physician: "That speech of Clark's has unquestionably sounded the death knell of the Reciprocity Pact, and it was the plan nearest to my heart."[11]

147

On April 25 the House began debating the farmers' free list. Two days later Taft made an extended plea for reciprocity—for "the bill, the whole bill, and nothing but the bill." On May 8 the House rebuffed him by passing the farmers' free list by a vote of 236 to 109 and then discussing a reduction of the rates on wool. A week later, while the Democratic members of the Ways and Means Committee tried to reach agreement on reducing the wool tariff, Taft sent the Senate the Tariff Board's report on the printing paper industry in the United States and in Canada and, while officially entertaining the new senators, tried to convert them all— even the rabidly opposed Miles Poindexter—to reciprocity.

The Senate consumed almost three weeks in getting organized, with Robert M. La Follette and seven other Republican insurgents refusing to attend their party caucus and demanding one-fourth of the committee assignments. Once they were conciliated and given adequate assignments, Cummins announced that he would amend the House reciprocity bill by adding a free list including lumber, coal, iron ore, textiles and clothing, and meat and flour as well as manufactured implements, and La Follette let it be known that he opposed Taft's brand of reciprocity because it would sacrifice American farmers to Canadian competition, strengthen American trusts by giving them cheap raw materials, and in the end put Canadians at the mercy of American trusts. The Finance Committee held hearings on reciprocity for several weeks; it was expected that the Senate would devote the month of June largely to debate upon the bill. Taft meanwhile used golf games to convert various opposed senators he invited to play.

Assuming that the American Congress could not reach agreement on reciprocity before the middle of July, the Canadian Parliament on May 19 adjourned for two months, with Laurier going to attend an imperial conference at London.

Backed heartily by the newspaper fraternity, especially by William Randolph Hearst, Taft sought to have the Senate pass the reciprocity bill without amendments that might be rejected by the House and result in deadlock. When he met his new secretary of war, Henry L. Stimson, on May 15, he said to him: "I'll give you your first assignment as the baby member of the Cabinet. It will be your duty to speak before the Intercolonial Club of Boston on May 24 on the subject of reciprocity."[12] In a speech before the Western Economic Association at Chicago, he himself demanded that the Senate pass the bill as he wanted it; in New York he charged that opposition came primarily from the producers of lumber and of print paper and from those who allegedly represented the farmers' interests. However, on June 20 by a vote of 221 to 100 the House passed a bill that lowered the wool and woolen duties and let it be known that it would attack the cotton and various other schedules. Progressive Republican as well as Democratic senators applauded the blows given Taft, who now made matters worse by thanking Hearst, long known as a proponent of Canadian annexation, for spreading the "gospel of reciprocity."

"Well, we are in for an all-summer session," the president said to his brother Harry. "It begins to look from this action yesterday that the Democrats and the insurgents are combined to force a general tariff revision."

"What will you do if they send the Reciprocity Treaty with free wool tacked onto it?" asked his brother.

"I will veto it," said the president. "They think I will be afraid to veto a free wool bill, but I will show them I don't propose to be bulldozed by them. If they want to remain in Washington all summer I am willing to do so. If it becomes a game of bluff I can keep my cards off the table as long as they can."[13]

Taft breathed more easily when the Finance Committee declined to report the farmers' free list sent over by the House and reported adversely on the wool reduction bill, and the Senate killed a move by Joseph W. Bailey to add the free list to the Canadian reciprocity bill by amendment. If Taft rewarded those who favored Canadian reciprocity, the free list, and lower rates on certain schedules—he had earlier called the Payne-Aldrich wool and cotton schedules "indefensible"—he would appear to be more a Democratic than a Republican president. Said Underwood: "If the President signs the Wool Bill, or the Farmers' Free List Bill, or both, the protective system is gone; if he vetoes either or both of them, Mr. Taft is gone."[14] On the other hand, the Democrats, already embarrassed by not having a general tariff reduction bill ready, did not try to reduce the wood-pulp and print-paper tariff rates. In any event, while Taft waited in his office for the results of the voting, a coalition of Democrats and regular Republicans passed the Canadian reciprocity bill on July 22 by a vote of fifty-three to twenty-seven. He was pleased but not overjoyed, for the opposition vote consisted of twelve regular and twelve insurgent Republicans and three Democrats and he had the Democrats to thank for his victory.

What would Canada now do? And what would Taft do if the

Senate passed the free list and the wool bill, on which votes were set for July 26 and August 1, respectively?

The Underwood wool bill reduced the Payne-Aldrich rate of 44 percent to 20 percent. In the Senate, La Follette obtained a compromise which reduced the rate to 35 percent. Compromise was further evident when Underwood and La Follette agreed to 29 percent. The House adopted the conference report by a vote of 206 to 90 on August 14, and the Senate by a vote of 38 to 28 on the next day. Although the new rate was still moderately protectionist, in keeping with threats to veto any tariff reduction bills sent to him, Taft on the seventeenth vetoed it with a message prepared long in advance on the advice of such notorious protectionists as Senators Murray Crane, Boies Penrose, and Reed Smoot. Underwood immediately called for passing the bill over the veto but was not supported by two-thirds of the House. The farmers' free list and bills calling for reductions in the rates on cotton, iron and steel, chemicals, and other products passed the Senate rather easily, only to be vetoed too, on the grounds that they were improperly drawn and based upon imperfect information. Since tariff reform was popular and Taft seemed to care more for the form of revision than for revision itself, he further weakened his position with the people. Moreover, his resentment of criticism once his mind was made up was clearly indicated. His brother Horace once told him that he was a "theoretical pedant" by refusing to read the Hearst papers and the *New York World,* which criticized his vetoes, because they would make him angry. "You will never know what the other side is doing if you read only the [New York] *Sun* and the *Tribune,*" sagely remarked Mrs. Taft. He replied with some irritation: "I don't care what the other side is doing. I only know that I am going to hammer the life out of Underwood. . . ."[15]

III

The Canadian Parliament, which opened on July 18, made reciprocity the first order of business. Since the majority could not force closure on a question of this kind, Parliament was dissolved on July 29, new elections were called for September 21, and the meeting of the new Parliament was set for October 1. Taft on September 15 embarked on a two-month, twenty-eight-state, sixteen thousand-mile cross-country trip during which he spoke 380 times, most often on the tariff question. Archie Butt, for one, doubted that he gained politically from his trip and felt his cheeks burn when discourteous children shouted "Hello, Billy" and "Hello, Fatty," when they saw the president. On September 22, Taft learned that Laurier, who had made the consummation of reciprocity the only issue of a vigorous campaign and lampooned the annexation idea as a bogey, was defeated. Robert L. Borden, who would be the new premier, had made much of the danger of annexation and pictured "tricky Taft" as a designing villain plotting the destruction of his neighbor. He thus slighted the economic issue in favor of the political issue of loyalty.

Measured by the flood of memorials sent to Congress by state legislatures, chambers of commerce, boards of trade, and other organizations, the American people, particularly in their role as consumers, favored Canadian reciprocity, and Taft seemed to be carrying out their will. But the publication of the agreement threw it out of the realm of diplomacy into that of public discussion. While newspapers avid for free newsprint supported it, vested interests opposed it. If regulars supported it, insurgents opposed it, thus widening the intraparty breach. Taft had reopened the whole tariff issue and embarrassed himself and his party by applauding the Democrats in the special session for having made his success possible. But he had ignored personal warnings sent to him by Laurier that Canadians were extremely sensitive people and that Taft must avoid "creating any impression that there is political significance in this treaty. My political opponents are trying to make that an issue."[16] To this advice Taft said "bosh" and created an unfavorable stir by referring to "annexation" while on tour and being quoted in Canada as having said that "Before Canada is irrevocably fixed in a policy leading to consolidation and strengthening of the British empire we must turn her from her course."[17] But others shared the blame with him for the failure of reciprocity.

If no impairment would bar either Canadian commerce or friendly intercourse with the United States, and the Canadian reciprocity law remained on the American statute book until late 1919 as an invitation to Canada to establish freer trade relations, reciprocity was dead. Taft, the "father of reciprocity" who had so ruthlessly pushed his "pet measure" through Congress, had been repudiated by Canada. Any advantage in having supported reciprocity accrued to the Democrats rather than to him, for no mitigation of the iniquities of the Payne-Aldrich tariff had occurred. If he had made the election of a Republican Congress in 1910 unlikely because of the Payne-Aldrich tariff and the Ballinger-Pinchot squabble, he had now made Republican harmony upon a presidential candidate in 1912 impossible. Canada's refusal, he admitted, had hit him "between the eyes."[18] If Canadian reciprocity was designed as an escape from the true tariff revision he had promised, that escape route was now closed. The Democrats would henceforth assert that they alone could be trusted to reform the tariff and that they would do so without seeking the permission of a foreign country to adjust the schedules.

8

★★★★★

A "NONREFORM":
THE ANTITRUST CRUSADE

I

Upon assuming the presidency, William Howard Taft found that three Supreme Court judges were over seventy years of age and that five of them were too ill to do their work properly. He therefore determined to appoint only "good" men of younger years to the Court as soon as possible. The death or resignation of five judges during his term gave him the unusual opportunity to reconstitute the Court with a majority of new men who, he hoped, would help him to protect the Constitution from the insurgents if not from the Theodore Roosevelt of the New Nationalism. Extremely important to the people and of course to the interests involved was the attitude the Supreme Court would take on the many antitrust cases it would hear.

Harbingers of the antitrust policy of Taft's administration lay in a speech and in an action. In a speech Attorney General George Wickersham gave in New York City late in April 1909, he stated that business could no longer plead ignorance of the Sherman Antitrust Act and that bona-fide antitrust cases begun under Roosevelt would be continued. The action was the barring of the army by Secretary of War Jacob M. Dickinson from making contracts with trusts such as the Standard Oil Company and the American Tobacco Company. Taft himself took the position that the heretofore toothless if not gumless Sherman Act must be enforced pending the devising of improved legislation. As he had put it in a speech before the Ohio Society on December 16, 1908, he believed that railroads and other transportation media should be controlled under the Interstate Commerce Act. The Sherman Act, however, should be amended in two particulars. First, it should make illegal every combination of capital in interstate commerce. Second, use of the words "reasonable" and "unreasonable" should be avoided and businessmen should be told exactly what actions they could follow.[1]

In the second half of his special message of January 7, 1910, Taft dealt with improving the Sherman Act in order to prevent monopoly. He had no objections to the large size of a business, he said, but he would prevent abuses, in effect saying that he would leave business alone as long as it behaved itself. But he would let "good" trusts with a capitalization of $100,000,000 or more incorporate under a new federal law, thereby shifting the power of investigation into business practices from the Department of Commerce and Labor to the Department of Justice and exempting corporations from suits brought by states.

Taft's ideas were included in a bill introduced in both houses on February 7. He thus fulfilled promises made in many addresses since his inauguration, but congressional Democrats and insurgents spurned his suggestions, saying that their adoption would destroy the Sherman Act.

II

Taft's unrelenting antitrust crusade exceeded Roosevelt's by far—about seventy suits in four years compared with forty suits in seven years. When it would stop no one could say, for Wickersham stated that there were about a hundred trusts in addition to those against which the government had already brought suit. Not only did Taft misunderstand Roosevelt's antitrust policy; he caused himself and Roosevelt great personal embarrassment, as shown by the United States Steel and International Harvester cases, discussed later. By his compulsive upholding of the letter of the law he dealt a shattering blow to his relations with Roosevelt. Moreover, he alienated businessmen, provided an important issue for the campaigns of 1910 and 1912, and failed to win new legislation for the improved regulation of big business.

In 1906, the Roosevelt administration had brought suit against the Standard Oil Company of New Jersey, charging that it controlled over 75 percent of the refining and marketing of petroleum products and that it had engaged in such unfair practices as obtaining rebates from railroads. The suit asked that the organization be dissolved. In April 1909, the case was heard by a Court of Appeals, which in November unanimously decided that the company was in violation of interstate trade, that it had attempted to monopolize, and that it must dissolve. Wickersham declared the decision to be "one of the most important ever rendered in this country," and praise for it came from those convinced that a brilliant victory had been won against what the *New York World* called "the most powerful industrial combination known to civilization" and that the Sherman Act had been vindicated. Others predicted that even if the Supreme Court upheld the decision, no practical results would follow and that "it leaves the structure of Standard-Oil extortion unshaken and unthreatened."[2]

When his military aide, Archibald W. Butt, told Taft about the decision, he exclaimed "Bully for that!" Soon thereafter he heard something to the effect that the decision might boomerang and said to Wickersham, as Butt recalled, that "unless there was some remediable legislation the whole commercial structure of the country as now existing would go to pieces," and that "I want to read the business interests of this country a lecture, but it should have some warning before the law becomes too drastic. It should not be taken by surprise." Butt believed that Roosevelt would say in the circumstance that the Sherman Act was warning enough and hoped that Taft "is not going to take a backward step in this matter, for it would do more than anything else could to bring about a separation from Mr. Roosevelt."[3] Before the decrees of dissolution became effective, however, the case went to the Supreme Court. That Court heard argument in March 1910 but, because of vacancies, scheduled a reargument for early 1911, when Wickersham and Frank B. Kellogg, fully supported by Taft, would represent the government. The judges were nearly divided in their opinion on the case; the death of David J. Brewer removed a man who had heard the earlier pleadings; William Moody was too ill to serve; and Horace Harmon Lurton was too new an appointee to be able to judge the case. This left six or at best seven men to make the decision under the majority rule followed by the Court, meaning that five of them must agree on what principles would govern the very fabric of the nation's economic life.

The decision, announced on May 15, 1911, provoked both applause and rebuke. In its decree the Court, now containing the new justices Charles Evans Hughes, Joseph Rucker Lamar, Lurton, and Willis Van Devanter, demanded that each subsidiary company controlled by Standard Oil must revive its full corporate activity and that the parent company wind up its affairs in six months. On September 1 the company complied by announcing that the shares of the thirty-three subsidiary corporations would be distributed pro rata to them on or about December 1. Evidently a great trust had been crushed. But even more important and provocative of criticism and derision was the "rule of reason" opinion read into the decision. Chief Justice Edward White said that the Sherman Act must not be regarded as arbitrarily prohibiting all contracts and agreements that might on their face seem to restrain interstate trade but that in their nature were reasonable and not contrary to individual rights or the general welfare. The spirit rather than the bare letter of the law must rule. Put another way, the Court was assuming the power to decide whether a given restraint of trade was a "reasonable" or "unreasonable" one. Thus monopoly was criminal only if achieved in illegal ways, but in the end the Court would determine what restraints on trade might be allowed. John M. Harlan dissented, saying that White was importing into the law the word "reasonable," thereby violating both the plain wording of the act and the intention of its authors. Among many others, his contention was supported by the progressive Republican Robert M. La Follette and the liberal Democrat William Jennings Bryan. Elbert H. Gary meanwhile spoke for many businessmen in requesting a definition of the terms "reasonable" and "unreasonable," and George Perkins predicted chaos in the business world.[4]

On May 29, 1911, the Supreme Court announced its unanimous decision on the *American Tobacco Company* case, which Roosevelt had instituted in 1908 with charges against sixty-five corporations and twenty-nine individuals. The Court upheld the "rule of reason" announced two weeks earlier and found that the methods the company had used to achieve monopoly amounted to undue and unreasonable restraint of trade such as was clearly prohibited by the Sherman Act. Like Standard Oil, it too must dissolve. The only dissenter was again Harlan, who upheld the decision as to the dissolution of the trust but dissented vigorously on the application of the test of "reasonableness" agreed to by his eight colleagues. While the majority would permit reorganization, he would absolutely refuse to let the company reorganize or even to continue its operations. The company on October 16 offered a plan of dissolution in which none of the "separate and independent" companies involved would have control or dominance over the other. However, it found it exceedingly difficult to commit suicide and under color of reorganizing really retained its monopoly position. Taft called the decree as effective as any ever issued by an American court, La Follette characterized it as "judicial legislation," and Roosevelt believed that the "rule of reason" gave desired flexibility to interpretations of the Sherman Act even though it did "not reach the root of the matter." What was needed, he said, was an independent commission somewhat like the ICC empowered to regulate corporations by "continuous administrative action, and not by necessarily intermittent lawsuits."[5] The following year, however, the Democratic national platform condemned the rule of reason, and Roosevelt, as Progressive candidate for president, labeled it a "flagrant travesty of Justice."[6]

Roosevelt's break with Taft came in part because of Taft's suit against the United States Steel Corporation. In 1905, Roosevelt's Bureau of Corporations had begun investigating the corporation, which in confidence opened its books to the government. Believing it to be a "good" trust and knowing that a thorough investigation could not be made before he left office, Roosevelt had instituted no suit against it.

During the panic of 1907, bankers who met with J. P. Morgan decided to prevent more business failures by letting U.S. Steel acquire a large number of shares of the Tennessee Coal, Iron, and Railroad Company, thereby shoring up the brokerage house of Moore and Schley and restoring confidence in Wall Street. Morgan telephoned both Judge Elbert H. Gary, chairman of the Executive Board of U.S. Steel, and Henry Clay Frick. One version of the story is that Gary, Frick, and Morgan knew that the stock was worth no more than $60.00 a share but would have declined to buy it then at any price through fear that its acquisition would invite an antitrust suit similar to that pending against Standard Oil. On the other hand, its acquisition might avert further disastrous financial consequences for the nation. Gary then suggested that the president or the Department of Justice grant approval for the purchase, and he and Frick went to Washington and on November 4 saw Roosevelt and Elihu Root and then proceeded with the purchase on the basis that, as Roosevelt had put it, "while he could not advise them to take the action proposed, he felt it no public duty of his to interpose any objection." Wall Street and the nation had thus been saved.[7]

Still worried about a possible government suit, Frick spoke with Gary and also with Senator P. C. Knox about seeing Roosevelt and arranging to have the Standard Oil suit settled out of court and then have Congress pass a law providing for the supervision and regulation of big business, thereby eradicating business uncertainty. In reply to a letter from Frick, Roosevelt said that the Standard Oil counsel should speak directly with the Department of Justice, not with him, and Frick desisted.

In June 1911, hearings were held before the Augustus Owsley Stanley Committee of the House of Representatives established to investigate U.S. Steel. The committee sought the political limelight by attacking Perkins and John D. Rockefeller rather than seeking the truth about the trust and verged upon citing Perkins for contempt. Both Gary and Perkins defended the taking over of T. C. & I. in 1907 on the ground that it prevented the panic from worsening. Gary not only denied that his so-called Gary dinners were designed to fix the prices of steel products but advocated federal control over industrial corporations and even federal control of prices charged by them. Perkins's position was closely attuned. Denying that American business could maintain its world supremacy "under a technical enforcement of the Sherman law," he suggested that corporations be allowed to register with the federal government and open their records to the public, and that interstate corporations be brought directly under federal control.

In July, Herbert Knox Smith, commissioner of corporations, gave Taft his report on his investigation into U.S. Steel. He made no startling revelations and offered no recommendations. He had found that the company had squeezed a great deal of water out of its overcapitalization when first formed in 1901. Moreover, he offered statistics which showed that the company overvalued its ownership of unmined ores, possibly with the intent of preventing them from falling into the hands of competitors. While the company had provided about 60 percent of the nation's finished steel in 1901 and only 50 percent in 1910, its ownership of unmined ores had increased to about 2.5 trillion tons, or 75 percent of the known total, thus approaching a monopoly position in this respect, a monopoly protected by the corporation's control of ore transport in the Great Lakes region. Finally, its policies with respect to its labor force were notoriously bad.

The real fireworks were delayed until August 5, when in addition to Gary and the former head of the corporation's finance committee, Perkins, Roosevelt was asked to testify in New York to the part he had played in permitting U.S. Steel to acquire T. C. & I. Roosevelt assumed full responsibility for what had transpired. With the country facing a dangerous financial situation, he "did exactly right," and the result had "justified my judgment." As to whether the steel executives were more anxious to provide a public service or to absorb a rival business, he could not say.[8] However, the Taft administration's bringing suit against the corporation implied that he had fostered monopoly and had been duped by clever industrialists and marked a final break between him and Taft.

In the most sweeping antitrust action ever brought by the Department of Justice, the government's dissolution suit, filed on October 26 without Taft's having read the bill of particulars, demanded that independence be granted to more than a hundred companies. Among the best known defendants were Morgan, Rockefeller, Andrew Carnegie, Charles M. Schwab, Perkins, Gary, John D. Rockefeller, Jr., and Frick. Basing their charge in part on the hearings of the Stanley Committee, government lawyers intended to make the acquisition of T. C. & I. the nub of their contention that transactions of this kind enabled the steel corporation to obtain monopoly status, the understanding between Roosevelt and Gary and Frick notwithstanding. Roosevelt, the government lawyers contended, was deceived as to the facts of the transaction and the motives which animated Gary and Frick. Had he known the facts, he never would have permitted U.S. Steel to acquire a competitor and thus become the largest steel corporation in the country. The corporation, these lawyers argued, had "unlawfully acquired a power which is a menace to the welfare of the country and should be destroyed." Roosevelt privately excoriated Taft, for he recalled that as secretary of war Taft had discussed the merger in cabinet and highly praised it. In an editorial in the *Outlook*, of which he was a contributing editor, he asserted that Gary had not deceived him and, without mentioning Taft, went on to criticize his administration's proceedings. The suit, he said, "has brought vividly before our people the need of reducing to order our chaotic government policy as regards business. . . . To attempt to meet the whole problem by a succession of lawsuits is hopeless. . . . It is practically impossible to break up all combinations merely because they are large and successful and to put the business of the country back into the middle of the eighteenth century." The shotgun method of attacking all trusts, "good" and "bad," merely because of their size, would not work. Moreover, the oil and tobacco suits still left the companies to their original owners, a result "lamentable from a standpoint of justice," for "none of the real offenders have received any punishment." The "rule of reason" did not tell every businessman exactly where he stood in relation to the Sherman Act, and he concluded that the administration should ask for a law granting the federal government the power to regulate and supervise businesses engaged in interstate commerce, even to the point of "regulating the prices charged by monopolies."[9]

Although the steel suit was the most spectacular of Taft's antitrust suits, the general public was less hostile to U.S. Steel than to a number of other trusts. Even independent competitors who apparently were being championed by the government sided with it, for their business had grown while that of the "trust" had declined in recent years. Wickersham was no longer sure that business could thrive under the Sherman Act, and despite Taft's stating that the act was "clear," business would proceed in suspense and uncertainty until it was rewritten or amended so as to permit a degree of consolidation and concentration fitting the verities of modern business life. Pictured as being courageous in bringing suit against the greatest industrial combination in the country, Taft nevertheless alienated the conservative interests of the country and damaged himself politically. Since Roosevelt disagreed with him on conservation, on his international arbitration treaties, and now on antitrust policy, numerous editors and politicians questioned whether Roosevelt was not preparing to enter the ring in 1912 as the "Wall Street candidate." Bryan pointed out that during his seven years as president, Roosevelt had made the criminal clause of the Sherman Act a dead letter, and asserted that the greatest single need of the hour was "protection of the people from exploitation at the hands of predatory corporations."[10]

Court decisions on old cases, such as those against the powder trust and beef trust, were handed down only a little more slowly than Wickersham entered new suits, as against the sugar trust, National Electric Lamp Company, and the soft coal trust. None of these cases involved Taft or Roosevelt, but the International Harvester Company suit did.

As in the case of U.S. Steel, Roosevelt had investigated but not brought suit against the Harvester company. Wickersham's suit against the company, or "farm machinery trust," filed in April 1912 and involving the hearing of twelve hundred witnesses, resulted in a decree that the company dissolve into three parts.

Superficially, the Harvester company had been on trial. In popular opinion, however, three defendants had awaited the verdict, the trust, Taft, and Roosevelt, because in their bitter contest for the presidential nomination Taft and Roosevelt made the case a leading issue. As president, Roosevelt had used the Sherman Act to break up large corporations because Congress had refused to give him authority to control them by means of a federal board similar to the ICC. Apparently on "technical grounds," he had delayed the execution of this "good" trust, good to him, that is, and Taftites asserted that this Morgan interest went unscathed because of gross executive favoritism, as proved by the support now being given Roosevelt by Perkins and the McCormick family. But Taft was tainted by the accusation that he had acquiesced as a cabinet member in Roosevelt's inaction and then waited until Roosevelt contended with him for the nomination to attack a trust that supported him. Moreover, although he had refused a demand by the Senate to provide it with the papers he had on the Harvester trust, in late April Taft complied with alacrity to a second demand at a moment when he was doing very poorly in the presidential primaries. The papers proved that Roosevelt had been patient in giving the trust time to rectify certain practices complained about by the ICC before he entered suit against it. Taftites charged that he had acted improperly, but Roosevelt blasted them by saying that he had taken the same action in the Harvester case that he had in other cases, that he had had the approval of all of his cabinet including Taft, and that Taft had let three and a half years of his administration go by before filing his suit.[11] To try to label him as a friend of trusts was simply too Herculean a task.

Perkins had been instrumental in creating the Harvester trust, whose stock was first placed on the market in 1908, and had been one of Roosevelt's many advisers on how to write an acceptable corporation control bill. In 1908 he had strongly supported Taft, indeed conducted a drive that raised a million dollars for him. Perkins had helped to compose the "gentlemen's agreements" between Roosevelt and the "House of Morgan."[12] Despite the failure in Congress of the corporation control bill he had helped to write, he had predicted that with the election of Taft, "we are going to have a more comfortable time."[13]

Busy with tariff reform, the crisis over conservation, and mending the split in his party, Taft not only ignored the "gentlemen's agreements" but failed to answer Perkins's demands to fulfill the Republican national platform pledge on the regulation of business without enforcing the Sherman Act "literally." In 1910, Perkins had withdrawn from the Morgan company to devote himself to "corporation work and work of a public nature." This work entailed a plan to get businessmen to cooperate under government regulation rather than to compete—under penalty of sending culpable corporation directors to jail—and the suggestion of profit-sharing between capital and labor. Taft's bringing suit against both U.S. Steel and International Harvester drove Perkins out of the Republican party and into the arms of Roosevelt.

In a transcontinental tour of the country lasting throughout October 1911, Taft told audiences what he thought they should hear, not what they wanted to hear, so that he could not be charged with seeking to promote either his nomination or election in 1912. He explained the Supreme Court's decisions in the major antitrust cases and declared that the word "unreasonable" which the Court read into the law did not mean that it would regard monopoly and the restraint of trade as reasonable. Neither he nor the Court believed that competition was impossible under modern business conditions. Since he could not, as various others did, see government control as a middle point between "individualism" and "combinations," and since the law was "clear," "businessmen must square themselves to that necessity. Either that or we must proceed [by price fixing] to State Socialism and vest the Government with power to run every business." In sum, because the Supreme Court had made the meaning of the Sherman Act "clear," the act should not be amended. However, he urged legislation on federal incorporation with supervision over interstate business by a executive bureau of the government.[14]

Either because it was unwilling to be left out of the antitrust crusade or because of the Supreme Court's "rule of reason" decision, the Senate Committee on Interstate Commerce began hearings on November 15, 1911, on whether changes should be made in the Sherman Act. Should Congress pass a law providing for federal regulation of interstate corporations? Should one company by law be forbidden to hold stock in another? Would the legislators agree with the demands of Taft or with those of Representative Martin W. Littleton, Senator La Follette, and Bryan, who advocated repeal of the Sherman Act, the substitution for it of a law that prohibited specified unfair business practices and required federal licensing before a corporation could engage in interstate commerce? This was in essence the plan Perkins discussed personally with Taft on November 25. Roosevelt publicly approved of regulating big businesses in the public interest rather than breaking them up. His good friend Henry L. Stimson agreed, asserting that while federal regulation was necessary, "government by indictment" was a poor way to reach this goal. Thus Roosevelt's way of treating big business as subordinate to the government was contrasted with the Taft way of exterminating it.

The *New York World* made a point when it stated that the "conversion" of big business "would be more genuine if Evangelist Taft had a few trust magnates in jail to serve as an example to others."[15] Despite Taft's saying that the "epoch-making . . . 'rule of reason'" had made the meaning of the Sherman Act "clear," businessmen were more uncertain than ever before about what practices were permissible under the law and claimed that they could not guarantee prosperity as long as they must work under the threat of grand jury action and the shadow of the penitentiary. Taft declared that "business must square itself to the Antitrust Law," adding that he had no discretion but to execute the law as it stood and could not "withhold criminal prosecutions . . . just to help business." To enforce the Sherman law in its present form, retorted Perkins, who spoke for big business, is to "throttle business."[16]

III

For twenty years the Sherman Act had neither prevented monopoly nor secured fair play. Rather than keeping his platform's pledge of 1908 to give the government the power to regulate corporations, Taft had adopted Bryan's idea of breaking them up so that they could not become monopolies. In reality, the Supreme Court rather than he or Congress was breaking up trusts. Since it was exceedingly difficult to know in advance what was legal or illegal, businessmen called for a commission that would establish the rules of fair competition and supervise business in such a way as to assure the worker, the consumer, and the investor that business dealings were honest. The *Wall Street Journal* asked why a man almost unanimously supported for president in 1908 by the business community should try to destroy the prosperity of the country. It was also said that business would no longer support Taft and the Republican party and would instead turn to Judson Harmon in 1912 as the "most conservative" (i.e., most friendly to big business) of the Democratic hopefuls.

By the end of 1910, the Taft administration had entered

seventeen antitrust suits. Because of these, two defendants had been imprisoned and fines amounting to $88,000 had been assessed. By the end of 1911, Wickersham could report that he had entered six civil suits in addition to the seventeen already under way, and twenty-three criminal suits in addition to the eleven already being prosecuted. Of eight civil suits completed during 1911, the government had won four, of criminal suits four also, and in addition Wickersham had started forty-six prosecutions against railroads for illegal discriminations and rebates. The questions therefore might well be raised: Had the Sherman Act been adequate to prevent monopoly or was it being used merely to undo evil already done? Had it solved the problems of "badness" as well as "bigness"?

In December 1911, in a special message on trusts, Taft made three "sanely progressive" proposals that found general favor in Wall Street and in all political quarters: (1) that the Sherman Act not be amended; (2) that a supplemental law should be enacted "which shall describe and denounce methods of competition which are unfair and badges of the unlawful purpose denounced in the Anti-trust law"; and (3) that government control of trusts be strengthened by federal incorporation and by the creation of a "special bureau of commission" in the Department of Commerce and Labor. This commission would number among its duties the reformation of bad trusts, supervision of trusts submitting their form of organization and business methods to it, and the supervision of the issuing of stocks and bonds.[17] He thus combined the two ideas of "government by indictment" and of reform legislation, but his comments on the latter were largely overlooked because they followed a lengthy disquisition on the former. As Root told Stimson, "No one really knows what the President's position on the trust question is."[18] Given this situation, could Taft expect Congress to enact his program?

The first regular session of the Sixty-second Congress, which met in December 1911, would sit until the eve of the national conventions. Since it had a strong Democratic majority in the House and a small Republican majority in the Senate, it was unlikely that it would pass many of the measures demanded by Taft. But Taft sent it a message during the first week of its life which, like Cleveland's tariff message of 1887, was devoted wholly to one topic— a "Message of the President of the United States on the Anti-Trust Statute"—with messages on other topics promised at later times. Although he used judicial terms to express his views, he offered the three suggestions mentioned above, enough to put him on record as willing to fight for the legislation he wanted.

In mid-March 1912, the Supreme Court by a vote of four to three upheld the right of the A. B. Dick Company by an "agreement of notice" with a purchaser of its duplicating machines to stipulate that he must use prescribed ink and paper lest he violate its patent rights. This interpretation of the Sherman Act so obviously guaranteed the company a monopoly position that Congress bestirred itself to amend those patent laws which supported monopoly and hindered the enforcement of the Sherman Act, but it did nothing to pass the antitrust laws Taft demanded.

In sum, Taft's efforts to revive the Sherman Act stabilized the trusts rather than destroyed them, weakened rather than strengthened the act, and failed to win from Congress legislation either telling business exactly what methods it could use or establishing a supervisory body to enforce fair play. Thus, Taft's efforts tended to drive businessmen away from him, and won the opposition of Roosevelt and the Progressives in 1912.

9

★★★★★

MAN OF PEACE

I

Never a bellicose man, William Howard Taft succeeded in settling various international disputes by peaceful methods during his term. During his last two years, moreover, he sought Senate approval for treaties of unlimited arbitration, which he believed would make world peace a practical reality. In the case of the Panama Canal tolls question, however, he reversed himself and rejected the British suggestion of arbitration. Most importantly, with a tremendous amount of tact and patience he maintained a steadfast neutrality toward the civil war that began in Mexico in 1910 and threatened to invite forcible American intervention.

By the time of Taft's inauguration, Russia had stopped pogroms against her Jews but instituted instead a system of "peaceful extermination" which included a refusal to recognize American passports issued to Jews, Roman Catholic priests, and Protestant ministers. Taft accepted the demand of the American Jewish community and various American churches that he get Russia to live up to its treaty obligations and stop repressing Jews, but he put no further pressure on Russia after being informed in June 1911 that the Duma would remove the restrictions on American Jews traveling in Russia. On December 14, however, the House of Representatives passed with only one dissenting vote a resolution abrogating the general Russian-American commercial treaty. Taft declined to officially communicate the resolution to Russia, which could read it in the press, and on the next day informed Russia of his own intent to abrogate the treaty. Yet he expressed his willingness to write a "modern" treaty, one that would be "perfectly responsible to the interests of both Governments." Both House and Senate approved of his stand. Theodore Roosevelt, too, applauded, for while he objected to general arbitration treaties this was one instance in which an interpretation of a treaty clause—that dealing with passports—could be submitted to arbitration. In the end, late in 1912 Taft abrogated the treaty, with resultant harm to American business and no benefit to American Jews because he failed to write a new treaty.

II

Various disputes with Great Britain were settled by pacific means. The pelagic sealing question was handled by a four-power conference, that of the Newfoundland fisheries by arbitration, and that of the United States–Canadian boundary in part by arbitration.

In accordance with an arbitral decision of 1892, the United States and Great Britain had restricted their sealers from hunting closer than sixty miles from the Pribilof Islands in the Bering Sea. Canadian and particularly Japanese pelagic sealers nevertheless threatened the seals with extinction. Conservationists demanded that their herd be protected, for it was down from about four million in 1867 to a mere one hundred thousand in 1910. On March 15, 1910, Taft sent Congress a special message on the subject and also a bill granting the secretary of commerce authority to handle it.

After long preparations, a conference was convened in the summer of 1911 at Washington attended by representatives of Great Britain, Japan, Russia, and the United States, the four countries that bordered the North Pacific and which had quarreled over seals for twenty-five years. When Japan proved reluctant to agree with its conclusions, Taft took the unusual step of appealing directly to the Mikado, with the result that the North Pacific sealing Convention adopted a kind of "international game law." According to the Convention, on which the delegates completed work on July 7, the four powers would prevent their nationals from engaging in pelagic sealing and the United States would pay to the other signatories a stipulated percentage of its regulated land kill. Thus the seal herd would be "conserved," with great future growth expected.[1] Although admittedly glad to see the end of a source of international friction, Japan felt that since Canada used only five ships in the Pribilof area while she used fifty, the granting of 15 percent of the catch to both her and Canada was unfair and caused her to suffer considerable economic loss. Nevertheless, the convention served for almost thirty years, until Japan terminated it in 1940.

Taft asserted in his annual message of 1909 that the controversy with Great Britain over the Newfoundland fisheries had existed for more than eighty years since the Anglo-American Convention of 1818 and should be settled. At issue was the demand by American fishermen for freedom from irritating regulations imposed by Newfoundland authorities on the use of their ports and inshore waters. Under the general treaty of arbitration between the United States and Great Britain of April 11, 1908, Secretary of State Elihu Root had entered a special agreement for the submission of the question to a tribunal to be formed from members of the Permanent Court of Arbitration at The Hague. Although now a senator from New York, Root journeyed to The Hague as an American counsel at the request of Taft and of his secretary of state, Philander C. Knox. The decision of 1910 satisfied both countries and was confirmed in the Anglo-American Convention of 1912, which among its provisions established a permanent body to adjust disputes as they arose. Although the processes of settlement had begun under Roosevelt, both countries had for long years resisted every other form of diplomacy. The final steps were taken under Taft and redounded to his credit, although he generously submitted that the argument presented at The Hague by Root had helped to achieve the desired results.[2]

Finally, a treaty between the United States and Great Britain of April 11, 1908, concerning the boundary with Canada, authorized the appointment of two commissioners to define and mark accurately the international boundary between Maine and New Brunswick in Passamaquoddy Bay which had been in dispute since 1783. When the commissioners failed to act upon briefs submitted in the six-month period provided, resort was had to arbitration. Under the Boundary Waters Treaty with Britain of January 11, 1909, a permanent joint commission was established to settle disputes arising over navigation and other questions in the waterways along the mutual boundary. With agreement on a new boundary in Passamaquoddy Bay reached under the treaty of May 21, 1910, the need for arbitration passed.

III

Roosevelt had sought peace through strength. Except for questions of honor and of vital interest, however, he favored the principle of arbitration. John Hay had written nine "special agreements" calling for the president by executive agreement with the signatories to commence arbitration procedures whenever trouble brewed. Jealous of its prerogatives, the Senate had substituted "special treaties" for "special agreement," thereby requiring Senate action before arbitration could begin. An irate Roosevelt thereupon dropped the agreements. Three years later, Root wrote treaties with twenty-four nations. These covered all questions except "vital interests, the independence, or the honor of the countries involved," and became operative only if two-thirds of the senators agreed to a special treaty concerning each specific dispute.

Like Root, William Jennings Bryan, Andrew Carnegie, Edward Ginn, and various others in the burgeoning organized peace movement, Taft saw world peace not as a Utopian dream but as a practical possibility by means of treaties providing for the unlimited adjudication on any question, not excepting "vital interests" and "national honor," that could not be settled by negotiation. In January 1910, Knox pleaded for the establishment of a genuine judicial tribunal for the adjudication of differences among the powers. In October Taft spelled out the details of a broad arbitration treaty to British Ambassador James Bryce. In an address before the American Society for the Judicial Settlement of International Disputes on December 18, he went on to suggest treaties of unlimited arbitration. He told Archie Butt in April 1911 that an unlimited arbitration treaty "will be the great jewel of my administration. But just as it will be the greatest act during these four years, it will also be the greatest failure if I do not get it ratified . . . ," adding that "there are men up in the Senate, Archie, who would try to kill it just because I advocated it." He then revealed how he had come to adopt his policy:

> It is strange how one happens on this sort of thing. When I made that speech in New York advocating the arbitration of questions, even those affecting the honor of a nation, I had no definite policy in view. I was inclined, if I remember rightly, merely to offset the antagonism to the four battleships for which I was then fighting, and I threw that suggestion out merely to draw the sting of old Carnegie and other peace cranks, and now the sug-

gestion threatens to become the main fact of my four years as president.[3]

Discounting loud cries on both sides of the Atlantic that arbitration meant alliance and the sacrifice of sovereignty as well as of national pride, British Foreign Secretary Sir Edward Grey directed Bryce to tell Knox that he would be pleased to receive a specific proposal. While he was motivated by a desire for peace, he also sought an escape valve from the obligations of the Anglo-Japanese Alliance. Yet even the leader of the opposition Conservative party, Arthur Balfour, supported such a treaty.

While peace advocates throughout the world and the churches particularly of the United States and of Great Britain cheered enthusiastically, Ireland and Germany were unhappy. Indeed, Germany asserted that the "proposed confederation" between the United States and Great Britain was a scheme aimed principally at her. British imperialists charged that Taft was motivated largely because of fear of a Japanese invasion of the United States; and Japan felt that unlimited arbitration between Great Britain and the United States spelled the end of the Anglo-Japanese Alliance.

Taft's offer to submit a treaty to any country that desired one was followed by a belated explanation that such a treaty would call for the submission of all "justiciable" differences to the Hague tribunal or some other body provided and that "nonjusticiable" differences would be submitted to commissions of inquiry composed of nationals of the two governments who were members of the Hague court. Were a commission to recommend arbitration, its decision for arbitration would be considered binding. Such a commission would, however, at the request of either government, delay its recommendations for one year to give opportunity for diplomatic settlement, and the arbitration itself would be subject to the advice and consent of the Senate.

By including France, Germany, Japan, and other nations, Taft dispelled the charge that he sought an Anglo-American alliance and heightened the sincerity of his demand for world peace. Knowing how the Senate had treated the Hay and Root treaties, Knox had specified that a two-thirds vote would be required for each specific arbitration. He also soothed many opponents by pointing out that arbitration would be used as a last resort, only if diplomatic negotiations failed. In addition, Taft spoke of the great progress toward world peace being made in the Declaration of London and in the North Pacific Sealing Convention,

Taft had not counted on Roosevelt, the Nobel Peace Prize winner who now emphatically declared that "the United States should never bind itself to arbitrate questions respecting its honor, independence and integrity." He excluded Great Britain, with whom the United States had been at peace for ninety-six years and which had reached a point in civilization where she could be trusted. In other cases, however, the United States should not give up its right to self-defense. Nor did he think much of the idea, he wrote Henry Cabot Lodge, of "allowing a commission which as you say might consist of foreigners, to take away power which belongs both to the President and the Senate," an idea he highlighted in three articles in the *Outlook*.[4] Of the European nations, Germany applauded Roosevelt most and raised questions sure to be embarrassing to Taft, as whether he would submit the immigration policy of the United States or the Monroe Doctrine to arbitration. Meanwhile, George Washington was often misquoted by American editors who spoke of his having advised the avoidance of "entangling alliances." With August 3, 1911, marked as a red-letter day by peace advocates, Knox, Bryce, and French Ambassador Jules Jusserand signed treaties of unlimited arbitration. Taft was correctly credited with the accomplishment, and most of the American press believed that the value of the treaties was so great the Senate must approve them with a minimum of deliberation.

While Taft's signing of the treaties and submitting them to the Senate was probably the most popular action of his entire administration, he and Knox overlooked the strenuousness with which the Senate would defend its constitutional prerogatives in the treaty-making process. He had not submitted the treaties for their prior consent, and many senators now spoke of them as being breeders of war rather than harbingers of peace. Other critics spoke of another "blunder by the unhappy Taft administration," one that made its "farcical incompetence" in handling Manchurian and Central American problems "appear to be inconsiderable."[5]

The majority report of the Foreign Relations Committee, written by Lodge and endorsed by all but Root and two other members, who provided a minority report, recommended that the first paragraph of the treaty, which provided for referring arbitral matters to a Joint High Commission apart from the Senate, be struck out. Furthermore, it declared that the empowering of a high court of inquiry to determine whether a question was arbitrable deprived the Senate of its constitutional power in the treaty-making process and that such policies as the Monroe Doctrine could be questioned by signatory powers. It then added an amendment offered by Senator Augustus Bacon (Democrat, Georgia), which listed issues that could not be submitted to arbitration:

> . . . the Senate would not submit to arbitration any question which affects the admission of aliens into the United States, or the admission of aliens to the educational institutions of the several States, or the territorial integrity of the several States of the United States, or concerning the question of the alleged indebtedness or moneyed obligation of any State of the United States, or any question which depends upon or involves the maintenance of the traditional attitude of the United States concerning American questions, commonly described as the Monroe Doctrine, or other purely governmental policy.[6]

Since Southern Democrats and West Coast insurgent Republicans in particular voted for the amendment, it was clear that it was designed to embarrass Taft. Thus fatally amended, the treaties with Great Britain and France both passed by a vote of 76 to 3, but they would have to be rewritten before they were resubmitted to them. With the Senate apparently putting its prerogatives above peaceful arbitration, Taft proved willing to fight hard for a matter close to his heart and determined through a vigorous speaking tour to let the people decide whether those prerogatives were more sacred than his. Alerted that he meant to cut the ground out from under them, senators stood firm. While he believed that he could more likely get the Senate to change its mind after the campaign of 1912 had ended than he could obtain agreement from abroad, the treaties were actually dead. In resignation, he stated that "we shall have to begin all over again." Later he quipped that he had hoped that "the senators might change their minds, or that the people might change the Senate; instead of which they changed me."[7]

IV

Stating that the Panama Canal was an American canal constructed mainly to increase the effectiveness of the navy, Taft demanded that it be fortified. As for the amount of toll to be charged, he wanted above all to be reasonable. Were the venture a commercial one, he would demand a return on the investment of $400,000,000, but the canal would also benefit the navy, greatly increase the trade facilities of the United States, and lower transportation rates between the East and West coasts. Therefore, he suggested a rate of $1 per ton, barely enough to cover interest charges and operating costs. He would have the government rather than private hands manage the canal, and he would prohibit American railroads from owning or controlling ships engaged in the Panama Canal trade.

During the summer of 1912 the Senate took up a bill providing for the opening of the canal. It gave the president power to fix toll rates, but prohibited him from collecting tolls from American ships engaged in the coastwise trade of the United States. Should "coastwise trade" include ships that engage in overseas trade, say, a ship that went from New York to San Francisco and on to Japan? If so, American ships would be given a national monopoly on voyages between any two American ports on different coasts, and other nations would be discriminated against. Moreover, the British read the second Hay-Pauncefote Treaty to mean that they would enjoy equality of rates with the United States, for it stated that like the Suez Canal, the Panama Canal would be open to the vessels "of all nations on terms of entire equality." Taft and most of his cabinet preferred to think that "all nations" meant "all other nations," but Root, who had sat next to Hay when the treaty was negotiated and next to Roosevelt when it was signed, disagreed and moved to strike out of the bill the provision granting special exemption to American ships. His motion defeated, the bill passed on August 9. Taft, who signed it on the fourteenth, could not see what ground Root had to stand on and wrote to Knox that he had found a "defect" in Root's career.[8] Taft suggested supplemental legislation enabling an alien to enter suit against the United States on the ground that his payment of toll was discriminatory and allowing the courts to decide the issue; but his suggestion came too late. Furthermore, Ambassador Whitelaw Reid had reported from London on August 7 that the news that the United States contemplated exempting her ships from toll payment was received "with amazement mingled with incredulity."[9] On December 11, Sir Edward Grey of the British Foreign Office formally remonstrated and suggested arbitration of the matter under the Root arbitration treaty of 1908. Now not only the tolls question but the principle of arbitration was at stake. Taft feared to submit the issue to arbitration because he felt that all of Europe was against him and that impartial judges would be impossible to find. He thus countered his own loudly touted demand for arbitration and made Britain "almost willing to see a Democratic President" in 1912.[10]

V

Mexico was far more important to the United States strategically, politically, and economically than any other Western Hemisphere country. Except for a few extradition cases, Mexican-American relations had been friendly since the United States had massed troops along the border to speed the collapse of Maximilian's empire, and Taft sent special embassies to Mexico as well as to Argentina and Chile to help celebrate the centennial anniversary of their independence from Spain. Moreover, he consented to arbitrate the question of the ownership of the Chamizal tract on the Texas-Mexican border which had been hanging fire since 1897. He did not give up hope of settlement when negotiations broke down in 1911, although he never suspected that the problem would not be settled until the late 1960s.

The eighty-year-old Porfirio Díaz, absolute ruler of Mexico, looked forward to being elected to an eighth term as president in the elections of 1910. In part because of lavish concessions granted foreigners, he had greatly increased the industrial and agricultural production of his country. American investments in Mexico had doubled between 1900 and 1910, when it was estimated that Americans owned about 43 percent of Mexico's property, other foreign nations 24 percent, and the fifteen million Mexicans the remaining 33 percent. Hence it was appropriate for the young radical idealist, Francisco I. Madero, to contest the election of 1910 with Díaz on a platform of "land for the landless and Mexico for Mexicans." Díaz had Madero arrested but, after winning the bogus election, permitted him to escape north of the border, whence he continued to call for a revolt.

Taft, who stated that Díaz had done more for the people of Mexico than any other Latin American had done for any of his people, disliked the antilandlordism and antiforeignism of Madero. He feared that the billion-dollar American investment in Mexico would be endangered if Díaz died before leaving office. Rather than making plans in anticipation of Díaz's death, he transferred Minister Henry Lane Wilson from Belgium to Mexico City and depended upon him to keep Mexican-American relations upon an even keel. Wilson had served earlier in Chile and knew Spanish and the Latin American psychology. But he was connected with large American corporations doing business in Mexico and deplored a revolution whose leaders were inspired by hatred for the United States.[11]

During revolutionary disturbances in Mexico against Díaz, some Mexicans crossed the border in various places and seized horses and supplies. Taft recognized what he called an "exceedingly delicate and difficult situation created along our southern border" and the need "for taking measures properly to safeguard American interests." At the moment, however, his primary advisers on foreign affairs were absent. Knox was on a good-will tour in Central America. Henry Wilson had gone from Washington to visit his ill mother. Moreover, Congress was in recess. "It seemed to me," he wrote Knox on March 3, "my duty was clear. Under all conditions it was quite within my province as Commander-in-Chief to order the army out for maneuvers; so I put that face upon it. . . . Simultaneously I took care to assure the Mexican authorities that the move had no significance which could be tortured into hostility to the government of Mexico. . . ."[12] He not only ordered twenty thousand troops to assemble at various posts along the Mexican-American border but directed warships and transports to mass at San Diego, California, and Guantánamo, Cuba. He made it clear, however, that there would be no intervention unless the Mexican government proved negligent in protecting American lives and property and that the troops were sent to the border to enforce the neutrality laws. Moreover, he told Army Chief of Staff Leonard Wood that troops would enter Mexico only if Congress so directed. He had enough money to conduct these "exercises" for three months, and if Mexico quieted down he would remove the troops at the end of that time. "I suppose, Mr. President," Butt said to him on May 8, "you hate to contemplate what may be the outcome of this Mexican business." Taft replied: "I'll tell you what I am going to do, Archie. I am going to sit tight on the lid, and it will take a good deal to pry me off."[13]

By the end of 1911, Taft could happily relate that his massing of American troops had had good effect in Mexico—that is, had helped Díaz by stopping filibustering expeditions and the smuggling of arms across the border. However, this first step in his seeking to insulate the United States from the Mexican civil war did not prevent Madero from finally toppling Díaz. A second step was Taft's remonstrance with both federal and insurrectionary Mexican authorities to stop their fighting in such areas as Agua Prieta, Mexico, where in April 1911, their bullets crossed the border and killed two Americans and wounded twelve others in downtown Douglas, Arizona.

After Díaz resigned, on May 25, 1911, and went into exile,

Madero was elected as president and entered upon his office on November 6, only to be faced with new insurrections. Taft never could enforce neutrality to the satisfaction of Madero or of the factions which contended with him. Madero was unable to exercise authority in various states; his impotent federal troops could not control roving bodies of brigands and insurgents led by Emiliano Zapata, Pancho Villa, and others; American property was being confiscated "through legal methods which would be a disgrace to the civilization of the Middle Ages"; and Americans were being thrown into filthy jails upon frivilous charges.[14] Acting Secretary of State Francis M. Huntington Wilson thereupon instructed Henry Wilson to insist to Madero that Americans in Mexico not be forced to surrender their arms either to his forces or to anti-Maderista insurrectionaries, but for the moment he left it up to the judgment of the Americans to decide whether their safety required them to flee Mexico. Continued civil war in Mexico soon led Huntington Wilson to state that "intervention which is not thorough and which will not secure permanent guaranties will be resented by Americans in Mexico," and to suggest that American warships be stationed off major Mexican port cities on both coasts. By early March 1912, the situation had deteriorated to the point that Taft granted him discretionary authority to warn Americans to flee areas where their lives and property were endangered. Taft, however, was as determined to let the Mexicans settle their problems in their own way and utterly to avoid intervention as he was to keep the issue out of the campaign of 1912.

When Madero and various foreign governments complained that Taft did not stem the flow of American munitions into insurgent hands, Huntington Wilson took the technically correct position that peace, not belligerency, was the legal status in Mexico, that trade in munitions was therefore permissible, and that Madero himself must enforce any laws applicable to such traffic within his own jurisdiction. Taft, however, on March 14 approved of a congressional joint resolution making the munitions traffic contraband and proclaimed that he would prosecute its violators. As Huntington Wilson quickly notified him, the prohibition extended to the Madero government as well as to its enemies. Indeed, Congress had given Taft power to make or unmake governments that depended upon American military supplies, and the anti-American feeling in Madero's camp increased. It was further exacerbated when Huntington Wilson refused to permit "exceptions" to the contraband resolution and allow Madero to obtain munitions from

177

the United States, and when Taft, following a ruling of the attorney general, included dynamite, vitally needed for mining and industrial purposes, in the contraband list and exempted only arms asked for by Americans in Mexico.

On April 14, Huntington Wilson stated that the United States "must hold Mexico and the Mexican people responsible for all wanton or illegal acts sacrificing or endangering American life or damaging American property or interests there situated."[15] Madero on the seventeenth replied that he was doing all that he could to restore order and could not be responsible for the acts of the rebel leaders. On the twentieth, Knox, now returned from his tour of Central America, snapped that if Mexico did not assume a "more obliging disposition" his department would reject further requests for exceptions for arms to reach the Madero government. A week later he asked the secretary of war to send a transport to the west coast of Mexico to receive refugees, but to avoid offense to Mexico he sent warships to Mexican ports only after Britain and France did so.

By late August, the rumor was heard that Madero, his hopes for unifying and pacifying his country dead, would resign, and on September 4 Taft had a long interview with the Mexican ambassador. He stressed American friendship for Mexico, the change in the neutrality laws that now banned the export of munitions to Mexico, thus denying them to revolutionaries, and the inability of the Mexican government to protect American lives and property. In return for American patience and friendship, he expected more hearty consideration for American interests in Mexico and more energetic and zealous action by Madero against the rebels. Indeed, were Madero not better able to protect American interests, he must ask Congress to consider how to deal with the situation. He spoke kindly, but his extreme earnestness was apparent, particularly when he said that his great patience should not be confused with weakness.

In keeping with Taft's feelings, on September 15 Henry Lane Wilson sent to the Mexican minister of foreign affairs a very long note which he deemed "a distinctly new departure" in dealing with Mexico. In it he recited all the grievances the United States could possibly have with Madero and Mexico in language certain to offend even people less sensitive than Mexicans. If Mexico did not bestir herself in setting her house in order, he concluded, she

> must furnish as promptly as possible a comprehensive and categorical statement as to the measures the Mexican

Government proposes to adopt: (I) To effect the capture and adequate punishment of the murderers of American citizens; (II) to put an end to the discriminations against American interests, . . . and (III) to bring about such an improvement in general conditions throughout Mexico that American settlers in the country will no longer be subjected to the hardships and outrages attendant upon a more or less constant state of revolutions, lawlessness, and chaos.[16]

In a sharp retort, the Mexican minister for foreign affairs denied that Mexico had been lax in fulfilling its international obligations toward American citizens (of whom forty-seven were killed between 1910 and 1912) and then brushed aside as unwarranted the accusation that the personnel of the government were not doing all possible to bring the civil war to an end.

In January 1913, while additional American warships were being sent to Mexican waters, Henry Lane Wilson prepared a draft memorandum, in keeping with the "distinctly new departure" note of September 15, 1912. In it were embodied the presentations that should be made to Mexico. This differed from an ultimatum only in that it contained no prescribed limitation of time for the performance of the specific demands made to satisfy American grievances. He did not believe in occupying Mexico, he said. However,

the American Government is reluctantly forced to state that should there not be observed an immediate improvement in the attitude of the present Government of Mexico toward American interests it will be obliged to withdraw its troops from the border, to allow the resumption of traffic in arms and ammunition across the border without restriction, and to cease its efforts to keep justly indignant foreign nations who have suffered much from Mexico in the last two years from insisting on that reparation for their wrongs which up to now only the attitude of the United States has been successful in restraining.[17]

On February 9, the not unexpected revolution against Madero began in Mexico City. On the next day, although Knox asked that several battleships be dispatched to Mexican ports to provide protection for foreigners and their interests, he indicated to Secretary of the Navy George Meyer that the request indicated no change in Taft's policy of strict impartiality between the contending factions. Two days later he asked the secretary of the treasury to help him to stop the flow of munitions to the Mexican government and so informed Taft. However, when Henry Lane Wilson requested instructions of a "menacing character" with which he might negotiate a settlement with Mexico, Taft declined to provide them lest their disregard lead to forcible intervention.

On February 14, Henry Lane Wilson met with the British, German, and Spanish ministers and concluded that even without instructions they should ask Madero to resign and turn the executive power over to his Congress, thus stopping the bloodshed and avoiding possible international complications. When the Spanish minister delivered this advice, Madero replied that he had no right to interfere in a domestic question and that he would die in defense of his rights as president rather than resign. At a personal meeting with Madero and General Victoriano Huerta on the fifteenth, Wilson won agreement on troop dispositions that would not endanger the American embassy and on an armistice during which foreigners could flee the city.

On February 17, Huerta told Henry Lane Wilson that plans were fully matured to "remove Madero from power." The knowing Wilson requested only that "no lives be taken except by due process of law."[18] True to his word, the double-crossing Huerta had Madero and his cabinet arrested and Wilson let him know that he trusted him to restore order as provisional president. "I have the honor to inform you that I have overthrown this Government. The forces are with me, and from now on peace and prosperity will reign," Huerta telegraphed Taft.[19] Upon learning of Huerta's coup, Venustiano Carranza of Coahuila was the first state governor to repudiate it and to decree that his state was sovereign and independent. The civil war was over only to begin again under new leaders, for Madero would soon be shot dead.

Should Taft recognize the new provisional government, as Henry Wilson urgently suggested? On February 21, Knox directed that recognition be extended upon receipt of assurances from Huerta that the differences between the two countries as outlined in the Department of State's note of September 15, 1912, be settled. However, when the British refused to recognize Huerta because of the murder of Madero and said they would recognize only a "permanent" rather than provisional president, Wilson was directed by Taft to follow suit. Wilson was embarrassed, for he was very friendly with Huerta, but Knox cautioned him to exercise extreme circumspection in dealing with the culpable Huerta, particularly since he had not yet furnished the required assurances with respect to settling differences with the United States. At the close of a friendly interview with the new foreign minister, Francisco de la Barra, whom he had known for years, Wilson told him that ". . . if it should become evident that I could not accomplish promptly and effectively the instructions of my government in these matters I intended to tender my resignation, as I had been working for two years to get justice and was not disposed to wait two weeks longer." To Knox he added: "This latter statement seemed to cause a profound impression, as I intended it should."[20] Because the Taft administration would end on March 3, 1913, however, Wilson had only time to join with the other members of the diplomatic corps in Mexico City and secretly offer Huerta's government an avenue of communicating with them but not to proffer formal recognition.

A man of peace, Taft had nudged Russia very lightly in the matter of her discrimination against American Jews and left the problem unsolved. Although he had settled every longstanding problem with Great Britain by amicable means and had made Britain the key to his arbitration treaty plan, he had renounced arbitration of the Panama tolls question. Despite great exertion on the hustings and upon various senators, he had been unable to sustain his contention that his prerogatives in the field of foreign affairs were better or stronger than those of the Senate. He also left the Mexican problem unsolved.

While eminently fitted by legal experience for technical negotiations, Knox appeared in the Mexican imbroglio more as an attorney for the defense than as a statesman. Equally legalistic, Taft had nevertheless been extremely sympathetic and patient with Mexico. American investors had much to lose south of the border, yet he had rejected the demands of Huntington Wilson and especially of Henry Wilson to intervene and enforce peace upon Mexico, knowing from his experiences in the Philippines and elsewhere how costly in American lives and dollars such an attempt would be. He had tried to preserve domestic order by applying the embargo on munitions to Madero's enemies alone, and by his mobilizing of troops along the border and sending warships to both coasts of Mexico he revealed his determination to protect American interests. Madero had been painfully slow in replying favorably to the demands of September 15, 1912, for the settlement of American claims against his government, even under the threat that the arms embargo might be lifted, thus permitting arms to flow to his opponents. Horrified by the assassination of Madero and the assumption of power by Huerta, Taft had found time too short in which to act before he left office. But it had been evident even in 1911 that the internecine warfare within his party took much effort and time he might have given to the Mexican problem. After his defeat in November 1912 he followed a hands-off policy lest he bequeath Woodrow Wilson a specific program.

10

★★★★★

DOLLAR DIPLOMACY

I

William Howard Taft relied heavily upon the advice of his secretary of state, Philander C. Knox, in both domestic and foreign affairs. Taft gave him full credit, telling the nation in his second annual message to Congress that "all I can claim is the merit of selecting him for the task" and adding privately that "the comfort I have in your management of the State Department I cannot exaggerate."[1] Taft may have referred to Knox's legal capacity, for he was an excellent lawyer. Yet he lacked qualities of statesmanship.

Knox's relations with Taft and with his own subordinates were excellent. Like Taft's, however, his relationships with the Senate and the press were not. Moreover, he dealt poorly with most foreign diplomats, especially those from Latin America. Detesting administrative duties, he delegated these in order to be free to engage in top-level planning. Once he had determined upon policies and plans, he let subordinates carry them out until a crisis demanded his personal intervention. The result was that he left most of the work to be done by Francis M. Huntington Wilson, the first assistant secretary. Kind to his subordinates, Huntington Wilson nevertheless had such a capacity to antagonize people that he made a poor diplomat.

Taft agreed with Knox that the Department of State needed overhauling. Knox turned the task over to Huntington Wilson, who expanded the politico-geographic divisions to include those for Western Europe, the Near East, and Latin America in the most

183

sweeping departmental reorganization since the days of Hamilton
Fish in the 1870s. Two new senior positions, of counselor and of
resident diplomatic officer, were also created. Finally, a new Division of Information provided information to overseas missions and
published the volumes of the *Papers Relating to the Foreign
Relations of the United States*. At the end of 1909, the department
consisted of 35 ranking officers, 135 clerks, and 40 menial jobholders
for a total of 210 persons. Only some twenty-five new employees
had been added, but this number represented an addition of approximately one-sixth to the department's personnel force.

Taft, Knox, and Wilson agreed upon much more than departmental reorganization. They must provide for the strategic defense of the Panama Canal, then being built, in part by promoting
the safety, peace, and prosperity of Central America and of the
Caribbean area. As for the Monroe Doctrine, said Knox bluntly,
"It does not depend upon technical right, but upon policy and
power."[2]

Taft, Knox, and Wilson were also agreed that they must not
intervene in the affairs of Europe. They would go a far step beyond the mere protection of life and property abroad, however,
and would actively support American investments overseas by both
the diplomatic and consular corps. Not only would the investments
earn profits; they would help to promote economic and political
stability in the areas of investment and would promote world peace.
Here were the ingredients of dollar diplomacy as applied to Latin
America and the Far East. Latin American nations in debt to
Europe invited forcible intervention that might challenge the independence of these nations, the Monroe Doctrine, and perhaps the
strategic security of the United States. Such intervention could be
avoided if the administration could find private American bankers
to invest in these nations funds with which to buy up the foreign
debt. The American investor now would enjoy a practically monopolized investment market, cause for European intervention and
economic competition would be removed, the more prosperous
borrower would move in the political and economic orbit of the
United States, and peace and stability would be preserved. Economic, or "nonimperialistic" imperialism, would thus supplant
territorial imperialism, and gold would replace guns. Moreover,
Pan Americanism would be supported as a device to foster peace,
the pacific settlement of disputes, and trade. Taft himself said that
"the diplomacy of the present administration has sought to respond

to the modern idea of commercial intercourse. This policy has been characterized as substituting dollars for bullets."[3]

The Latin American policy of Taft and Knox differed from that of Roosevelt and Root in motivation rather than in objective. A typical businessman's lawyer, Taft served his clients without breaking precedents or making them. In Knox he had a bird of the same feather, "a skilled lawyer whose conception of his place was that he was employed by the United States to represent her material interests [and to] push American business interests."[4] The cold logic and legal reasoning of businessmen's attorneys who in addition exhibited patronizing and supercilious manners replaced the cordiality and cooperation Elihu Root had exhibited in dealing with the nations south of the border while he was secretary of state under Theodore Roosevelt.

Roosevelt's intervening in Panama and Santo Domingo had generated a tremendous amount of ill will which Root had valiantly but not too successfully tried to overcome. While retaining Roosevelt's strategic motive for continued control of the Caribbean, Taft and Knox aggravated the Latin Americans by aggressively seeking commercial advantages particularly in Central America, in establishing financial protectorates, and in using their diplomatic and consular agents to find new fields for American enterprise. This was carried even to the point of putting pressure upon the governments of Latin America to have their warships constructed in United States yards.

In his successive annual messages to Congress, Taft detailed the progress made by using the Department of State as a field agency for commercial enterprise. It was that department, he declared in 1910, that obtained contracts from Argentina to build battleships and railway equipment and from Cuba to build various ships. He was pleased to ask Congress to continue to support the department in its efforts to expand American trade still further.[5] In 1911 he could report a gain of $300,000,000 in exports over the previous fiscal year. In his last message, of 1912, he noted that the export trade, up another $200,000,000, was a very real factor in the economic welfare of the United States. The policy of dollar diplomacy "is one that appeals alike to idealistic humanitarian sentiments, to the dictates of sound policy and strategy, and to legitimate commercial aims." It had not only increased the export trade of the United States, but, lest it be thought to have none but materialistic aims, had been used to support peace in South America, to uphold the Open Door in China, and to help such Central American countries as Nicaragua and Honduras to "help themselves" and at the same time to support the Monroe Doctrine and improve the strategic defense of the Panama Canal. To further foster American trade, he asked for legislation authorizing the establishment of American banks and branch banks abroad and for the subsidizing of the American merchant marine.[6]

In support of the derivation of the policy of dollar diplomacy, it must be said that conditions south of the border were occasionally very challenging to American interests. Particularly in Central America, politics were corrupt, economic development lagged badly, financial indebtedness was prevalent, and revolutions were endemic to those countries that did not have oppressive dictators. Colombia, Honduras, and Nicaragua are the best examples of the working of dollar diplomacy south of the border.

Root had sought an accord with Colombia in which she would be recompensed for her appreciable loss of Panama. In January 1909, the so-called Root-Cortés-Arosemena treaties were written, one between the United States and Colombia, another between the United States and Panama, and the third between Colombia and Panama. All three were to stand or fall together. While the United States and Panama promptly approved the treaties, Colombia stalled; she was so bitter toward the United States that she rejected as "inopportune" a proposed visit by Knox, who was making an official tour of Central America. She nevertheless renewed her call for the arbitration of differences. Upon receiving favorable reports from United States Minister James T. Dubois, Knox assured him in December 1912 that "direct negotiations upon some reasonable basis would now be welcome."[7]

In his first and last conference with the Colombian minister of foreign affairs, Francisco José Urrutia, Dubois offered him $10,-000,000 for Colombia's approval of the tripartite treaties, the good offices of the United States in settling Colombia's disputes with Panama, and various minor concessions. As a salve for bruised feelings he prefaced the whole with the expression that the United States "honestly regrets anything should have occurred" to interrupt international friendship. Urrutia rejected the terms. Asked what he would accept, he replied: "The arbitration of the whole Panama question, or a direct proposition from the United States to compensate Colombia for all of the moral, physical, and financial losses sustained by her because of the separation of Panama." When

Dubois inquired if that were the last word of the Colombian government, Urrutia replied simply, "Yes."[8] Two days later, Dubois raised the financial offer to $25,000,000 and dropped the request for options and privileges, but again Urrutia refused. Knox thanked Dubois for his efforts and reported them to Taft. Next day, February 28, 1913, Julio Betancourt, the Colombian minister to the United States, told Knox that since "perfect justice" was not available to his country, "there will remain no other recourse but to arbitrate."[9] Taft thus left office without settling the Colombian problem.

In a Convention of 1907, the Central American republics had pledged to settle disputes among themselves through a permanent Central American Court of Justice and also to respect the neutrality of Honduras, which was being challenged by the dictators of Nicaragua and of Guatemala and was long in arrears on interest owed to European bondholders. Although the United States and Mexico had sponsored the Convention of 1907, neither had signed it and Mexico declined to help the United States to support it. Thus, Taft and Knox proceeded unilaterally with a plan probably formulated by Huntington Wilson to seek American bankers willing to lend Honduras monies with which to liquidate her mainly English-held foreign debt of $110,000,000. The loan was to be secured by American control of the custom houses. At the same time that Lionel Carden was trying to refund obligations owed to British bondholders, representatives of J. P. Morgan and Company, J. and W. Seligman and Company, and Speyer and Company talked with Huntington Wilson, and the Morgan Company soon made arrangements with the bondholders. The British thereupon withdrew from the field. Both Taft and Knox then asked the Senate to approve of the Knox-Paredes loan convention of January 11, 1911, but the Foreign Relations Committee refused to do so.

At the behest of the administration, the American bankers had entered upon a risky loan venture which promised little profit and depended upon the official loan convention to provide for the regular payment of interest and sinking fund by an American collector general of customs. When a revolution broke out in July 1911, the landing of naval detachments from two American warships was followed by Taft's sending of special envoy Thomas C. Dawson to arbitrate differences. Despite armed intervention, the settlement of differences, and Knox's renewed pressure on the Senate to confirm the loan convention, the Morgan Company withdrew its loan proposals and the convention died. Knox complained that private American enterprise would not enter Honduras without an official treaty and offered new loan arrangements, but Honduras refused to agree to the convention. All Taft could say in his last annual message, of December 3, 1912, was that despite four years of effort no loan or convention had been made but that the administration and American bankers stood ready to aid Honduras whenever she needed help.

American relations with Nicaragua best illustrate the workings of dollar diplomacy south of the border. If American investments in Nicaragua were small, Nicaragua had an alternate canal route which must not fall into unfriendly domestic or foreign hands. Its unscrupulous dictator-president, José Santos Zelaya, became increasingly objectionable to the United States by threatening to cancel certain American commercial concessions, in one of which Knox was reported to be a heavy stockholder. He also granted unconstitutional commercial concessions to political partisans and to foreigners as well, borrowed freely from Europe, and at least hinted that he might grant canal rights to Great Britain or Japan. In October 1909, a revolt instigated and financed by American interests broke out, and three days later Juan J. Estrada became president of a provisional government.

Knox became very angry when he learned that during the revolution against him Zelaya had executed two Americans who were serving with the insurgents, saying that the United States "will not for one moment tolerate such treatment of American citizens."[10] He thereupon put into effect what was popularly called the "Hard Knox Policy." He arranged to have naval vessels speed to both Nicaraguan coasts and withdrew recognition from Zelaya. In his annual message to Congress, Taft then noted that the Panama Canal and heavy American financial investments in Central America gave the United States a "special position" in the Caribbean area and that it must restore order therein. Privately he told Knox that he was distressed over the Central American situation and wished he had "the right to knock their [governors'] heads together until they should maintain peace between them."[11]

Zelaya was succeeded by Dr. José Madriz. On March 3, 1910, both Madriz and Estrada asked the United States to mediate their differences, stating that they would agree to its designating a provisional president other than they and to holding free elections under American supervision. In addition they promised that the government would recognize the public debts incurred by the revolution and abolish the unconstitutional monopolies granted by

Zelaya. Knox refused to recognize Madriz and insured his defeat by having two gunboats prevent his reaching Estrada's rebels at Bluefields, on the ground that fighting would endanger American lives and property therein, and by having a hundred marines stationed in the city. Estrada's ragged army fought its way into the capital, Managua, on August 22, with Knox's spirit, it was alleged, marching with it. Taft denied Madriz's accusations that the continuance of strife was due to American policy, whereas he in truth had been grossly unneutral.

In September, Estrada sought recognition from the United States, promising to hold a general election within a year and to punish those responsible for the death of the two Americans. He also wished to rehabilitate the nation's finances with a loan it would seek through the Department of State, such loan to be secured by a percentage of the customs revenues. The door to dollar diplomacy having been opened, Dawson, then American minister to Panama, proceeded to Managua as the special agent of the United States to insure that Estrada's promises were effectuated. Terms were agreed upon by early November, and late that month Estrada was elected president by his Congress, and Adolfo Díaz became vice-president.

Convinced that the revolution against Zelaya represented the wishes of the majority of the Nicaraguan people and believing that the "Dawson Agreements" between Estrada and other revolutionary leaders promised political peace, Taft recognized Estrada on January 1, 1911. Knox then quickly took advantage of the terms Estrada had offered, for by stabilizing Nicaragua's finances the canal site would be safe, a secured American loan would enable Nicaragua to pay off its foreign debtors, and American control over customs collections would remove these from the grasp of would-be revolutionaries. When Estrada was overthrown on May 9, in part because of machinations by American Minister Elliott Northcott, his successor, Díaz, adhered to these terms, only to come under fire from political opponents who felt that by its prospective loan and financial arrangements the United States was helping him to remain in power. When Nicaragua finally agreed to the loan contracts, on October 11, Knox sent to Managua various financial experts and a new minister, George T. Weitzel. The consummation of the financial arrangements and peace treaties with Nicaragua's neighbors, said Taft, would provide "a complete and lasting economic regeneration . . . of inestimable benefit to the prosperity, commerce, and peace of the Republic. . . ."[12] But bad luck brewed. During widespread disorders in 1912 in which insurgents seized various American properties, Taft sent several warships and about 2,700 marines to protect American lives and property. The marines engaged in a sharp engagement at León and then occupied the capital and principal cities of the interior. Although most of them left by the end of the year, a legation guard remained—until 1933! Evidently a president could be kept in power in Nicaragua only by the use of American marines. Also, the Knox-Castrillo Convention, embodying the financial sections of the Dawson Pacts, although approved by the Díaz government, was rejected by the American Senate, to which ten additional Democrats had been added by the elections of 1910.

On May 6, 1911, the Nicaraguan Assembly had approved of a loan of up to $20,000,000 from private American sources. Taft had asked the Senate three times to approve of a loan convention with Nicaragua and of the similar one with Honduras, calling them imperative. The Senate refused to act. With Nicaragua on the verge of bankruptcy and the American Red Cross furnishing food to impoverished natives, Weitzel passed on to Washington the suggestion of Díaz for a treaty. Díaz proposed that the United States give Nicaragua $3,000,000 in return for an option upon the canal route and certain other concessions which would make Nicaragua virtually a financial protectorate of the United States, indeed permit the United States to intervene in Nicaraguan internal affairs. The proposal was distasteful not only to Díaz's opponents, who in July began a revolution against him, but to Salvador and Costa Rica as well, who said Nicaragua was transgressing their treaty rights in the canal matter. Although Taft submitted the Weitzel-Chamorro Treaty to the Senate on February 24, 1913, no action was taken on it before he left office.

Knowing that his policies were unpopular in Latin America, Knox followed Taft's suggestion and made a good-will tour of most of the Caribbean republics, including Nicaragua, early in 1912. "I beg to assure you . . ." he asserted in one speech, "that my Government does not covet an inch of territory south of the Rio Grande."[13] Fine words, but they did not conceal the fact that dollar diplomacy as practiced by him and Taft included economic imperialism, American customs control, even armed intervention.

That the substitution of dollars for bullets did not result in political stability was best illustrated in Nicaragua, where a president ruled only because he was supported by United States marines. Nor did dollar diplomacy sit well with the Senate, which defended the traditional American policy of nonintervention by refusing to approve of the treaties with Honduras and with Nicaragua in part because they contained protectorate features. Despite the stated objectives south of the border of economic improvement, political stability, and peace, dollar diplomacy added greatly to the ill will already generated by Roosevelt. Knox was largely responsible for the ill will, for as Root put it, he was "absolutely antipathetic to all Spanish-American modes of thought and feeling and action, and pretty much everything that he did with them was like mixing a Seidlitz powder."[14] Taft fully accepted Knox's advice, however, and in the end was responsible for the policy of dollar diplomacy.

Under Taft, Pan-Americanism made no progress. While Brazil attempted at the Fourth Pan-American Conference at Buenos Aires in 1910 to win an endorsement of the Monroe Doctrine, the delegates made it quite clear that they wished to limit United States influence in the Caribbean. While upholding the principle of arbitration, Knox excluded from consideration by this method such concrete cases as Colombia.

Finally, the Lodge Corollary to the Monroe Doctrine sat as badly with Latin America as it did with Taft. The superficial reason for its enunciation was to prevent foreign corporations from obtaining land grants and other concessions in Latin America. Specifically, Lodge stated that the landholdings sought by a Japanese fishing company in Lower California adjacent to Magdalena Bay might be turned over to the Japanese government. The public became excited over the issue, as did George von L. Meyer, the secretary of the navy, and the members of the General Board of the Navy. But it was Germany perhaps even more than Japan that was in Lodge's mind. Denmark had granted a concession to a private corporation to develop the harbor of St. Thomas island into a formidable naval base and the authority to sublet it. When Rear Admiral Stephen B. Luce, U.S. Navy, wrote to Lodge that "this is a notice, I presume, to Germany to keep out of the Danish West Indies rather than to Japan to keep out of Magdalena Bay,"[15] Lodge replied that "the immediate cause of the resolution was Magdalena Bay, the attempt of the Japanese, through private individuals and the medium of corporations or syndicates, to get control of it. However, I had St. Thomas in mind also. . . ."[16] Taft took the Lodge Corollary—which stated that strategic sites in the Americas could not be transferred to non-American control—to be merely an expression of opinion by the Senate that he was under no obligation to follow. Nevertheless, its enunciation caused ill feeling not only in Latin America but in Germany and Japan as well.

II

When he became president, Theodore Roosevelt was already committed by the Open Door policy to the maintenance of equal commercial opportunity in China and to the preservation of China's administrative and territorial integrity. Knowing that he could not force Great Britain, France, Germany, Japan, and Russia, all with spheres of interest in various parts of China, to abide by the Open Door, he determined to balance Great Britain and Japan, allied since 1902, against the expansionist proclivities of Russia in Manchuria and Korea. Fearing that Japan, after defeating Russia in their war of 1904–1905, might become the primary power in the Far East and close the Open Door, he adroitly succeeded at the Portsmouth Conference in getting Japan and Russia to mediate their differences. Yet he paid a price, for the terms of settlement stated that Japan would enjoy "predominant" interest in Korea and in certain formerly Russian economic interests in Manchuria. When Taft, his secretary of war, called at Tokyo in the summer of 1905, he won Japan's assent to an agreement in which she would take over Korea on her promise of nonaggression towards the Philippines. If the Open Door was maintained in Manchuria, Roosevelt had permitted its closing in Korea, with Taft as his agent.

The Taft-Knox policies for the Far East were logical extensions of those of Roosevelt and Root. But Taft and Knox went beyond their predecessors by using the Open Door not only as a political means to protect China but also to insure that the door would remain open in the future for the export of excess American production and to allow America to acquire financial supremacy in China and Manchuria. If they found little European competition in creating an American financial hegemony in Latin America, they challenged vested European and Japanese interests in the Far East. In addition, rather than seeking to conciliate Japan, as Roosevelt had done, they exacerbated Japanese-American relations by trying to strengthen China so that she could resist foreign encroachments. Unable to force enough private American capital where it would not go of its own accord, they naïvely hoped to receive support from Britain and Europe. In the end, their bullying yet clumsy tactics not only failed to achieve their objectives but also raised questions about their motives.[17]

United States trade with the Far East when Roosevelt became president, while second only to that of Great Britain, never fulfilled the loudly touted claims of the expansionists of 1898. Trade with China, for example, amounted to only $20,000,000, or less than 10 percent of American trade. Among the most important American firms in China during Roosevelt's presidency was the American China Development Company, a railroad-building syndicate including E. H. Harriman, J. P. Morgan, and Jacob Schiff. An important adviser to this company was Willard Straight, American consul general in Mukden from 1906 to 1908. When brought home to serve as chief of the Division of Far Eastern Affairs of the Department of State, he carried with him plans for the purchase of the Chinese Eastern Railway from Russia and the South Manchurian Railway from Japan. If Japan did not sell, a competing road would be built from Chinchow to Aigun. While Roosevelt rejected his plans, Taft, Knox, and Huntington Wilson accepted them with alacrity. Straight, now the representative of Kuhn, Loeb and Company in China, linked the Department of State with the American bankers, and at the invitation of the department these bankers organized the American Banking Group for China.

The Manchu dynasty had long proved unable to fend off western imperialism. It had submitted to the creation of spheres of interest following China's defeat by Japan in 1895, and in 1907 the rapprochement of Russia and Japan and an agreement by them with Britain practically closed the door in North China, Korea, and Mongolia. Apparently the only remaining instrument left with which to counter Russia and Japan was military power, but this Taft would not use. Nevertheless, his interest in the Far East provoked a reorganization of both the diplomatic and consular branches of the Department of State and a reorganization of the naval fleets. His administration was marked by an attempt to expand American financial and political influence in China, and a coming of age, as it were, of the United States as a Pacific power.

Because of his personal knowledge of the Far East and acquaintance with its political leaders, Taft was expected to have a very large voice in the determination of policy for that area. China looked to him for protection especially from Japan and Great Britain and for loans for railroad construction, currency reform, education, and other undertakings. The Japanese were equally sure that he would grant generous terms on the immigration rights of Japanese to the United States and upon other matters when the expiring American-Japanese treaty of amity and commerce came to be rewritten in 1911.

Taft would neither give up American rights of extraterritoriality nor heed China's requests that the law barring the naturalization of Chinese in the United States be rescinded. On the other hand, he carefully noted Japan's attempt to continue her encroachment upon Manchuria. When, for example, an agreement signed between China and Japan on September 4, 1909, gave Japan joint mining rights near the Mukden-Antung Railroad, Knox asked whether the mining privilege was a monopoly or would be extended to Americans and other foreign nationals. China mollified him by saying that third parties could be admitted if they found minerals in the area.

Late in May 1909, meanwhile, Knox had learned that a British, French, and German consortium had offered to lend China funds for the construction of a portion of the Hankow-Szechuen Railway —the Hukuang Loan—and asked China whether American capital would be admitted into it. When the Chinese Foreign Office said that it was "probably too late"—the agreement had been initiated in the previous September—but that China welcomed American capital investments, Knox retorted that the United States had not relinquished the right granted it in 1904 to provide loans to China. He also directed Ambassador Whitelaw Reid, at London, to tell British Foreign Secretary Sir Edward Grey that the addition of the United States to the consortium was necessary to protect the Open Door.[18] When members of the consortium suggested that his request had come too late, Knox told China that she was showing an unfortunate lack of appreciation for the consideration the United States had long shown her. He then authorized Chargé Henry Fletcher, at Peking, to sign the agreement on behalf of the American Group he had quickly gotten together and demanded to know how much railroad building material the United States could supply for the project.

When the European and American bankers failed to agree and China urged the conclusion of the original agreement, Taft took an unusual step and cabled Prince Chun, the young Prince Regent of the Chinese Empire, for equal participation by American capital in the railway loan, adding that

I have an intense personal interest in making the use of American capital in the development of China an instrument for the promotion of the welfare of China, and an increase in her material prosperity without entanglements or creating embarrassments affecting the growth of her independent political power and the preservation of her territorial integrity.[19]

On the same day, Knox "warned" China that the American Group would gain admission to the consortium as a matter of "dignity and moral right" and that if the foreign bankers did not agree to American participation the United States would welcome an opportunity to arrange for the whole loan.[20]

On July 18, Taft waxed happy when the prince regent told him that he soon could expect a favorable decision. However, dickering over details continued between the consortium representatives, so that it was not until May 1911 that Knox won his point and all parties concerned agreed to American participation.

On October 7, 1909, Chargé Fletcher sent Knox a copy of a preliminary agreement by the viceroy of Manchuria, the governor of Fengtien, the American Group, and the British construction firm of Pauling and Company, for the financing, construction, and operation of a railway from Chinchow to Aigun in Manchuria. A month later, Knox cabled Ambassador Reid, with information copies to the American ambassadors in Russia, France, and Germany, to obtain Grey's reaction to a daring new plan by which to support the Open Door in Manchuria. This plan, drafted by Straight, would, according to Knox, "bring the Manchurian highways, the railroads, under an economic, scientific, and impartial administration by some plan vesting in China the ownership of the railroads through funds furnished for that purpose by the interested powers willing to participate."

"Audacious," "grandiose," "fantastic," said some Americans; a violation of the traditional policy of isolation, said others.[21]

By an earlier arrangement with Russia, Great Britain had agreed not to build railroads north of the Great Wall if Russia would not build south of it. Now Grey told Knox that China should be aided by an international consortium to acquire and control foreign-dominated railroads in Manchuria, that the creation of another international consortium should await the conclusion of the Hukuang Loan, and that Knox should have China admit Japan into the building of the Chinchow-Aigun line. Knox sounded out not only Japan but Russia, Germany, and France. Although China's leaders saw that the neutralization proposal could put China under the joint control of the participating powers, they believed that Manchuria was lost anyway and took Knox's suggestion as a misguided but sincere attempt to help China. American economic interests in Manchuria were insufficient to warrant strong diplomatic support, however, and in the end Knox's "essential hypocrisy" in using the Open Door as a financial weapon was detected and he was defeated by diplomatic means. Japan and Russia strenuously objected to the obvious challenge to their primacy in Manchuria. Moreover, if Germany took a "lively interest" in Knox's proposal, France could not see any challenge to the Open Door by either the Japanese or the Russians in Manchuria.

Russia controlled 1,100 miles of track in north Manchuria, Japan, 500 in the south. Both now notified China that they must be consulted before agreeing to the construction of the Chinchow line, for it would parallel Japan's South Manchurian Railway and Russia was extremely unhappy with its leading toward her undefended frontier at Aigun. China thereupon declared that in keeping with an agreement with Russia of 1899 of which Knox was unaware, any railway built from Peking to the north or to the northeast toward the Russian border would be built by Chinese capital under Chinese supervision or, if built by any other nation, by Russia. Knox pressured Russia to reconsider and at least to agree to the building of the first stages of the line out of Chinchow, and China put a survey party to work with its report expected in July. By this time everyone knew that Knox's plan was dead.

In his annual message to Congress of December 6, 1910, Taft noted that American capitalists had succeeded in lending money to China and that negotiations for a currency reform loan were almost concluded. If Knox's plan to neutralize the Manchurian railroads was opposed by Japan and Russia, the Chinchow-Aigun project was "still the subject of friendly discussion." In mid-March 1911, he learned that Straight, who represented the American-Chinese Syndicate, had finally won China's agreement to the currency reform loan and was trying to overcome China's objection to the appointment of an American financial adviser on the ground that its sovereignty would be violated.

How well, then, had Taft and Knox helped China? How well had they supported the Open Door? By the late spring of 1911 both the Hukuang Loan and the Currency Loan negotiations had been concluded. The Hukuang Loan earned the American Group barely enough profit to pay its cable bills, but its signing had helped provoke a revolutionary outbreak in China. When Yuan Shih-k'ai, provisional president of the Chinese Republic, sought loans with which to finance military operations against the rebels, loans which the American Group would not make, he turned elsewhere, and by wishing to support him against the rebels Knox seemed to counter the American public demand for the recognition of a Chinese republic.

Unlike the other major Pacific powers, the United States had neither pressing security considerations nor great economic interests in China. Taft and Knox nevertheless had sought to give "new life and practical application" to dollar diplomacy by an economic penetration of China that would secure the United States a strong position therein. It turned out to be nothing but a "shopkeeper diplomacy."[22] The Manchurian railroad neutralization proposal particularly had an aura of the big stick and, instead of gaining the entry of American capital into Manchuria, drove Japan and Russia and their respective allies Great Britain and France into a close defensive alliance. The American Group had cooperated with the administration in seeking to invest in an area where American capital would not go of its own accord. Since it made little if any profit, Taft and Knox revealed their inability to separate private from national interest.

Finally, the dollar diplomacy policy had provoked such criticisms as that Taft, like Lord Curzon with respect to India and Lord Cromer in India and Egypt, had become "Orientalized." Sent by Roosevelt to "subjugate a dependency in Asiatic waters," he had lost touch with democratic processes and become a despot, even though a benevolent one. Knox also had his detractors at home and abroad, who charged that he never meddled but he muddled, that he lacked the imaginative faculty, that he blundered, was utopian, naïve and the like, and that instead of supporting the Open Door he had brought Japan and Russia closer together in common defense of their Manchurian interests than they had been since the Portsmouth Conference.

Additional proof of the "American Defeat in the Pacific" came in statistics portraying declining American exports to China from $58,000,000 in 1905 to $15,500,000 in 1910. While Japan and Germany had increased their trade with China and Britain had held her own, the United States had fallen far behind because she had not successfully blended diplomacy with economic policy. Thus, it was alleged, she left the sale and distribution of her cottons, flour, steel, and the like in the hands of foreigners, gave no official support to her traders, as in subsidizing her merchant marine, and offered financing in no fields outside of railroads.[23]

Taft kept a sharp eye upon efforts being made to change the imperial government of China into a constitutional republic. Provincial assemblies were to be organized in 1909 and a new constitutional assembly was to be opened in 1910, with a two-house parliament to begin functioning in 1913. Frequent antigovernment and antiforeign riots in 1909 and 1910, which threatened American lives and damaged American property, caused him to use the ships of the Pacific Squadron—after 1910 of the Asiatic Fleet—in defense and to use the American diplomatic and consular corps to seek indemnification for losses incurred. Then, on December 29, 1911, revolutionary leaders chose Dr. Sun Yat-sen as provisional president of the Republic of China. In consequence of this revolution, the Manchu Emperor abdicated, on February 12, 1912, and appointed Yuan Shih-k'ai to organize a republican form of government. Dr. Sun abdicated in Yuan's favor and a call was issued for holding a constitutional convention late in 1912.

The Manchu government's weakness in permitting Russia and Japan to expand in Manchuria, widespread fear that foreign powers were planning to partition China, the granting of railroad building concessions to foreigners, and the acceptance of foreign loans were some of the causes of the revolution. As Minister John Calhoun told Knox on February 12, 1912, the English and Japanese worked together, as did the French and Russians, leaving the Germans and Americans very much to themselves. Moreover, the other foreigners suspected that Taft and Knox sought special privileges in China which they would not share with them. With cogent reasoning he added with reference to the American Open Door policy: "Diplomacy, however astute, however beneficent and altruistic it may be, if it is not supported by the force which not only commands but demands respect and consideration, will avail but little."[24] Overseas Chinese asked Taft to remain neutral in the movement to establish popular government in China while the Chinese foreign minister hoped that the United States would urge international intervention in order to prevent selfish independent action by any one power. Should the United States follow a unilateral policy of recognition or, as the other five major powers operating in China suggested, act in concert and recognize only a government pledged to maintain order, to respect treaties in force, and to assume its foreign debts? Although the House of Representatives on February 29 passed a resolution wishing the Chinese godspeed in their attempt to establish a republican form of government, Knox warned Americans in China that this resolution was not to be equated with recognition, proceeded to deal with China on a de facto basis, and opted for concerted action, thereby denying the administration any flexibility in the matter.

Under pressure from American public opinion to recognize the provisional government of China unilaterally, on July 20, 1912, Knox asked the powers whether they believed it to be stable enough to merit formal recognition. The replies were negative. On January 2, 1912, however, Senator Augustus Bacon, of Georgia, had introduced a joint resolution providing for the immediate recognition of Yuan's government as being representative, permanent, and stable, which in fact it was not, and his supporters argued that the administration was violating the traditional American policy of recognizing de facto governments. Taft stated in his annual message of 1912 that the United States was, according to precedent, maintaining de facto relations with the provisional government *pending* the completion of the steps leading to a republican form of government—but by this time the shadow of the Wilson administration lay over Washington.

Taft followed Roosevelt's policy with respect to the exclusion of Chinese and Japanese immigration. The Japanese immigration "menace," almost exclusively a problem to the West Coast states, was handled by Taft in the rewriting of the expiring Japanese-American treaty of commerce and navigation. This was signed on February 21, 1911, and ratified and proclaimed as in effect on April 5, 1911. Article I was quite specific in the matter of reciprocal treatment of nations:

> The citizens or subjects of each of the High Contracting Parties shall have liberty to enter, travel and reside in the territories of the other to carry on trade, wholesale and retail, to own or lease and occupy houses, manufactories, warehouses and shops, to employ agents of their choice, to lease land for residential and commercial purposes, and generally to do anything incident to or necessary to trade upon the same terms as native citizens or subject, submitting themselves to the laws and regulations there established.[25]

Nothing was thus said about the right of land ownership. The treaty, however, had been written on the understanding that the American prohibition upon the immigration of Japanese into the United States remained unchanged from the regulations established in Roosevelt's Gentlemen's Agreements and that Americans could own land in Japan and Korea if the United States obtained the consent of its states to reciprocity in the matter. Rather than seeing this arrangement as a courteous deference to Japanese national pride, the people of the West Coast flared up. The California Senate urged Taft to withdraw the treaty from the Senate and also asked the Senate not to approve of "a compact fraught with so much danger to our citizens, to our industrial development, and to our civilization." Taft wired Governor Hiram Johnson that the arrangements on immigration were the same as those he had explained to him earlier in person, Pacific Coast senators to whom he explained the situation quieted their people down, and Japan was satisfied that the restriction of immigration rested with her and she would not suffer the humiliation of having it enforced by the United States. During Taft's last days in office, however, California proposed to permit land ownership only to "aliens eligible to citizenship under the laws of the United States," thereby barring Japanese and other Orientals. As with the case of the recognition of China, however, the crisis arose so late in his term that Taft left its solution to the incoming Wilson administration.

11

★★★★★

COMMANDER IN CHIEF

I

One might assume that because William Howard Taft had been secretary of war, as president he would take special interest in the army. This was not the case. Rather than increasing the size of the army, he wished to economize in government spending. Nor did he strongly support recommendations for reforms in army organization suggested by his first secretary of war, Jacob M. Dickinson. A tremendous amount of political infighting over organizational and administrative doctrine took place during his term in both the army and Congress. In the battle between conservatives and reformers with respect to army reorganization, he tended to side with the reformers, who were led by his second secretary of war, Henry L. Stimson, and Chief of Staff Leonard Wood. The result was that if the army was not quite ready to fight a successful war, it verged upon being made so.

Except for aid given Philippine civil authorities to chastise some unruly Moros, the army engaged in no operations worthy of mention in 1909. At the time, it was short 7,350 of the 81,778 officers and men authorized by law. In an address at Gettysburg on May 31, 1909, Taft paid tribute to the regular army. However, in his annual message, of December 7, he stated that he had lowered the War Department estimates for fiscal year 1910 by $45,000,000 over 1908 in the interest of immediate economy even if this cut would suspend for the year "all progress in military matters." The measure would be temporary, until the revenues improved, and he promised to send Congress special suggestions for a "definite military policy."[1]

When Taft failed after several months to furnish Congress his promised "definite military policy," Representative James Mc-Lachlin introduced a resolution calling upon the secretary of war to submit to the Military Affairs Committee "information concerning national defense . . . with the least possible delay."[2] Just at this time Major-General Leonard Wood succeeded Major-General J. Franklin Bell as chief of staff of the army. Wood, not yet fifty years of age, had commanded Theodore Roosevelt's Rough Riders and for years had preached reform with the zeal of a religious crusader. An avowed Republican, he had good political support from such friends as Elihu Root and Henry Cabot Lodge and particularly from Roosevelt, and Taft acknowledged that he named him to be chief of staff because "Roosevelt was anxious to have it done."[3] What kind of an army did he head?

Whoever read the annual reports of the secretary of war, books such as Homer Lea's *The Ignorance of Valor* (1909), the *Army and Navy Journal,* and the *Infantry Journal* knew that the army was underofficered, deficient in specially trained men, unprepared for field service, and out of date in its transportation because no automobiles or trucks were being used.

Not long after succeeding Dickinson, Stimson asserted that the army was unprepared for anything but peace, the major reason being the post system. Forty-nine posts, located during Indian troubles that no longer existed or in answer to local political demands, were scattered over twenty-four states and territories. Since most of them were unable to support more than a single regiment and only one could handle a brigade, concentration was impossible. Therefore he recommended that units be concentrated, that terms of enlistment be shortened from three to two years in order to build up a cadre of reserves, and that more shells be furnished for field guns. He was of course parroting Wood's ideas. However, as with the tariff and public works appropriations, congressmen with posts in their districts saw economy as a noble thing when practiced elsewhere but deplorable when it touched home.

As soon as Wood entered his new office, on July 19, 1910, he prepared an "Answer" to the McLachlin resolution. Wood stated that the army was undermanned, short of munitions, had poor quartermaster and commissary departments and an even poorer militia, and was so badly organized as to be unable to concentrate. Moreover, a permanent Council of National Defense was needed.

His conclusions were supported by an appendix replete with devastating statistics.

Although Dickinson, still secretary, fully agreed with the Answer, Wood sent a copy of it to Taft's secretary late in November in hope that Taft would use it in writing his annual report to Congress. Anxious to increase the army's appropriations, he sent copies to various congressmen and also obtained Dickinson's permission to give copies to the press associations. Thus the people, aroused over the poor status of national defense, would demand his reforms. But when Representative Richmond Pearson Hobson asked James A. Tawney, chairman of the Appropriations Committee, to support the suggestions in Wood's Answer, Tawney rushed to the White House to demand if Taft had approved of it. Taft said he knew nothing about it, for it still lay in his secretary's desk. Tawney then warned Taft that it would upset the public and force the lid on appropriations. With his budget in the red, the public concerned about the high cost of living, his stock low as a result of the elections of 1910, and several arbitration treaties being negotiated, Taft too became alarmed. He vetoed the Answer as politically inexpedient and asked the press associations not to print it. But in giving testimony before the House Committee on Military Affairs, on December 14 and 15, Wood was able to make public the Answer Taft wished kept secret. Taft became angry, overlooking the fact that there was negligence in his own office. Calling Dickinson to the White House, he reprimanded him for the "indiscretion" of his subordinate, Wood, then reprimanded Wood himself.

Since what Wood was saying was common knowledge at home and abroad, military men applauded him and sneered at Taft, whose attempt to suppress the Answer had advertised the army's weakness throughout the world. Taft slammed back with a speech on December 17 in which he charged that some men would start a war scare in order to force defense appropriations from Congress. He not only was satisfied with the current defense posture; he also assumed that the arbitration treaties being negotiated would make war less possible than ever before.

The flurry now over, Wood settled down to seeking an effective defense and to reorganizing the army to make it more efficient. In so doing he faced the opposition of Major General Frederick Ainsworth, the bureau chiefs, and their congressional supporters.

At the apex of the army stood the general staff. This was composed of a chief of staff and forty-four other officers freed of administrative duties in order that they might make policy, prepare plans for national defense and for mobilization in time of war, report on the state of preparation for military operations, and perform whatever tasks the president might prescribe. Until Wood became chief of staff, the general staff was divided into three divisions lacking clearly defined duties. Moreover, certain offices, like those of the inspector general and the Bureau of Pensions and Records, were not included in its purview. The result was a spate of committees and subcommittees that engaged in little beyond busy work while Ainsworth, who according to Taft's military aide, Archibald W. Butt, had "more personal influence in Congress than any man in the government, including the President of the United States," ran the army and challenged Wood's authority to do so.[4] A similar situation existed within the Army War College, which was charged with aiding the general staff to prepare plans for national defense. Wood reorganized the general staff into four divisions—the Mobile Army, Militia Division, Coast Artillery, and War College Division—and put in charge of each an assistant chief of staff who would take action on routine matters without referring them to his personal attention. Then, in keeping with Taft's Efficiency Commission, he established a War Department Board on Business Methods, Ainsworth chairman, to recommend procedures that would effect economies. A prime target was Ainsworth's own office, which spewed out and received tons of paper work. Ainsworth declared open war, but the amount of paper work dropped immediately and the Army War College began to prepare war plans rather than writing additional memoranda. By thus having the general staff act as a coordinating agency, Wood of course intruded upon administrative details and even upon operations.

Rather than training only a few elderly professionals, Wood would train large numbers of young men and discharge them into a reserve force. In contrast, military conservatives and West Point graduates preferred to have enlistments raised to five years and to encourage reenlistments. Among Wood's opponents were Ainsworth, Ainsworth's good friend James Hay (Democrat, Virginia), chairman of the House Military Affairs Committee, and officers in the field, men Wood charged were "stupid fools."[5] But in 1912 these "stupid fools" compromised by establishing two enlistment plans, one for four years without reserve duty and one for three years of active duty and four more with the reserves. That the latter failed to appeal was demonstrated when after two years there were only sixteen men in the reserve force.

With the backing of Taft and of Stimson, Wood meanwhile used general orders to decentralize authority away from Washington and to liberalize the army's penal system. More importantly, he tried to make the army mobile and capable of concentrating by improving its tactical organization. A test was provided when Taft personally directed Wood on March 6, 1911, to send a division, twenty thousand men, or a fourth of the entire army, to patrol the Mexican border from the mouth of the Rio Grande to San Diego. A mobilization which should have been completed in five days took ten, with maximum strength not achieved for almost ninety. Because most of the men were from Fort D. A. Russell, Cheyenne, Wyoming, the commander from Washington, the chief of staff from New York, and staff officers from all over the country, they did not work well together in improvising a division administration and supply system. This poor performance led Wood to divide the army into four districts, one of which was in the Philippines, and to subdivide them into departments. Each district would contain all the necessary adjuncts to form a division; each district commander was also charged with the supply and administration of his division. Thus each division could move and operate independently of the others. One order to a division commander would be enough to have him use that brigade or those divisional units needed to accomplish his tasks. By late 1911, Wood's reforms made it possible to speak of a new, progressive army.

In contrast to the mobilization of 1911 was that of early 1913. At 2:00 A.M., one morning, Wood received a call to go to the White House, where Taft was talking with Secretary of State P. C. Knox, Secretary of the Navy George Meyer, Stimson, and Rear Admiral Bradley A. Fiske, Meyer's aide for operations. The American embassy had been fired upon in Mexico City. How long, Taft asked Stimson, would it take him to organize a relief expedition? Stimson replied that all he had to do was to send a telegram to the commanding general of the division nearest the troop transports at Newport News, Virginia, who would have his men on their way to Veracruz within a few hours.

Despite Stimson's support, Wood's attempt to shift army posts to more strategically located places so as to make concentration possible ran into local and congressional hostility. When Wood said he would abandon eighteen posts immediately and seven more as soon as possible, congressmen faced with losing posts banded together. They attached a rider to an army appropriation bill that created by name a commission of five officers and two members of each house of Congress to report on the location and distribution of army posts, and forbade the president from changing existing posts until the commission submitted its report. Furthermore, it limited the term of enlistments, reestablished the office of adjutant general as the key post in the War Department, and in other ways countered the recommendations of Wood, Stimson, and Taft. Finally, it provided that no line officer could be chief of staff unless he had served at least ten years in grades below brigadier general. As Root told the Senate, "The provision could not better accomplish its purpose if it read that . . . no man whose initials are L. W. shall be Chief of Staff."[6]

In order to obtain Taft's support for his plans and especially for the removal of Ainsworth from his post, Wood took Archie Butt into his confidence. Butt opposed his plans yet wanted to avoid a Wood-Ainsworth quarrel that might mushroom into another controversy like those between Ballinger and Pinchot and between Wickersham and Wiley. Taft saw the point and told Butt to hint to Wood to avoid providing the administration with a scandal in the War Department.

Ainsworth so resisted Wood's directives in so many matters in the summer of 1911 that Stimson assumed responsibility in the battle. With the concurrence of Taft and Root, he contemplated having Ainsworth court martialed for insubordination and sent him home to await orders. "Stimson, it has fallen to you to do a dirty job which your predecessors ought to have done before you," said Taft. Ainsworth escaped a possible court martial and saved Taft a lot of trouble by offering to resign his commission, at which Taft chuckled and happily agreed.[7] Harmony now reigned in the War Department because victory for the general-staff concept heightened Wood's control over the bureau chiefs.

Hay slapped back with an investigation by his committee. Its report naturally upheld Ainsworth against Wood, Stimson, and Taft, and the authority of Congress rather than of the president over the army. With just two weeks before the end of the fiscal year in which to consider the army appropriation bill, Taft was in a dilemma. If he vetoed the bill, delegates who favored Wood might line up for Wood's friend, Roosevelt, in the Republican national convention. If he signed it, the popular Wood would be ousted as chief of staff. In a courageous move, he vetoed the bill and may have gained some political advantage by doing so. Unwilling to leave the troops unpaid, Congress passed the original bill without the rider, thereby saving Wood but lessening the support

Taft could expect from conservatives in the national convention. Moreover, Congress would not vote sufficient monies to put Wood's reform program into operation.

Rebuffed by Congress, Stimson and Wood nevertheless went on record with a study made by the War College Division of the general staff entitled "Report on the Organization of Land Forces of the United States." Stimson then directed Wood to suggest an adequate military policy. In July 1912, Stimson, Wood, various congressmen, and a military historian named Frederick Huidekoper held a series of conferences at the War Department on principles of military organization, how best to reorganize the army with the men and materials at hand, and what could be done in the future to improve the army. The result was that "for the first time in our history a sound and definite policy in respect to the military branch of our services was formulated," asserted Huidekoper.[8] In addition to endorsing Wood's reform program, the "Stimson Plan" asked for the definition and implementation of a comprehensive defense policy. While the navy must defeat enemy forces far at sea and defend home ports, the army must back up local defense and also hold the Philippines as long as possible until the fleet reached the far side of the Pacific. Only a highly trained army could defeat other trained armies, the report went on, and enough soldiers must be at hand to protect the overseas dependencies of the United States. Although many copies of the report went to members of Congress as well as to regular and National Guard officers, Congress failed to act on the report until 1915, when the Wilson administration undertook its preparedness program and used it in part to win approval for the National Defense Act of 1916. Meanwhile, Congress increased appropriations for providing more and better army horses, fortifications and munitions for the Panama Canal, and $100,000 with which to start an army air service.

II

As with the army, so with the navy, Taft kept tight reins upon appropriations. Even if only tangentially involved, he supported Secretary of the Navy Meyer and those naval officers who desired a general naval staff rather than conservatives who would retain the old bureau system. As parsimonious with the navy as with the army, Congress declined to provide enough money for ships or dry docks or for bases in the Middle and Western Pacific. Largely because of reforms instituted by Meyer with Taft's blessing, the navy reached a high peak in efficiency. Although the navy of 1913 was considered to be sufficiently strong to protect the widespread interests of the United States, Taft let it drop a notch as a world naval power.

With the exception of the General Board of the Navy (hereafter cited as the G. B.) created in 1900 by a Navy Department General Order, the organization of the Department of the Navy at Taft's inauguration differed little from that of 1842, when the first five bureaus were established. The civilian secretary must depend for the carrying out of the recommendations of the G. B. upon the—now eight—firmly entrenched bureau chiefs, who courted happy relations with Congress because it appropriated their funds and approved their nominations to four-year terms. Efforts to force the bureaus to cooperate, as by providing for a general staff over them that would plan for war and direct it when it came, sat badly with those who feared being "Prussianized" and especially with the quasi-independent bureau chiefs. Moreover, in the absence of higher administrative levels, any squabble between the secretary and his leading officers must be referred to the president. Too, the fact that secretaries came and went, with Roosevelt, for example, using six in seven years, meant that they were not in their job long enough either to learn it or to place restraints upon the bureau chiefs. An exception came with Taft's appointment of Meyer, who remained in office throughout his term, and who through a system of aides, as discussed below, sought to insure that the recommendations of the G. B. would be carried out by the bureaus.

Admiral of the Navy George Dewey remained as president of the G. B. from its inception until his death in 1917. He was also chairman of the Joint Board of the Army and Navy, created in 1903, which dealt with all matters calling for the cooperation of the two services. While he favored a slow, "evolutionary" approach toward establishing a general naval staff, he looked kindly upon certain insurgent officers, especially Stephen B. Luce, Alfred Thayer Mahan, Richard Wainwright, Albert Lenoir Key, Philip Andrews, William Sowden Sims, and Fiske, who demanded a "revolutionary" approach. To this end, some of them, especially Sims, criticized everything they could find wrong with the navy in the hope of popularizing their favored reform. In best position to influence Meyer to adopt a general staff was the great naval inventor Fiske, who late in Taft's term became aide for operations.

Naval war plans made by the G. B. with the aid of the Office of Naval Intelligence were tested at the Naval War College. With the same membership as that established in 1900, the G. B. under Taft could not produce plans to protect the worldwide interests of the United States and the employment of naval forces three times more numerous than those of 1900. More importantly, many of the plans simply could not work because the bureaus were unwilling or unable to provide the men, ships, and weapons they called for.

The G. B. based its plans in Taft's day, as in Roosevelt's, upon the assumption that war with the nations of Latin America, with Great Britain, or with France was inconceivable, and that war was most probable with Germany in the Atlantic Ocean and with Japan in the Pacific. Since it did not envisage a war against both simultaneously, it kept 70 percent of the battleships in the Atlantic. In 1906, however, in keeping with Roosevelt's policy to keep the fleet concentrated, all battleships were stationed in the Atlantic, and on March 3, 1909, he gave Taft his "one closing legacy," that is, "Under no circumstances divide the battleship fleet between the Atlantic and Pacific oceans prior to the finishing of the Panama Canal. . . . There were various factors which brought about Russia's defeat [in 1905] but most important by all odds was her having divided her fleet between the Baltic and the Pacific. . . ."[9]

The Black (Atlantic) War Plan assumed that in case of war between America and Germany, an American and German fleet engagement would take place somewhere in the Caribbean near Culebra, Puerto Rico. A very general plan which sought to cover numerous contingencies, it was recommended for study by fleet commanders but not imposed upon them, for they were expected to exercise their own initiative in their operations.

The Orange (Asiatic) War Plan, completed late in 1906, recognized the weakness of the United States in the Pacific. Some ships of the Pacific Fleet, which was based upon the west coast of the United States, were organized as the Asiatic Squadron when stationed in the western Pacific. The power they could exert against Japan was small indeed, even after they were reconstituted as the Asiatic Fleet for strategic and administrative reasons in 1910. The plan therefore called for the stout defense of Guam and for the army to hold Corregidor as long as possible while American warships withdrew to Hawaii. Those ships would wait for reinforcements from the Atlantic Fleet before countering the Japanese fleet and then reconquering the Philippines, which it was presumed had fallen to the Japanese. Part of the weakness in the Pacific stemmed from the unwillingness of Congress to appropriate funds for the ships needed there or for the logistic support necessary for extended operations. Congress refused, for example, to build and maintain adequate Pacific coast navy yards and forward bases at Guam and in the Philippines as recommended by the G. B. Another part of the problem was the continuing interservice squabble in which Taft, as secretary of war, had supported the army in demanding the use of Manila Bay while the navy wanted to use Subic Bay, with the result that nothing was done at either place. As president, Taft still favored Manila; therefore the navy let do with what it had at Subic and at defenseless Guam but planned to build up Pearl Harbor from a mere coaling station to the "Gibraltar of the Far East" by 1913. Another weakness in the war planning process stemmed from the paucity of the naval attachés sent abroad and the poor information they often sent home.

The time was rapidly approaching, the Joint Army and Navy Board told Taft in November 1909,

> when because of the increased size of the battle ship fleet it may be divided and a part of it stationed in the Pacific. Such a fleet, more powerful than that of any possible enemy in the Pacific, and based on the Pacific yards and on the new naval station which is being developed at Pearl Harbor, would control the Pacific and provide a strategic defense against the invasion of the Philippines by land.[10]

However, with Germany displacing Japan as the prime threat after 1911, with Roosevelt's parting advice to keep the fleet concentrated in mind, and with the completion of the Panama Canal in the offing, Taft kept the fleet concentrated in the Atlantic.

If Navy Department organization remained largely unchanged until the advent of Taft and Meyer, the same cannot be said about the numbers and kinds of American warships. In 1902, based upon battleship and cruiser strength, the United States ranked seventh among the world's naval powers. In 1903, the G. B. stated that the navy should have a fleet strength one and a half times that of Germany and recommended a building program which by 1920 would provide forty-eight battleships, major indices of naval power, and the other ships needed to make up a balanced fleet. According to this program, two battleships must be built each year through 1919. When a given twenty-year life was taken into account, however, more than two a year must be built. The new dreadnought type must also be considered.

In consequence of Roosevelt's policy of building at least one first-class battleship a year, by 1907 the United States had advanced from third to second place as a world naval power. In 1908, when Germany's amended Fleet Law called for overtaking the United States in dreadnoughts, the G. B. called for the building of four battleships and thirty-seven ships of other types. However, Congress failed to provide the funds and continued its control over the building program by the practice of making only annual appropriations. In 1912, Dewey called for an "emergency" building program to cost $100,000,000 each year. Meyer approved, for he would equal the strength of the German fleet; but Congress did not.

The *Delaware,* completed in 1910, was the first American dreadnought and the most powerful ship in the world. She displaced twenty-one thousand tons, had a top speed of twenty-one knots, and had a main battery of ten twelve-inch guns. In contrast to their efforts to increase shipbuilding, the insurgents failed to interest either the navy or Congress in providing fleet, or seagoing, submarines as opposed to coastal defense boats, or even in building aircraft until the very end of Taft's term, with the G. B. not accepting the airplane as a proven instrument of war until 1913.

In January 1908, only a month after the Great White Fleet had left to reveal to the world the naval power of the United States, *McClure's Magazine* published an article by the respected naval authority Henry Reuterdahl which well voiced the insurgents' charges that American battleships were badly designed, indeed dangerous to their crews in certain respects and short of ordnance in others. It also pointed an accusing finger at the conservatism in the bureaus which precluded change for the better. The widely copied article brought what many officers already knew to the attention of a public heretofore ignorant. Roosevelt stood by Sims, who had provided Reuterdahl with technical details. Eugene Hale, chairman of the Senate Committee on Naval Affairs, felt impelled to investigate Reuterdahl's charges, which the bureau chiefs of course denied. Hale stood by the bureaus, did not publish a report on his investigation, and then introduced legislation to abolish the G. B., which had long made the same charges as Reuterdahl and the insurgents. Although not convinced that a general staff would be a good thing, Roosevelt called a conference of naval officers. Their conclusions supported enough of Reuterdahl's charges to provoke the demand that future ship designs be submitted to a special board of officers for examination and recommendations. However, change in what Roosevelt felt was lack of initiative and flexibility in administration was left for his last secretary of the navy, Truman H. Newberry, to handle. Newberry, who took office on December 1, 1908, suggested that the G. B. be enlarged by adding to it members from the bureaus, while members of the G. B. would be added to the Bureau of Construction, his major objective being to make the enlarged G. B. a general staff. In part because Sims advised him not to adopt any plan which would enlarge bureau influence, Roosevelt scotched the Newberry plan and on January 27, 1909, appointed the William Moody Commission to look into the navy's organizational needs.

In its report, made in late February 1909, the Moody Commission recommended that the Navy Department be divided into five functional areas under men who could be held personally rather than corporately responsible. One of these would be headed by a chief of naval operations who would be the secretary's major military adviser and have the G. B. report to him rather than to the secretary. As expected, Roosevelt in his last month in office did nothing about the report and Congress declined to act upon it, in great part because of the power it would give a chief of naval operations.

Several factors favored Meyer's being a good secretary. He was familiar with the working of the highest levels of government and had discussed naval problems while he was postmaster general in Roosevelt's cabinet. He won the respect of high ranking officers because, although he kept the power to run the navy at his own desk, he made it plain in his first annual report that "the Navy Department business has today grown beyond effective control under the present organization."[11] He also dignified the G. B. by being the first secretary to attend its meetings fairly regularly.

After reviewing the many naval reorganization plans in his files, Meyer on July 13, 1909, urged a board of line officers chaired by Rear Admiral William Swift to produce a plan of organization with which to execute naval policies. Like the Moody Commission, the Swift Board recommended the granting of sufficient power to a single officer to define policy and to have the bureaus carry it out. Moreover, in the matter of war plans this officer could refer questions or problems to the G. B. for its advice. But the G. B. was denied the right it had possessed since 1900 to initiate recommendations. Meyer compromised. Rather than creating a general staff, he would appoint four rear admirals as aides to give him professional advice and information on fleet operations, materiel, inspections, and personnel. The first two aides would also be members of the G. B. Since the aides had no legal status, they could not be given executive or administrative duties. Rather they would seek to "coordinate" the work of relevant bureaus. Because Meyer already had authority in law to put the reorganization into effect, he did so without having to hazard an appeal to Congress. With Taft's approval, he put the system into effect on December 1, 1909. Congress took no adverse action, and the Meyer system lasted throughout his four years in office, indeed until it was superseded by the creation of the Office of the Chief of Naval Operations in 1915.

How well did the Meyer system work? Meyer forced three of the eight bureau chiefs out before they were due for retirement and won authority from the congressional naval committees to consolidate bureau functions. By directing that all official correspondence reach him via the appropriate aide, he kept informed on all happenings and drastically cut down the amount of paper work. In daily meetings with his aides he formulated legislative and administrative policies and general orders, reached decisions on the recommendations of the G. B., and decided upon the duty assignments for admirals and captains. The aide for operations, Rear Admiral Richard Wainwright, reorganized both the battleship and torpedo fleets so that the load of repair work in the navy yards was evened out and in addition brought war plans and strategic studies up to date. Meanwhile the aides for materiel and for inspections decided whether repairs to ships could be justified by their military value. Meyer could thus claim that the aide system had resulted in increased military efficiency and improved administration with an economy befitting the character of the Taft administration. By using his aides as a council of advisers or "strategy board," he came as close as he dared to creating a general staff for the navy and led the way toward the creation of the Office of the Chief of Naval Operations. He also supported the plan to create a council of national defense to be composed of members representing the cabinet, Congress, and the military services—a plan finally adopted in 1916.

Meyer was particularly interested in navy yard administration. After visits to most of the continental yards, he consolidated various functions therein and also caused them to adopt the best cost accounting procedures of the day. Resulting lower costs helped him to operate within the ten-million-dollar cut Taft prescribed for the navy in 1910 alone. On the other hand, Taft's penchant for penny-pinching and Congress's refusal to approve of the closing of "useless" navy yards meant that no extensive improvements were made in even the most important yards. Two results followed. First, there were too few dry docks and no dry docks that could handle the new first-class battleships of twenty thousand and even twenty-six thousand tons being built except at Boston and Norfolk. Second, except for Pearl Harbor, little was done to provide the logistic support required by ships in the Pacific.

A mark of Meyer's capability was that, although he was denied adequate funds, as of March 15, 1912, almost fifty battleships and cruisers had had yard overhauls and all of the battleships were for the first time in recent years ready for service.

Although Taft supported international arbitration as a substitute for war and deplored the naval arms race sweeping the world, he was determined to keep pace with the building programs of Britain and Germany, in part, though he did not publicize the point, to provide the balance of power between Britain and Germany. Domestic problems, however, severely mitigated against a large building program. First, neither he nor Meyer could provide the political leadership, as Roosevelt had, to cajole Congress into answering their demands. Second, the panic of 1907 had left the Treasury Taft inherited quite bare, and Taft's parsimoniousness caused one journal at least to talk about "Substituting the Pruning Hook for the Big Stick."[12] Third, "insurgents" in both the House and Senate sundered their party by opposing Taft on tariff, income tax, conservation, and railroad reforms. Moreover, the winning of the elections of 1910 by the Democrats presaged two or three lean years for the navy and the admittedly lazy Taft preferred personal ease to a fight. Rather than subscribing to Roosevelt's interventionist policies, he sought security for the United States in the time-honored policy of nonintervention.

Throughout his four years, Taft strongly urged economy. In 1909 he cut military appropriations severely, with the army getting $45,000,000 and the navy $38,000,000 less than in 1908. Similar if less drastic cuts were made in 1911. In 1910, Taft obtained two first-class battleships, one repair vessel, and a few minor ships only after a bitter fight with congressional opponents of the navy. He got two additional battleships in fiscal year 1911 but only one in 1912. Nor did Congress respond to his request following his defeat in 1912 for authority to build three battleships in order that the United States keep its relative position as a world naval power.

Moreover, in consequence of the understandable concentration on building battleships, the navy of Taft's day was more unbalanced than ever. Nevertheless, it was deemed to be fully adequate to defend the interests of the United States.

Poor executive leadership, the split in the Republican party, the control of Congress in 1911 and 1912 by the Democrats, and the threat by southern Democrats not to vote building funds as long as Meyer threatened to close their naval facilities hindered naval progress in many ways other than in the building program. Congress refused Taft's suggestion to relieve the "hump" in the officer promotion pipe line, to merge Pay Corps and Construction Corps officers with the line, and to abolish restrictions on the employment by the department of retired officers in a civilian capacity. In contrast, it authorized the immediate commissioning of graduates of the Naval Academy rather than having these men first serve two years at sea.

Other reforms came by the administrative route. Meyer on October 4, 1909, established a postgraduate school of marine engineering at Annapolis. In 1910 and 1911 he revitalized the course offerings at both the Naval War College and the Naval Academy. A new personnel reorganization plan gradually brought the navy the number of men it needed in peacetime. He won approval for a bill that permitted navy and Marine Corps personnel to retire after sixteen, twenty, or twenty-five years rather than after thirty years only. Finally, he greatly increased the amusement and recreation facilities at navy yards and stations and liberalized the naval penal system. In contrast, Congress declined his suggestions to establish a naval reserve program, improve the naval militia program, and give the Marine Corps the men and equipment it vitally needed. But Congress accepted his idea of reserve fleets for the Atlantic and Pacific. By 1911 there were ten ships in the former and a few less in the latter. At his recommendation, too, Taft established two naval oil reserves in southern California.

American naval aviation even at the close of Taft's term ranked fourteenth in the world on the basis of its expenditures and had but fourteen aviators and four aircraft. However, progress was achieved in days made memorable by the exploits of Curtiss and Wright planes piloted by pioneers like Eugene Ely. By landing upon and then taking off from a platform built on the afterpart of the *Pennsylvania*, Ely took a key step in the development of the carrier.

The reviews of the Atlantic Fleet Taft held off New York City in 1911 and 1912 revealed the impressive naval might of the nation, for they were the largest and most powerful collections of ships ever assembled under the American flag. In Roosevelt's review of 1906, forty-five ships including eighteen battleships had taken part. In 1911 there gathered twenty-four battleships; in 1912 there were thirty-one active or reserve battleships, among them the new twenty-six-thousand-ton *Wyoming* and *Arkansas,* at the moment the largest and fastest ships in the world. Thus, at the end of his term Taft could state that the fleet was decidedly stronger and in more efficient condition than ever in its history, advances he credited to the reorganization undertaken by Meyer as well as to the work of the officers of the fleet, particularly of Wainwright. On the other hand, the terribly imbalanced fleet was particularly short of seagoing submarines and aircraft and still lacked a naval reserve force and an adequate Marine Corps. Whereas Roosevelt had asked Congress for four battleships in the hope of getting two, Taft and Meyer asked for only what they needed, and a parsimonious Republican Congress in 1909–1911 and an anti-navy Democratic Congress in 1911–1913 permitted the navy to fall from second to third place.

12

★★★★★

THE ELEPHANT AND THE
BULL MOOSE

I

After the elections of 1910, William Howard Taft began preparing his annual message to Congress and planning an inspection trip to Panama. He also asserted that it would not take the Democrats who controlled Congress long "to convince everybody of their incapacity."[1] With his good nature rapidly restored, and as though unaware that Theodore Roosevelt had parted company with him, he wrote Roosevelt an extremely cordial letter in which he suggested that as private citizens in 1913 they visit the completed canal, and invited him to call at the White House. When he sent him proof of his annual message and asked for his advice on the Japanese problem, Roosevelt responded as graciously as his pugnacity would permit and won his consent to raise a cavalry division if war came with Mexico. While patting the progressives with one hand, Roosevelt honeymooned with Taft until mid-1911.

In mid-January 1911, with what Archie Butt suspected were tears in his eyes, Taft confessed that he was more distressed than anyone could ever know "to think of [Roosevelt] sitting there at Oyster Bay alone and feeling himself deserted. I know just what he feels," for he pictured him as cut out by those who had formerly looked upon him as an idol, lacking the power which he loved, and unable to fight for what he thought was best for the country. He asked Butt, "Well, do you see where I could have acted differently?" Butt replied: "I don't see how you could have done differently," then wondered whether he had lied.[2]

Criticism of Taft following the elections of 1910 was quite severe and sometimes unwarranted. Rather than keeping his promise to serve as an executive officer concerned solely with efficient administration, he had written bills for Congress to enact and like a British prime minister had actively sought to influence party matters and used the patronage to this end. For one with almost unparalleled qualifications to be president, he had succeeded neither in driving his program through Congress nor in keeping his party united and strong.

Believing that his legislative accomplishments of the past year and a half had answered the demands of the progressives, Taft proceeded to administer the government with the aid of regular Republicans. If he thus countered the demands of progressives for the purification of America's institutions by the admission of more democratic processes, he nevertheless won the support of the regulars for his legislative program and for his renomination in 1912. However, if he was satisfied with what he had accomplished thus far, the election of 1910 showed that the country was not. The Payne-Aldrich tariff continued to draw criticism. He had failed to obtain reciprocity with Canada, and the attempt alone had won him the opposition of the Northwest farmer especially. Moreover, the Supreme Court decisions in the great antitrust cases sat badly with the business community and so angered Roosevelt that they played an important part in his decision to run against Taft for president. Several of the measures for which Taft took credit, such as the Mann-Elkins Act and the Postal Savings Bank Act, owed much to the insurgents. Rather than letting the insurgent and conservative factions of his party fight out their differences, he had intervened on the side of the conservatives and sought to excommunicate those he considered to be heterodox. He had then proved his inconsistency and confessed his error by announcing that he would not hunt heretics any more but allow them to share the patronage and other party honors. The result of his attempt to punish men of principle had been to split his party and to lose the elections of 1910. Since insurgents could not stomach his death-bed repentance and conservatives could not live with the Roosevelt of Osawatomie, Republican defeat in 1910 had been expected in advance and was predicted for 1912.

Following the elections of 1910, Taft tried to restore harmony in his party and to appear as the leader of the progressive forces of the nation. He invited all the insurgents to the White House to discuss patronage. All came except the grim Robert M. La

Follette, who told Mrs. La Follette that he would not go where "all the plots to destroy me have been hatched," and that Taft was trying to appear "in sympathy" with the progressives solely in order to "promote the renomination and reelection of Taft."[3]

In the winter of 1910, danger appeared to Taft from two quarters. The first loomed from the Congress which assembled in December 1910 and would remain in session until March 4, 1911. Democrat Champ Clark would be the new Speaker, and the Ways and Means Committee promised a new tariff bill. Forty-six insurgents refused to be bound by the decisions of the Republican caucus in the House, while the ten to fourteen insurgent Republicans held the balance of power between the Democrats and the Taft Republicans in the Senate. How well would Taft fare at the hands of such a Congress?

The second danger came from La Follette and his fellow insurgents. La Follette explained his ideas in Ohio, Illinois, and Michigan during the Christmas recess and through the press to the country. "The great issue before the American people today," he said, "is the control of their own Government," and the purpose of the progressive movement was to restore popular sovereignty, to modify wherever necessary Constitution, statutes, courts, and administration so as to carry out the will of the people. He would control unfair business competition by specifically prohibiting all methods which made possible unfair competition and the restraint of trade, and have a commission ascertain the physical value of the property of any corporation and true costs of its production in order to determine whether its prices were yielding extraordinary profits. He wanted tariff rates based upon differences in the cost of production in the United States and competing countries; a permanent, nonpartisan tariff commission; direct primaries not only for candidates to office but for delegates to presidential conventions and in addition a presidential preference primary. He called for the adoption of the initiative, referendum, and recall, including the recall of judges, and for the development of Alaska by having the government provide its communication facilities and by supervising the mining of its coal.

Having explained his ideas, La Follette next drew up a Declaration of Principles, a constitution, and a plan of organization for a National Republican League which would support progressive legislation on both the national and state levels. He included the word "Republican" in the title to avoid the charge that he was launching a third-party movement. After he had accepted modifications offered to the Declaration by Senators Jonathan Bourne and Joseph Bristow, however, it proposed only five policies: the popular election of United States senators, direct primaries for all state offices, direct election of delegates to national conventions, the adoption of the initiative, referendum, and recall, and a thorough corrupt practices act.

Believing that the league was a vehicle to promote a presidential nomination for La Follette either in a contest against Taft or in a third-party movement, Roosevelt declined invitations from La Follette and Bourne to adhere to it.

At an organizational meeting held at La Follette's home in Washington on January 21, Bourne was elected as president, Frederic C. Howe as secretary, and Charles R. Crane as treasurer of the National Progressive Republican League. Among the charter members were nine senators, six governors, thirteen representatives, and many other prominent national figures. The league grew so rapidly in numbers and influence that it was soon described as "the culmination of the progressive movement in the Republican Party and the beginning of the new Progressive Party."[4] Both Taft and Roosevelt must take it into account. Even if the league were not to run a member for president in 1912 it could concentrate about one of them all those who opposed Taft's renomination. Critics compared it to the old Populist party and predicted its early demise, while Democrats of course smiled in satisfaction over the evident rift in the opposition ranks. When stalwart Republican senators utterly refused La Follette's demand that Progressives be given membership on committees in proportion to their number, one out of four, it became obvious that there were three rather than two parties in Congress.

Although they saw La Follette as the strongest of their kind they could put up against Taft, Progressives were rebels generally unamenable to cohesive action or discipline albeit fiercely loyal one to the other. Few of them believed that La Follette could defeat Taft even though they named him as their candidate, on April 30. After he obtained promises of political and financial support, La Follette announced his candidacy in June. Headquarters were soon opened in Washington, Progressive Clubs were formed in a number of states, and his cause made gains among agrarians in the Middle- and Far West. No man was more "progressive" than "the most insurgent of them all." A great orator with much more persistence than patience, he launched an acrid attack on the deeds, purposes, and motives of the Taft administration. Perhaps like William Jennings Bryan, however, he was too much the crusader, too much the evangelistic reformer to win election even if he were named. He was very well understood in the West but misunderstood in the East, and his demand for the recall of judges was not accepted by all insurgents as Progressive doctrine. Quite brashly he alleged that "the President's course has been vacillating and without definite policy, because, apparently, there has been throughout his Administration no deep conviction other than the hour makes appear expedient."[5] But he and his advisers could not shake off the feeling that his leadership of the league depended upon whether Roosevelt waived his claim to it.

La Follette could probably put Wisconsin, Kansas, Washington, Oregon, and California in his column. However, he was feared by the businessmen of the country, his "Frenchy" name repelled some people, and his being a "radical" still others. Even friends and supporters disliked his vehemence, narrowness, and lack of humor. An insurgent distrusted by the regulars, he was still a Republican and thus unable to win support from partisan Democrats except on matters that would hurt the Republican party. Taft's absolute control over the delegates to be chosen to the national convention told against him on the one hand; on the other, he was no match in the popular mind with Roosevelt, even though Roosevelt's progressivism differed from his.

Moreover, Taft did not stand still. Early in September he delivered a so-called keynote address at Hamilton, Massachusetts, in which he attacked the insurgents and Democrats, defended his veto of the three Democratic tariff reduction bills, and criticized La Follette, Speaker Champ Clark, and Majority Leader Oscar W. Underwood for their "political logrolling" and "irresponsible legislation."[6] During September and October, he tried to stem the revolt against him by delivering two hundred speeches in one hundred fifteen cities during a thirteen-thousand-mile tour of the West, concentrating upon the insurgent strongholds of Wisconsin, Minnesota, South Dakota, Iowa, Kansas, and Washington. He then extended his trip to seventeen thousand miles to include Virginia, West Virginia, Tennessee, and Kentucky, with knowing ones suggesting that he sought to nail down southern delegates for the national convention. Opinion on the effect of his trip varied, with Republican newspapers saying he had revealed himself incapable of dealing with the tariff or trust questions and provided no constructive suggestions for bringing genuine relief to the ordinary worker, who was becoming increasingly dissatisfied with his administration. Although he was patently honest and utterly lovable as a man, his accounts of his battles against Aldrichism, Cannonism, and Lorimerism sounded weak, and his popular reception was a tribute more to his office than to him personally. Perhaps because of this last fact, rather than cheering and encouraging his followers in the coming conflict, he dampened their enthusiasm by conceding impoliticly in a speech at Chicago that he would be defeated in November 1912. Upon returning to Washington, he wrote to his brother Horace:

> When I went West I was going into enemy country; now that I return, I seem to be coming back into the enemy's country, due to the enforcement of the antitrust law by George Wickersham's prosecutions. . . .
>
> As to the outlook I do not know. If the New York papers do not cease to be hostile, if Woodrow Wilson does not cease to attack me for the enforcement of the [antitrust] law, and if Bryan does not cease to attack me for the appointment of our judges, they may elect me to the Presidency. I am pursuing the middle of the road policy as well as I can. . . .
>
> I am only conscious of my defects and weaknesses. I am content with one term and get through with it; but if they do not look out, as I said, they may drive me into a second term against their will. . . .[7]

Taft appealed to conservatives, La Follette to progressives, but Roosevelt to many in both camps. Roosevelt had taken a long speaking tour of the country beginning in March 1911. There was no mistaking the fact that the New York gubernatorial campaign of 1910 had left him in a sorry plight politically. The 1911 trip restored his self-confidence to a marked degree. But he stated over and over again from his return from Africa until January 1912 that he was not a presidential candidate, that Taft would be renominated and defeated, and that the proper strategy must be to reform their party for 1916. When he changed his mind and threw his hat in the ring, both La Follette and Taft felt betrayed. What made him change his mind? Why did most progressives drop La Follette for him? And what difference did it make to Taft whether La Follette or Roosevelt challenged him for the nomination?

II

While there is no one particular point at which Taft and Roosevelt consciously parted company, Roosevelt was unhappy with the sluggish campaign Taft had waged in 1908 and his failure to help him during his battle with his last Congress. Although not at first resentful of Taft's cabinet choices, he came to feel that Taft, by allying himself with the Old Guard, had turned his back upon his policies in the attempt to reform the House rules and in both the tariff and conservation controversies. Most important were Taft's insistence upon following a limited, legal concept of presidential leadership, his attempt to achieve world peace through unlimited arbitration treaties, and his suit against United States Steel, in which it had been made to appear that Roosevelt had been duped in 1907. For his part, Taft was grievously hurt when, upon his return from Africa, Roosevelt honeymooned with the insurgents and in his New Nationalism appeared to be an enemy of the Constitution. Had he known that Roosevelt wanted him to help him during his last Congress, he would have done so. Had he asked for particular cabinet appointments, he would have made them. Having entered the presidency unwillingly, he would now be happy to leave it. To Otto T. Bannard, an old friend, he wrote on January 22, 1912:

> I am afraid I am in for a hard fight without any knowledge of military strategy, and with very little material for organization, but I am going to stay in anyhow. . . . I believe I represent a safer and saner view of our government and its Constitution than does Theodore Roosevelt, and whether beaten or not I mean to continue to labor in the vineyard for those principles.[8]

After completing his speaking tour on April 16, Roosevelt wrote to his son Ted in part: "I found that the great majority of the progressives felt as I did, that is, they disapproved of Taft, felt that they would like to see some other man nominated, and did not feel that a third party would be wise." While "it looks as if the Republican Party was disintegrating at the moment, I feel that my nomination would be a calamity to me. . . ."[9] In August, however, a change in attitude became perceptible, for while he would not support Taft's nomination, he would support his election.

After talking with Roosevelt in New York, Herman H. Kohlsaat, the newspaper publisher from Chicago, lunched at the White

House and repeated what he had learned about Roosevelt's feelings toward Taft. Taft said with considerable emotion,

> You are a great friend of Colonel Roosevelt's. Through some misunderstandings he feels hurt with me. I must have done something that displeases him very much. Knowingly I have done nothing to hurt his feelings. I may have been tactless, but not intentionally did I do anything to displease him. I owe him everything. He is responsible for my being President. I am so disturbed it keeps me awake nights.

When Kohlsaat suggested that perhaps Roosevelt was angry because of the letter he sent him via Butt in which he coupled Brother Charley's name with his, Taft replied: "But I didn't send any such message!" Kohlsaat went on to suggest that Roosevelt was angry over his failure to appoint James Garfield and Oscar Straus to his cabinet as he had promised, and "that made him mad." Taft replied: "But I didn't promise to appoint them!" adding, "I don't know where you get your information, but you are entirely wrong." To prove his point, he showed Kohlsaat all his correspondence with Roosevelt since 1908. Kohlsaat went away unable to fathom Roosevelt's telling him about an incident Taft denied and had records to support. As noted earlier, Roosevelt confused Taft's thanking of him and of Brother Charles in a letter of November 1908 with the letter Butt brought to his ship on March 22, 1909.[10]

The two hundred delegates to the first National Progressive Republican Conference, held at Chicago on October 16, endorsed La Follette for president, resolved in favor of presidential primaries, and urged Republican leaders in states lacking them to provide primaries as alternatives to state conventions. Taft men, who controlled the party machinery, naturally opposed changing the rules for selecting delegates. On the trust issue the delegates resolved that industrial corporations should be given a new law which would provide definite rules by which to conduct their business. Taft men naturally resented this slap at Taft's antitrust policies.

While Roosevelt asserted that he would not take sides between La Follette and Taft, on October 27 he wrote in reply to a letter from Governor Hiram Johnson, of California, that he would insist upon the right of the people to have an open primary in which to express their views for the presidential nomination. He added in confidence that Taft had never once said anything "in consonance with humanity," held the business community in higher regard than all others, and preferred the Old Guard to Progressives. There was more to life than mere business and material well-being, and on this point Taft had not "gone wrong" but had "stayed wrong." Therefore, "as for my ever having any enthusiasm for Taft again, it is utterly impossible." On the other hand, La Follette seemed to proceed on the principle of following a majority, even if it were wrong. He himself would be a "weak candidate," and he asked Johnson "to do everything possible to prevent not merely my nomination but any movement looking toward my nomination."[11] One wonders whether he did not protest too much!

As yet the political situation remained pat. The few elections held in November shed no light on the hopes of either Republican or Democratic presidential contenders for 1912. Taft was so firmly in control of his party's machinery that only a major revolution could upset him, yet there was also the possibility that he might run only to be defeated. Meanwhile questions of power, prestige, and progressive politics filled Roosevelt's mind. He alone seemed to be the popular choice, the cleansing of a number of leading conservatives from Congress would make it easy now to work with it, the spurting forward of the progressive movement promised the enactment of many reforms in addition to those accomplished under Taft, and he more than anyone else could bring back together the wings of the Republican party at the moment being led by Taft and La Follette. In writing to Judge Ben Lindsey on December 5, therefore, he discounted the third-term tradition on the ground that it meant a "consecutive" third term. He thus indicated that he was open for a draft. While he declined requests by La Follette's friends to announce that he would refuse the nomination if offered to him, he still feared that "Taft may redeem himself," for "it is possible that the Democrats in Congress may play the fool, and give him the chance to appear as the strong leader, the man who must be accepted to oppose them."[12]

Some progressives would send delegations to the national convention pledged either to Taft or Roosevelt. Others would leave their delegates free to vote for either La Follette or Roosevelt. When asked by some men to declare that he was not a candidate in the interest of La Follette and by others that he was not a candidate in the interest of Taft, Roosevelt replied that "no man has been authorized by me to put my name on any ballot, or to get up any petition in my interest, or to take any action on my behalf."[13] He was of course being disingenuous, for friends were already hard at work establishing headquarters for him at Chicago and New York.

Roosevelt's day of decision was apparently January 9, 1912, for he let it be known on that day that he would speak before the Constitutional Convention in Ohio in February and "then put out my platform" and subsequently make a short statement stating that he would "under no circumstances . . . lift my hand to get the nomination, but that if it comes to me as a genuine popular movement of course I will accept. . . ."[14] Then, upon deciding in favor of an open announcement, he began to plan how best to make it. Several governors had recently asked him to announce. "What do you think," he asked Chase S. Osborn, "of having you and Governor Glasscock, of West Virginia, Governor Stubbs of Kansas, Governor Osborn of Michigan, and Governor Bass of New Hampshire, write me a letter to which I can answer. They could merely write that the people of their states wish me to run and ask whether I would refuse a nomination."[15]

An incident which no doubt weighed heavily in Roosevelt's decision to run was the temporary breakdown of La Follette. Suffering from a digestive disturbance, worried about a daughter who on the morrow would undergo a serious operation, and perhaps in anguish because of the growing Roosevelt boom, in an address at Philadelphia on February 2 he rambled on at unconscionable length in almost incoherent fashion. As has been suggested, his performance "was the excuse for, not the cause of," the flight of such progressives as Gifford Pinchot, Medill McCormick, and many others from him to Roosevelt.[16] He was hurt but did not, as often alleged, withdraw from the race. "Poor La Follette! As you say, that was a pitiable tragedy," Roosevelt wrote to Governor Stubbs on February 8 and then indicated that if public sentiment for himself existed, it must be granted a chance for expression.[17] Meanwhile he selected the men who would direct his campaign for the nomination. By seeking that nomination he exploded the myth that the Republican party, which had ruled perpetually since 1896, was invincible and did much to rehabilitate Taft in the eyes of the country even if the business community proved lukewarm in his support.

III

On November 24, 1911, it being clear to him that La Follette could not be nominated and that the progressives were turning to

Roosevelt, Taft told Mrs. Taft that things had looked equally black four years earlier.

"Yes," she said, "but I was always hopeful then. I am not hopeful now. Things are different."

Taft looked worried and asked: "Well, you are not hopeless about the nomination?"

She replied slowly, as though searching for the proper words: "No, I think you will be renominated, but I don't see any chance for the election."

"Well," he concluded, "I am chiefly interested in the renomination, so don't get disconsolate over that. If we lose the election I shall feel that the party is rejected, whereas if I fail to secure the renomination it will be a personal defeat."[18]

Taft had more power over the party machinery than he believed, however, and as usual when angered he fought hard. As Secretary of Commerce Nagel put it, "He had the stubbornness of an uncertain man."[19] He practically demanded a loyalty oath from Victor Rosewater, who would be second in command at the national convention, and from Frank H. Hitchcock, the postmaster general who he suspected might try to use the patronage in his own behalf or for Roosevelt. On December 12, 1911, he gave a dinner for the members of the national committee. Although the proceedings were consummated in the spirit of arranging funeral services, Taft smoothed the way for the selection of officers at the convention who would be friendly to him, and for some time his outlook improved. Two weeks later, however, he plunged back into depression, for he said to Butt: "It is very hard to take all the slaps Roosevelt is handing me at this time, Archie. . . . I could not subordinate my administration to him and retain my self-respect, but it is hard, very hard, Archie, to see a devoted friendship going to pieces like a rope of sand."[20] Even if the breach with Roosevelt was beyond healing, he felt that "I am going to defeat [Roosevelt] in the Convention. He may defeat me for reelection and he probably will, but I think I will defeat him in the Convention."[21]

The first president ever to stump in a primary campaign, Taft abandoned what he considered the "dignity" of the office of president and became an aroused circuit rider in his popular contest with Roosevelt. "Whether I win or lose is not important, but I am in this fight to perform a great public duty—the duty of keeping Theodore Roosevelt out of the White House," he told Charles W. Thompson, reporter for the *New York Times*.[22] To another he said that he would stay in the fight for two reasons. First, "I believe

I represent a safer and saner view of our government and its Constitution than does Theodore Roosevelt." Whether defeated or not, he would continue to support those constitutional principles and stamp out the "pernicious theory" that the way to reform representative government was to admit additional democratic processes into it. Second, "I am not conscious of having done anything which disentitles me to stand as a candidate for a second term or requires a departure from the time-honored and very safe tradition against a third term."[23]

In a Lincoln Day speech in New York City headlined as "Taft Fires on His Opponents," Taft first attacked Progressive Republicans. He opposed their demand for direct political action by the people, including direct selection of candidates. Of the advocates of direct popular government he said that "such extremists would hurry us to a condition which would find no parallel except in the French Revolution." These extremists "are not progressives; they are political emotionalists or neurotics." Moreover, he regarded discussion of the position of the judiciary as profane meddling with things sacred, for judges were "the high priests who administer justice." Second, he spoke contemptuously of the Democratic party and alluded to the Republican defeat in 1910 as merely a popular reminder that the Republican organization get into condition to win an overwhelming victory in 1912.[24]

Although Taft subsequently asserted that he did not have Roosevelt in mind when he delivered his speech, Roosevelt thought that he did and took great offense at his remarks.

In various other speeches, Taft admitted that judges sometimes invalidated social reform statutes of which he approved and even gave wrong construction to statutes. However, he denied that judges were bound "to follow the will of a majority in respect of the issue for their decision." Judicial recall, moreover, "would deprive the judiciary of that independence without which the liberty and other rights of the individual cannot be maintained against the Government and the majority." Nor did he care for the recall of judicial decisions by submitting them to a vote of the electors, for this "lays the ax at the foot of the tree of well-ordered freedom, and subjects the guarantees of life, liberty, and property without remedy to the fitful impulse of a temporary majority of an electorate."[25] He would thus preserve things as they were, and in consequence the Old Guard strongly supported him as the conservative "regular" against the "progressive" Roosevelt. That the term "progressive" by this time provoked myriad connotations is revealed in Walter Hines Page's writing to Ray Stannard Baker that "we now have Progressives, Halting-Progressives, Ultra-Progressives, Progressive Conservatives, Conservative Progressives, and TR."[26]

Upon Taft's return from his six-day stumping tour of New York and Ohio, Butt screwed up enough courage to talk to him about his health. As he had noted on February 9, 1912,

> He looks terribly. His flesh looks like wax, and his lips are thin, and he is getting those unhealthy bags under his eyes. I begged him to see a specialist, for I felt sure that all his drowsiness was due to some toxin in his system and that during his campaign he would need every bit of vitality to take him through.

Taft had slapped him on the back and said "Archie, you go to hell! I will not be hauled and pulled about by specialists. . . ."[27] A great part of Taft's trouble of course was that Roosevelt was so much on his mind. He felt that Roosevelt would soon declare himself a candidate, and with each passing hour he grew more bitter against him because he thought Roosevelt had no real cause for resentment.

Roosevelt finally dropped the mask he had been wearing for several months and began his preconvention campaign with an exceedingly long "Charter of Democracy" address before the Ohio Constitutional Convention. He placed human rights above all other rights, asserted that "wealth should be the servant, not the master, of the people," demanded that there should be a "fair distribution of property" and direct nominations including presidential primaries, and also advocated the recall of judicial decisions involving constitutional interpretations on the state level—a sound legal principle quickly corrupted, however, into the "recall of judicial decisions."[28] He may have hoped by his address to win over La Follette's supporters; he also made himself appear as a radical to the East and drove moderates as well as conservatives into Taft's camp. Businessmen particularly backed Taft because they wished the judiciary to continue to shield them from state social and economic legislation. As Henry Cabot Lodge told Brooks Adams, "Roosevelt's Columbus speech has turned Taft into a man of principle."[29]

Just before speaking to the Ohio convention, Roosevelt told a reporter, "My hat is in the ring," but little notice was taken of his statement except by George Harvey, whose *Harper's Weekly* asserted that "hate, not hat, is in the ring" and that Roosevelt would "intercept" rather than "accept" the nomination.[30] Then when the governors he had asked to do so made their "spontaneous appeal" that he run, he replied on February 24 that "I will accept the nomination for President if it is tendered to me. . . ."[31] His declaration provoked genuine distress particularly for La Follette but also for men like George Meyer, Henry L. Stimson, and Butt, who were friends of both Roosevelt and Taft. Such a lifelong friend of Roosevelt as Lodge remained neutral in the contest, as did Roosevelt's son-in-law, Nicholas Longworth, and most Republican congressmen, although Lodge's son-in-law, Augustus Gardner, ably defended Taft against Roosevelt's charges. Taft's attitude is best expressed by his reply to Governor Osborn, of Michigan, who asked both him and La Follette to drop out in favor of Roosevelt or someone else who could win in November: "Nothing but death can keep me out of the fight now."[32]

At dinner on February 25, Taft was handed an Associated Press announcement that Roosevelt had answered the letter from seven governors to the effect that he would accept the nomination if offered to him. Taft showed the note about the table. Mrs. Taft was the first to break the silence, saying, "I told you so four years ago, and you would not believe me."

Taft laughed good-naturedly and replied: "I know you did, my dear, and I think you are perfectly happy now. You would have preferred the Colonel to come out against me than to have been wrong yourself."[33]

Seven progressive governors had asked Roosevelt to run. A week later, nine conservative governors endorsed Taft for renomination. Republicans now must choose between alternative men and issues. As the *Outlook*, which supported Roosevelt, said, they must choose between two tendencies, "the tendency to conservatism and the tendency toward progress, the tendency toward distrusting the popular judgment and the tendency toward giving the popular judgment larger play, the tendency toward restraining democracy and the tendency toward curing the ills of democracy by more democracy." A second issue was that between the public records of Taft and Roosevelt, one "legalistic," the other "of temperament."[34]

Taft used his secretary, Charles D. Hilles, as his preconvention manager until February, when he replaced him with Congressman William B. McKinley, of Illinois, who nevertheless kept his position as chairman of the Republican Congressional Campaign Committee. He thus acted as the chairman of a committee that spoke for the entire party and also as Taft's private campaign director. Following Taft's directions, conservative leaders held state conventions before Roosevelt's followers could organize and began to corral delegates wherever and however they could, with abundant lashings of the patronage whip.

All of the 64 delegates to the national convention chosen in February were pledged to Taft, but many of them were contested by Roosevelt men, who charged that they had been overrun by the "steam roller, or machine political power." An additional 190 delegates would be chosen in March, many of them from southern states where there was no real Republican party and not a single electoral vote could be expected. The southern "brokerage corporations dealing in federal patronage" could give Taft 252 of the total of 1,072 delegates, with 537 needed to control the convention, thus giving him almost half of his strength and making him virtually impregnable.

The first northern state to hold primaries, North Dakota, gave Taft only 1,543 votes while Roosevelt got 19,101 and La Follette, who had been regarded by most of the press as being out of the race, 28,620. La Follette thus appeared as the choice of progressives, Roosevelt of the standpatters. As expected, La Follette won Wisconsin by almost three to one over Taft, but at the end of March Taft had 274 of the 537 delegates needed to nominate. In April, however, Oregon and Nebraska went to Roosevelt in what Mrs. La Follette called a "body blow,"[35] while Taft received the delegates from a number of southern states. Late in April, Taft won Rhode Island and New Hampshire and picked up 4 delegates at large in Iowa. In all, Taft got 16 Iowa delegates and favorite son Albert B. Cummins 10 progressive men who probably would support Roosevelt. Missouri, and Kansas, however, went to Roosevelt, and Taft became deeply worried.

Until early May the preconvention campaign was conducted on the basis of the issues rather than of personalities, with Taft maintaining his resolve to keep the campaign for the nomination on the highest possible plane. Fearing that a victorious Roosevelt would change the Republican party from a "party of moderate liberalism" to a "radical party," he told a brother that "if I am defeated, I hope that somebody, sometime, will recognize the agony of spirit that I have undergone."[36]

Saying that he did so reluctantly, Taft was the first to refer in personal terms to his major opponent. He told whistle-stop audiences that he was on his way to Boston "to reply to an old friend of mine, Theodore Roosevelt, who has made many charges against me. I deny those charges. I deny all of them. I do not want to fight Theodore Roosevelt, but sometimes a man in a corner fights. I am going to fight."[37] In speeches in Boston and elsewhere in Massachusetts, after acknowledging Roosevelt's aid in securing his nomination and election and revealing details that opened the eyes of many as to Roosevelt's methods, he defended the record of his administration and slashed at Roosevelt because of what he had said in his address to the Ohio Constitutional Convention on February 21, particularly because of his "alarming" advocacy of the recall of judicial decisions. As has been well said, "this was the Gethsemane of all his crowded years in public life."[38]

"This wrenches my soul," said Taft as he submitted a twelve-point bill of particulars. First, Roosevelt misquoted, garbled, and misrepresented his language. Second, how could Roosevelt charge the administration with providing government at the hands of an oligarchy of state bosses when he was dealing with these bosses himself and as president had cooperated with Aldrich, Cannon, Penrose, and others? Third, he resented the charge that he had "interfered" with the prerogatives of the Senate in the Lorimer case. Fourth, when he had consulted Roosevelt on the value of Canadian reciprocity ten days before the agreement was signed, Roosevelt had blessed his efforts. But in reading the confidential letter he had written to Roosevelt on January 10, 1911, Taft revealed that he had said that one of the advantages of "free trade" with Canada would be, with respect to the resulting "current of business between Western Canada and the United States," to make Canada "only an adjunct of the United States," a revelation to which Canadian Conservatives and the English government now took umbrage. Taft then asserted that Roosevelt's "recanting" of his approval for reciprocity was obviously a political trick to win the farmers from him and "not a square deal." Fifth, if Roosevelt believed that fraud had been perpetrated in certain primaries, he should take his case to the courts. Sixth, while he had suggested to Congress that the patronage be taken out of politics, Congress had not acted. Roosevelt was again violating the square deal by seeking the support of federal officeholders while criticizing him for doing the same thing. Seventh, Roosevelt himself had suggested that he take counsel with such "reactionaries" as Aldrich and Cannon on his legislative program. He had taken their advice, with the result that the Payne-Aldrich tariff and other legislation could be considered "progressive." With but one exception, moreover, Roosevelt had approved of all the sections of the Mann-Elkins Act which he now criticized. Roosevelt as president had begun to prosecute the trusts; as a presidential candidate he was "coming the other way" and denouncing their prosecution and objecting to a rise in the price of oil in consequence of a decree of dissolution drawn up by Roosevelt's own attorney general. Roosevelt's antitrust policy, furthermore, amounted to nothing more than a "benevolent despotism." Roosevelt charged him with "standing with the interests." Taft replied that his antitrust suits showed that he played no favorites. Under the eleventh head, Taft stated that Roosevelt should not be chosen as the candidate because the policies he had set forth in his Columbus speech were so radical as to amount to a "threatened undermining of our Constitutional Government." Finally, Taft warned against violating the third-term tradition and concluded "sorrowfully" that "one who so little regards Constitutional principles, especially the independence of the judiciary; and one who is so naturally impatient of legal restraints and of due legal procedure, and who has so misunderstood what liberty regulated by law is, could not be safely trusted with successive Presidential terms."[39]

It was a sledgehammer attack, but it admitted so many things that Taft insured that the one issue on which the campaign would be fought would be the merits of his own administration. He had also been hurt. That evening he returned to his train tired and shaken, his usually light step ponderous, his face almost lifeless, and sat down on a lounge. Louis Seibold of the *New York World* found him "slumped over, with his head between his hands." Taft looked up at him, blurted out "Roosevelt was my closest friend," and wept.[40]

Roosevelt replied in similar personal terms the very next day, saying that "it is a bad trait to bite the hand that feeds you," that "the Republican Party would have died of dry-rot if we had not made this fight," and "this is not a dress parade, but a fight to the finish."[41] Soon Taft was calling Roosevelt a "dangerous egotist" and "a demagogue" and Roosevelt calling the man he made president a "puzzlewit" and "fathead." Based as it was upon personality rather than principle, the Taft-Roosevelt contest became a sorry spectacle that approximated a national disgrace. Even if each tried to tell the truth about the other man, each accused the other of hypocrisy and falsification. The commitment of private offenses, of real or fancied slights, of pique, and of offended dignity rather than questions of public policy aroused resentment. Should Taft be denied renomination and reelection solely because Roosevelt disliked him? Or because he had declined to retain members of Roosevelt's cabinet? Or because Wickersham in the Steel antitrust suit had made it appear that Roosevelt once had been hoodwinked? Or because he had been "insubordinate" and tried to be president in his own right and refused to follow his predecessor's policies? The result of the battle of personalities was to degrade the office of president and to lower the esteem of both men in the eyes of the public.

The Massachusetts primaries were inconclusive largely because of the use of an ambiguous primary law which, as Roosevelt put it, caused some voters to think they could "vote both for Taft and for me or against us both."[42] The presidential preferential vote went to Taft, the 8 delegates at large to Roosevelt. Of the district delegates, 10 were for Roosevelt and 18 for Taft. Roosevelt had received a total of 86,000 votes and Taft 81,000, yet Taft claimed victory with 22 delegates against 14 for Roosevelt. A mess had been created that would have to be untangled in the national convention itself, yet Taft's nominal victory served to dampen the enthusiasm for Roosevelt in other states.

Roosevelt won 66 delegates to the state convention in Maryland and Taft 63. Taft carried Connecticut, Indiana, Colorado, New York, and Kentucky by what Roosevelt called a "criminal farce," while Roosevelt took 20 of the 22 delegates from Kansas, 56 of the 58 men in Illinois, and 67 of the 76 in Pennsylvania. Disorder was so rife in Michigan that police and even state militia were called. When the Taft forces obtained control, the Roosevelt men bolted and chose a contesting delegation. The best that can be said of Indiana is that Roosevelt men stole the delegates from Taft and Taft men then stole them back. By the latter part of April, 450 of the 1,072 delegates had been selected. Since both Taft and Roosevelt managers claimed everything in sight and there were no fewer than 148 contested delegates, no one really knew how many the one or the other had. Agreement was possible only upon the fact that La Follette had 36 delegates and Cummins 10, for Roosevelt men charged Taft's managers with fraud, intimidation, and trickery in various states and demanded that the convention system of selecting delegates be discarded in favor of primaries— in which Roosevelt did best. Nevertheless, if it was true that "as New York and Indiana go, so goes the nation," Roosevelt was doomed and Taft would go on to win.

In the second week in May, four states with 28 delegates went to Taft (Montana, Wyoming, Nevada, and Utah) and four with 80 delegates to Roosevelt (California, Minnesota, West Virginia, and North Carolina). Having won all but two of the state's delegates for Roosevelt, the California Progressives believed that Hiram Johnson would be a real contender for the vice-presidential nomination.

Taft had said that the vote of Ohio would be decisive in determining the result in the national convention. Roosevelt had stumped the state. Taft himself on two trips covering three thousand miles had delivered more than a hundred speeches, often to unfriendly audiences. He received a terrific blow when the voters clearly repudiated him by giving Roosevelt 34 delegates to his mere 8, with 6 additional delegates to be chosen in the state convention. The results provoked predictions that his chances for the nomination were nearly if not quite impossible, whereas in fact he already had enough delegates to name him.

In Washington, on May 15, the Republican State Central Committee tossed out enough Roosevelt delegates to the state convention to give Taft a majority therein. In the last contests held, New Jersey went heavily to Roosevelt; Arizona's 6 delegates went to Taft and were promptly contested by Roosevelt men; and South Dakota went for Roosevelt. Taft sent a telegram to the Ohio state leaders asserting that delegates favorable to him must be elected in the state convention. These leaders so manipulated the convention that even though Roosevelt had carried the preference vote by 30,000 the 6 delegates at large were obtained for Taft.

Even as the last states held their primaries, the national committee, on which Taft had a majority, met at Chicago and on June 6 began to decide the 105 contests involving 254 seats, many of them evidently manufactured by "practical" Roosevelt men in the attempt to show that he had great delegate strength. The thirteen states using presidential preferential primaries had given La Follette 36 delegates, Taft 48, and Roosevelt 278, with 74,716 votes for Taft, and 1,151,397 for Roosevelt, thus making Roosevelt appear to be the truly popular choice. States using the convention system had generally gone to Taft. Taft had among his delegates 283 men from southern states. Roosevelt's 350 delegates came from twenty-five normally Republican states. Roosevelt's adherents naturally asked whether the National Committee and the convention itself would listen to the voice of the people or, by manipulating the party machinery, thwart that will and select Taft? To Roosevelt, the issue "is simply whether or not we shall permit a system of naked fraud, of naked theft from the people, to triumph." More specifically, he said that "practically the attempt is being made by the Taft managers to use the present National Committee for the purpose of unseating honestly elected delegates and of seating enough fraudulently elected delegates, especially from States where there is no real Republican party, to secure the nomination for Mr. Taft."[43]

But Roosevelt overlooked the fact that he had sanctioned the work of the national committee in 1904 and 1908, when he had controlled it and refused to reform it, and La Follette's people at least stated that he should not complain when Taft used methods he himself had taught him. Moreover, he could not blame Taft because of the retirement for various causes between 1908 and 1912 of 17 regulars out of 39 and 9 Roosevelt men out of 13. Nor could he explain away the fact that in some contested cases, Indiana for example, the national committee decided by *unanimous* vote that there was not a shred of evidence to support his charges of fraud by Taft. Finally, as that expert in conventions, Bryan, observed, Roosevelt would have dealt with Taft men in the same way if he had had a majority in the national committee.[44]

Roosevelt filled the newspaper headlines; Taft wielded power in the party organization. The National Committee decided the contested cases by steam-roller tactics and gave Taft 235 delegates and Roosevelt only 19. The 72 delegates Roosevelt said were denied him were then placed on the temporary roll of the convention. When Roosevelt men protested, Taft men indicated that no business was in order until after the convention itself was organized. Thus the national committee gave Taft a majority in a convention which Mr. Dooley correctly predicted would be a "combination iv th' Chicago fire, St. Bartholomew's massacre, the battle iv th' Boyne, the life iv Jesse James, and the night iv th' big wind." In a drama of passion and principle, friendships crumbled and men divided between the "amiable island," Taft,[45] and the "bull moose," Roosevelt.

Roosevelt took an unprecedented step for a candidate by going to Chicago and personally assuming direction of the battle. On convention eve, June 17, he aroused an audience of twenty thousand persons to frenzy with a speech that ended with his saying ". . . we stand at Armageddon, and we battle for the Lord."[46]

The diminutive Victor Rosewater, acting chairman of the national committee, opened the convention on June 18. James Watson was Taft's floor leader; Governor Herbert S. Hadley, of

Missouri, Roosevelt's. Hadley quickly moved to seat 72 delegates in place of Taft delegates on the temporary roll. His defeat put Taft in control for the rest of the convention, a control to be made doubly sure when the Committee on Credentials sustained the national committee and Roosevelt at best could count on but 344 delegates. Had he been given 72 more, he would have had 416, still 31 short of a majority. He suffered an additional setback when Elihu Root was chosen as both the temporary and permanent chairman.

Roosevelt's managers failed to interest La Follette in a plan to name Governor Francis E. McGovern, of Wisconsin, as temporary chairman. The intransigent La Follette hated Roosevelt too much to make a deal or alliance with him, and Roosevelt knew that he would never get La Follette's 36 delegates. The vote between McGovern and the Taft candidate, Root, was close, 502 to 558, but it was a great victory for Taft even though it appeared that both he and Roosevelt would need La Follette's men in order to win a majority.

In his keynote address Root damned not the Democrats but his fellow Republican Roosevelt. If the minority would not agree with the majority, he implied that it had the option to bolt. He stressed that "the Republican Party will uphold at all times the authority and integrity of the courts," and the overall tenor of his address favored conservative and restraining action rather than radical reforms, hence was unacceptable to the Progressives.[47]

Root tried to be fair in the votes taken on seating contested delegates and to be just in unraveling problems caused when state primary laws and the rules of the party conflicted. In the end, with the reports of the National Committee and of the Committee on Credentials confirmed by the floor, enough Roosevelt delegates were thrown out to give Taft control of the convention. Every time Root ruled in favor of Taft, Roosevelt's delegates shouted derisively "Toot! Toot! All aboard! Choo Choo!" and rubbed pieces of sandpaper together to imitate the sound of a locomotive. George Perkins, for one, felt "very much as a man does toward someone who has murdered his parents or outraged his sister" and was ready to support a third party.[48]

The short platform was adopted after La Follette failed to substitute his own for it and without Roosevelt delegates voting on it at all, evidence that they no longer intended to participate in the proceedings. It dealt more with generalizations than with specific recommendations. While it upheld the authority of the courts it also called strongly for judicial reforms that would speed up justice and make both civil and criminal cases less costly. While it condemned the recall of judges, it asserted that some simple means must be found to remove those unfit. It then went on to declare for international peace and arbitration; the suppression of monopoly and privilege; a reasonably protective tariff; an investigation of the high cost of living; better banking currency; a civil service based on merit and tenure of office based on good behavior and efficiency; publicity for campaign contributions; conservation of natural resources; the reclamation of arid lands and the opening of Alaska coal mines on a leasehold system; a general parcel post; the protection of American citizens in foreign countries; an efficient navy; ship subsidies; federal action in controlling the Mississippi River; economy and efficiency in government; and high moral standards in civic and political life. That it had not been influenced by the Progressives was illustrated by its failure to call for presidential primaries. According to critics, Taft could stand on the platform only on the basis of expediency, only because he believed that he was defending the country from a great national calamity and that the end justified the means. Since Taft would rather lose the election and even destroy his party than see Roosevelt nominated, Chauncey Depew said that "the only question now is which corpse gets the most flowers."[49]

After many rumors about a possible compromise candidate, say Hadley, had been squelched, only the names of Taft and Roosevelt were placed in nomination, with Warren G. Harding's description of Taft as "the greatest Progressive of the age" received with derisive howls by many delegates. At Roosevelt's direction, his 344 delegates refused to participate in the proceedings, and the first ballot resulted in 561 votes, or a majority, for Taft, 107 for Roosevelt, Cummins, 17, La Follette, 41, and Hughes, 2. Taft's renomination came as an empty honor, for there was no enthusiasm for him at Chicago. The fight was not for him but against Roosevelt.

Rather than turning the wrath of the Progressives and progressives away by choosing a running mate acceptable to them, Taft alienated them by insisting upon James Sherman again.

After Sherman was named and the convention ended, at 10:30 P.M., June 21, men shouting "We Want Teddy" gathered at Orchestra Hall a mile away to pledge support to their hero in the greatest open revolt against the Republican party since the Silver Republicans defected in 1896. Once the millionaires Frank Munsey and

George Perkins offered to "see him through," Roosevelt declared himself a presidential candidate and announced the formation of a third party. On June 22 a committee composed of representatives from twenty-two states named him for president. On the next day, a convention held in Orchestra Hall ratified the nomination and issued a call for the formation of Progressive state organizations which would send delegates to a new national convention.

Meanwhile, in a statement made to the *New York Times,* Taft told the people of the great danger facing the nation.

> Never before in the history of the country was such a preconvention campaign fought. Precedents or propriety were broken in a President's taking the stump . . . but the emergency was great and the course thus taken was necessary to avoid a National calamity, and in view of the result it was justified. . . .
>
> The question here at stake was whether the Republican party was to change its attitude as the chief conservator in the nation of constitutional representative government and was to weaken the constitutional guaranties of life, liberty and property, and all other rights declared sacred in the Bill of Rights, by abandoning the principle of the absolute independence of the judiciary, especially to the maintenance of these rights. . . .

It was not necessary, he concluded,

> to speak of the result in November or of the issues which will arise between the Republican and Democratic parties in the Presidential campaign to follow. . . . It is enough now to say that, whatever may happen in November, a great victory for the Republican party and the people of the United States has already been won.[50]

The operation at Chicago had been a success. Would the patient survive?

IV

Bryan, who attended the Republican national convention as a newspaper reporter, was convinced that the Republican split imperatively demanded the naming against Taft of a progressive at the Democratic national convention to be held at Baltimore. While he could not altogether be ruled out as a presidential possibility, he was determined that the mantle of leadership in the Democracy should pass to another. Having evaluated the careers and characters of the major presidential contenders, Champ Clark, Judson Harmon, Oscar W. Underwood, and Woodrow Wilson, he had decided that Wilson, the remarkably capable reform governor of New Jersey, was the most progressive.

At Baltimore, as at Chicago, the majority of the delegates were progressive while the party machinery was controlled by conservatives. With his great parliamentary skill and superb oratorical powers, Bryan destroyed the hopes of Clark, who at one point obtained a majority of the ballots, by preventing him from obtaining the necessary two-thirds. In thoroughly dispassionate manner he killed the ambition of a friend and supporter of twenty years in favor of one who was more loyal to principles than to persons, even to close friends.

The Baltimore platform, the fifth Bryan had written for his party, contained moderate pronouncements designed to avoid giving offense to either the conservative right or the radical left. Among its major demands were those for tariff reform, banking and currency reform, and legislation which would regulate business competition rather than business monopoly. Interested more in general ideas than in specific details, Wilson planned to campaign almost exclusively upon these paramount causes, which he believed would appeal to the small entrepreneur who was fighting a losing battle with the large corporations. Thus he and Roosevelt, who would soon adopt a similar reform platform, differed little on political fundamentals and by contrast made Taft appear as the lonely conservative.

V

Taft's formal notification of his nomination, on August 1, should have been routine, but Root created a mild public sensation by denying that the methods used at the Chicago convention were other than just. In his speech of acceptance, Taft stood squarely, honestly, and boldly as the conservative candidate for president. He staked everything upon the presumed desire of sober men for calmer politics, stable government, and business tranquillity. He mentioned many matters but spoke particularly of the need to preserve the Constitution and the institutions of the country, to revise the tariff but to keep it protective, to improve upon the antitrust law, and to beware of the peddlers of panaceas. He thanked those who at Chicago had saved the Republican party for future usefulness, criticized the Progressives for having attempted "to violate the two-term tradition," and joined them to the Democrats as causative agents in what he considered a tendency toward socialism. In his customary way, weighty but not piercing, occasionally impressive but never thrilling, using tame rather than fighting words, he neglected to assail either Roosevelt or Wilson and to provide a stirring war cry for his own followers. He thus failed to reveal himself as a political man of resources, vigor, and skill, one with a certain élan of leadership needed in this crisis of the Republican party. A week later he issued a forty-thousand-word pamphlet defending the Chicago convention from the charges of fraud leveled against it.

Meanwhile on August 5 the National Progressive party held its promised convention at Chicago, where the two thousand delegates, including women but lacking many ward heelers and professional politicians, spoke of the need for "social brotherhood," "representative government," and "an undivided nation." Under the motto of "Pass Prosperity Around," the new "Moosevelt" party would make human living easier, free the hands of honest business, make trade and commerce sound and healthy, protect womanhood, save childhood, and restore the dignity of manhood. But Roosevelt vetoed the acceptance of Negroes, particularly those from the South, as members of the party, and most of them went for Taft; and few noticed that the proceedings were as arbitrarily managed by their leaders as the steam roller had worked for Taft. When the "Battle Hymn of the Republic" was preferred by the Bull Moosers as their national anthem to "Columbia, the Gem of the Ocean," it was clear that there was in the making a religious revival rather than a political meeting. When Albert J. Beveridge concluded his keynote speech, rather than applauding him the delegates again sang the "Battle Hymn." On the next day Roosevelt gave his "confession of faith" speech, and on the third and last day Hiram Johnson was chosen as his running mate. Unaware of the differences of viewpoint existing in inner circles, as between Perkins and Amos Pinchot, the delegates then adopted the most progressive political and social platform in the history of the nation. It called for the direct primary; a presidential preference primary; short ballot; initiative, referendum, and recall, including the recall of judicial decisions; woman suffrage; the registration of lobbyists; more publicity for campaign funds; and a "more easy and expeditious method of amending the Constitution." On social issues it called for legislation on minimum wage standards, child labor, industrial health and accidents, social insurance, agricultural credit

241

and cooperation, and a national Department of Labor. While it called for strengthening the Sherman Antitrust Act, that plank was deleted before the platform went to press; and it wanted a tariff no higher than the cost of production at home and abroad. With a rampant Bull Moose on their banners, the delegates dispersed with great hopes for winning over the electorate.

On August 26, 1912, Taft wrote to Mrs. Taft:

> As the campaign goes on and the unscrupulousness of Roosevelt develops, it is hard to realize that we are talking about the same man whom we knew in the presidency. . . . He is seeking to make his followers "Holy Rollers," and I hope that the country is beginning to see this. . . . I have not any feeling of enmity against Roosevelt or any feeling of hatred. I look upon him as an historical character of a most peculiar type in whom are embodied elements of real greatness, together with certain traits that have now shown themselves as unfitting him for any trust or confidence by the people. I look upon him as I look upon a freak, almost, in the zoological garden, a kind of animal not often found. So far as personal relations with him are concerned, they don't exist—I do not have any feeling one way or the other.[51]

Roosevelt during a ten-thousand-mile tour of the West and South spoke about the need to increase the powers of the federal government, wrote Taft off as undeserving of debate, and attacked Wilson. Coached by Bryan, the precise, intense, and eloquent Wilson spoke first in the East and later in the Middle West about "important" things only—of the need for tariff reform to a tariff-for-revenue-only basis, of banking and currency reforms, of regulating business competition rather than preventing monopolies, and of the need for labor to organize. He not only preached political righteousness but suggested practical methods for reform. He aimed at keeping the progressive Democratic vote and winning over the progressive Republican vote, for he correctly saw the contest as one between himself and Roosevelt.

Taft retired to Beverly at the end of the congressional session late in August and abandoned his party. Neither he nor the members of his cabinet actively participated in the campaign even though he contested with Roosevelt and Wilson for the presidency and with Roosevelt for control of the Republican party. In September, Vermont preferred Taft to a Roosevelt Republican and Ohio amended its constitution along unmistakably progressive lines. Early in October Taft asserted that the Progressive platform was a "crazy quilt" made up of "new fads and theories, many of which are preposterous and impractical," and that the country was too prosperous and contented to be attracted by it. Had he rested on the general argument, he might have ended the campaign in dignity. Instead he ascribed the prosperity to tariff protection.

Many questioned the utility of Taft's reelection because the new House of Representatives promised to be Democratic and the Senate anti-Republican. Moreover, he was charged with having played constantly for partisan advantage, shifted his responsibilities, evaded his duties, and kept the nation in turmoil. Since he had lost the confidence of the voters and failed to unify his party, the insurgents had bearded him with impunity while the Democrats in Congress harassed him until he seemed to be shorn of power. While friends like John Hays Hammond stated that he was a patriotic, honest, and honorable man who recognized the limitations fixed by the Constitution and was a conscientious administrator, others like George Harvey asserted that his record as president was nevertheless "a register of failure, not because he is a man of straw, but because he is not a man of iron."[52] On the other hand, he was the recognized head of his party, had upheld the no-third-term tradition, and had battled for what he considered right. He had achieved his objective of denying Roosevelt the nomination, thus saving his administration from rejection. Apparently satisfied with what he had accomplished, he would do no more.

Despite the defection of most leading Progressives to Taft, Roosevelt continued his campaign. On October 14 in Milwaukee a demented would-be assassin gave him a severe gunshot wound in the chest. In heroic vein, he insisted upon delivering a scheduled speech before submitting to medical care and said that the fight would go on whether he lived or died. With keen political sense, Wilson sent words of sympathy and announced that he would refrain from campaigning until Roosevelt was well. With equally good political sense, Roosevelt declined the gesture. Taft received the news of the attack in New York, where he had gone to attend a banquet. With little visible emotion he told a *New York Times* reporter, "I am delighted to learn that the dastardly attack was unsuccessful. The resort to violence is out of place in our twentieth-century civilization and under our form of government." However, he also sent Roosevelt a telegram saying that he was praying for his speedy recovery. About a week after he had been shot, Roosevelt returned to Oyster Bay. He recuperated enough to be able to speak at a huge election-eve rally at Madison Square Garden.

In the meantime, the death of Sherman, on Wednesday, October 30, caused Taft many anxious moments, for he believed that the voters would be confused and shun his ticket. After conferring with numerous advisers and considering several potential candidates, he decided to leave the office of vice-president vacant. He had recently given an exclusive interview to A. V. Pinci, of *Harper's Weekly,* in which he had favorably summarized the domestic and diplomatic accomplishments of his administration and added that whether he won or lost in November he would be grateful to the American people for having bestowed upon him their greatest honor.[53] Because the interview failed to say anything about the campaign, Taft agreed to give Louis Seibold, of the *New York World,* an interview on the issues of the campaign and on his relationship with Roosevelt that could be printed on Saturday, just two days prior to election day. On Friday, Seibold accompanied him from Washington to New York—Taft was going on to attend Sherman's funeral at Utica—and gave him the result to edit. But Taft then wished to obtain the advice of Root, Wickersham, and Barnes, at New York, with respect to some of the statements he had made about Roosevelt.

"I'm afraid that's too late," said Seibold.

"But Roosevelt was my closest friend," replied Taft, who would not release the interview for publication. Indeed, when Seibold, after the election, asked him for a copy of the interview, he said that there was none and that he had ordered his secretary to burn his notes.[54] Thus Taft failed to grasp a last opportunity to tell his version of his relationship with Roosevelt and to favorably affect the voting. Betting odds on election eve stood at 1 to 4 for Roosevelt, 1 to 3 for Taft, and 4 to 1 for Wilson.

In 1910, insurgent Republican disaffection with Taft especially over tariff reform, railroad reform, and conservation had been notable in the East and Middle- and Far West. Instead of trying to win the insurgents to his side, Taft had campaigned against them and split his party. Only their partisan support of the Republican organization had saved it from a worse drubbing than it received. After 1910, a Democratic House and a Senate in which progressive Republicans held the balance of power either objected to his legislative demands or changed them so as to make them more liberal. His retort sometimes took the form of a veto. While Taft continued to cooperate with Cannon and with Aldrich until his retirement, first La Follette and then Roosevelt led the Progressive Republican movement against him. Thus, the results in 1912 were predictable because of the split in the party and the fact that two progressive candidates challenged Taft.

In 1908, Taft had won 7,600,000 popular votes, Bryan 6,400,000, and Eugene V. Debs 400,000, with Taft taking 321 of the 483 electoral votes. Based upon the reapportionment of 1910, there were now 531 electoral votes. In the elections of November 5, 1912, the Democrats won their greatest triumph since 1852. They obtained control of the presidency and both houses of Congress for the first time since 1892, and Democrats were elected in twenty-one of the thirty-five states that held gubernatorial contests. Although Wilson did not win a majority of the popular vote, the split between Taft and Roosevelt made Wilson president and provided a victory for Wilsonian rather than Rooseveltian progressivism. Taft received most of the votes of conservative Republicans and also of some conservative Democrats and ran best in the least industrialized states. Roosevelt won the Progressive Republicans, especially in the Middle West, but failed to win either anti-conservation westerners, the progressives in the Democracy, or those Republicans who, like William Borah, were progressives rather than Progressives and preferred to reform their party from within, not to build a third party. La Follette, who campaigned in Wisconsin only, had ferociously attacked Roosevelt and brought many Republicans over to Wilson. The most spectacular gains were made by Debs, who more than doubled his vote of 1908 to an impressive 900,000 votes, outpolled Taft in seven states (Arizona, California, Florida, Louisiana, Mississippi, Nevada, and South Dakota), and revealed the extent of the belief that capitalism was wholly evil and was incapable of being reformed by either Progressive Republicans or Democrats. To put it another way, the country did not go Democratic because Taft and Roosevelt together polled 1,311,444 more votes than Wilson. But adding Debs's vote to the 4,119,507 votes given Roosevelt and the 6,293,019 given Wilson plainly showed 11,314,399 progressive votes against Taft's 3,484,946. If the 23.15 percent of the vote given Taft may be considered conservative, then 75.26 percent of the vote was progressive. Since third parties other than the Socialist party won only 1.5 percent of the votes, most of their members apparently voted progressive too. The electoral vote was 435 for Wilson; 88 for Roosevelt, who carried six states (Pennsylvania, Michigan, Minnesota, South Dakota, Washington, and California); and a mere 8 for Taft, who carried only Vermont and Utah in the worst drubbing a presidential candidate had yet received (his record would not be matched until 1936, when Alf M. Landon carried only Maine and Vermont against Franklin D. Roosevelt). "What I got," he commented ruefully, "was the irreducible minimum of the Republican Party."[55]

A brief summary of the popular vote by sections reveals that geography played an important part in the elections. In 1908, Taft had carried all of the eastern states over Bryan by a vote of almost two to one, with third parties negligible except in the most industrialized states—Massachusetts, New York, and Pennsylvania. In 1912 he carried only Vermont. Although he did better than Roosevelt in six of the nine states, Wilson carried eight of them.

In 1908, Taft had squeezed by Bryan in the Border States of Delaware, Maryland, and Missouri by very close votes, won handily in West Virginia, and lost Kentucky. In 1912 he lost every one of these states and Roosevelt received more votes in Maryland and in West Virginia than he did.

Taft had lost the entire South in 1908, yet he had run strong in the upper South (Virginia, North Carolina, and Tennessee), polled a third of the vote of Florida and Alabama and almost a fourth of that of Texas, and lost Oklahoma by only twenty thousand votes. In 1912, seven southern states increased their Democratic vote and five decreased it, with the exodus of votes going to Roosevelt rather than to Taft. In 1908, third-party votes had totaled 71,725; in 1912 they totaled 359,477. Except for Oklahoma, which gave Taft twice as many votes as Roosevelt, Roosevelt obtained 50 to 200 percent more than Taft in the other states. In 1908, for example, North Carolina had given Taft 114,887 votes and third parties 345; in 1912, it gave 29,129 to Taft and 70,273 to third parties. Taft did worse than Roosevelt in eight of the twelve states and received only 15.7 percent of the votes cast in the South.

In 1908, Taft had carried all the states of the Middle West, most of them by very large pluralities. In 1912 there was a shifting of votes out of the Democratic party by lows of from two to three thousand in Wisconsin and Minnesota to a high of eighty thousand in Ohio. But the votes went to third parties rather than to Taft. In the seven states, 1,339,556 votes were cast for Progressives, 1,150,086 for Republicans, and 1,718,602 for Democrats. Both Michigan and Minnesota gave pluralities to Roosevelt. In Ohio, 573,312 votes had been cast for Taft in 1908 and 46,519 for third parties; in 1912, the Republican vote was reduced to 278,168 while the third-party vote escalated to 334,112. In percentages, Wilson won 40.96, Roosevelt 22.16, Taft 26.82, and Debs 8.6 of the Middle West. Excluded are percentages for the minor third parties.

In the Far West, while Utah supported Taft, three states went to Roosevelt (California, Washington, and South Dakota) and eleven went Democratic. To take a prime example, in 1908 California had cast 127,492 votes for Democrats, 214,398 for Republicans, and 44,707 for third parties. In 1912, the Democratic vote increased to 283,436, the Republican dropped to a mere 3,914, the Socialist vote increased from 28,659 to 79,201, and Roosevelt carried the state with 283,610 votes. All in all, Taft received only 18.3 percent of the vote in this section, or a 60 percent reduction over 1908.[56]

While Roosevelt with pardonable pride pointed to what had been accomplished by Progressives in the few months between June and November, Taft, privately and in an interview published in the *New York World,* hid his bitterness and said that he was not greatly disappointed in the results of the election, adding that hundreds of thousands of Republicans had voted for Wilson in order to defeat Roosevelt. He had been glad to serve as president and had improved the government, not by great and notable measures but by steady progress in small ways. He showed little patience with the "quacks" who were Progressives and urged Republicans, once tired of the Democrats, to restore their party to power. In the drawn battle, he had made Roosevelt's nomination impossible, while Taft's chances for reelection had been destroyed by the man who had made him president. As the *Nation* put it, "He brought his fate upon himself. When in 1908 he allowed Theodore Roosevelt to force him upon the Republican party and his country as President, he put his official life at the mercy of one man. Placed in the White House by grace of Theodore Roosevelt, he is now expelled from it as revenge of Theodore Roosevelt."[57]

13

★★★★★

CONSTITUTIONAL CONSERVATOR

I

Throughout the months during which the primary contests and the national conventions of 1912 were held, Congress was continuously in session. As far as the general public was concerned, it might not have been sitting at all, or it might have been meeting in Uganda. Once the rules were adopted, the House Democrats proceeded to put sugar on the free list. To make up for the loss of $60,000,000 a year in duties, they suggested either an income tax the Supreme Court would approve or an excise tax on corporations. Late in January 1912, the House by a nearly two-thirds vote adopted a bill lowering the wool duties and another which reduced the steel duties to a tariff-for-revenue-only basis and also enlarged the free list on manufactured steel imports. The Senate agreed to this last bill, to a bill reducing the wool duties similar to one President William Howard Taft had already vetoed, and to a cotton bill which cut the old rates in half. By revealing their intention to continue revising the tariff schedule-by-schedule on the basis of tariff-for-revenue-only and without waiting for the "scientific" data from the Tariff Board, the Democrats openly invited Taft's vetoes. The House quickly passed both the vetoed wool and steel bills over Taft's head by large majorities containing many Republicans, but the Senate held firm in both cases.

For all their hustle and bustle, the Democratic majority and their progressive Republican allies had failed to lower the tariff. But they had lured Taft into a trap. If he would not permit tariff revision without the advice of the Tariff Board, why had he overlooked its counsel in the case of Canadian reciprocity? Moreover, in one case he was hoist by his own petard when Germany and the Scandinavian countries complained that free entry of print paper was denied to them but granted to Canada. In part because of pressure by American newspapers, he had quietly, almost secretly, implemented the clause of the Canadian reciprocity bill that permitted free entry of Canadian print paper. By refusing to permit use of the most-favored-nation clause in treaties with European countries he provoked an international dispute and revealed himself inconsistent in his policy of revising the tariff only on the recommendations of the Tariff Board. As progressives saw it, he wanted only tariff reductions that would help the manufacturer at the expense of the farmer.[1]

In early February 1912, the Senate passed a bill creating a Children's Bureau in the Department of Commerce and Labor. Support for it came mainly from those who would prohibit employers from exploiting child labor, but these misread the bill, which called merely for an agency that would gather and disseminate information relating to the welfare of children. Once the House agreed to the bill, in April, Taft chose Miss Julia C. Lathrop —formerly with Jane Addams at Hull House and later with the Illinois State Board of Charities—to head the bureau, the first time in American history that a woman had been selected to head a federal bureau. Shortly thereafter Taft was happy to learn that the Senate had passed a bill he had outlined providing for employers' liability for workmen injured in interstate commerce. Although Congress was too rushed to pass all of the appropriation bills by June 30, it did pass four of them and, in addition, the Phosphorous Matches Act, a constitutional amendment providing for the direct election of senators, and an act providing for an eight-hour day on all government work. Although Taft succeeded in lowering a new pension appropriation from $75,000,000 to $35,000,000, this amount was still in violation of his preachments concerning economy and smacked of political expediency.

In early August 1912, Taft vetoed a bill granting the Dixie Power Company the right to construct a dam across the White River in Arkansas. The House had passed a "wide open" bill which the Senate had amended by giving the state of Arkansas the right to regulate the rates charged for electrical power generated by the dam. Accepting the advice of Henry L. Stimson, secretary of war, Taft stated that he would veto all bills that did not provide some method of remunerating the government and limiting the right of private corporations. In this instance, the president of the National Conservation Association, Gifford Pinchot, supported Taft and Stimson.

In mid-August, Taft refused to sign the Legislative, Executive, and Judicial Appropriations bill because it contained two riders, one putting a seven-year limit upon civil service, the other abolishing the Commerce Court. Within an hour of the veto of the bill abolishing the Commerce Court, the House repassed it by a three-to-one margin, but the Senate refused to agree. In its closing moments Congress provided that two radio operators rather than one must serve on passenger liners, an outgrowth of the *Titanic* tragedy; placed all radio communications under federal control; and prohibited the making of any "false or fraudulent statement" as to "any curative or therapeutic effect" on a drug package label.[2]

Although the second session of the Sixty-second Congress sat from December 4, 1911, to August 26, 1912, expended a billion dollars, and talked twenty-six million words, it did no truly outstanding work. One of the reasons for its extensive prolongation was the desire of its members to play politics in a presidential election year; another, the differences between the two houses; a third, the endlessly recurring differences between the houses and Taft, who got along better with the Democratic House than with the Republican Senate. In the eyes of a host of observers, by vetoing appropriation bills and tariff reduction bills he seriously imperiled his chances for a second four years in the White House.

Although defeated in November, Taft meant to battle it out with the third and final session of the Sixty-second Congress, which would meet in December and sit until March 3, 1913. It was evident, moreover, that his defeat took a heavy burden from his shoulders and restored his zest for life and sense of humor. Unlike many men in high office, he did not consider himself indispensable, saying in one instance that if he and his cabinet disappeared the bureaucracy could continue to administer the government. Nor did he harbor ill-feelings or resentment over his defeat, as exemplified in a speech he gave to the Lotus Club in New York City on November 16.

Taft had accepted the invitation before the election. Now that he was about to be shorn of office, he could speak only of what had been rather than of the present or the future. He nevertheless accepted the invitation, he said, because the diners were "organized to furnish consolation to those who would forget, an opportunity for a swan song to those about to disappear." He continued half-serious, half-humorous, by denying that the discretion allowed a president by the Constitution made him more powerful than kings or emperors in Europe. Indeed, "the consciousness of such power is rarely, if ever, present in the mind of the ordinary individual acting as president, because what chiefly stares him in the face in carrying out any plan of his is the limitation upon that power and in its extent." With perhaps Roosevelt in mind, but without mentioning his name, he added:

> Of course, there are happy individuals who are able nevertheless to ignore those limitations both in mind and practice, and as to them the result may be different. But to one whose training and profession is subordinate to law, the intoxication of power rapidly sobers off in the knowledge of its restrictions and under the prompt reminder of an ever-present and not always considerate press, as well as the kindly suggestions that not infrequently come from [Congress].

He then offered several suggestions for improving the government. A single six-year term for president was preferable to the present system because the incumbent need not divide his time between public service and playing politics looking to reelection. Second, to bring the executive and legislative branches more closely together he would give cabinet members nonvoting seats in both houses. Finally, he would free the president of much of the time and effort devoted to the patronage by placing postmasters and consular officials under civil service.

In another passage revealing of his character, he said that the presidency was not a position to be enjoyed by a sensitive man because it was subject to criticism from the moment a man entered it until he left it. "I don't know that this evil has been any greater in this administration than in a previous administration," he added. "All I know is that it was my first experience and that it seemed to me as if I had been more greatly tried than most presidents by such methods."

The office of president, Taft went on, was a great one to hold, at the same time an honor and a great pleasure, and also a mark for misrepresentation and false attack, and he closed on this point with a blast at the muckrakers, whose heyday he correctly predicted was about over.

The only satisfaction a president had, Taft continued, was "the thought that one has done something permanently useful to his fellow countrymen. . . ." He felt deep gratitude to the American people for having given him the honor of being president and hoped that enough progress had been made during his tenure to warrant their confidence. He regretted that he had not accomplished more. His chief regret was the failure of the Senate to ratify the general arbitration treaties with France and Great Britain, treaties which would have been steps toward general world peace, but he did not despair of their ultimate success.

What should be done with former presidents? Taft then asked. One could chloroform them, thereby assuring the people that they need never fear their attempt to return to office. Second, there was William Jennings Bryan's suggestion of giving them nonvoting seats in the Senate and, as Taft put it, having them "expire under the anaesthetic effects of the debates." He disagreed with Bryan and preferred the chloroform. Finally, with the diners all on their feet, he gave a toast to "the next President of the United States."

Taft had given one of the best speeches of his presidential career. Without mentioning either Roosevelt or Woodrow Wilson, he had paid his compliments to the one and wished the other well. Gay rather than morose, looking and acting as happy as a boy out of school, he revealed himself free of ill-feelings and resentment over his defeat. By showing himself to be a good loser he reinstated himself in the affection of the people, and public opinion henceforth was more kindly toward him.[3]

When the third session of the Sixty-second Congress met on December 2, Taft and its members were in an anomalous if not absurd position, for he and many of them had been repudiated at the polls. Wilson would assume the presidency on March 4, 1913, but the new Congress just elected would not have met until December had he not stated that he would call it into extra session about April 15 to reform the tariff. Taft of course sent the Congress his annual message and a number of special messages, among them one which asked that it confer upon cabinet members the right to sit and talk in either house. Meanwhile Congress suggested a pension plan for former presidents and passed bills providing for the physical valuation of railroad properties as the basis for rate making and endorsed Taft's placing of fourth-class postmasters in the classified service. Taft's placing of the postmasters and also of twenty thousand navy yard workers under civil service was looked upon by some as part of his plan to take the patronage out of politics, by others as evidence that he wished to keep Republican incumbents in their positions. Progressives became angry, moreover, because he also dismissed a number of postmasters for alleged "pernicious political activity" during the campaign, saying that he was now removing them for doing what he had required them to do in order to make his renomination possible.

Taft had planned to return to Cincinnati upon the expiration of his term to seek employment as general counsel rather than to enter active legal practice, and to serve the Republican party as an elder statesman. By mid-December, however, he had accepted an offer by his alma mater, Yale University, to become a professor of law.

While Congress recessed for the holidays, Taft boarded the battleship *Arkansas* for an inspection trip of the Panama Canal. On January 4, 1913, in a major address, he defended the policies of his administration, now favored the arbitration of the dispute with Great Britain over the Panama Canal tolls, and urged the adoption of the reciprocity agreement with Canada and of the arbitration treaties with France and Great Britain—to no avail. As he saw it, the Republican party had succeeded in its purpose because it had averted the danger of Roosevelt's election, and he now invited all men, regardless of party, to join in supporting the Constitution. He also made his last appointments to office, including the members of the Commission on Industrial Relations. He directed the commission to investigate the conditions that provoked such violent labor disturbances at those at Lawrence and Lowell, Massachusetts, and at Passaic, New Jersey, in which the International Workers of the World loomed large, and to recommend solutions to industrial problems lest they add fuel to the fire of the Socialists.

Upon its return to duty, meanwhile, Congress prohibited corporations from making contributions to political conventions and primaries and limited the amount of individual campaign contributions. By the Edwin Y. Webb bill it prohibited the shipment in interstate traffic of liquor intended for sale in dry states. While it authorized the construction of a single battleship, it received too late to do anything about it the Pujo Committee Report on its investigation of the money trust. When Taft vetoed the Webb bill, Congress passed it over his veto; when he vetoed a restrictive immigration bill, the Senate overrode the veto but the House upheld the veto by a mere five votes. Among his last acts as president, Taft sent Congress a special message proposing the adoption of a federal budget and an announcement that the Sixteenth Amendment had been ratified and now would be added to the Constitution.

II

On March 4, 1913, half a million people gathered for the inauguration of Woodrow Wilson in fair weather much different from the storm during which Taft had taken his oath. "I'll be glad to be going—this is the loneliest place in the world," Taft told Wilson. What had Taft accomplished?

Taft and Mrs. Taft had set a good table, entertained frequently, and made the White House a center of good cheer during four of the most prosperous years in American history. However, Mrs. Taft so overexerted herself with social and charitable affairs that she broke down physically. While Taft's devotion to her further endeared him to a public that liked him personally if not politically, her long illness placed a great burden upon him for over a year and deprived him of the advice of his most capable and interested critic.

No great scandal or corruption marked Taft's term. Nor did he take any steps backward, yet he remains the gigantic symbol of standpattism—the champion of privilege, of property rights as the bulwark of civilization, and of the status quo—and as the opponent of both direct and social democracy. His legislative record does not wholly warrant such a picture, for it included many solid achievements. He had undertaken the first tariff revision since 1897. The Payne-Aldrich tariff retained the protective principle, yet its corporation tax feature was deemed to be "progressive." He had placed Roosevelt's conservation work on a legal basis and even improved upon it, made a real advance in railroad regulation, launched an antitrust crusade to which Roosevelt's paled in comparison, and nearly completed the Panama Canal. Among other achievements, his administration created postal savings banks and parcel post systems, added two states to the Union and two amendments to the Constitution, established a Department of Labor separate from Commerce, regulated corporate campaign contributions, provided a Children's Bureau, passed a white slave act, abolished the manufacture of phosphorous matches, limited work on federal projects to eight hours a day, and strengthened the Pure Food and Drugs Act. Taft's appointments to the federal judicial system—he named six new Supreme Court justices and a total of 45 percent of the federal judiciary—were excellent, and he made notable contributions in seeking efficiency and economy in government and in suggesting the adoption of a federal budget. Conservatives also praised him for vetoing a number of measures which they believed either violated the Constitution or advanced a welfare state.

The results of Taft's choice of conservative corporation lawyers for his cabinet were that they advised him neither to sponsor progressive domestic measures nor to adopt foreign policies more conciliatory than those of Roosevelt. Nothing memorable was accomplished by the Democrat, Franklin MacVeagh, at the Treasury Department, certainly not in the way of banking and currency reform. If Charles Nagel, at the Department of Commerce, did anything remarkable, it was to place his agency more than ever before at the disposal of America's businessmen. Secretary of Agriculture James Wilson gave a black eye to his department in the Dr. Washington Wiley affair. George Wickersham won the enmity of the business community because of his antitrust crusade and battle against progressive railroad regulations, and Richard Achilles Ballinger furnished the ingredients for one of the most bitterly fought intergovernmental squabbles not only of Taft's term but of American history. Frank Hitchcock, who managed to place the Post Office on a paying basis, was feared by Taft until the eve of the national Republican convention of 1912 as a potential presidential rival or as one who would throw the influence of the patronage to Roosevelt. Not until Stimson succeeded Jacob Mc-Gavock Dickinson and Leonard Wood became army chief of staff was firm and capable leadership given the War Department. Taft's best secretary was George Meyer, who reformed the navy in many ways and brought the fleet to a new point in efficiency. It was Taft's luck that like so many of his colleagues Meyer preferred Roosevelt to him and gave him only perfunctory support in the campaign of 1912.

Roosevelt had been his own secretary of state. Although he had realistically backed water in the Far East before obvious Japanese strength, by using his Big Stick he had impressed American power especially upon the countries of the Caribbean area. At Algeciras and elsewhere he had revealed his consciousness that a nation as vital and strong as the United States must play a responsible part in world affairs. Criticism he received for playing power politics was often virulent, but in the end it was respectful because he played the game hard and, if not always completely honestly, well and in keeping with the international posture of his country.

Under Taft, Philander C. Knox and Francis M. Huntington Wilson had undertaken a needed reorganization of the Department of State and of the consular service and largely established the foreign policies Taft followed. Not satisfied with merely seeking strategic advantages in expanding American power in the Caribbean, Taft had gone beyond Roosevelt in seeking commercial advantages especially in Central America. Through dollar diplomacy supported by military intervention and attempts to establish protectorates he had greatly added to the ill will of Latin America for the United States. Similarly, in seeking to expand the market for American capital in the Far East he won the ill will of Japan and Russia without strengthening the Open Door with respect to China. American productivity and salesmanship rather than diplomatic dickerings caused foreign trade to increase during his term except, paradoxically, in China. The end result of using the Department of State as a field agency for commercial enterprise was failure—failure either to earn profits for American bankers or to create the economic and political stability needed to obtain peace in the countries to which it directed its attention. Finally, Taft's intrusive "shopkeeper" diplomacy was resented by such nations as Britain, Japan, and Russia, while his insistence upon keeping rather than freeing the Filipinos appalled the anti-imperialists and liberals of his day. On the other hand, he had settled by pacific means all important disputes with foreign countries except the one with Great Britain over the Panama tolls, which he belatedly agreed to arbitrate; the one with Colombia over Panama; and the one with Russia over the right of Americans to freedom of travel. In addition, he launched the most ambitious attempt yet made to obtain world peace through arbitration. He not only declined to intervene in world politics but steadily maintained a policy of neutrality toward Mexico.

In part because of his parsimoniousness, in part because of his devotion to peace, Taft starved the military services. Reforms undertaken by both the army and navy were consummated by departmental administrative directive in order to evade the danger of a congressional veto for reorganizations requiring legislative sanction. During his term the army remained static in numbers, was refused financial support for an aviation program, and failed to obtain adequate training facilities and procedures for the militia. However, Stimson and Chief of Staff General Leonard Wood so reorganized the regular army that it was able to concentrate and also furnished a military policy useful in time of war.

Roosevelt had built the navy up from seventh to second place. As Stimson had done in the army, so Meyer undertook reorganization of the navy by administrative rather than congressional action, with the result that naval administration improved greatly. However, Congress would not grant funds either for the ships or naval aircraft needed or for the fortification of forward bases west of Hawaii. The result was that the United States dropped to third place as a world naval power and was incapable of defending its interests in the Pacific.

If Taft could point to a fairly laudable legislative record, how does one account for the political revolution against him? First, he perhaps dared too much. Rather than resting on his party's record, he tried to carry out the pledges he had made in his campaign speeches and in his platform. Second, he failed with respect to the Payne-Aldrich tariff, Canadian reciprocity, and his general arbitration treaties; in letting the interdepartmental disagreement between Ballinger and Pinchot balloon far out of proportion and raise questions about the efficiency of the bureaucracy; and in bullheadedly rejecting tariff reform schedule-by-schedule unless framed on the recommendations of his pet Tariff Board. Third, he allowed himself to be counseled and represented by such men as Nelson Aldrich, Joseph Cannon, Murray Crane, and Boies Penrose, men in whom the country lacked confidence. By allying himself with the Old Guard he appeared to repudiate Roosevelt's policies, thereby losing the support not only of the progressives in his own party but of the people in the elections of 1910. Thereafter he tried to be a harmonizer when the people wanted a fighter against bosses, and he sanctioned political methods condemned by the American people when he won renomination at the hands of the party organization and especially of southern delegates when a majority of the people opposed him. Challenged by the New Nationalism on one side and New Freedom on the other, he had retreated to a defense of conservative constitutionalism.

In the tariff, conservation, and railroad regulation battles, Taft had supported a minimum of reform and doggedly resisted proponents of additional reformation. He had also used the patronage against congressional insurgents—in his view they could not be loyal Republicans—and thus widened the split between the conservative and progressive wings of his party. Believing the few insurgents powerless to affect his programs adversely, he had sought support from the more numerous and much more congenial congressional conservatives. While this tactic endeared him to the latter, it drove insurgents to request a vote of confidence from their constituencies. The elections of 1910 not only provided this vote of confidence but brought a majority of Democrats into the House and strengthened the Democratic and progressive Republican forces in the Senate. For the rest of his term, Taft had to deal with a Democratic-progressive Republican coalition that blocked such of his major proposals as Canadian reciprocity, sought tariff and other reforms, and drove him often during his last year to govern negatively by veto. The same people who elected him as president gave him an opposition Congress yet held him responsible for failing to carry out the mandate they gave him.

Taft was not a bad president but a rather good one. We should therefore seek reasons for his inability to achieve more than he did in areas outside of his legislative accomplishments.

Of singular charm, Taft was an unpretentious democrat with simple personal desires. He liked to converse, to dance, particularly to waltz, to play golf, to travel, attend the theater, root at a baseball game. If he read at all, he chose biography. Of absolute integrity, high-minded, just-minded, and clean-minded, he was in no way devious. He never posed, had small capacity for self-delusion, and was completely free of the arts and practices of the demagogue. Somewhat like Warren G. Harding, he was affable, humble, kind, and conciliatory. Unlike Harding, he rarely if ever drank liquor and had only one love, his own wife. Big as he was, he was a sensitive soul who wanted affection and approval and suspected that other men with greater ability, say Charles Evans Hughes, would be a better president than he. He was not a pleasant politician like McKinley, a professional boss like Quay, a business politician like Hanna, or a congenital politician like Roosevelt. Like Ulysses S. Grant, whose peace of mind required that he be shielded from the complicated side of anything, he detested competitiveness. A national campaign for the presidency appeared to him as a "nightmare." He lacked political ambition. As he told Mrs. Taft, "Politics, when I am in it, makes me sick," and he complained that in the executive office there was too much to do and too little time to do it in. Out of office he revealed great political judgment; in office he lost his bearings. He knew that his administration must differ somehow from Roosevelt's, even if he merely carried out the same programs more efficiently, but like Herbert Hoover later, he was no renovator or innovator. Moreover, he sometimes forgot what he had said and occasionally missed appointments he had made. Slow-moving, easy-going if not lazy, never yearning for the strenuous life, he had a placid nature that craved the sort of tranquillity best obtained in the cloistered serenity of a high court. And his powerful penchant for procrastination frequently let him play bridge until the wee hours of the morning or play golf while important papers piled up on his desk or speeches to be delivered remained unwritten until the very last moment. He himself confessed: "My sin is an indisposition to labor as hard as I might; a disposition to procrastinate, and a disposition to enjoy the fellowship of others more than I ought."[4]

By virtue of his very existence, Roosevelt posed for Taft a deeply personal as well as political problem. Although Taft said he had the same ideas, ideals, and objectives as Roosevelt, he could not be another Roosevelt, as Roosevelt had led the nation to believe and expect. Nor could he be a mere echo when he was faced with solving new problems. He revealed great courage, for example, in initiating tariff reform, Canadian reciprocity, and general arbitration treaties. A better interpreter of laws than administrator of laws, he should have been a judge rather than president. To a degree, his shortcomings can be blamed on Roosevelt, upon whose record he ran and who made him president, and comparisons with Roosevelt are inevitable even though no attempt can be made here to deal fully with Roosevelt. In fairness, too, Taft's should be compared with Roosevelt's first rather than second administration. Roosevelt succeeded to the presidency by accident and for three years cooperated with the Old Guard in order to be renominated and elected in 1904. His dynamism was better revealed between 1905 and 1908, yet opposition Congresses placed a great damper upon his reform demands, especially upon those of his last two years. Taft suffered because he was Roosevelt's "appointee" but differed from him in his conception of presidential power and procedures. Less brash than Roosevelt by nature, he took a more cautious approach to administration than Roosevelt. Whether he would have been a more dynamic leader had he been elected for a second term is a question that may be raised but must go unanswered.

Roosevelt saw the presidency as a position of leadership from which he could control the destinies of men; Taft, as a position from which like an engineer he could make the organizations of government work smoothly together. Taft did not thrill or inspire men, bind men to himself by passionate admiration. Roosevelt was picturesque, indifferent to precedent, audacious in method, occasionally a prevaricator. But he made things happen while Taft waited for things to happen. Roosevelt was energetic, aggressive, dynamic; Taft was static, dilatory, sometimes indolent, and had an obstinateness that verged upon perverseness. He never could be hurried, with the result that he belatedly tried to catch up with situations after it was too late. A patrician by birth and democrat by choice, Roosevelt pitted interest groups against each other and usually obtained what was politically possible. A conservative by education and choice, Taft did not understand the dynamics of pressure groups, did not know how to be a politician in the best sense of the word, how to mobilize power in the political system, to balance the advocates of reform against those of reaction. As his brother, Horace, said, "There is no question that my brother was a very poor politician. He loathed the arts of that trade and when, of necessity, he had to practice them he was very clumsy."[5] In defending Ballinger, for example, he broke with Pinchot; in trying to help reelect James A. Tawney in 1910, he provoked great opposition by the insurgents to himself; in demanding Canadian reciprocity he violated the deep attachment of the Republican party to the principle of tariff protection; at a time when he was under attack from progressives he invited attack from rich conservative businessmen by undertaking his antitrust crusade; in the suit against United States Steel he cast aspersions on Roosevelt; and in seeking general arbitration treaties he seemed to criticize the arbitration treaties Roosevelt had negotiated while president. Roosevelt eventually forgave men who crossed him, including Taft. Taft hated certain men who did so, particularly Robert M. La Follette.

Roosevelt sought advice from many men; Taft from few, and those few included his brothers, the strict constructionist lawyers in his cabinet, congressional conservatives, and such personally conservative friends as John Hays Hammond. Roosevelt had an instinctive showman's feel for publicity that would magnify his office and himself; Taft disdained publicity and lacked flair for engaging the public's emotion. "I don't want any forced or manufactured sentiment in my favor," he once said. When a visitor at the White House urged him to undertake a press campaign so that the people could better know his ideas and aims, he replied: "I simply can't do that sort of thing. That isn't my method. I must wait for time and the result of my labors to vindicate me naturally. I have a profound faith in the people. Their final judgment will be right."[6] To Mrs. Taft he wrote, on July 20, 1912:

> The truth is it is not the height of my ambition to be popular. I have even become quite philosophical with respect

to the dislike the people may feel for me, because generally I have attributed it to some misrepresentation. . . . There are other and better things than being extremely popular. . . . I have held the office of President once, and that is more than most men have, so I am content to retire from it with a consciousness that I have done the best I could, and have accomplished a good deal in one way or another. I have strengthened the Supreme Bench, have given them a good deal of new and valuable legislation, have not interfered with business, have kept the peace, and on the whole have enabled people to pursue their various occupations without interruption. It is a very humdrum, uninteresting administration, and it does not attract the attention or enthusiasm of anybody, but after I am out I think that you and I can look back to some pleasure in having done something for the benefit of the public weal.[7]

Nevertheless, his lack of respect for the newspaper fraternity earned him a bad press. Unable to get news from him, reporters obtained it from his opponents. The muckraking magazines used him as a perpetual target, yet the most devastating criticism came not from them but from the *Atlantic Monthly*.[8]

Believing that the people would support him if he could present his case to them in person, Taft became one of the most peripatetic of presidents, covering 150,000 miles during his term. Rather than winning the people over, however, he won criticism for neglecting his work at Washington. By election time 1912, he could obtain neither campaign funds from the rich nor votes from the poor.

Roosevelt made up his mind quickly; Taft was torn by indecision at critical times. When subjected to opposing pressures he took the path of least resistance and did nothing, thereby being master neither of men nor of himself and revealing a lack of political astuteness and of self-confidence. His conceptions lacked vividness. He had a kind of grocer-intellect that operated like a weighing machine that was apt for business-like administration but showed little of fire or imagination. As early as April 29, 1909, Henry Cabot Lodge had written to Roosevelt: "[Taft] is all we believed him to be and I have great affection and respect for him, but I am surprised that he had not, in all his years of public life, learned more about politics, and you will understand that I do not mean this in any bad sense of the word, but as one of the conditions with which a man has to deal, especially a President."[9] Roosevelt would probably have told Pinchot and Ballinger to "drop it," stop their squabbling, or get out of government service. Taft fired Pinchot because of what he regarded as contempt of court, then used the congressional investigation into the differences between him and Ballinger much as a judge uses a jury.

Roosevelt wrote his speeches beforehand, painted broad pictures with sweeping phrases, premeditated upon the effect of his utterances, and accepted suggestions for improvement from those he asked to read them. Taft was a witty and humorous conversationalist, but he literally wrote his speeches "between trains," as was the case at Winona. His ponderous writing style and soporific public-speaking style won him a deserved reputation for malapropism and for political blunderings. With frank and unstudied naturalness he said what he thought without the slightest regard for how it would sound in speech or read in print, and he often said things in private that should have been made public and said publicly what better should have remained private.

Roosevelt embodied the presidency with his personality. Taft could not distinguish between himself as president and as a private person. If Roosevelt could not achieve his purpose on the basis of some constitutional or legal power, he would ask if a contemplated move were anywhere prohibited. If it was not, he would act. Trained in the law, Taft took a conservative and legalistic approach to government. He must find authority in the Constitution or in law prior to acting. There was no "undefined residuum of power" which he could use merely because the public interest required it. Since he viewed a president's power as stemming from the Constitution alone, he narrowly construed that power and denied that it involved either the exercise of political leadership or even initiative with respect to legislation. Although very late in his term he suggested that the presidential and legislative branches be brought closer together by giving cabinet members nonvoting seats in Congress, he believed that the executive and legislative branches should have equal power. Rather than the presidency, he idolized the court system as the greatest protector of property rights and needed brake on democracy, and he looked upon its critics as anarchists or communists.

With the counsel of the corporation lawyers in his cabinet and of congressional conservatives, all of whom highly respected the rights of the business interests of the country, Taft concerned himself with materialistic rather than social or moral matters. Except for tariff reform, he at first believed that he needed only to put the reforms initiated by Roosevelt upon a legal basis. No call then, to launch a reform program of his own. He not only believed that the legislation provided by the Sixty-first Congress substantially fulfilled the demands of his platform; he saw a positive value in the stalemate that might arise between President and Congress after the midterm elections, saying that "a system in which we may have an enforced rest from legislation for two years is not bad. It affords an opportunity for proper digestion of legislation and for the detection of its defects."[10] Then, when he tried to obtain congressional sanction for such ideas of his own as Canadian reciprocity and general arbitration treaties, he was defeated. Moreover, he countered two major progressive demands, one to transfer the power of government from the hands of the few to those of the many, the second to legislate advances in social justice. He did nothing to help Americanize the millions of foreigners still flocking in, to advance the status of the Negro or of the common worker, to lower the cost of living which increased during every one of his four years, to devise tax programs that would cause a more equitable distribution of the national wealth. Rather he demanded support for the documents, political machinery, and traditions of the past, opposed the extension of democracy by such methods as direct primaries, and cared little for such progressive reforms as prohibition, woman suffrage, or the initiative, referendum, and recall. Like Elihu Root, it has been said, his greatest service was "to the cause of conservative constitutionalism, which [he] defended steadfastly against the assaults of direct democracy."[11] Lacking comprehension of the changing character of his own country, he failed to lead the people in the progressive direction in which they wished to go. In answer to his personal appeals to the people to reverse their verdict against his administration, they gave him their respect, perhaps their affection, but not their confidence. As one writer put it, "Psychologically, he has failed to hit it off with his fellow countrymen, and that is much more disastrous to a public leader than to have made a botch of it politically."[12]

Of seven personal qualities a keen student of the presidency believes are needed by a president—bounce, affability, political skill, cunning, the newspaper habit, a sense of history, and a sense of humor[13]—Taft had only two—affability and a sense of humor. He lacked bounce, that "extra elasticity" that would have enabled him to thrive on a harsh diet of work and responsibility; political skill, as in winning popular support for his programs, dealing with powerful rivals in Congress, and with party and interest groups; the cunning to know when to be silent, when to speak out, when to lead the people and when to follow them; the newspaper habit, for he preferred to hear cheerful rather than discouraging news and read only those newspapers that supported him; and a sense of history to detect what the people of his time wanted done in order to provide a better life for themselves and for those to follow.

Taft and his friends declared that once time had set aside the turbulent passions and prejudices of the moment, the calmer future judgment of history would reverse the evaluation of him as a failure. After discarding the misrepresentations and vilifications heaped upon him, historians would discover what his truly memorable accomplishments were. It is easy to picture him as a victim of circumstances, as the scapegoat of a people desiring to end the rule of his party: he had faced unsolved and insoluble problems, served at a time of great discontent and ferment, his party had split before his eyes as a result of the operations of a venomous calumny machine, and he had been subjected to the vengeful and supreme disloyalty of his best friend. But such a picture would appeal as much to pity as to history and include his personal characteristics yet evade his qualities as a public figure. Was he a poor politician because he was victimized or because he lacked the foresight and imagination to notice the storm brewing against him in the political sky until it broke and swamped him? Did he not fail to see the political danger in refusing to help unhorse Cannon, in the Payne-Aldrich tariff, and in the Ballinger-Pinchot controversy, start wrong, and then find it impossible to right himself? Did he not stumble before correcting himself in the Lorimer and Wiley affairs? Can any other time but his administration be given to the breakup of the Republican party? And though he was renominated, was he not defeated, thereby ending the rule of a Republican dynasty, Cleveland excepted, which began in 1860?

The conventional image of Taft remains unflattering, but history has not been too unkind to him. When he left office, contemporary opinion evaluated his place as president as "far from the bottom, tho not near the top."[14] Research into the relative "greatness" of presidents supports this conclusion. Not a "great" president like Washington, Jefferson, Jackson, Lincoln, Wilson, or Franklin D. Roosevelt, neither was he a "failure" like Grant and Harding. Although not a "near great" like Theodore Roosevelt, he was as "average" as John Quincy Adams, Madison, Monroe,

Van Buren, Andrew Johnson, Arthur, McKinley, Benjamin Harrison, and Hoover.[15] Once he was sobered by the responsibility of the presidency and no longer subject to Roosevelt's personal influence, he for a time followed a middle course between the progressive and conservative forces in his party, then returned to his philosophical conservative self. In troubled times in which the people demanded progressive change, he saw the existing order as good. Rather than seeing the presidency as the center to which the people turned for inspired directions for conducting their lives, he acted as a bookkeeper engaged in making merely mechanical arrangements and computations.

Unable to win legislative reforms from a three-party Congress that floundered about in a bog of contrary purposes, unable to win decisions from federal judges in keeping with their increasingly liberal judgments, the American people demanded a president who would provide strong leadership both in congressional and party matters. Rather than expanding the presidential power, Taft narrowed it. When viewed as being president between two progressive presidents, Roosevelt and Wilson, he is best remembered as a constitutional conservator.

Notes

CHAPTER 1

1. For the Taft family and the Cincinnati of Taft's day, see especially Zane L. Miller, *Boss Cox's Cincinnati: Urban Politics in the Progressive Era* (New York: Oxford University Press, 1968); Ishbel Ross, *An American Family: The Tafts, 1678–1964* (Cleveland: World Publishing Co., 1964); and Mrs. William Howard Taft, *Recollections of Full Years* (New York: Dodd, Mead & Co., 1914), pp. 1–31.

2. Butt to his sister Clara, Mar. 21, 1909. Archibald Willingham Butt, *Taft and Roosevelt: The Intimate Letters of Archie Butt, Military Aide*, 2 vols. (Garden City, N.Y.: Doubleday, Doran & Co., 1930), 1:21.

3. Joseph Benson Foraker, *Notes of a Busy Life*, 2 vols. (Cincinnati: Stewart & Kidd Co., 1917), 2:398.

4. Henry F. Pringle, *The Life and Times of William Howard Taft*, 2 vols. (New York: Farrar & Rinehart, 1939), 1:96.

5. Taft to Helen Taft, July 6, 1894, ibid., 1:128.

6. Butt, *Taft and Roosevelt*, 2:441.

7. Taft to Mrs. Taft, Oct. 21, 1901, William Howard Taft Papers, Manuscripts Division, Library of Congress.

8. Taft to A. P. Wilder and J. J. Cherry, May 20, 1901; Roosevelt to Taft, July 15, 1901; J. B. Bishop to Taft, June 24, 1904, ibid.

9. Root to Leonard Wood, June 4, 1904, Theodore Roosevelt Papers, Manuscripts Division, Library of Congress. See also Roosevelt to John Hay, May 6, 1905; Roosevelt to Root, May 13, 1905, ibid.

10. Letter of May 13, 1905, ibid.

11. Roosevelt to Charles W. Eliot, Apr. 4, 1909, ibid.

12. Roosevelt to H. C. Lodge, July 11, 1905, ibid. Why Roosevelt associated Taft with the West is difficult to fathom, for both Taft and Ohio are considered to be eastern. Moreover, Taft thought that Roosevelt had been too hard on the business community.

13. Roosevelt to Taft, Aug. 21, 1907, Taft Papers.

14. A. W. Butt to his mother, July 24, 1908, Lawrence Abbott, ed., *The Letters of Archie Butt: Personal Aide to President Roosevelt* (Garden City, N.Y.: Doubleday, Page & Co., 1924), p. 67.

15. Taft to C. M. Heald, Dec. 25, 1907, Taft Papers (italics added).

16. Letter of Nov. 6, 1908, Roosevelt Papers.

17. Herbert Agar, *The Price of Union* (Boston: Houghton Mifflin Co., 1950), p. 639.

18. Pringle, *Taft*, 1:341–343.

19. Theodore Roosevelt, *An Autobiography* (New York: Charles Scribner's Sons, 1913), p. 389.

20. Roosevelt as cited by George Fort Milton, *The Use of Presidential Power, 1789–1943* (New York: Octogon Books, 1965), p. 195.

21. William Howard Taft, *Our Chief Magistrate and His Powers* (New York: Columbia University Press, 1916), pp. 139–140.

22. Pringle, *Taft*, 1:365.

23. Paolo E. Coletta, *William Jennings Bryan: I. Political Evangelist, 1860–1908* (Lincoln: University of Nebraska Press, 1964), 375–380.

24. Taft to Roosevelt, July 16, 1907, Roosevelt Papers.

25. Taft to W. R. Nelson, Jan. 18, 1908, Taft Papers.

26. William Howard Taft, *Popular Government: Its Essence, Its Permanence, and Its Perils* (New Haven:

Yale University Press, 1913), pp. 35–36.

27. William Howard Taft, *Present Day Problems: A Collection of Addresses Delivered on Various Occasions by William Howard Taft* (New York: Dodd, Mead & Co., 1908), pp. 245–246.

28. Taft, *Popular Government*, pp. 90–91.

29. Ibid., pp. 29, 85, 188.

30. Ibid., pp. 28, 29. See also pp. 85–86, 182.

31. Alpheus Thomas Mason, *William Howard Taft: Chief Justice* (London: Oldbourne, 1964), pp. 13–14.

32. Chief Usher Irwin Hood ("Ike") Hoover, *Forty-two Years in the White House* (Boston and New York: Houghton Mifflin Co., 1934), pp. 40–41.

CHAPTER 2

1. Robert H. Wiebe, *Businessmen and Reform: A Study of the Progressive Movement* (Chicago: Quadrangle Paperback, 1968), pp. 6–8.

2. Ibid., pp. 104–107; Louis Galambos, *Competition and Cooperation: The Emergence of a National Trade Association* (Baltimore: The Johns Hopkins University Press, 1966), pp. 3, 4, 8–10, 25, 28–29, 46–47.

3. See chapter 8.

4. Albro Martin, *Enterprise Denied: Origins of the Decline of American Railroads, 1897–1917* (New York: Columbia University Press, 1971), pp. 18–21, 79–80, 83–91, 111–121.

5. Samuel Haber, *Efficiency and Uplift: Scientific Management in the Progressive Era, 1890–1920* (Chicago: University of Chicago Press, 1964), p. 70; Wiebe, *Businessmen and Reform*, pp. 16–41.

6. The term "progressive" meant different things to different people. One definition is that progressives were "liberals in all parties who were seeking to advance social justice through political action." Oscar Theodore Barck, Jr., and Nelson Manfred Blake, *Since 1900: A History of the United States in Our Times*, 4th ed. (New York: Macmillan Co., 1965), p. 33. Russel B. Nye, *Midwestern Progressive Politics: A Historical Study of Its Origins and Development, 1870–1950* (East Lansing: Michigan State University Press, 1951), p. 197, says that "'Progressivism' . . . simply meant that the rule of the majority should be expressed in a stronger government, one with a broader social and economic program and one more responsive to popular control." Some autobiographers, such as Roosevelt and La Follette, and some admiring biographers of them and of others, chose events that cast their heroes in a progressive role. Some historians, among them Matthew Josephson and Louis Filler, used as their test whether a reformer opposed big business, while Daniel Aaron and Louis Hartz refuse to see this as part of a truly "liberal" tradition. Richard Hofstadter and George E. Mowry saw progressives as urban, middle-class Americans who felt their status challenged by big business, organized labor, and political machines. Wiebe, *Businessmen and Reform*, pp. 211–224, calls a progressive whoever tried "to provide the underprivileged with a larger share of the nation's benefits; to make governments more responsive to the wishes of the voters; and to regulate the economy in the public interest." By this definition, most businessmen were not progressives except when they boosted civic improvement or supported programs calling for the federal control of business. In contrast, James Weinstein, *The Corporate Ideal in the Liberal State: 1900–1918* (Boston: Beacon Press, 1968), argues that "the ideal of a liberal corporate social order was formulated and developed under the aegis and supervision of those who then, as now, enjoyed ideological and political hegemony in the United States: the more sophisticated leaders

of America's largest corporations and financial institutions" (p. ix). While he does not go that far, Gabriel Kolko, *The Triumph of Conservatism: A Reinterpretation of American History, 1900–1916* (New York: Free Press of Glencoe, 1963), holds that many big businessmen wanted government, especially the federal government, to intervene in economic matters so as to provide for stability in the marketplace.

7. See John William Gibson, *Progress of a Race*, rev. and enl. by J. L. Nichols and H. Crogman (Naperville, Ill.: J. L. Nichols & Co., 1929), esp. chap. 12–15.

8. Ray S. Baker, *Following the Color Line* (New York: Doubleday, Page & Co., 1908); George Kibbe Turner, "Daughters of the Poor," *McClure's Magazine,* 34 (Nov. 1909): 45–61.

9. Allan H. Spear, *Black Chicago: The Making of a Negro Ghetto, 1890–1920* (Chicago: University of Chicago Press, 1967); George B. Tindall, *The Emergence of the New South, 1913–1945* (Baton Rouge: Louisiana State University Press, 1967), pp. 143–151; Ray S. Baker, "The Negro's Struggle for Survival in the North," *American Magazine,* 65 (Feb. 1908):474–475, 477–485; Gilbert Osofsky, "Progressivism and the Negro: New York, 1900–1915," *American Quarterly,* 16 (Summer 1964):153–168.

10. See Robert W. Shufeldt, *The Negro, A Menace to American Civilization* (Boston: R. G. Badger, 1907); William McDougall, *An Introduction to Social Psychology* (Boston: J. W. Luce & Co., 1908); and C. Vann Woodward, *The Strange Career of Jim Crow,* 2d rev. ed. (New York: Oxford University Press, 1966).

11. William Howard Taft, "Address at Howard University, Washington, D.C.," May 26, 1909, in W. H. Taft, *Presidential Addresses and State Papers of William Howard Taft, from March 4, 1909, to March 4, 1910* (New York: Doubleday & Co., 1910), pp. 111–116. See also Taft, "Industrial Education of the Negro"

(Hampton Institute, Hampton, Va., Nov. 20, 1909), ibid., pp. 444–446; Taft, "Southern Democracy and Republican Principles" (Lexington, Ky., Aug. 22, 1907), in W. H. Taft, *Present Day Problems: A Collection of Addresses Delivered on Various Occasions by William Howard Taft* (New York: Dodd, Mead & Co., 1908), pp. 221–240.

12. Haber, *Efficiency and Uplift,* pp. ix–x, 75–98.

13. See C. C. Regier, *The Era of the Muckrakers* (Chapel Hill: University of North Carolina Press, 1932).

14. Mark Sullivan, *Our Times: The United States, 1900–1925,* 6 vols. (New York: Charles Scribner's Sons, 1926–1935), 4:123.

15. William G. McLoughlin, Jr., *Billy Sunday Was His Real Name* (Chicago: University of Chicago Press, 1955); Walter Rauschenbusch, *Christianity and the Social Crisis* (New York: Macmillan Co., 1907), *Christianizing the Social Order* (New York: Macmillan Co., 1912), and *The Social Principles of Jesus* (New York: Association Press, 1917); John A. Ryan, *A Living Wage* (New York: Macmillan Co., 1906).

16. "President Taft on Woman Suffrage," *Outlook,* 94 (Apr. 23, 1910):860–861; Editorial, "President Taft and the Suffragettes," *Independent,* 68 (Apr. 21, 1910):879; "The President on Woman Suffrage," *Literary Digest,* 41 (Apr. 30, 1910): 830.

17. See Samuel P. Hays, *The Response to Industrialism, 1885–1914* (Chicago: University of Chicago Press, 1957), pp. 94–109, 152–158, and "The Politics of Municipal Reform in the Progressive Era," *Pacific Northwest Quarterly,* 55 (Oct. 1964): 157–169; James B. Crooks, *Politics and Progress: The Rise of Urban Progressivism in Baltimore, 1895 to 1911* (Baton Rouge: Louisiana State University Press, 1968); Weinstein, *The Corporate Ideal in the Liberal State,* pp. 92–116.

18. Haber, *Efficiency and Uplift,* pp. 99–100, 115; Wiebe, *Businessmen and Reform,* pp. 9–10.

19. Woodward, *The Strange Career of Jim Crow*, pp. 90–92; Arthur S. Link, "The Progressive Movement in the South," *North Carolina Historical Review*, 23 (Apr. 1946):172–195.

20. Wiebe, *Businessmen and Reform*, pp. 8, 68.

21. See Robert M. La Follette, *La Follette's Autobiography: A Personal Narrative of Political Experiences* (Madison: La Follette Publishing Co., 1913), pp. 176–318; Louis G. Geiger, *Joseph W. Folk of Missouri* (Columbia: University of Missouri Press, 1953), pp. 86–132.

22. Haber, *Efficiency and Uplift*, pp. 108–109.

23. William Jennings Bryan, ed., *The Commoner* (Lincoln, Neb., 1901–1923), Mar. 1, 8, 15, May 10, 24, June 14, 21, Oct. 11, 1907.

24. *The Commoner*, Oct. 11, 1907; Bryan to Josephus Daniels, n.d., but 1908, Josephus Daniels Papers, Manuscripts Division, Library of Congress.

25. Cortez A. M. Ewing, *Presidential Elections from Abraham Lincoln to Franklin D. Roosevelt* (Norman: University of Oklahoma Press, 1940), pp. 17–19, 45–107, 189–218; Edgar Eugene Robinson, *The Presidential Vote, 1896–1932* (Stanford: Stanford University Press, 1947), pp. 31, 34; Hays, *The Response to Industrialism*, pp. 15–17.

26. Wiebe, *Businessmen and Reform*, p. 69.

27. See Paolo E. Coletta, ed., *Threshold to American Internationalism: Essays on the Foreign Policies of William McKinley* (New York: Exposition Press, 1970).

28. Samuel Flagg Bemis, *A Short History of American Foreign Policy and Diplomacy* (New York: Henry Holt & Co., 1959), p. 299.

CHAPTER 3

1. Henry F. Pringle, *Theodore Roosevelt, a Biography* (New York: Harcourt, Brace & Co., 1931), pp. 476–477.

2. Taft to Roosevelt, Jan. 2, 1909, Roosevelt Papers.

3. Taft to W. R. Nelson, Feb. 23, 1909, Taft Papers.

4. Mark Sullivan, *Our Times: The United States, 1900–1925*, 6 vols. (New York: Charles Scribner's Sons, 1926–1935), 4:331–332.

5. Ibid., 4:343.

6. Ibid., 4:344; Alice Roosevelt Longworth, *Crowded Hours, Reminiscences of Alice Roosevelt Longworth* (New York and London: Charles Scribner's Sons, 1933), pp. 164–165; Philip Jessup, *Elihu Root*, 2 vols. (New York: Dodd, Mead & Co., 1938), 2:137–138.

7. "Measuring Taft by His Inaugural," *Literary Digest*, 38 (Mar. 13, 1909):405–408; "Mr. Taft's Excellent Address," *American Review of Reviews*, 39 (Apr. 1909):392.

8. Taft to Jacob Schmilapp, n.d., in Herbert S. Duffy, *William Howard Taft* (New York: Minton, Balch & Co., 1930), p. 22.

9. Jessup, *Elihu Root*, 2:138.

10. Lodge cited in William Manners, *TR and Will: A Friendship That Split the Republican Party* (New York: Harcourt, Brace & World, 1969), p. 73.

11. Letter of Jan. 27, 1909, Elting E. Morison et al., eds., *The Letters of Theodore Roosevelt*, 8 vols. (Cambridge, Mass.: Harvard University Press, 1951–1954), 6:1487.

12. Letters in Taft Papers.

13. Duffy, *Taft*, pp. 244–245.

14. Joseph Benson Foraker, *Notes of a Busy Life*, 2 vols. (Cincinnati: Stewart & Kidd Co., 1917), 2:400; Francis E. Leupp, "President Taft's Own View: An Authorized Interview by Francis E. Leupp," *Outlook*, 99 (Dec. 2, 1911):811, 812.

15. Taft to Roosevelt, Mar. 21, 1909, Henry F. Pringle, *The Life and Times of William Howard Taft*, 2 vols. (New York: Farrar & Rinehart, 1939), 1:400–401 (italics Pringle's).

16. Roosevelt to Taft, Mar. 23, 1909, Taft Papers.

17. James E. Watson, *As I Knew Them: Memoirs of James E. Watson, Former United States Senator from Indiana* (Indianapolis: Bobbs-Merrill Co., 1936), pp. 144–145.

18. Taft to Charles P. Taft, Sept. 10, 1910, Taft Papers.

19. Henry L. Stimson and McGeorge Bundy, *On Active Service in Peace and War* (New York: Harper & Brothers, 1947), p. 14.

20. William Allen White, *Masks in a Pageant* (New York: Macmillan Co., 1928), p. 328.

21. Arthur W. Dunn, *From Harrison to Harding: A Personal Narrative Covering a Third of a Century, 1888–1921*, 2 vols. (New York: G. P. Putnam's Sons, 1922), 2:111–112. See also Oscar King Davis, *Released for Publication: Some Inside Political History of Theodore Roosevelt and His Times, 1898–1918* (Boston and New York: Houghton Mifflin Co., 1925), pp. 94–95, 127.

22. Ray S. Baker, *Woodrow Wilson: Life and Letters*, 8 vols. (Garden City, N.Y.: Doubleday, Doran & Co., 1927–1939), 3:181.

23. Claudius O. Johnson, *Borah of Idaho* (New York: Longmans, Green & Co., 1936), p. 114.

24. Frank W. Taussig, *The Tariff History of the United States*, 8th ed. (New York: G. P. Putnam's Sons, 1931), pp. 363–368.

25. *New York Times*, Mar. 5, 1909.

26. Claude G. Bowers, *Beveridge and the Progressive Era* (Boston: Houghton Mifflin Co., 1932), pp. 333–334.

27. James Holt, *Congressional Insurgents and the Party System, 1909–1916* (Cambridge, Mass.: Harvard University Press, 1967), p. 29.

28. Blair Bolles, *Tyrant from Illinois: Uncle Joe Cannon's Experiment with Personal Power* (New York: W. W. Norton & Co., 1951), p. 11.

29. Letter of Nov. 25, 1908, Taft Papers.

30. Taft to Root, Nov. 25, 1908, ibid.

31. Butt to his sister, Clara, in Lawrence F. Abbott, ed., *The Letters of Archie Butt, Personal Aide to President Roosevelt* (Garden City, N.Y.: Doubleday, Page & Co., 1924), pp. 379–380.

32. Letter of May 29, 1909, Whitelaw Reid Papers, Manuscripts Division, Library of Congress.

33. Horace Samuel Merrill and Marion G. Merrill, *The Republican Command, 1897–1913* (Lexington: University Press of Kentucky, 1971), pp. 243–298.

34. Kenneth W. Hechler, *Insurgency: Personalities and Politics of the Taft Era* (New York: Columbia University Press, 1940), p. 92.

35. George W. Norris, *Fighting Liberal: The Autobiography of George W. Norris* (New York: Macmillan Co., 1945), p. 103.

36. Taft to J. B. Farwell, Apr. 13, 1909, Taft Papers.

37. Robert M. La Follette, *La Follette's Autobiography: A Personal Narrative of Political Experiences* (Madison: La Follette Publishing Co., 1913), pp. 439–441.

38. Lodge to Roosevelt, Apr. 29, 1909, Henry Cabot Lodge, *Selections from the Correspondence of Theodore Roosevelt and Henry Cabot Lodge, 1884–1918*, 2 vols. (New York: Charles Scribner's Sons, 1925), 2:330–335.

39. La Follette, *Autobiography*, pp. 450–451. See also "Republican Revolt against the Aldrich Tariff," *Literary Digest*, 38 (May 15, 1909): 830–832.

40. La Follette, *Autobiography*, pp. 448–449.

41. *New York World*, July 16, 1909.

42. Watson, *As I Knew Them*, p. 141.

43. Taft to Mrs. Taft, July 18, 1909, Taft Papers.

44. Archibald Willingham Butt, *Taft and Roosevelt: The Intimate Letters of Archie Butt, Military Aide*, 2 vols. (Garden City, N.Y.: Doubleday, Doran & Co., 1930), 1:58.

45. Ibid., 1:58. On July 23, La Follette wrote to his wife that he would "do the thing that conscience

dictates—being very careful to confine *my attack to the bill*—nothing on the *President* unless it be to commend *if I can* his *effort*." Belle Case La Follette and Fola La Follette, *Robert M. La Follette, June 14, 1885–June 18, 1925*, 2 vols. (New York: Macmillan Co., 1953), 1:277–278 (hereafter cited as La Follette, *La Follette*).

46. Taft to Mrs. Taft, July 25, 1909, Taft Papers.

47. M. A. DeWolfe Howe, *George von Lengerke Meyer: His Life and Public Services* (New York: Dodd, Mead & Co., 1920), p. 442.

48. Butt, *Taft and Roosevelt*, 1: 124–127.

49. Ibid., 1:144–146 (July 18, 1909).

50. John E. Lathrop, "The Views of Champ Clark," *Outlook*, 101 (May 11, 1912):70.

51. Butt, *Taft and Roosevelt*, 1: 162–164.

52. Hammond, *Autobiography*, 2: 555.

53. Lodge to Roosevelt, July 31, 1909, Lodge, *Correspondence*, 2:343. See also "The President's Belated Intervention," *Independent*, 67 (July 29, 1909):259–261, and "Final Passage of the Tariff Bill," ibid., 67 (Aug. 12, 1909):329–330.

54. "What the New Law Really Is," *American Review of Reviews*, 40 (Sept. 1909):259.

55. Taft to Mrs. Taft, Aug. 11, 1909, Taft Papers.

56. Butt, *Taft and Roosevelt*, 1: 185.

57. Ibid., 1:3.

58. Taft to Mrs. W. H. Taft, telegrams, Sept. 16, 17, 1909, Taft Papers.

59. *New York Tribune*, Sept. 18, 1909.

60. Oscar King Davis, *Released for Publication*, pp. 164–166; Sullivan, *Our Times*, 4:369, 371; Charles W. Thompson, *Presidents I've Known and Two Near-Presidents* (Indianapolis: Bobbs-Merrill Co., 1929), pp. 213–217.

61. La Follette, *La Follette*, 1: 282.

62. See the excellent account of Taft's thinking in Stanley D. Solvick, "William Howard Taft and the Payne-Aldrich Tariff," *Mississippi Valley Historical Review*, 50 (Dec. 1963): 424–442.

CHAPTER 4

1. Arthur Henry Chamberlain, *Thrift and Conservation* (Philadelphia: J. B. Lippincott Co., 1919); Roy M. Robbins, *Our Landed Heritage* (Princeton: Princeton University Press, 1942), pp. 301–343; J. Leonard Bates, "Fulfilling American Democracy: The Conservation Movement, 1907–1921," *Mississippi Valley Historical Review*, 44 (June 1957): 29–57.

2. Samuel P. Hays, *Conservation and the Gospel of Efficiency: The Progressive Conservation Movement, 1890–1920* (Cambridge, Mass.: Harvard University Press, 1959), pp. 12–15.

3. Ibid., pp. 1–5, 16–26, 36–39, 66–72, 138–140, 265–266, 271; A. Hunter Dupree, *Science in the Federal Government: A History of Politics and Activities to 1940* (Cambridge, Mass.: Harvard University Press, 1957), pp. 232–246; Samuel Haber, *Efficiency and Uplift: Scientific Management in the Progressive Era, 1890–1920* (Chicago: University of Chicago Press, 1964), p. 14n; Elmo R. Richardson, *The Politics of Conservation: Crusades and Controversies, 1897–1913* (Berkeley: University of California Press, 1962), pp. vii–viii, 1–5, 121.

4. James Penick, Jr., *Progressive Politics and Conservation: The Ballinger-Pinchot Affair* (Chicago: University of Chicago Press, 1968), pp. 12–18; Dupree, *Science in the Federal Government*, pp. 251–252.

5. Richardson, *The Politics of Conservation*, pp. 17–46.

6. Taft quoted in John Lovelle

Withers, "The Administrative Theories and Practices of William Howard Taft" (Ph.D. diss., University of Chicago, 1956), p. 44.

7. Alan Brant Gould, "Secretary of the Interior Walter L. Fisher and the Return to Constructive Conservation: Problems and Policies of the Conservation Movement, 1909–1913" (Ph.D. diss., West Virginia University, 1969 [microfilm]), pp. 31–34; Roosevelt quoted in Hays, *Conservation and the Gospel of Efficiency*, p. 125.

8. "State or National Conservation," *Literary Digest*, 41 (Sept. 17, 1910):525–526.

9. Penick, *Progressive Politics and Conservation*, pp. 19–40, 186–187; Richardson, *The Politics of Conservation*, pp. 50–55.

10. Richardson, *The Politics of Conservation*, p. 61.

11. Penick, *Progressive Politics and Conservation*, pp. 43–76; Hays, *Conservation and the Gospel of Efficiency*, pp. 152–165.

12. Hays, *Conservation and the Gospel of Efficiency*, p. 152.

13. Penick, *Progressive Politics and Conservation*, p. 184. See also Richardson, *The Politics of Conservation*, pp. 65–76.

14. Gifford Pinchot, *Breaking New Ground* (New York: Harcourt, Brace & Co., 1947), p. 417.

15. Ibid., pp. 417–418.

16. Ibid., pp. 420–424; M. Nelson McGeary, *Gifford Pinchot: Forester, Politician* (Princeton: Princeton University Press, 1960), p. 130.

17. Archibald Willingham Butt, *Taft and Roosevelt: The Intimate Letters of Archie Butt, Military Aide*, 2 vols. (Garden City, N.Y.: Doubleday, Doran & Co., 1930), 1:348–349 (May 15, 1910).

18. Ibid., 1:350.

19. Hays, *Conservation and the Gospel of Efficiency*, pp. 28–48; Pinchot, *Breaking New Ground*, pp. 1–390; Harold T. Pinkett, *Gifford Pinchot: Private and Public Forester* (Urbana: University of Illinois Press, 1969).

20. Roosevelt to Pinchot, Mar. 2, 1909, Pinchot, *Breaking New Ground*, pp. 380–381.

21. McGeary, *Pinchot*, pp. 113–114; Pinchot, *Breaking New Ground*, pp. 375–376.

22. William Henry Harbaugh, *Power and Responsibility: The Life and Times of Theodore Roosevelt* (New York: Farrar, Straus and Cudahy, 1961), p. 384.

23. McGeary, *Pinchot*, pp. 69–77, 121–125; Penick, *Progressive Politics and Conservation*, pp. 43–76; Pinchot, *Breaking New Ground*, pp. 389, 408–413.

24. Harbaugh, *Roosevelt*, p. 384. See also Hays, *Conservation and the Gospel of Efficiency*, pp. 132–138, 147–150; "Mr. Ballinger and Mr. Pinchot," *Independent*, 67 (Sept. 9, 1909):563–564.

25. Butt, *Taft and Roosevelt*, 1: 193.

26. Alpheus T. Mason, *Brandeis: A Free Man's Life* (New York: Viking Press, 1946), p. 255, and *Bureaucracy Convicts Itself: The Ballinger-Pinchot Controversy of 1910* (New York: Viking Press, 1941), pp. 16–17.

27. Taft to Ballinger, Sept. 13, 1909, copy to Pinchot, Taft Papers. See also Mason, *Bureaucracy Convicts Itself*, pp. 74–78, and "The President and Ballinger," *Literary Digest*, 39 (Sept. 25, 1909):465.

28. Taft to Pinchot, Sept. 13, 1909, Taft Papers; Pinchot, *Breaking New Ground*, pp. 430–431.

29. W. H. Taft to H. W. Mabie, Oct. 4, 1909, Henry F. Pringle, *The Life and Times of William Howard Taft*, 2 vols. (New York: Farrar & Rinehart, 1939), 1:496; "Mr. Taft's Hand in the Pinchot Fray," *Literary Digest*, 39 (Oct. 9, 1909): 560–562.

30. Butt, *Taft and Roosevelt*, 1: 208 (Nov. 14, 1909).

31. Taft to Pinchot, Sept. 13, 1909, Taft Papers.

32. Pinchot, *Breaking New Ground*, pp. 432–436; "The Power Site Controversy," *Independent*, 67 (Sept. 30, 1909):725–726.

33. Pinchot to Taft, Nov. 4, 1909, Taft Papers.
34. Taft to Pinchot, Nov. 24, 1909, ibid.
35. Pinchot to Dolliver, Jan. 5, 1910, *Breaking New Ground*, pp. 448–449; Thomas Richard Ross, *Jonathan Prentiss Dolliver: A Study in Political Integrity and Independence* (Iowa City: State Historical Society of Iowa, 1960), pp. 270–271.
36. "Secretary Ballinger and Conservation," *Outlook*, 93 (Dec. 4, 1909):748–749; Gifford Pinchot, "The A B C of Conservation," ibid., 93 (Dec. 4, 1909):770–772.
37. Butt, *Taft and Roosevelt*, 1: 245 (Jan. 7, 1910).
38. Ibid., 1:254–256.
39. Taft to Pinchot, Jan. 7, 1910, Taft Papers.
40. Pinchot, *Breaking New Ground*, p. 451.
41. Taft to C. H. Kelsey, Jan. 10, 1910, Taft Papers.
42. Pinchot, *Breaking New Ground*, pp. 450–451.

43. Butt, *Taft and Roosevelt*, 1: 235–236.
44. Norman Hapgood, *The Changing Years: Reminiscences* (New York: Farrar & Rinehart, 1930), p. 183.
45. Taft to W. R. Nelson, May 15, 1910, Taft Papers.
46. Pinchot to Roosevelt, Dec. 31, 1909, Pinchot, *Breaking New Ground*, pp. 498–500.
47. Taft to Roosevelt, May 26, 1910, Roosevelt Papers.
48. Butt, *Taft and Roosevelt*, 2: 461 (Aug. 3, 1910).
49. Richardson, *The Politics of Conservation*, pp. 129–131.
50. Butt, *Taft and Roosevelt*, 2: 462 (Mar. 11, 1911).
51. Richardson, *The Politics of Conservation*, pp. 111–113, 132.
52. Ibid., pp. 137–144. For Fisher, see Gould, "Secretary of the Interior Walter L. Fisher and the Return to Constructive Conservation," pp. 112–538.
53. Penick, *Progressive Politics and Conservation*, p. 185.
54. Harbaugh, *Roosevelt*, p. 388.

CHAPTER 5

1. Walter Johnson, ed., *Selected Letters of William Allen White, 1899–1943* (New York: Henry Holt & Co., 1947), pp. 105–106.
2. William Allen White, *The Autobiography of William Allen White* (New York: Macmillan Co., 1946), pp. 425–426.
3. *Chicago Tribune*, Feb. 14, 1910; " 'The Return from Elba,' " *Literary Digest*, 40 (Mar. 5, 1910):427–428.
4. "Mr. Taft on the Party's Crisis," *Literary Digest*, 40 (Feb. 26, 1910): 375–379; "Taft among the Snags," ibid., pp. 381–382; and "Republican Disaffection," ibid., 40 (Apr. 2, 1910):627–630.
5. Archibald Willingham Butt, *Taft and Roosevelt: The Intimate Letters of Archie Butt, Military Aide*, 2 vols. (Garden City, N.Y.: Doubleday, Doran & Co., 1930, 1:335.
6. Roosevelt to Lodge, Apr. 11, 1910, Henry Cabot Lodge, *Selections*

from the Correspondence of Theodore Roosevelt and Henry Cabot Lodge, 1884–1918, 2 vols. (New York: Charles Scribner's Sons, 1925), 2: 367–374.
7. Philip Jessup, *Elihu Root*, 2 vols. (New York: Dodd, Mead & Co., 1938), 2:160; Henry F. Pringle, *The Life and Times of William Howard Taft*, 2 vols. (New York: Farrar & Rinehart, 1939), 1:546–547.
8. Roosevelt to Lodge, May 5, 1910, *Correspondence*, 2:379–382.
9. Butt, *Taft and Roosevelt*, 1: 312–313.
10. Ibid., 1:327–328.
11. Taft to Roosevelt, May 26, 1910, Taft Papers.
12. Roosevelt to Taft, June 8, 1910, ibid.
13. Butt, *Taft and Roosevelt*, 2: 435 (July 6, 1910).
14. Taft to Dickinson, Wicker-

sham, Meyer, et al., July 7, 1910, Pringle, *Taft*, 1:553.

15. Butt, *Taft and Roosevelt*, 1: 417–431.

16. Roosevelt to Pinchot, June 29, 1910, Roosevelt Papers.

17. Butt, *Taft and Roosevelt*, 1: 416.

18. Ibid., 2:435. See also "Little Journeys to Oyster Bay," *Literary Digest*, 41 (July 23, 1910):117–119.

19. Butt, *Taft and Roosevelt*, 2: 434–436.

20. Ibid., 2:479.

21. Ibid., 2:480–481 (Aug. 17, 1910).

22. Taft to Representative William McKinley, Aug. 20, 1910, Pringle, *Taft*, 2:565.

23. Roosevelt to Pinchot, Aug. 17, 1910, Elting E. Morison et al., eds., *The Letters of Theodore Roosevelt*, 8 vols. (Cambridge, Mass.: Harvard University Press, 1951–1954), 7: 113–114; Gifford Pinchot, *Breaking New Ground* (New York: Harcourt, Brace & Co., 1947), pp. 385–386; "Mr. Roosevelt at Osawatomie," *Independent*, 69 (Sept. 8, 1910):505–506.

24. Butt, *Taft and Roosevelt*, 2: 496–497 (Aug. 25, 1910).

25. Taft to Edward Colston, Sept. 8, 1910, Taft Papers.

26. Taft to Charles P. Taft, Sept. 10, 1910, ibid.

27. Taft to Horace D. Taft, Sept. 16, 1910, ibid.

28. Butt, *Taft to Roosevelt*, 2: 503 (Sept. 2, 1910).

29. Taft to Mrs. W. H. Taft, Sept. 28, 1910, Pringle, *Taft*, 2:578.

30. Roosevelt to Root, Oct. 21, 1910, Roosevelt Papers.

31. Jessup, *Root*, 2:164–165; "The President's View of the Patronage," *Outlook*, 96 (Sept. 24, 1910):

133–134; Editorial, "Secretary Norton's Letter," ibid., 69 (Sept. 22, 1910):658–659.

32. Butt, *Taft and Roosevelt*, 2: 511 (Sept. 13, 1910).

33. "Are the Insurgents Traitors?" *Literary Digest*, 41 (Apr. 23, 1910): 792–793; "Dolliver's Defense of Insurgency," ibid., 41 (June 25, 1910): 1248.

34. "What Congress Did," *Literary Digest*, 41 (July 2, 1910):1–3.

35. Homer E. Socolofsky, *Arthur Capper: Publisher, Politician, and Philanthropist* (Lawrence: University of Kansas Press, 1962), p. 63; "Insurgent Victories in the West," *Independent*, 69 (Aug. 11, 1910):272–274.

36. Butt, *Taft and Roosevelt*, 2: 513; Howard W. Allen, "Miles Poindexter: A Political Biography" (Ph.D. diss., University of Washington, 1959), p. 109.

37. "Advance of the Insurgents," *Literary Digest*, 41 (Oct. 15, 1910): 629–630.

38. Butt, *Taft and Roosevelt*, 2: 556.

39. Ibid.

40. "Mr. Roosevelt's Position," *Outlook*, 96 (Nov. 19, 1910):607.

41. Butt, *Taft and Roosevelt*, 2: 555.

42. Letter of Nov. 11, 1910, Lodge, *Correspondence*, 2:394.

43. See the excellent article by George E. Mowry, "Theodore Roosevelt and the Election of 1910," *Mississippi Valley Historical Review*, 25 (Mar. 1939):523–534; and Oscar King Davis, *Released for Publication: Some Inside Political History of Theodore Roosevelt and His Times, 1898–1918* (Boston: Houghton Mifflin Co., 1925).

44. "Meaning of the Republican Waterloo," *Literary Digest*, 41 (Nov. 19, 1910):915–917.

CHAPTER 6

1. A *Chicago Tribune* poll of Republican editors in twenty-six states west of the Alleghenies showed that 2,686 of them disapproved of Taft's contention and that only 812 agreed with him. Editorial, "Mr. Taft's Speech," *Independent*, 68 (Feb. 17, 1910):373.

2. Archibald Willingham Butt, *Taft and Roosevelt: The Intimate Letters of Archie Butt, Military Aide,* 2 vols. (Garden City, N.Y.: Doubleday, Doran & Co., 1930), 1:222–223.

3. Ibid., 1:307–308 (Mar. 26, 1910).

4. Taft to Otto T. Bannard, Mar. 2, 1910, Taft Papers.

5. Taft to F. Lockley, Feb. 8, 1910, ibid.

6. Albro Martin, *Enterprise Denied: Origins of the Decline of the American Railroads, 1897–1917* (New York: Columbia University Press, 1971), pp. 68–69.

7. Butt, *Taft and Roosevelt,* 1: 303.

8. Taft speech at Milwaukee, Wis., Sept. 17, 1909, cited in Henry F. Pringle, *The Life and Times of William Howard Taft,* 2 vols. (New York: Farrar & Rinehart, 1939), 1: 518.

9. Anne W. Lane and Louise H. Wall, eds., *The Letters of Franklin K. Lane, Personal and Political* (Boston: Houghton Mifflin Co., 1922), pp. 68–69.

10. Samuel Haber, *Efficiency and Uplift: Scientific Management in the Progressive Era, 1890–1920* (Chicago: University of Chicago Press, 1964), pp. 52–54.

11. *New York Times,* June 4, 1910, p. 1.

12. John Lovell Withers, "The Administrative Theories and Practices of William Howard Taft" (Ph.D. diss., University of Chicago, 1956), pp. 76–77.

13. George Kibbe Turner, "An In-terview with the President," *Mc-Clure's Magazine,* 35 (June 1910): 220–221.

14. Withers, "Administrative Theories and Practices of Taft," pp. 106–125, 171–204.

15. See the extensive treatment of this issue in Joel Arthur Tarr, *A Study in Boss Politics: William Lorimer of Chicago* (Urbana: University of Illinois Press, 1971).

16. "The President on the Tariff," *Outlook,* 99 (Sept. 9, 1911):53–54.

17. "The Speaker on the Tariff," ibid., 99 (Sept. 9, 1911):54.

18. Concentrated Banking and a 'Money Trust,'" *Literary Digest,* 43 (July 22, 1911):121–122.

19. Withers, "Administrative Theories and Practices of Taft," pp. 205–221, 224–240.

20. Francis E. Leupp, "President Taft's Own View: An Authorized Interview," *Outlook,* 99 (Dec. 2, 1911): 811–818.

21. "Senator Cummins' 'Bill of Particulars,'" ibid., 99 (Sept. 16, 1911):96–97.

22. By the Editor [George Harvey], "President Taft's 'Volte Face,'" *North American Review,* 194 (Aug. 1911):177–183.

23. 'The President and His Administration," *Outlook,* 100 (Feb. 10, 1912):300–301. See also Alpheus Thomas Mason, *William Howard Taft: Chief Justice* (London: Oldbourne, 1964), pp. 41–65, and Erwin C. Hargrove, *Presidential Leadership: Personality and Political Style* (New York: Macmillan Co., 1966), pp. 77–96.

CHAPTER 7

1. U.S., Department of State, *Papers Relating to the Foreign Relations of the United States, 1910* (Washington: Government Printing Office, 1915), pp. XVI–XVII.

2. Taft to Roosevelt, Jan. 10, 1911, Taft Papers; Roosevelt to Taft, Jan. 12, 1911, ibid.

3. Charles Callan Tansill, *Canadian-American Relations, 1875–1911*

(New Haven: Yale University Press, 1943), pp. 412–462.

4. Taft to William O. Bradley, Feb. 27, 1911, Taft Papers.

5. Claude G. Bowers, *Beveridge and the Progressive Era* (Boston: Houghton Mifflin Co., 1932), p. 412.

6. Ibid.

7. Archibald Willingham Butt, *Taft and Roosevelt: The Intimate*

Letters of Archie Butt, Military Aide, 2 vols. (Garden City, N.Y.: Doubleday, Doran & Co., 1930), 2:594–596 (Feb. 14, 1911).

8. Champ Clark, *My Quarter Century of American Politics,* 2 vols. (New York: Harper & Brothers, 1921), 2:7.

9. Richard Bolling, *Power in the House: A History of the Leadership of the House of Representatives* (New York: E. P. Dutton & Co., 1968), p. 92.

10. Ibid., p. 90; "The New Congress," *Outlook,* 97 (Apr. 15, 1911): 797.

11. Richard C. Baker, *The Tariff under Roosevelt and Taft* (Hastings, Neb.: Democrat Printing Co., 1941), p. 159; Charles E. Barker, *With President Taft in the White House:*

Memories of William Howard Taft (Chicago: A. Kroch, 1947), pp. 33–34.

12. *New York Sun,* May 16, 1911.

13. Butt, *Taft and Roosevelt,* 2: 684–685.

14. "Tariff Tangles," *Literary Digest,* 43 (Aug. 12, 1911):230.

15. Butt, *Taft and Roosevelt,* 2: 749.

16. John Hays Hammond, *The Autobiography of John Hays Hammond,* 2 vols. (New York: Farrar & Rinehart, 1935), 2: 575.

17. Arthur W. Dunn, *From Harrison to Harding: A Personal Narrative Covering a Third of a Century, 1888–1921,* 2 vols. (New York: G. P. Putnam's Sons, 1922), 2:146.

18. Taft to Horace D. Taft, Sept. 15, 1911, Taft Papers.

CHAPTER 8

1. Thomas Thacher, "Mr. Taft and the Sherman Act," *North American Review,* 189 (Apr. 1909):513; "Standard Oil Loses a Customer," *Literary Digest,* 40 (Jan. 1, 1910):4.

2. "How the Standard-Oil Verdict Is Received," *Literary Digest,* 39 (Dec. 4, 1909):991–993.

3. Archibald Willingham Butt, *Taft and Roosevelt: The Intimate Letters of Archie Butt, Military Aide,* 2 vols. (Garden City, N.Y.: Doubleday, Doran & Co., 1930), 1:220–221 (Nov. 25, 1909).

4. Paolo E. Coletta, *William Jennings Bryan: II. Progressive Politician and Moral Statesman, 1909–1915* (Lincoln: University of Nebraska Press, 1969), 24; Belle Case La Follette and Fola La Follette, *Robert M. La Follette, June 14, 1885–June 18, 1925,* 2 vols. (New York: Macmillan Co., 1953), 1:336; "The Rule of Reason," *Outlook,* 98 (July 8, 1911): 513; "The Supreme Court Decisions," *North American Review,* 194 (July 1911):1–95.

5. William Henry Harbaugh, *Power and Responsibility: The Life and Times of Theodore Roosevelt* (New

York: Farrar, Straus and Cudahy, 1961), p. 404.

6. "The Growth of a Great Monopoly," *Outlook,* 98 (June 10, 1911): 272–273.

7. John Garraty, *Right-Hand Man: The Life of George Perkins* (New York: Harper & Brothers, 1960), pp. 210–214; G. Wallace Chessman, *Theodore Roosevelt and the Politics of Power* (Boston: Little, Brown & Co., 1969), pp. 149–150.

8. "The Steel Corporation and the Panic of 1907," *Outlook,* 98 (Aug. 19, 1911):849, and "The Government and the Steel Corporation," ibid., 99 (Nov. 4, 1911):547.

9. "Mr. Roosevelt's Attack on the Taft Trust Policy," *Literary Digest,* 43 (Nov. 25, 1911):959–961.

10. Ida M. Tarbell, *The Life of Elbert H. Gary: The Story of Steel* (New York and London: D. Appleton & Co., 1925), pp. 230–240; C. M. Harger, "William Jennings Bryan on the Political Situation," *Outlook,* 100 (Jan. 6, 1912): 23.

11. "Mr. Roosevelt and the Harvester Trust," *Outlook,* 101 (May 4, 1912):1–2, and "Mr. Roosevelt's

Statement on the Harvester Trust," ibid., 101 (May 4, 1912):2.

12. Robert H. Wiebe, "The House of Morgan and the Executive, 1905–1913," *American Historical Review*, 65 (Oct. 1959):49–60.

13. Perkins to J. P. Morgan, Jr., Nov. 10, 1908, cited in Robert H. Wiebe, *Businessmen and Reform: A Study of the Progressive Movement* (Chicago: Quadrangle Paperback, 1968), pp. 81–82.

14. "President Taft on the Trusts and the Tariff," *Outlook*, 99 (Sept. 30, 1911):249–250, and "The President and the Trusts," ibid., 99 (Nov. 11, 1911):595–596.

15. "Mr. Taft's Firm Antitrust Stand," *Literary Digest*, 43 (Sept. 30, 1911):518–519.

16. "George W. Perkins on 'World Business,'" *Outlook*, 97 (Jan. 7, 1911):2–3; "Dissolved Trusts under Scrutiny," *Literary Digest*, 44 (June 15, 1912):1240–1241.

17. "President Taft's Trust Message," *Outlook*, 99 (Dec. 16, 1911):895–896.

18. Henry L. Stimson and McGeorge Bundy, *On Active Duty in Peace and War* (New York: Harper & Brothers, 1947), pp. 45–46. See also James C. German, Jr., "The Taft Administration and the Sherman Antitrust Act," *Mid-America*, 54 (July 1972):172–186.

CHAPTER 9

1. William Howard Taft, "Message of the President" (Dec. 7, 1911), in U.S., Department of State, *Papers Relating to the Foreign Relations of the United States, 1911* (Washington, D.C.: Government Printing Office, 1918), p. XXIII (hereafter cited as *For. Rel.*, with year); Thomas A. Bailey, "The North Pacific Sealing Convention of 1911," *Pacific Historical Review*, 4 (1935):1–14.

2. *For. Rel., 1909*, p. IX; *For. Rel., 1910*, pp. XII, 544–578; "The Fisheries Decision," *Outlook*, 96 (Sept 17, 1910):93–94; "The Fisheries Dispute with Canada Settled," *Literary Digest*, 41 (Sept. 17, 1910):431–432.

3. Archibald Willingham Butt, *Taft and Roosevelt: The Intimate Letters of Archie Butt, Military Aide*, 2 vols. (Garden City, N.Y.: Doubleday, Doran & Co., 1930), 2:635.

4. Letter of Aug. 14, 1911, in Henry Cabot Lodge, *Selections from the Correspondence of Theodore Roosevelt and Henry Cabot Lodge, 1884–1918*, 2 vols. (New York: Charles Scribner's Sons, 1925), 2:406.

5. "The General Arbitration Treaties," *Outlook*, 98 (Aug. 26, 1911):914, and "The Senators and the Arbitration Treaties," ibid., 100 (Mar. 1912):561–562.

6. Senator Augustus O. Bacon, "The Senate Amendments to the Arbitration Treaties," *North American Review*, 195 (May 1912):673–686.

7. Henry F. Pringle, *The Life and Times of William Howard Taft*, 2 vols. (New York: Farrar & Rinehart, 1939), 2:755.

8. Taft to Knox, Jan. 27, 1912, Taft Papers.

9. Reid to Taft, Sept. 6, 1912, ibid.

10. William S. Coker, "The Panama Canal Tolls Controversy," *Journal of American History*, 55 (Dec. 1969):555–564.

11. See the ambassador's apologia in Henry L. Wilson, *Diplomatic Episodes in Mexico, Belgium, and Chile* (Garden City, N.Y.: Doubleday, Page & Co., 1927).

12. Letter, P. C. Knox Papers, Manuscripts Division, Library of Congress.

13. Butt, *Taft and Roosevelt*, 2:645.

14. American Ambassador to the Secretary of State, Jan. 31, 1912, *For. Rel., 1912*, pp. 713–715.

15. The Acting Secretary of State to the American Ambassador, Apr. 14, 1912, ibid., p. 787.

16. The Secretary of State to the American Ambassador, Sept. 15, 1912, ibid., pp. 828–834.

17. The American Ambassador to

the Minister of Foreign Affairs, Jan. 18, 1913, with enclosures, *For. Rel., 1912,* pp. 886–892.

18. The American Ambassador to the Secretary of State, Feb. 17, 1913, ibid., p. 718.

19. General Huerta to the President, Feb. 18, 1913, ibid., p. 721.

20. The American Ambassador to the Secretary of State, Feb. 28, 1913, ibid., pp. 748–749.

CHAPTER 10

1. Alexander DeConde, *The American Secretary of State, an Interpretation* (New York: Frederick A. Praeger, 1962), p. 81. For a character sketch of Knox, see Walter V. Scholes and Marie V. Scholes, *The Foreign Policies of the Taft Administration* (Columbia: University of Missouri Press, 1970), pp. 6–10.

2. Knox quoted by J. Reuben Clark, *Memorandum on the Monroe Doctrine,* Senate Document No. 114, 71st Cong., 2d sess., 1930, p. 176.

3. Message of the President, Dec. 3, 1912, U.S., Department of State, *Papers Relating to the Foreign Relations of the United States* (Washington, D.C.: Government Printing Office, 1919), p. X (hereafter cited as *For. Rel.,* with year).

4. Albert Bushnell Hart, *The Monroe Doctrine: An Interpretation* (Boston: Little, Brown & Co., 1916), p. 234. See also Scholes and Scholes, *The Foreign Policies of the Taft Administration,* pp. 105–106.

5. Message of the President, Dec. 6, 1910, *For. Rel., 1910,* pp. XVII–XXVII.

6. Message of the President, Dec. 3, 1912, *For. Rel., 1912,* pp. VII–XVII.

7. Dubois to Knox, Nov. 25, 1911, National Archives, Washington, D.C., State Department Decimal File, SD711.21/64; and Sept. 30, 1912, Knox Papers; Knox to Taft, Nov. 29, 1911, Knox to Dubois, Dec. 6, 1911, Knox Papers.

8. Dubois to Knox, Feb. 17, 1912, SD711.21/137; J. Fred Rippy, *The Capitalists and Colombia* (New York: Vanguard Press, 1931), p. 105.

9. Knox to Dubois, Feb. 20, 1913, SD711.21/137; Taft to Knox, Feb. 27, 1913, SD711.21/42; Julio Betancourt

to Knox, Feb. 28, 1913, SD711.21/137. Dubois's report is printed in *For. Rel., 1913,* pp. 297–308.

10. The Secretary of State to Consul Caldera, telegram, Nov. 8, 1909, *For. Rel., 1909,* p. 446.

11. Taft to Knox, Dec. 22, 1909, Taft Papers.

12. Message of the President, Dec. 7, 1911, *For. Rel., 1911,* p. XVI.

13. *Speeches Incident to the Visit of Philander Chase Knox, Secretary of State of the United States of America, to the Countries of the Caribbean, February 23 to April 17, 1912* (Washington, D.C.: Government Printing Office, 1913), p. 17.

14. Philip Jessup, *Elihu Root,* 2 vols. (New York: Dodd, Mead & Co., 1938), 2:250–251. See also William S. Coker, "Dollar Diplomacy versus Constitutional Legitimacy," *Southwest Quarterly Review,* 6 (July 1968): 428–437.

15. Letter of Aug. 5, 1912, in Rear-Admiral Albert Gleaves, *Life and Letters of Rear-Admiral Stephen B. Luce, U. S. Navy, Founder of the Naval War College* (New York and London: G. P. Putnam's Sons, 1925), p. 308.

16. Letter of Aug. 7, 1912, ibid., pp. 308–309.

17. Scholes and Scholes, *The Foreign Policies of the Taft Administration,* pp. 247–248.

18. The Secretary of State to Minister Rockhill, May 4, 1909, *For. Rel., 1909,* pp. 144–145; The Secretary of State to Ambassador Reid, June 2, 1909, ibid., pp. 145–146; The Secretary of State to Ambassador Reid, June 9, 1909, ibid., p. 146. Although the incumbent minister, William W. Rockhill, was an eminent Sinologist, he was more concerned with maintain-

ing the territorial integrity of China than in providing equality of economic opportunity therein. Desiring to replace him with someone who believed that increased American trade with China was possible, Taft originally chose Charles R. Crane, of Chicago. When Crane leaked Taft's instructions to him, Taft chose a man of better judgment, William J. Calhoun.

19. The President of the United States to Prince Chun, Regent of the Chinese Empire, telegram, July 15, 1909, *For. Rel., 1909*, p. 178.

20. The Secretary of State to Ambassador Reid, Nov. 6, 1909, ibid., pp. 234–235.

21. "Propping up the Open Door in Manchuria," *Literary Digest*, 40 (Jan. 22, 1910):131.

22. Charles Vevier, *The United States and China, 1906–1913* (New Brunswick: Rutgers University Press, 1955), p. 214. Jerry Israel, *Progressivism and the Open Door: America and China, 1905–1921* (Pittsburgh: University of Pittsburgh Press, 1971), sees foreign policy largely as an extension of domestic policy. His questionable thesis is that American policy toward China could follow either "a fiercely competitive, independent posture or an efficient, cooperative, rationalized position" (p. 31). Cooperation meant trimming sail to suit Japan, competition opposing Japan, with the New Nationalism favoring cooperation and the New Freedom preferring competition. He concludes that Taft, although looked upon as one who could reconcile the "competitors" and the "cooperators," widened rather than closed the rift between them.

23. Paul A. Varg, *The Making of a Myth: The United States and China, 1879–1912* (East Lansing: Michigan State University Press, 1968), pp. 126–127, and "The Myth of the China Market, 1890–1914," *American Historical Review*, 73 (Feb. 1968):742–758.

24. The American Minister to the Secretary of State, Feb. 12, 1912, *For. Rel., 1912*, pp. 64–65.

25. "The New Treaty with Japan," *Literary Digest*, 42 (Mar. 4, 1911): 394–395; "Treaty with Japan," *Army and Navy Journal*, 48 (Mar. 4, 1911): 784.

CHAPTER 11

1. "Message of the President," U.S., Department of State, *Papers Relating to the Foreign Relations of the United States, 1909* (Washington, D.C.: Government Printing Office, 1914), pp. XXVII–XXVIII (hereafter cited as *For. Rel.*, with year).

2. J. C. Lane, "Leonard Wood and the Shaping of American Defense Policy, 1900–1920" (Ph.D. diss., University of Georgia, 1963), p. 62.

3. Henry F. Pringle, *The Life and Times of William Howard Taft*, 2 vols. (New York: Farrar & Rinehart, 1939), 1:541.

4. Archibald Willingham Butt, *Taft and Roosevelt: The Intimate Letters of Archie Butt, Military Aide*, 2 vols. (Garden City, N.Y.: Doubleday, Doran & Co., 1930), 2:780.

5. Major General Otto L. Nelson, Jr., *National Security and the General Staff* (Washington, D.C.: Infantry Journal Press, 1946), pp. 151–163.

6. "Ousting General Wood," *Literary Digest*, 44 (June 22, 1912): 1287.

7. Henry L. Stimson and McGeorge Bundy, *On Active Service in Peace and War* (New York: Harper & Brothers, 1947), pp. 33–37; "The Charges against the Adjutant General," *Outlook*, 100 (Feb. 24, 1912): 378–379.

8. Frederick Huidekoper, *The Military Unpreparedness of the United States: A History of the American Land Forces from Colonial Times until June 1, 1915* (New York: Macmillan Co., 1916), p. 411.

9. Elting E. Morison et al., eds., *The Letters of Theodore Roosevelt*, 8 vols. (Cambridge, Mass.: Harvard University Press, 1951–1954), 6:1543.

10. Report of the Joint Board of the Army and Navy, Nov. 8, 1909, General Board Records, GB File 405,

Navy Department Operational Archives, Washington, D.C.

11. U.S., Navy Department, *Annual Reports, 1909* (Washington, D.C.: Government Printing Office, 1910), p. 5.

12. *Literary Digest*, 39 (July 17, 1909):78–80.

CHAPTER 12

1. Taft to W. G. Harding, Nov. 25, 1910, Henry F. Pringle, *The Life and Times of William Howard Taft*, 2 vols. (New York: Farrar & Rinehart, 1939), 2:580.

2. Archibald Willingham Butt, *Taft and Roosevelt: The Intimate Letters of Archie Butt, Military Aide*, 2 vols. (Garden City, N.Y.: Doubleday, Doran & Co., 1930), 2:580–581.

3. Belle Case La Follette and Fola La Follette, *Robert M. La Follette, June 14, 1885–June 18, 1925*, 2 vols. (New York: Macmillan Co., 1953), 1:314 (hereafter cited as La Follette, *La Follette*).

4. Benjamin Parke DeWitt, *The Progressive Movement: A Non-partisan, Comprehensive Discussion of Current Tendencies in American Politics* (New York: Macmillan Co., 1915), p. 70.

5. "Senator La Follette as a Candidate. A Poll of the Press," *Outlook*, 100 (Jan. 20, 1912):120–122.

6. "Opening the 1912 Campaign," *Literary Digest*, 43 (Sept. 9, 1912): 379–381.

7. Letter of Nov. 5, 1911, Taft Papers.

8. Ibid.

9. Letter of May 5, 1911, Elting E. Morison et al., eds., *The Letters of Theodore Roosevelt*, 8 vols. (Cambridge, Mass.: Harvard University Press, 1951–1954), 7:260–261.

10. Herman Henry Kohlsaat, *From McKinley to Harding: Personal Recollections of Our Presidents* (New York: Charles Scribner's Sons, 1923), pp. 184–188.

11. Letter of Oct. 27, 1911, Roosevelt Papers.

12. Morison, ed., *Letters of Theodore Roosevelt*, 7:450–452.

13. See Roosevelt to George W. Norris, Jan. 2, 1912, Roosevelt Papers.

14. Roosevelt to Henry Beach Needham, Jan. 9, 1912, ibid.

15. Letter of Jan. 18, 1912, ibid.

16. Morison, ed., *Letters of Theodore Roosevelt*, 7:489 n2. See also Robert M. La Follette, *La Follette's Autobiography: A Personal Narrative of Political Experiences* (Madison: La Follette Publishing Co., 1913), pp. 556–558, 602–609; La Follette, *La Follette*, 1:399–409.

17. Letter of Feb. 8, 1912, Morison, ed., *Letters of Theodore Roosevelt*, 7:499.

18. Butt, *Taft and Roosevelt*, 2: 767–768.

19. Charles Nagel to Henry F. Pringle, Oct. 25, 1934, Pringle, *Taft*, 2:762.

20. Butt, *Taft and Roosevelt*, 2: 804.

21. Ibid., 2:812–814 (Jan. 15, 1912).

22. Charles W. Thompson, *Presidents I've Known and Two Near-Presidents* (Indianapolis: Bobbs-Merrill Co., 1929), p. 219.

23. Taft to an unnamed addressee, undated, in Herbert S. Duffy, *William Howard Taft* (New York: Minton, Balch & Co., 1930), pp. 276–277.

24. "The President Aggressive," *Outlook*, 100 (Feb. 24, 1912):376–377; "The Republican Feud," *Literary Digest*, 44 (Feb. 24, 1912):357–358; "Taft Fires on His Opponents," *American Review of Reviews*, 45 (Mar. 1912):271.

25. "President Taft on the Recall of Judges," *Outlook*, 100 (Mar. 23,

1912):604; "Mr. Taft's Boston Speech," ibid., 100 (Mar. 30, 1912): 706–707.

26. Letter of Feb. 23, 1912, Ray Stannard Baker Papers, Manuscripts Division, Library of Congress.

27. Butt, *Taft and Roosevelt*, 2: 839.

28. "A Charter of Democracy," *Outlook*, 100 (Mar. 2, 1912):476–477; Harold Remington, "Mr. Roosevelt's 'Recall of Judicial Decisions,'" *American Review of Reviews*, 45 (May 1912):567–569.

29. Lodge cited in Richard M. Abrams, *Conservatism in a Progressive Era: Massachusetts Politics, 1900–1912* (Cambridge, Mass.: Harvard University Press, 1964), p. 278.

30. "To Be Accurate," *Harper's Weekly*, 55 (Apr. 20, 1912):4.

31. "Mr. Roosevelt and the Presidential Nomination," *Outlook*, 100 (Mar. 2, 1912):475.

32. Henry L. Stoddard, *As I Knew Them: Presidents and Politics from Grant to Coolidge* (New York: Harper & Brothers, 1927), p. 388.

33. Butt, *Taft and Roosevelt*, 2: 850.

34. "Principles and Personalities," *Outlook*, 101 (May 4, 1912):11–12.

35. La Follette, *La Follette*, 1:431.

36. Taft to Horace D. Taft, May 12, 1912, Taft Papers.

37. Sidney Warren, *The Battle for the Presidency* (Philadelphia: J. B. Lippincott Co., 1968), p. 186.

38. Pringle, *Taft*, 2:775.

39. "Mr. Taft's Boston Speech," *Outlook*, 100 (Mar. 30, 1912):706–707; "President Taft's Denunciation of Mr. Roosevelt," *Literary Digest*, 44 (May 4, 1912):922–923.

40. Pringle, *Taft*, 2:781–782.

41. Victor Rosewater, *Backstage in 1912: The Inside Story of the Split Republican Convention* (Philadelphia: Dorrance & Co., 1932), pp. 60–61; "The Massachusetts Speeches—A Review:II—Mr. Roosevelt's Speech at Worcester," *Outlook*, 101 (May 4, 1912):18–21.

42. Roosevelt to Lodge, May 2, 1912, Henry Cabot Lodge, *Selections from the Correspondence of Theodore Roosevelt and Henry Cabot Lodge, 1884–1918*, 2 vols. (New York: Charles Scribner's Sons, 1925), 2: 425; "The Political Campaign in Massachusetts," *Outlook*, 101 (May 11, 1912):47–48.

43. Theodore Roosevelt, "A Naked Issue of Right and Wrong," *Outlook*, 101 (June 15, 1912):327–336.

44. William Jennings Bryan, *A Tale of Two Conventions* (New York: Funk & Wagnalls Co., 1912), pp. xxi–xxiii.

45. The descriptive phrase is from the title of Chapter LX in William Allen White, *The Autobiography of William Allen White* (New York: Macmillan Co., 1946).

46. *Official Report of the Proceedings of the Fifteenth Republican National Convention, Held in Chicago, Illinois, June 18, 19, 20, 21, and 22, 1912* (New York: Tenny Press, 1912), pp. 377–403.

47. Ibid., pp. 88–100; Bryan, *Tale of Two Conventions*, pp. 37–43; Rosewater, *Backstage in 1912*, pp. 186–194.

48. John Garraty, *Right-Hand Man: The Life of George Perkins* (New York: Harper & Brothers, 1960), p. 262.

49. Mark Sullivan, *Our Times: The United States, 1900–1925*, 6 vols. (New York: Charles Scribner's Sons, 1926–1935), 4:530–531.

50. "President Taft's Attitude," *Outlook*, 101 (June 29, 1912):445.

51. Taft Papers.

52. John Hays Hammond, "Why I Am for Taft," *North American Review*, 191 (Oct. 1912):449–459; By the Editor [George Harvey], "Roosevelt or the Republic!" ibid., 196 (Oct. 1912):433–435.

53. A. V. Pinci, "Mr. Taft on the Issues," *Harper's Weekly*, 56 (Oct. 26, 1912):9–10.

54. William Manners, *TR and Will: A Friendship That Split the Republican Party* (New York: Harcourt, Brace & World, 1969), pp. 289–290; Pringle, *Taft*, 2:838.

55. *New York World,* Nov. 6, 1912.

56. The returns are presented in Edgar Eugene Robinson, *The Presidential Vote, 1896-1912* (Stanford: Stanford University Press, 1934), Table IX; Cortez A. M. Ewing, *Presidential Elections from Abraham Lincoln to Franklin D. Roosevelt* (Norman: University of Oklahoma Press, 1940), passim, but especially pp. 79, 95-96; and Svend Petersen, *A Statistical History of American Presidential Elections* (New York: Frederick Unger Publishing Co., 1963), pp. 74-79. For the election in Mississippi, typical of that in the rest of the southern states, see Paul D. Casdorph, "The 1912 Republican Presidential Campaign in Mississippi," *Journal of Mississippi History,* 33 (Feb. 1971):1-19. See also Paul Lewinson, *Race, Class, and Party: A History of Negro Suffrage and White Politics in the South* (New York: Oxford University Press, 1932), and George E. Mowry, "The South and the Progressive Lily White Party of 1912," *Journal of Southern History,* 6 (May 1940):237-247.

57. "The Week," *Nation,* 95 (Nov. 7, 1912):421.

CHAPTER 13

1. "The President and the Duty on Paper," *Outlook,* 100 (Feb. 12, 1912):339-340.

2. "Scotching the Patent Medicine Fakers," ibid., 101 (Aug. 31, 1912):992-993.

3. *New York Times,* Nov. 17, 1912, pp. 1, 3; "The Three Presidential Candidates," *Outlook,* 102 (Nov. 30, 1912):702-703.

4. "Sizing Up Mr. Taft's Record," *Literary Digest,* 46 (Mar. 15, 1912): 559.

5. Horace Dutton Taft, *Memories and Opinions* (New York: Macmillan Co., 1942), p. 116.

6. "Wilson-Taft-Roosevelt: The Candidates Compared—An Intimate Evening with Each," *World's Work,* 24 (Sept. 1912):572. See also Elmer E. Cornwell, Jr., *Presidential Leadership of Public Opinion* (Bloomington: Indiana University Press, 1965): pp. 13-30.

7. Taft Papers.

8. See "President Taft," *Atlantic Monthly,* 109 (Feb. 1912):164-171.

9. Henry Cabot Lodge, *Selections from the Correspondence of Theodore Roosevelt and Henry Cabot Lodge, 1884-1918,* 2 vols. (New York: Charles Scribner's Sons, 1925), 2:334.

10. William Howard Taft, *Our Chief Magistrate and His Powers* (New York: Columbia University Press, 1916), p. 12.

11. "The Retiring President," *Outlook,* 103 (Mar. 8, 1913):520-522.

12. "President Taft," *Atlantic Monthly,* 109 (Feb. 1912):171.

13. Clinton L. Rossiter, *The American Presidency* (New York: Harcourt, Brace & Co., 1956), pp. 135-137.

14. "Sizing up Mr. Taft's Record," *Literary Digest,* 46 (Mar. 14, 1913): 558.

15. James MacGregor Burns, *Presidential Government: The Crucible of Leadership* (Boston: Houghton Mifflin Co., 1966), pp. 79-81. Unanimity on the "greatness" of presidents cannot be expected. Morton Borden, ed., *America's Ten Greatest Presidents* (Chicago: Rand McNally & Co., 1961), for example, lists Washington, John Adams, Jefferson, Jackson, Polk, Lincoln, Cleveland, Theodore Roosevelt, Wilson, and Franklin D. Roosevelt. Both Burns and Borden base their conclusions largely upon research conducted by the late Professor Arthur M. Schlesinger and published in *Life,* Nov. 1, 1948, and in "Our Presidents: A Rating by 75 Historians," *New York Times Magazine,* July 29, 1962, p. 12. See also Thomas A. Bailey, *Presidential Greatness: The Image and the Man from George Washington to the Present* (New York: Appleton-Century, 1966), esp. pp. 12-34.

Essay on Sources

MANUSCRIPTS

The William Howard Taft Papers in the Manuscripts Division, Library of Congress, remain the best source of information on Taft's efforts as president. They have been supplemented by a number of other collections. The Theodore Roosevelt Papers, Library of Congress, contain much correspondence dealing with Roosevelt's break with Taft. The labor of plowing through them heightens the researcher's regard for their superb editing by Elting E. Morison et al., *The Letters of Theodore Roosevelt*, 8 vols. (Cambridge, Mass.: Harvard University Press, 1951–1954). Much of the material encompassed in the *Autobiography* by Robert M. La Follette and in the biography of him by his wife and daughter is revealed in the Robert M. La Follette Papers, Library of Congress, which were finally opened to scholarly researchers in 1970. The Ray Stannard Baker Papers, in the same repository, throw light upon the efforts of an outstanding muckraker of Taft's time. The George W. Norris Papers, at the same place, illustrate the *modus operandi* of a leading insurgent, while those of Joseph G. Cannon, at the Illinois State Historical Society, Springfield, Illinois, contain the record of a conservative. At the Library of Congress, the William E. Borah Papers detail the political strivings of a Republican progressive who was not a Progressive; those of William Jennings Bryan reveal the great efforts made to insure that a progressive presidential candidate would be named at the Baltimore convention. Considerable light on the convention is also shed by the Josephus Daniels and the Woodrow Wilson Papers. The Andrew Carnegie Papers are valuable for the peace crusade of Taft's day; those of Edwin Y. Webb, at the University of North Carolina Library, for the prohibition crusade. The difficulties experienced by a Democrat and southerner in Taft's cabinet are illustrated in the Jacob McGavock Dickinson Papers, Tennessee Archives and Library, Nashville.

In the realm of foreign affairs, the Philander C. Knox Papers and those of Elihu Root, Chandler P. Anderson, and Whitelaw Reid, all in the Library of Congress, proved quite rewarding, as did those of Francis Mairs Huntington Wilson, Ursinus College, Collegeville, Pa. (microfilm).

Information on the reforms undertaken in the army in Taft's day lies in part in the Leonard Wood Papers, Library of Congress. Similar information on reforms in the navy is found in the papers of Josephus Daniels, of Admiral William S. Benson, used by permission of his son, Commodore H. H. J. Benson, U.S. Navy (Ret.), and of William S. Sims, in the Library of Congress. The William Veazy Pratt Papers and the Records of the General Board of the Navy were used at the Navy Operational Archives, Naval History Division, Washington, D.C. The George von Lengerke Meyer Papers were used at the Navy Department Records, National Archives, Washington, D.C.

OFFICIAL DOCUMENTS

Materials on the conduct of foreign affairs by the Department of State were consulted in the National Archives, Washington, D.C. (State Department Archives, Decimal File Series). These supplemented Taft's annual messages to Congress and the selected dispatches and documents which are printed in the U.S., Department of State, *Papers Relating to the Foreign Relations of the United States* (1909–1912). Addresses by Taft and by Knox and congressional hearings on the writing of treaties helped to round out the picture.

Details on the status of American economic and social life during Taft's term were obtained in part in the *Thirteenth Census* reports, *Statistical Abstract of the United States, 1910* (Washington, D.C.: Government Printing Office, 1911), and *Yearbooks* of the Department of Agriculture. Additional information was garnered from testimony given at hearings held on the Payne-Aldrich tariff and in Taft's messages to Congress either suggesting legislation or containing vetoes. Pertinent for an understanding of tariff reciprocity with Canada are: *Reciprocity with Canada* (62d Cong., 1st sess., House Report No. 3, 1911); U.S., Tariff Commission, *Reciprocity and Commercial Treaties* (Washington, D.C.: Government Printing Office, 1919); and *Reciprocity with Canada: A Study of the Arrangement of 1911* (Washington, D.C.: Government Printing Office, 1920).

Invaluable for military matters are the *Annual Reports* of the War Department and of the Navy Department and congressional hearings held on the annual appropriation bills and other subjects.

The bible for those seeking light on the Ballinger-Pinchot affair is *Investigation of the Department of the Interior and of the Bureau of Forestry* (61st Cong., 3d sess., Sen. Doc. No. 719, 13 vols., 1911), that on Taft's attempt to obtain efficiency in government in his *Message of the President of the United States Transmitting the Reports of the Commission on Economy and Efficiency* (62d Cong., 2d sess., House Doc. No. 1262, 1913).

NEWSPAPERS AND JOURNALS

Republican newspapers such as the *Chicago Tribune, New York Tribune,* and *Washington Post* generally upheld Taft. The Democratic *New York Times* and *New York World* opposed him. The *Wall Street Journal* was most often critical, while the independent *New York Herald* was persistently and vehemently opposed.

American, European, and Far Eastern opinion concerning Taft was ascertained from the news items and editorial comments in a number of journals. The *American Review of Reviews* and the *Literary Digest* provided excellent summaries of both American and foreign newspaper opinion. Generally opposed to Taft were the *Century Magazine, Collier's Weekly,* the *Commoner, Current History,* the *Forum, Harper's Weekly,* the *Independent,* the *Nation,* the *North American Review,* the *Outlook* (Roosevelt's organ, and therefore of especial value), and the *World's Work.* However, Bryan's *Commoner,* the *Independent,* and the *Nation* strenuously supported Taft's efforts for world peace. The *Army and Navy Journal* reflected the distaste of its editor for the manner in which Taft starved the military services. Although the *Atlantic Monthly* is best known as a vehicle for good literature, some of the most acutely perceptive and derogatory studies of Taft as a political figure appeared in its pages.

An extremely selective list follows of the most useful signed articles in the journals mentioned and in others. Ray S. Baker, "The Negro in a Democracy," *Independent,* 67 (Sept. 6, 1909): 584–588, pleads for the elevation of the position of the Negro. Claude E. Barfield, " 'Our Share of the Booty': The Democratic Party, Cannonism, and the Payne-Aldrich Tariff," *Journal of American History,* 57 (Sept. 1970):308–323, shows that many Democrats as well as Republicans favored tariff protection. J. O. Bayleu, "American Intervention in Nicaragua, 1909–1913: An Appraisal of Objectives and Results," *Southwestern Social Science Quarterly,*

35 (Sept. 1954):128–154, is very critical of the Taft-Knox policy of intervention. Bruce Bliven, "Robert La Follette's Place in Our History," *Current History*, 22 (Aug. 1925):716–722, speaks of a devoted public servant whose ego was perhaps somewhat inflated. George Harvey was very critical of Taft in two pieces: By the Editor, "President Taft's 'Volte-Face,'" *North American Review*, 194 (Aug. 1911):177–183, and "Roosevelt or the Republic!" *North American Review*, 196 (Dec. 1912):443–448. Jonathan Dolliver, "The Downward Revision Hoax," *Independent*, 69 (Sept. 8, 1910):512–517, and "The Forward Movement in the Republican Party," *Outlook*, 96 (Sept. 24, 1910):161–172, excoriates Taft for his tariff policy, and persecution of insurgents. A favorable view of Taft is provided in Francis E. Leupp, "Taft and Roosevelt: A Composite Study," *Atlantic Monthly*, 106 (Nov. 1910):648–653, "President Taft's Own View: An Authorized Interview by Francis E. Leupp," *Outlook*, 99 (Dec. 2, 1911):811–818, and "President Taft on Tariff-Making. Common Sense vs. Haphazard Methods: An Authorized Interview by Francis E. Leupp," *Outlook*, 100 (Mar. 2, 1912):495–501. George E. Mowry, "Theodore Roosevelt and the Election of 1910," *Mississippi Valley Historical Review*, 25 (Mar. 1939):523–534 is an excellent assessment of the dilemma Roosevelt faced in 1910. Gifford Pinchot, U.S. Forester, "The A B C of Conservation," *Outlook*, 93 (Dec. 4, 1909):770–772, spells out the Pinchot-Roosevelt attitude toward conservation. Theodore Roosevelt, in "The Steel Corporation and the Panic of 1907," *Outlook*, 98 (Aug. 19, 1911):865–868, and "The Trusts, the People, and the Square Deal," *Outlook*, 99 (Nov. 18, 1911):649–656, defends himself against Taft's charges that he let U.S. Steel monopolize the steel industry and that he was friendly toward trusts. In a third article, "A Charter of Democracy: Address Before the Ohio Constitutional Convention," *Outlook*, 100 (Feb. 24, 1912):390–402, Roosevelt foreshadowed the Progressive Party platform of 1912. Stanley D. Solvick, "William Howard Taft and the Payne-Aldrich Tariff," *Mississippi Valley Historical Review*, 50 (Dec. 1963):424–442, and "William Howard Taft and Cannonism," *Wisconsin Magazine of History*, 48 (Autumn 1964):48–58, very perceptively assesses Taft's thinking with respect to tariff reform and liberalization of the House rules. Robert H. Wiebe, "The House of Morgan and the Executive, 1905–1913," *American Historical Review*, 65 (Oct. 1959):49–60, shows that Taft rejected the modus vivendi Roosevelt had achieved with Morgan, while Woodrow Wilson, "The Tariff Make-Believe," *North American*

Review, 190 (Oct. 1909):535–556, and "Hide-and-Seek Politics," *North American Review,* 191 (May 1910):585–601, excoriates Republican tariff philosophy and the politics Republicans played to preserve protection.

PERSONAL HISTORIES OR PUBLISHED CORRESPONDENCE

Taft's relations with contemporary state and national leaders are described in a large number of personal histories. Listed below are the autobiographies, biographies, statements or speeches, personal recollections, or published letters only of those with whom Taft had intimate or important connections.

Older biographies of Taft are those by Herbert S. Duffy, *William Howard Taft* (New York: Minton, Balch & Co., 1930), and Francis McHale, *President and Chief Justice: The Life and Public Services of William Howard Taft* (Philadelphia: Dorrance & Co., 1931). Much, much better is Henry F. Pringle, *The Life and Times of William Howard Taft,* 2 vols. (New York: Farrar & Rinehart, 1939). William Manners, *TR and Will: A Friendship That Split the Republican Party* (New York: Harcourt, Brace & World, 1969), is popularly written. Very disappointing because it tells little about his administration's policies or politics is Mrs. William Howard Taft, *Recollections of Full Years* (New York: Dodd, Mead & Co., 1914). Horace Dutton Taft devotes a chapter to his brother and another to Theodore Roosevelt in *Memories and Opinions* (New York: Macmillan Co., 1942). Some insights into Taft's politics are offered in James E. Watson, *As I Knew Them: Memories of James E. Watson, Former United States Senator from Indiana* (Indianapolis: Bobbs-Merrill Co., 1936); in John Hays Hammond, *The Autobiography of John Hays Hammond,* 2 vols. (New York: Farrar & Rinehart, 1935); and in excellent scholarly fashion in George E. Mowry, *Theodore Roosevelt and the Progressive Movement* (Madison: University of Wisconsin Press, 1946) and *The Era of Theodore Roosevelt, 1900–1912* (New York: Harper & Brothers, 1958). Of greatest value, nevertheless, remains Archibald Willingham Butt, *Taft and Roosevelt: The Intimate Letters of Archie Butt, Military Aide,* 2 vols. (Garden City, N.Y.: Doubleday, Doran & Co., 1930). Unfortunately the observations end with 1912, for Butt went down on the *Titanic.*

Claude G. Bowers, *Beveridge and the Progressive Era* (Boston: Houghton Mifflin Co., 1932), tells how Beveridge opposed Taft in most instances but supported his quest for a Tariff Commission.

Champ Clark, *My Quarter Century of American Politics,* 2 vols. (New York: Harper & Brothers, 1921), found Taft to be misinformed and naïve on tariff and tariff reciprocity matters and lacking in tactical political skill. Paolo E. Coletta, *William Jennings Bryan: II. Progressive Politician and Moral Statesman, 1909–1915* (Lincoln: University of Nebraska Press, 1969), shows that Bryan supported Taft whenever Taft agreed with the demands of the Democratic platform of 1908 and especially when he sought agreements on international arbitration. John A. Garraty, *Right-Hand Man: The Life of George Perkins* (New York: Harper & Brothers, 1960), provides insight into a big businessman who developed a social conscience and preferred Roosevelt's way of handling of trusts to Taft's. Kenneth S. Hechler, *Insurgency: Personalities and Politics of the Taft Era* (New York: Columbia University Press, 1940), deals with Taft's political and legislative problems. Robert M. La Follette, *La Follette's Autobiography: A Personal Narrative of Political Experiences* (Madison: La Follette Publishing Co., 1913), and Belle Case La Follette and Fola La Follette, *Robert M. La Follette, June 14, 1885–June 18, 1925,* 2 vols. (New York: Macmillan Co., 1953), are important because they detail La Follette's opposition to Taft and his part in the creation of the Progressive organization. Gifford Pinchot, *Breaking New Ground* (New York: Harcourt, Brace & Co., 1947), gives Pinchot's version of the conservation controversy and is very critical of Taft.

That every major newspaper reporter of Taft's time who left reminiscences was critical of Taft is revealed in the quasi-autobiographical works of Oscar King Davis, *Released for Publication: Some Inside Political History of Theodore Roosevelt and His Times, 1898–1918* (Boston and New York: Houghton Mifflin Co., 1925); Arthur W. Dunn, *From Harrison to Harding: A Personal Narrative Covering a Third of a Century, 1888–1921,* 2 vols. (New York: G. P. Putnam's Sons, 1922); Henry L. Stoddard, *As I Knew Them: Presidents and Politics from Grant to Coolidge* (New York: Harper & Brothers, 1927); Charles W. Thompson, *Presidents I've Known and Two Near-Presidents* (Indianapolis: Bobbs-Merrill Co., 1929); and Oswald Garrison Villard, *Prophets True and False* (New York: Alfred A. Knopf, 1928), and *Fighting Years: Memoirs of a Liberal Editor* (New York: Harcourt, Brace & Co., 1939).

WORKS OF GENERIC VALUE

William R. Braisted, *The United States Navy in the Pacific, 1909–1922* (Austin: University of Texas Press, 1970), skillfully relates Taft's efforts to provide for an adequate Navy. Wilfrid Hardy Callcott, *The Caribbean Policy of the United States, 1890–1920* (Baltimore: The Johns Hopkins Press, 1942), is critical of the Taft-Knox dollar diplomacy south of the border, as is Dana G. Munro, *Intervention and Dollar Diplomacy in the Caribbean, 1900–1921* (Princeton: Princeton University Press, 1964). The delightfully written Albro Martin, *Enterprise Denied: Origins of the Decline of American Railroads, 1897–1917* (New York: Columbia University Press, 1971), finds a rapid decline of these railroads during Taft's term. Horace Samuel Merrill and Marion Galbraith Merrill, *The Republican Command, 1897–1913* (Lexington: University Press of Kentucky, 1971), neatly synthesize the Taft administration. Mark Sullivan, *Our Times: The United States, 1900–1925*, 6 vols. (New York: Charles Scribner's Sons, 1926–1935), presents social and cultural as well as political data. Exhaustive coverage is given to tariff reciprocity with Canada in L. Ethan Ellis, *Reciprocity, 1911: A Study in Canadian-American Relations* (New Haven: Yale University Press, 1939), and Charles Callan Tansill, *Canadian-American Relations, 1875–1911* (New Haven: Yale University Press, 1943). Charles Vevier, *The United States and China, 1906–1913* (New Brunswick: Rutgers University Press, 1955), concludes that Taft's objectives in China were purely materialistic. Walter V. Scholes and Marie V. Scholes, *The Foreign Policies of the Taft Administration* (Columbia: University of Missouri Press, 1970), stands in a class by itself because it is the only study devoted entirely to the subject even though it does not completely cover it.

UNPUBLISHED SOURCES

A number of unpublished sources throw light upon Taft or upon the movements with which he was connected. The most useful doctoral dissertations consulted were: Howard Wilson Allen, "Miles Poindexter: A Political Biography" (University of Washington, 1959); Commander Daniel J. Costello, U.S. Navy, "Planning for War: A History of the General Board of the Navy, 1900–1914" (Fletcher School of Diplomacy, 1968); Alan Brant Gould, "Secretary of the Interior Walter L. Fisher and the Return to Constructive Conservation: Problems and Policies of the Conservation Movement, 1909–1913" (West Virginia University, 1969); J. C. Lane, "Leonard Wood and the Shaping of American Defense Policy, 1900–1920" (University of Georgia, 1963); and John Lovelle

Withers, "The Administrative Theories and Practices of William Howard Taft" (University of Chicago, 1956, microfilm).

SELECTED WRITINGS
OF WILLIAM HOWARD TAFT

Perhaps in answer to Roosevelt's doctrine of virtually unlimited presidential power, Taft wrote more extensively on the institution and character of the presidency than did any other president. Not all of the titles listed below deal with the period 1909–1913. However, the ones published in 1913 and later help to explain the development of Taft's ideas as expressed during his presidency: *Four Aspects of Civic Duty* (New York: Charles Scribner's Sons, 1906); *Present Day Problems: A Collection of Addresses Delivered on Various Occasions by William Howard Taft* (New York: Dodd, Mead & Co., 1908); *Political Issues and Outlooks: Speeches Delivered between August 1908 and February 1909* (New York: Doubleday, Page & Co., 1909); *Presidential Addresses and State Papers of William Howard Taft, from March 4, 1909, to March 4, 1910* (New York: Doubleday & Co., 1910); *Popular Government: Its Essence, Its Permanence and Its Perils* (New Haven: Yale University Press, 1913); *The Anti-Trust Act and the Supreme Court* (New York: Harper & Brothers, 1914); *Ethics in Service: Addresses Delivered in the Page Lecture Series, 1914, before the Senior Class of the Sheffield Scientific School, Yale University* (New Haven: Yale University Press, 1915); *Our Chief Magistrate and His Powers* (New York: Columbia University Press, 1916).

A NOTE ON THE CRISIS OVER CONSERVATION

Rose Stahl, "The Ballinger-Pinchot Controversy," in *Smith College Studies in History* (Northampton, Mass., 1915–), 11 (1926):65–126, established the theme that conservationists were part of the progressive movement and sought to counter corporate wealth; she supported Pinchot and his associates. In his biography of Taft, published in 1939, Henry F. Pringle upheld Taft and Ballinger against Pinchot but did not distinguish sufficiently between the conservation views of Taft and of Ballinger. Secretary of the Interior Harold L. Ickes, in an article in the *Saturday Evening Post*, May 25, 1940, and in an official report, *Not Guilty: An Official Inquiry into the Charges Made by Glavis and Pinchot against Richard A. Ballinger, Secretary of the Interior, 1909–1911*

(Washington, D.C.: Government Printing Office, 1940), also upheld Ballinger and excoriated Pinchot. In his *Bureaucracy Convicts Itself: The Ballinger-Pinchot Controversy of 1910* (New York: Viking Press, 1941), Alpheus T. Mason tried to steer a middle course even though Pinchot let him use his papers. In chapter 3 of his *Theodore Roosevelt and the Progressive Movement,* George Mowry tries to be fair but, like Mason, questions the sincerity of Ballinger's devotion to the cause of conservation. Pinchot's version may be found in his autobiography, *Breaking New Ground* (New York: Harcourt, Brace & Co., 1947); and he has received some sympathy at the hands of a biographer, M. Nelson McGeary. Samuel P. Hays, *Conservation and the Gospel of Efficiency: The Progressive Conservation Movement, 1890–1920* (Cambridge, Mass.: Harvard University Press, 1959), shows that conservation, originally sponsored by scientific and technical men rather than by anticorporation crusaders, was heartily adopted by Theodore Roosevelt as part of his drive for efficiency in government. Only at the end of Roosevelt's term did it acquire political and especially moral overtones. Elmo R. Richardson, *The Politics of Conservation: Crusades and Controversies, 1897–1913* (Berkeley: University of California Press, 1962), provides a well-balanced account which includes thorough research into the attitude of the West on conservation. Two studies deftly relate the conservation crusade to the progressive movement: James Penick, Jr., *Progressive Politics and Conservation: The Ballinger-Pinchot Affair* (Chicago: University of Chicago Press, 1968), and Alan Brant Gould, "Secretary of the Interior Walter L. Fisher and the Return to Constructive Conservation: Problems and Policies of the Conservation Movement, 1909–1913" (Ph.D. diss., West Virginia University, 1969, copyrighted in 1970 by University Microfilms). Lawrence Rakestraw, "Conservative Historiography: An Assessment," *Pacific Historical Review* 41 (Aug. 1972):271–288, notes that Penick, by not dealing with the roots of the conservative battle, misunderstands both issues and men and "casts . . . Ballinger in the role of a latter day Jeffersonian democrat trying to turn the clock back to an earlier and less complex period."

Index